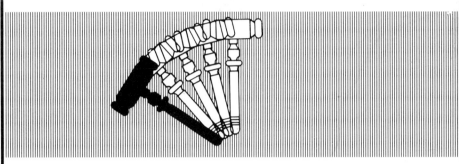

TORTS

George C. Christie
James B. Duke Professor of Law
Duke University
co-editor: *Cases and Materials on the Law
of Torts,* 2nd ed. (with Meeks)

and

Jerry J. Phillips
W.P. Toms Professor of Law
University of Tennessee
co-editor: *Tort Law: Cases, Materials, Problems,*
(with Terry, Maraist, and McCellan)

NORMAN S. GOLDENBERG
Senior Editor
PETER TENEN
Managing Editor

CASENOTES PUBLISHING CO., INC.
1640 Fifth Street, Suite 208
Santa Monica, CA 90401
(310) 395-6500

Third Edition, 1999
First Printing, 1999

ISBN 0-87457-177-4

With the introduction of *Casenote Law Outlines,* Casenotes Publishing Company brings a new approach to the legal study outline. Of course, we have sought out only nationally recognized authorities in their respective fields to author the outlines. Most of the authors are editors of widely used casebooks. All have published extensively in respected legal journals, and some have written treatises cited by courts across the nation in opinions deciding important legal issues on which the authors have recommended what the "last word" on those issues should be.

What is truly novel about the *Casenote Law Outlines* concept is that each outline does not fit into a cookie-cutter mold. While each author has been given a carefully developed format as a framework for the outline, the format is purposefully flexible. The student will therefore find that all outlines are not alike. Instead, each professor has used an approach appropriate to the subject matter. An outline on Evidence cannot be written in the same manner as one on Constitutional Law or Contracts or Torts, etc. Accordingly, the student will find similar features in each *Casenote Law Outline,* but they may be handled in radically different ways by each author. We believe that in this way the law student will be rewarded with the most effective study aid possible. And because we are strongly committed to keeping our publications up to date, *Casenote Law Outlines* are the most current study aids on the market.

For added studying convenience, the *Casenote Law Outlines* series and the *Casenote Legal Briefs* are being coordinated. Many titles in the *Casenote Legal Briefs* series have already been cross-referenced to the appropriate title in the *Casenote Law Outlines* series, and more cross-referenced titles are being released on a regular basis. A tag at the end of most briefs will quickly direct the student to the section in the appropriate *Casenote Law Outline* where further discussion of the rule of law in question can be found.

We continually seek law student and law professor feedback regarding the effectiveness of our publications. As you use *Casenote Law Outlines,* please do not hesitate to write or call us if you have constructive criticism or simply would like to tell us you are pleased with the approach and design of the publication.

Best of luck in your studies.

CASENOTES PUBLISHING CO., INC.

CASENOTE LAW OUTLINES — SUPPLEMENT REQUEST FORM

Casenotes Publishing Co., Inc. prides itself on producing the most current legal study outlines available. Sometimes between major revisions, the authors of the outline series will issue supplements to update their respective outlines to reflect any recent changes in the law. Certain areas of the law change more quickly than others, and thus some outlines may be supplemented, while others may not be supplemented at all.

In order to determine whether or not you should send this supplement request form to us, first check the printing date that appears by the subject name below. If this outline is less than one year old, it is highly unlikely that there will be a supplement for it. If it is older, you may wish to write, telephone, or fax us for current information. You might also check to see whether a supplement has been included with your *Casenote Law Outline* or has been provided to your bookstore. If it is necessary to order the supplement directly from us, it will be supplied without charge, but we do insist that you send a stamped, self-addressed return envelope. If you request a supplement for an outline that does not have one, you will receive the latest *Casenotes* catalogue.

If you wish to request a supplement for this outline:

#5000, TORTS by Christie and Phillips • (Third Edition, First Printing, 1999)

please follow the instructions below.

TO OBTAIN YOUR COMPLIMENTARY SUPPLEMENT(S), *YOU MUST FOLLOW THESE INSTRUCTIONS PRECISELY* **IN ORDER FOR YOUR REQUEST TO BE ACKNOWLEDGED.**

1. **REMOVE AND SEND THIS ENTIRE REQUEST FORM:** You *must* send this *original* page, which acts as your proof of purchase and provides the information regarding which supplements, if any, you need. The request form is only valid for any supplement for the outline in which it appears. *No photocopied or written requests will be honored.*

2. **SEND A STAMPED, SELF-ADDRESSED, FULL-SIZE (9" x 12") ENVELOPE:** *Affix enough postage to cover at least 3 oz.* We regret that we absolutely cannot fill and/or acknowledge requests unaccompanied by a stamped, self-addressed envelope.

3. **MULTIPLE SUPPLEMENT REQUESTS:** If you are sending supplement requests for two or more different *Casenote Law Outlines,* we suggest you send a return envelope for each subject requested. If you send only one envelope, your order may not be filled immediately should any supplement you requested still be in production. In that case, your order will not be filled until it can be filled completely, *i.e.,* until all supplements you have requested are published.

4. **PLEASE GIVE US THE FOLLOWING INFORMATION:**

    Name: _____ Telephone: (____) _____ - _____

    Address: _____ Apt.: _____

    City: _____ State: _____ Zip: _____

    Name of law school you attend: _____

    Name and location of bookstore where you purchased this *Casenote Law Outline:* _____

    _____

    Any comments regarding *Casenote Law Outlines?* _____

    _____

CASENOTES PUBLISHING CO., INC., 1640 Fifth Street, Suite 208, Santa Monica, CA 90401
TELEPHONE (310) 395-6500

E-Mail Address - casenote@westworld.com • Website - www: http://www.casenotes.com

LAW
OUTLINES

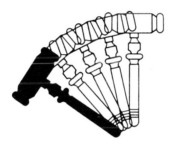

TORTS

To our students

TABLE OF CONTENTS

TC

CAPSULE OUTLINE

CAPSULE OUTLINE

CHAPTER 1 **CHAPTER 1: INTRODUCTION**

I. **THE AMBIGUITY OF THE LAW**

    A. **The Role of Rules:** Although there are many rules of law, most of them are ambiguous, particularly as applied to the facts of a case. The search for certainty in the law is a search for a chimera.

II. **TAKING A LAW EXAMINATION**

    A. **Issues and Analysis:** Likewise, any distinction between issue identification and analysis is misleading. Analysis involves an identification of issues.

    B. **Some Do's and Don'ts for Taking Law Exams:** Don't assume facts that are not fairly implied by the question. Don't catalog possible torts without relating them in detail to the question. Do read the question carefully, stick to the facts given, and answer only those things asked for by the question.

III. **REVIEW**

    A. **The *Sine Qua Non*:** Review regularly throughout the term. Pay particular attention to those matters the professor emphasizes in the course.

CHAPTER 2 **CHAPTER 2: INTENTIONAL TORTS AND DEFENSES**

I. **ASSAULT**

    A. **Definition:** An assault is the intentional causing of one to be put in apprehension of an imminent harmful or offensive bodily contact.

        1. The necessary intent is a desire to cause the consequences, or a belief that such consequences are substantially certain to occur.

    B. **The Nature of the Harm:** The threatened contact must be imminent. A past or future threat is not an assault.

        1. *The apprehension need not incite fear.* Offensiveness is sufficient.

        2. The apprehended contact need not be directly caused by the defendant.

    C. **The Nature of the Act:** Assault normally must be accompanied by some act or gesture that causes the plaintiff's apprehension.

II. **BATTERY**

    A. **Definition:** A battery is the intentional causing of an actual bodily contact that is harmful or offensive.

    B. **The Necessary Intent:** The intent here is the same as that necessary for an assault.

    C. **The Nature of the Act:** Assault normally must be accompanied by some act or gesture that causes the plaintiff's apprehension.

CO

    1. The bodily contact may be either with the plaintiff's person or with some object intimately associated with her person.

III. FALSE IMPRISONMENT

    A. Definition: False imprisonment is the intentional confinement of someone within specific boundaries without a privilege to do so.

    B. Intent: The necessary intent is to confine, without a privilege to do so.

        1. The courts recognize the doctrine of transferred intent for this tort, as well as for assault, battery, trespass to chattel, and trespass to land. The transferred-intent doctrine may possibly apply to other intentional torts as well.

    C. Plaintiff's Knowledge: The cases are divided on the question of whether the plaintiff must be aware of the confinement at the time it occurs in order to recover for solely dignitary harm resulting from the confinement. If physical injury results from the confinement, then the plaintiff should be able to recover even if he is not aware of the confinement until after it is over.

    D. Confinement: The confinement must be within boundaries fixed by the confiner and without any reasonable means of escape. The confinement need not be in a single place. Unlawful confinement in a moving car could be false imprisonment.

    E. The Act of Confinement: The confinement may, but need not, result from physical duress. It may occur as the result of unreasonable psychological duress as well.

    F. False Arrest: This involves the arrest or confinement of a person suspected of committing a crime. Generally a law enforcement officer has greater rights than an individual to arrest, and the officer's rights are further enlarged if he arrests with an apparently valid warrant.

IV. INTENTIONAL INFLICTION OF EMOTIONAL DISTRESS

    A. Definition: One who by outrageous conduct intentionally or recklessly causes severe emotional distress to another is liable for the resulting harm, whether physical or emotional.

    B. The Necessary Conduct: Words alone are sufficient to give rise to this tort, although it includes conduct as well.

    C. The Nature of the Damage: Liability does not normally extend to mere insult. Exceptions are insults by employees of common carriers or of public utilities.

        1. There may be liability for the improper handling or disposal of a dead body.

        2. A greater duty is owed to those known to be especially vulnerable or susceptible to emotional distress.

    D. Transferred Intent: The doctrine of transferred intent does not apply. Where emotional distress results from the defendant's injury of a third person, the issue of liability turns on the defendant's intent to cause emotional distress and on proximate cause (*e.g.,* how closely related, in time or otherwise, the distress is to the injury).

    E. The First Amendment Defense: The defendant may be entitled on appropriate facts to defend on grounds of free speech (especially if the plaintiff is a publicly prominent individual) or freedom of religion (especially if the resulting harm is only emotional).

V. **TRESPASS TO LAND**

   A. **Definition:** This tort occurs when one without privilege voluntarily enters, or causes another person or thing to enter, onto the land of another.

   1. The necessary intent here is to do the act, not to cause the harm.

   2. Good-faith mistake is no defense.

   3. The initial entry, although lawful, may become a trespass if the person refuses to leave after the right or privilege to be on the land has expired.

   4. Some courts require a physical entry in order for trespass to occur. These courts may find that intrusions of vibrations, gases, odors, and offensive sights or sounds and the like do not constitute trespass.

   B. **Trespass above and below the Land:** The traditional common law rule was that intrusions either above or below the ground constitute trespass. This rule has been modified to accommodate for modern-day air traffic and for subsurface extraction of oil and minerals.

   C. **Damages:** The traditional rule is that no actual damage is necessary; nominal damages are sufficient. This rule may give way where large public interests (*e.g.,* the continuation of an important industry) are at stake.

   D. **Risk-Utility Analysis:** There is a division of authority as to whether the risk of an activity should be weighed against its utility in determining liability.

   E. **Foreseeability:** While a defendant is not required to foresee the resulting damage in order to be liable, it is necessary that the risk itself be foreseeable.

VI. **TRESPASS TO CHATTEL**

   A. **Definition:** This tort results from the intentional dispossession or use of, or intermeddling with, another's chattel.

   B. **Intent:** Whether or not good-faith mistake is a defense depends on the magnitude of the interest asserted.

   C. **Degree of Harm:** There must be actual harm, although the degree of harm necessary for the tort is flexible depending on the importance of the interests involved.

VII. **CONVERSION**

   A. **Definition:** A conversion is the intentional and unauthorized exercise of dominion or control over another's chattel which so seriously interferes with the other's rights that the converter is required to pay full value for the chattel.

   1. A conversion may occur if the chattel of another is retained for a substantial period of time, if the owner is substantially inconvenienced by the retention, if the chattel is substantially damaged, or if the defendant intends to convert the chattel.

   B. **Intent:** Good-faith mistake is relevant, along with the extent of damage, in determining whether the tort has been committed and how damages are to be computed.

CO

1. Negligence is insufficient to give rise to the tort of conversion.

C. **Stolen Goods:** The general rule is that one cannot take good title to stolen goods. An exception to this rule is for stolen money or negotiable instruments payable to bearer, which can be transferred to a good-faith purchaser for value without liability for conversion by the transferee. One who obtains goods by fraud or deceit can transfer good title to a good-faith purchaser for value.

D. **Bailment:** A bailee is not strictly liable for keeping or transporting the goods of another. He will be strictly liable, however, if without authority he receives or transfers title to the goods of another or misdelivers the goods.

E. **Damages:** Damages are computed at market value as of the time of conversion, plus interest from the time of conversion to trial. Some courts allow recovery of the highest market value between conversion and trial. If there is no market value, then the cost of replacement or the value to the owner may be used.

1. If the goods are returned, recovery will be reduced by the value of the goods returned. If the converter offers to return innocently converted goods which have not been substantially damaged, the court may take this good-faith offer into account in computing damages.

VIII. DEFENSES

A. **Consent:** Consent is the willingness for conduct to occur.

1. It may be a complete defense to any tort, unless public policy invalidates the consent.

2. Consent may be express or implied, and it may be implied by words or conduct, by custom, or by law. Consent being a complete defense, the doctrine of comparative fault is inapplicable.

3. If the actor exceeds the consent given, then consent is no defense.

   a. Mistake will not invalidate the consent, unless the actor knows of the mistake or induces it by fraud, misrepresentation, or duress.

4. There are cases holding that one cannot consent to the commission of a crime.

   a. The modern view is that one can consent to the commission of a crime, unless the conduct was made criminal to protect a certain class of persons without regard to their consent.

B. **Self-Defense:** One is permitted to use reasonable force to protect oneself against threatened harm.

1. Force not threatening death or serious bodily harm may be used, without the necessity of retreat, if it is reasonably believed necessary for self-protection. Some courts hold that retreat is necessary, if reasonably possible, before using force threatening death or serious bodily harm to repel a like force. Others hold that retreat is unnecessary in this situation.

   a. The force must not be excessive (more than necessary for the occasion), and the actor will be liable for any damage caused by the use of such excessive force.

C. **Defense of Others:** A person is entitled to use the same force to defend others as she would be entitled to use to defend herself.

1. A division of authority exists as to the effect of good-faith mistake in this regard.

2. An arresting officer may use deadly force to prevent the escape of a felon reasonably suspected of posing a significant threat of death or serious bodily harm to the officer or to others.

D. Defense of Land or Chattels: One is privileged to use force, not intended to cause death or serious bodily harm, to prevent entry onto one's land or the taking of one's chattels. Force threatening death or serious bodily harm cannot be used for this purpose.

1. One can use mechanical means (such as barbed wire or a spiked fence) for this purpose if such means are reasonable and customary. Reasonable mistake as to whether or not another has a privilege to intrude is a defense if the intruder causes the mistake.

E. Recapture of Land or Chattels: One is privileged to recapture land or chattels, of which one has been wrongly deprived, by the use of timely and reasonable force that does not threaten death or serious bodily injury.

1. One is privileged to assist another in the recapture of her land or chattels if the other is herself privileged to effect the recapture.

F. Discipline and Order: One is privileged to use reasonable force to maintain discipline or to maintain order, safety, and the preservation of property.

CHAPTER 3

CHAPTER 3: NEGLIGENCE

I. INTRODUCTION

A. Negligence may be defined as the failure to take reasonable care to avoid a foreseeable risk of injury to another person. Alternatively, it is sometimes described as the breach of a duty of care owed to another person.

B. To establish a prima facie case, the plaintiff must allege and prove:

1. damage to the plaintiff,

2. fault on the part of the defendant, and

3. causation.

II. STANDARD OF CARE

A. The defendant is required to conform to the objective standard of a reasonable person in like circumstances.

1. Where a defendant is engaged in an activity that requires special skills, such as a physician or an attorney, the defendant will be held to the standard of what would be expected of a reasonable person with those skills.

2. Under the objective reasonable person standard, there will be some facts that the hypothetical reasonable person will be presumed to know or at least under a duty to find out.

3. Children are held to the standard of what it is reasonable to expect of a child of like age, intelligence, and experience.

a. Minors engaged in adult activities have been held to an adult standard.

       b.   Although often suggested, there is very little actual authority that a child is held to a higher standard when the child is the defendant than when the child is the plaintiff and the issue is the child's contributory negligence.

   4.   A mentally deficient adult is held to the objective reasonable adult standard, at least when such a person is the defendant in a negligence action.

   5.   What is reasonable conduct under the circumstances depends on many factors including whether the defendant was confronted with an emergency.

   6.   A physically handicapped person can only be required to exercise the skill and care of which such a person is physically capable, although in deciding what to do, such a person must take into consideration the handicaps from which he suffers.

       a.   There are a few cases holding that the presence of physically handicapped persons must be anticipated by others and some minimal precautions taken to protect them.

B.   The calculus of risk is used to determine whether the defendant has met the required standard of care. As enunciated by Judge Learned Hand, if the defendant's burden of protecting against the injury is less than the loss incurred times the probability of the loss being incurred, that is, if $B < PL$, the defendant is negligent.

   1.   The test cannot be taken too literally because it is hard to quantify the various factors involved.

C.   Determining what a defendant should have done in a particular situation is usually a question for the trier of fact — that is, the jury — but, since the ultimate conclusion that someone was negligent is not the sort of factual question that can be answered purely by observation, the courts will sometimes second-guess a jury and decide that, in the particular case before the court, no rational jury could find the defendant to be negligent.

D.   Sometimes the standard of care is set by the legislature. The courts will typically hold that a defendant who has violated a criminal statute is negligent *per se* even if the legislature has said nothing about what effect a violation of the statute should have in a civil case.

   1.   In a minority of states, violation of a statute is merely "evidence of negligence."

   2.   There is some division of authority on the question of whether a defendant can claim that a violation of the statute was "excused," even if the excuse would not have been valid in a criminal prosecution.

   3.   In order to base an action on a statutory violation, the plaintiff must be within the class of persons whom the legislature was trying to protect.

   4.   Some statutes impose absolute criminal liability, such as statutes prohibiting the sale of adulterated food or requiring motorists to have brakes in good operating condition. If the purpose of the statute is to protect people from a danger from which it is felt that they are unable to protect themselves, the courts will be inclined to impose absolute civil liability as well for a breach of these statutes.

E.   Evidence of custom is sometimes used in determining the standard of care and is often presented through the testimony of an expert.

   1.   In order to use expert testimony, the person presenting the testimony must first be qualified as an expert during a preliminary qualification procedure called the voir dire.

CO

2. Evidence of custom, except in certain types of medical and perhaps other professional malpractice actions, is not conclusive.

3. In cases involving medical malpractice, with some very few exceptions, a physician may not be held liable in a negligence action unless the applicable standard of care is established through the use of expert testimony.

   a. Traditionally, a physician was held to the standard of physicians practicing in the same community or, by extension, in similar communities.

      (1) The majority of jurisdictions have now probably abandoned the same or similar community standards in favor of a national standard where specialists are concerned.

      (2) There is a similar movement toward a national standard with regard to general practitioners, although a majority of states may still be applying the same or similar community standards.

      (3) The rising cost of medical malpractice insurance has led to some legislative attempts to regulate malpractice claims and/or set limits on the amounts that may be recovered in medical malpractice actions.

   b. The modern trend is to treat the question of the adequacy of information on the basis of which a plaintiff has consented to medical treatment as a question of negligence.

      (1) Under a negligence theory, even if a plaintiff establishes that he was not fully informed of the consequences of treatment, the plaintiff must usually show that a reasonable person in the plaintiff's position would have refused the treatment if an adequate disclosure had been made.

      (2) The modern trend in the United States is to answer the question of the adequacy of the information disclosed by the physician from the point of view of the reasonable person in the position of the plaintiff rather than from the perspective of what information it is customary for physicians to supply.

      (3) The courts have recognized that there may be some situations in which the need for treatment is very great and the provision of a detailed explanation might confuse, and possibly even increase, the patient's anxiety. It has been suggested that, in those circumstances, a full disclosure be made to the patient's relatives.

III. PROOF OF NEGLIGENCE

A. In the trial of all legal matters, questions of fact are sometimes determined by the use of circumstantial evidence. The term *res ipsa loquitur* describes the use of circumstantial evidence in circumstances in which the jury is specifically told that proof of the happening of an accident can be treated as proof of the defendant's negligence.

1. It is often said that the doctrine of *res ipsa loquitur* only applies when the defendant has had exclusive management or control of the instrumentality that caused the accident. It is more helpful to focus not upon whether the defendant had exclusive management or control of the instrumentality that caused the accident but upon whether the defendant had a sufficiently close connection with that instrumentality so that it is more likely than not that the defendant was negligent, given that an accident happened which normally does not occur in the absence of the negligence of someone in the defendant's position.

2. In most jurisdictions, invocation of the doctrine of *res ipsa loquitur* does not shift the ultimate burden of persuasion. That burden still remains with the plaintiff.

    a. In some jurisdictions, it is occasionally held that unless the defendant comes forward with evidence to negate the inference of negligence, the jury must decide the case for the plaintiff.

3. Although based on logical considerations, the doctrine of *res ipsa loquitur* is often justified because in most, although not all, cases in which it is invoked, the defendant has greater access to information as to how the accident occurred than does the plaintiff. Invocation of the doctrine encourages the defendant to come forward with information as to how the accident actually happened in order to exonerate himself.

    a. In pursuance of this policy, the doctrine of *res ipsa loquitur* has sometimes been used to permit patients who are injured while under general anesthesia to proceed against medical personnel whose connection with the plaintiff's injuries is rather remote.

CHAPTER 4: SPECIAL SITUATIONS

I. **NEGLIGENT INFLICTION OF EMOTIONAL DISTRESS**

    A. Practically all states now recognize some liability for the negligent infliction of emotional distress, even in the absence of some kind of physical impact with the plaintiff.

        1. Some states permit recovery if the plaintiff is within the "zone of danger," that is, within the area in which a reasonable person would perceive himself to be in danger of physical impact as a result of the defendant's negligence.

        2. Some jurisdictions have gone beyond the zone of danger test and permit some people who have witnessed the death or serious injury to others to recover for emotional distress. Factors that are considered are the proximity of the plaintiff to the scene of the accident, whether the shock resulted from a contemporaneous sensory observation of the accident, and whether the plaintiff and the victim were closely related.

            a. Some states have extended liability to close relatives who witnessed the immediate aftermath of an accident but not the accident itself.

                (1) In most states, liability only extends to close legally recognized relationships and not to people who cohabit with each other.

        3. Many jurisdictions have required that before a plaintiff can recover for severe emotional distress in the absence of a physical impact with the person of the plaintiff, the plaintiff must suffer some kind of physical injury or illness, although this injury can be rather attenuated.

        4. There are some cases holding that people who have suffered emotional distress as a result of conduct directed toward themselves, such as the recipients of telegrams mistakenly informing them of a close relative's death, can recover for the negligent infliction of emotional distress even without showing any physical injury.

II. **THE LIABILITY OF POSSESSORS OF LAND**

    A. A possessor of land is someone who occupies land with the intention to control it or who is entitled to immediate possession of the land. The liability of a possessor to persons injured on the land is still greatly influenced by the status of the person injured.

1. Persons who enter or remain on land without the consent of the possessor or without some legally recognized privilege are trespassers.

2. Persons who enter or remain on land without the consent of the possessor but who are not invitees are licensees. Persons who enter land by virtue of legally recognized privileges are also usually classified as licensees.

3. Persons who are invited to enter and remain on land for a purpose that directly or indirectly involves some kind of business dealing with the possessor are invitees or, as they are sometimes called, "business invitees." In recent years, there has been increasing recognition of a class of "public invitees," that is, of persons who, as members of the public, are invited to enter or remain on land that has been held open to the public, such as a shopping mall.

B. At common law, the extent of the duty owed by a possessor of land to those who are injured on the land depended upon the status of the person injured.

   1. The only duty owed to trespassers was to refrain from intentionally or negligently injuring known trespassers as a result of activity carried on upon the land and to warn known trespassers of highly artificial conditions which the trespasser was unlikely to appreciate, such as abandoned mine shafts.

      a. Although at one time the law made no distinction between children and adults, most states now give some added protection to child trespassers. In most jurisdictions, a possessor of land would be liable for harm caused to trespassing children from highly dangerous artificial conditions if the possessor knows or has reason to know that children are likely to trespass on the land and if there is a failure to exercise reasonable care to protect the children.

   2. A possessor of land owed to licensees all the duties owed to trespassers together with the additional duty to warn licensees of any activities being carried on upon the land or of any natural or artificial conditions on the land, of which the possessor is aware, that are dangerous and which licensees would be unlikely to discover on their own.

   3. A possessor of land owed invitees all the duties owed to trespassers and licensees and the further duties to use reasonable care to discover any dangerous conditions on the land that the possessor should expect that the invitees would not discover and to protect invitees from any such dangers from which invitees would be unable to protect themselves.

C. About ten jurisdictions have now completely abandoned the common law distinctions and ruled that the liability of a possessor of land should be based upon the reasonable person standard of reasonable care under the circumstances.

D. A number of jurisdictions have abandoned the common law distinctions between licensees and invitees but not the special doctrines affecting trespassers. Most states, however, have thus far refused to abandon the common law distinctions.

E. A number of states have enacted statutes limiting the liability of owners of land that is used, without payment of a fee, for recreational purposes.

F. A possessor of land is responsible for taking whatever measures are reasonably necessary to prevent excavations, structures, and other artificial conditions on the land from endangering persons outside of the land.

G. In a few states, the common law rule that a landlord who is not actually in possession of land only owes a tenant a duty to warn of hidden dangers of which the tenant was unaware and to maintain in proper repair those portions of the premises that remain in the landowner's control, such as common stairways and halls, is being expanded into a duty of reasonable care under the circumstances. Even under the common law rule, a landowner who leased premises for immediate public use, such as theaters or sports arenas, owed a duty of care to those who might use the premises.

1. Some jurisdictions have now read into leases of residential property an implied warranty of habitability under which a lessor is strictly liable for any unsafe conditions existing at the time of the lease.

III. FAILURE TO AID — AFFIRMATIVE DUTIES

A. In the absence of some sort of special relationship, such as employer/employee or teacher/student, the common law imposed no duty upon a person to come to the assistance of another person.

  1. One special relationship recognized by the common law was that between a tortfeasor and his victim.

    a. In recent years, the obligation of coming to the assistance of others has been extended to those who injure other people, even if the injury was not tortious.

    b. The law seems to be moving in the direction of recognizing some duty to aid business invitees, such as department store customers who become ill in a store.

    c. Vermont, by statute, imposes a general duty to come to the assistance of others when that can be done without danger or peril to the rescuer. A few other states have, by statute, imposed duties to help upon those who witness certain emergencies.

  2. There are a growing number of cases imposing some duty on psychiatrists and others to warn individuals whom they have reason to believe will be threatened with physical injury by a patient released from a mental institution or an inmate released from a public institution.

  3. Once a person had come to the assistance of another, at common law the rescuer had the full obligation of exercising reasonable care under the circumstances. In order to encourage rescuers, the Restatement (Second) of Torts has proposed that rescuers should only be liable for discontinuing their aid if they increase the danger of injury to the rescued person. With the same purpose of encouraging the rendition of aid, all jurisdictions have now enacted a form of "Good Samaritan" statute. Such statutes relieve physicians and/or others who come to the assistance of accident victims from either all liability or, more commonly, all liability for merely negligent behavior.

CHAPTER 5: PLAINTIFF'S MISCONDUCT

CHAPTER 5

I. CONTRIBUTORY NEGLIGENCE

A. At common law, the plaintiff's contributory negligence was a complete bar to an action seeking recovery from a negligent defendant. It is still the law in a few states, but the vast majority of jurisdictions has now adopted some general form of comparative negligence.

  1. At one time, the plaintiff had to prove that he was not guilty of contributory negligence, but now in most jurisdictions the burden is on the defendant to show that the plaintiff was guilty of contributory negligence.

2.   In order for the plaintiff 's contributory negligence to affect the plaintiff 's recovery, the contributory negligence must bear a causal relationship to the plaintiff 's injury.

B.   To ameliorate the harshness of the common law rule, a number of doctrines were evolved which, in certain circumstances, permitted even a contributorily negligent plaintiff to recover.

1.   If the defendant's conduct could be considered to be reckless (or intentional), the plaintiff 's recovery was not barred by contributory negligence. Now that most jurisdictions have moved to comparative negligence, there is a division of authority on whether, when the defendant is guilty of aggravated fault, the plaintiff 's contributory negligence will be ignored or whether it will be taken into account in comparing the fault of the parties.

2.   At common law, the plaintiff 's contributory negligence was no bar to an action if the defendant was found to have had the "last clear chance" to avoid the accident. If the plaintiff, through no fault of her own, had been rendered helpless and thus no longer able to avoid the accident by the exercise of reasonable care, a negligent defendant would be liable for failing to use with reasonable care his then-existing opportunity to avoid the harm when he knew of the plaintiff 's situation and thus realized, or had reason to realize, the plaintiff 's peril. Some jurisdictions also applied the doctrine in favor of a helpless plaintiff if the defendant should have realized the plaintiff 's peril had the defendant exercised due care.

a.   Some states even permitted an inattentive plaintiff to recover if the defendant actually knew of the plaintiff 's helplessness and then failed to use due care to avoid the accident.

b.   Most jurisdictions that have adopted comparative fault have now ostensibly abolished the doctrine of last clear chance.

II.   ASSUMPTION OF RISK

A.   At common law, assumption of risk was also a complete defense to a negligence action. Assumption of risk is often classified as being either express or implied.

1.   Express assumption of risk typically arises in situations in which the plaintiff has signed a release acknowledging the risk involved and absolving the defendant from any legal liability if injury ensues. When the defendant is providing what might be considered a necessary public service and there is a disparity in bargaining power, the courts have struck down such releases as contrary to public policy. Releases signed by race car drivers and others competing in sporting events have, on the other hand, generally been upheld. Even with the adoption of comparative negligence, the courts continue to recognize express assumption of risk as a complete defense to a negligence action.

a.   The concept of express assumption of risk has been extended by analogy to cover certain situations in which there was no actual formal agreement to assume the risk of injury, as for example, cases involving participants in sporting events. Because of the absence of a formal written agreement, these are probably instances of implied assumption of risk.

2.   Implied assumption of risk is the term used to describe the other situations in which a plaintiff, who might be said to have consciously accepted a risk, was barred from recovery. Because of dissatisfaction with the doctrine of implied assumption of risk, many courts, even before the advent of comparative negligence, merged the doctrine of implied assumption of risk with that of contributory negligence.

a.   Implied assumption of risk is sometimes used to describe a situation in which the courts would otherwise be inclined to hold that the defendant had no duty to the plaintiff, that is, was not negligent toward the plaintiff. Typical of these situations are cases in which a spectator at a baseball game was struck by a batted ball. A similar approach has been used to bar recovery by participants in formal games.

    b. Implied assumption of risk has also been used to describe situations in which the defendant was truly negligent toward the plaintiff but in which it was felt that the plaintiff was aware of the risk that had been created. It is these situations which many courts have been inclined to merge with the doctrines of contributory and comparative negligence.

III. COMPARATIVE FAULT

A. Most American jurisdictions have now adopted some form of comparative fault.

B. Comparative fault schemes generally fall into one of three basic types.

    1. The first is the so-called "pure" type under which even a plaintiff who is 99% at fault would be entitled to recover 1% of his damages against a defendant who is 1% at fault.

    2. The second type permits plaintiffs to recover at least some of their damages in situations in which a plaintiff's negligence was "less than" that of the defendant.

    3. The third and most popular form of comparative negligence scheme is that in which plaintiffs can recover at least some of their damages in situations in which the plaintiff's fault is "not greater than" that of the defendant. Under this type of "modified" scheme, if the defendant counterclaims and the trier of fact finds the parties to be equally at fault, both parties can recover against each other as they can under the pure type.

C. In jurisdictions which have adopted the so-called pure form of comparative fault, it frequently happens that the plaintiff and the defendant will each get a judgment against each other. Under traditional notions, these judgments should be set off against each other and one judgment entered for the balance due against one of the parties. A number of states, by judicial decision or statute, have declared that set-offs are only permitted when the parties are uninsured or the amounts awarded exceed policy limits.

D. In jurisdictions that have adopted one of the so-called modified comparative fault schemes, there is a division of authority, in cases involving more than one defendant, as to whether the plaintiff's fault must be compared to the fault of each defendant separately or to the combined fault of all the parties.

IV. THE SO-CALLED SEAT BELT DEFENSE

A. In about ten jurisdictions, either by statute or judicial decision, some reduction in damages is possible for a plaintiff's failure to wear a seat belt. In about half the states, no reduction in damages is made because of the plaintiff's failure to wear a seat belt and, in the remaining states, the law is unclear.

CHAPTER 6: MULTIPLE DEFENDANTS, CONTRIBUTION, AND INDEMNITY   *CHAPTER 6*

I. JOINT LIABILITY

A. Typical Situations: A cotortfeasor is jointly (fully) liable for an injury if the tort would not have occurred but for the act or omission of that cotortfeasor — or, as some courts say, if the cotortfeasor was a substantial cause of the injury. The plaintiff can collect all or any part of her damages from any one of the jointly liable defendants, but she can collect her full damages only once.

CO

1. Some courts do not impose joint liability (but rather, they impose several liability) if the injuries caused by different tortfeasors occur successively. The better rule imposes joint liability in this situation also, where the injuries are theoretically or practically indivisible.

II. SEVERAL LIABILITY

A. Abolition of Joint Liability: A number of jurisdictions have abolished joint liability, in whole or in part, in favor of several liability. Several liability means that each defendant is liable only for the damages caused by his own fault or responsibility.

    1. The impetus toward adoption of several liability has been fueled in part by the widespread adoption of comparative fault as between plaintiffs and defendants.

        a. Other jurisdictions have retained joint liability, even with the adoption of comparative fault. The reasons for such retention are that the plaintiff may be faultless, or his fault may be less culpable than that of the defendants, each of whom are fully responsible for all of the plaintiff's damages.

III. CONTRIBUTION

A. Types of Contribution: Where joint liability exists, many jurisdictions allow a defendant who has paid more than his fair share to seek recovery over by way of contribution against another defendant who has not paid her fair share.

    1. Where contribution is allowed, apportionment is made on: (1) an equal basis, (2) the relative degrees of fault, or (3) the relative degrees of causation. Some courts consider both fault and cause in making apportionment.

    2. Contribution between strictly liable and negligent cotortfeasors is widely allowed. Many courts do not, however, allow an intentional tortfeasor to seek recovery against a cotortfeasor.

    3. There is a division of authority as to whether a tortfeasor will be permitted to recover contribution from a cotortfeasor who is immune from liability to the tort victim.

B. Settlement: The traditional rule is that a release of one tortfeasor releases all cotortfeasors from liability to the tort victim, while a covenant not to sue does not release the other cotortfeasors from liability to the tort victim. The modern approach is that neither type of agreement releases the other cotortfeasors from liability to the tort victim, unless the intent to do so is apparent.

    1. A satisfaction by judgment, however, does release other cotortfeasors from liability to the tort victim.

    2. A settlement for the full amount due, or the satisfaction of a judgment, will entitle the payor to seek contribution against other cotortfeasors.

    3. If a tortfeasor settles for less than the full amount due, two approaches are taken: the settler remains liable to and able to make claims for contribution, or the settler is immune to and barred from claims for contribution. The latter is the more common approach.

        a. Where the settlor settles for less than the full amount and is immune from contribution, nonsettling cotortfeasors are then entitled to a credit against any liability they may have to the tort victim, an amount equal either to the amount of the settlement, or (under another approach) to the share of liability attributable to the settlor.

IV. INDEMNITY

    A. Basis and Effect: When one tortfeasor is vicariously liable, or passively at fault, and pays any part of the tort victim's claim, he can then seek recovery over for all of that payment from a cotortfeasor who is primarily liable or is actively at fault.

        1. The trend today is to abolish indemnity (full recovery over) in favor of contribution (partial recovery over), especially in the active-passive situation.

    B. Settlement: There is a division of authority as to whether release of the indemnitor automatically releases the indemnitee.

CHAPTER 7: ACTUAL CAUSE

I. IN GENERAL

    A. We ascribe causal relationships between two events as part of our attempt to understand those events and the extent of the relationship between them. If we could fully comprehend the cause of a particular event, we should, in theory at least, be capable of recreating that event by bringing into existence all the preceding events which caused the event in question.

        1. It is often impossible, however, even in theory, to completely recreate an event. Under such circumstances, we look for some prior event that could have been part of the cause of the event in question and then try to eliminate all other possible causes. Thus, by a process of elimination, some prior event, such as the defendant's negligence, becomes the most likely cause of the event in which we are interested.

        2. The inquiry is not purely an objective one because the causal inquiry will be affected by the level of generality at which the inquiry takes place. On a general level, there does not seem to be any correlation between driving a car in excess of the speed limit and the car's being hit by lightning. If, however, the events are described in greater detail so as to include precise time, atmospheric and wind conditions, etc., one would eventually reach a description of the two events in which there indeed was a correlation between the act of driving in excess of the speed limit and the striking of the vehicle by lightning. The determination of the appropriate level of generality with which the events are to be described depends largely on common sense as reflected in legal precedent.

    B. There are some anomalous situations in which the courts will find a causal connection between the defendant's negligence and the plaintiff's injuries when, as a matter of strict logic, it would be difficult to conclude that the proof permits that inference. Examples include cases in which two fires, each of which would have been sufficient to destroy the plaintiff's property, joined up before the plaintiff's property is destroyed by the combined fire. A strong argument could be made that either fire alone would have destroyed the plaintiff's property. Nevertheless, in such circumstances, most courts will allow recovery against a defendant whose negligence was responsible for one of the fires on the ground that the defendant's fire was a *substantial cause* of the plaintiff's injuries.

        1. The notion of substantial cause is also sometimes used to describe a situation in which the defendant's negligent conduct initially appears to have had only a low probability of causing the plaintiff's injuries, but the plaintiff has succeeded in eliminating other possible causal explanations. The courts may use the language of substantial cause in these situations because despite the elimination of other possible causes, they have some lingering doubts as to whether the plaintiff has shown that the defendant's conduct was, in point of fact, more likely than not the cause of the injury.

CO

C. *Actual cause* or *cause in fact* has also successfully been established in circumstances in which the plaintiff has shown that there are several possible causes, each of which alone is sufficient to account for the plaintiff's injuries, but the plaintiff is unable to establish which particular cause actually caused the injuries.

    1. These cases are sometimes explained in terms of "substantial cause," namely that the conduct of all the defendants was a substantial cause of the plaintiff's injuries, even if it is clear from the facts of the case, such as when the plaintiff is hit by a single shot but two or more defendants have discharged their weapons, that the plaintiff could only have been injured by one of the defendants. This explanation leaves much to be desired as a matter of strict logic.

    2. A more satisfactory explanation of such situations is that once it is shown that both defendants are negligent and that the plaintiff is unable to show which of the negligent defendants actually caused the injury, the burden of persuasion on the issue of causation shifts to the defendants. This doctrine encourages the individual defendants to come forward with evidence that will establish that one of the other defendants is the responsible party. In situations where such proof is unavailable, however, the effect of shifting the burden is to impose liability upon all the defendants even if it is clear that not all of them not caused the injury. As the number of defendants decreases, the imposition of liability upon all the defendants becomes more questionable both on the consideration of logic and fairness.

D. In recent years, the problem has arisen as to whether the plaintiff can bring an action against a defendant whose negligence has resulted in the plaintiff's loss of a chance to avoid some particular risk. A few courts have permitted at least some recovery in these situations. Some of these courts have suggested that recovery should be limited only to a portion of the plaintiff's injuries, namely the monetary value of the chance of recovery lost by the plaintiff. Because of the difficulty of evaluating the value of the loss of a chance, most courts are inclined to deny such recovery.

CHAPTER 8   **CHAPTER 8: PROXIMATE CAUSE**

I.   THE DIRECT CAUSE TEST

A. The older cases generally spoke in terms of the defendant being liable when the defendant's negligent conduct was the *direct cause* of the plaintiff's injuries. In the famous *Polemis* case, it was held that even if the plaintiff's injuries were unforeseeable, the defendants would nevertheless be liable if their conduct was the direct cause of the plaintiff's injuries.

    1. A difficulty with the direct cause test is that it suggests that a cause might not be "direct" if there are sufficient other "intervening causes" without adequately explaining what a sufficient intervening cause is.

II. THE REASONABLE FORESEEABILITY TEST

A. The modern trend is to accept that the reasonable foreseeability of the defendant's conduct resulting in injury to the plaintiff is not only relevant to the question of whether the defendant was negligent but is also relevant to the question of the extent of the defendant's liability.

    1. The most famous expositions of this view are contained in the two *Wagon Mound* cases decided by the Privy Council. In the second of these cases, it was held that even a relatively remote cause was sufficiently foreseeable to impose liability when the possible danger was very great and the injury could have been easily avoided.

        a. The recent American cases seem to adopt the reasonable foreseeability test, but if the foreseeability of a slight chance that the defendant's conduct will cause the injury is sufficient to satisfy the test, it does not seem to offer defendants much comfort.

b. There is some uncertainty in the authorities as to whether a defendant who threatens some particular interest of the plaintiff may be held liable for a completely unforeseeable injury to some other interest of the plaintiff.

c. There is no certain answer as to how foreseeable an injury must be in order to be "reasonably foreseeable." The courts will be guided by common sense and precedent and their perception of the importance of the interests involved.

2. It has sometimes been suggested that the question of proximate cause is ultimately a policy question, but courts have been reluctant to accept openly that the ascription of causation in an action for damages is ultimately a political question.

3. The courts have struggled with the question of exactly what has to be foreseen.

a. It is universally held that if damage of a certain type is foreseeable as a result of the defendant's negligent conduct, the defendant is legally responsible for all damage of that type suffered by the plaintiff, even if the extent of the damage actually inflicted was not reasonably foreseeable.

b. The causal inquiry will be affected by the manner in which the events in question are described. If the defendant must foresee the specific details of a particular accident, it is more likely that the accident will be held to have been unforeseeable. On the other hand, if the defendant must only be able to foresee an accident of some general type, it is easier to find that the defendant could reasonably have foreseen the plaintiff's injuries.

III. INTERVENING CAUSE

A. Even where a defendant's conduct is held to be a direct cause or a foreseeable cause of a plaintiff's injuries, the defendant may still escape liability if there are any superseding intervening causes.

1. Acts of God or of innocent or negligent third parties are universally held not to be superseding causes if the intervening acts can be said to have been "reasonably foreseeable." As a special application of this rule, a plaintiff may recover from a negligent defendant not only damage resulting from the initial injury but also damages resulting from the enhancement of those injuries in the course of subsequent medical treatment. By injuring the plaintiff, the defendant has exposed him to a foreseeable risk of injury by health care professionals.

2. The question of the effect of intentional or reckless acts of third persons is more difficult.

a. The modern tendency is to permit recovery despite the intervening, reckless, or intentional acts of third persons. In deciding whether an intervening act is a superseding act, the courts will consider the culpability of the intervening act and, more importantly, its foreseeability. The more foreseeable the intervening acts of a third party are, the more likely it is that the courts will hold the negligent defendant responsible for the ultimate result.

b. In recent times, the courts have sometimes allowed recovery on behalf of persons who have committed suicide on the ground that the original injuries caused by the defendant's negligent conduct had rendered such a person emotionally unstable.

CO

IV. **LIABILITY TO RESCUERS**

A. On the theory that "danger invites rescue," one who injures or subjects others to a serious risk of injury will be held to have caused the injuries incurred by someone making a reasonable rescue attempt.

1. In some jurisdictions, this principle is qualified by a doctrine that precludes recovery by "professional rescuers," such as police officers or firefighters.

CHAPTER 9 **CHAPTER 9: VICARIOUS LIABILITY**

I. **THE RATIONALE FOR THE RULE**

A. **Qui Facit Per Alium Facit per se:** Some courts give, as the basis for the rule, the respondent's right of control over the actor. Others view the basis as resting on the idea that the act is done in furtherance of the respondent's interests. In some instances, the respondent may authorize or ratify the act. The broadest basis for the rule is that the respondent should be liable for its agent's acts that are fairly characteristic of the respondent's enterprise or activity.

II. **TYPICAL SITUATIONS OF VICARIOUS LIABILITY**

A. **The Employment Relationship:** There are certain broad categories of tortious acts to which the doctrine typically applies. One (perhaps the most common) involves acts of employees committed within the scope of employment imposing liability on the employer.

B. **Partners and Joint Venturers:** Acts of partners or of joint venturers can make another partner or joint venturer liable.

C. **The Independent Contractor:** Acts of independent contractors involving nondelegable duties or apparent agency may give rise to liability of the principal.

D. **Bailers:** Acts of automobile bailees may make the bailor liable.

E. **Parents:** In certain circumstances, acts of children may result in parental liability.

III. **IMPUTED CONTRIBUTORY NEGLIGENCE**

A. **The "Both-ways" Rule:** In some instances, courts impute the contributory negligence of an agent to the principal, so as to bar or reduce the principal's claim against another. Common situations are in the employer-employee and joint venture contexts. Likewise, contributory fault may be imputed in derivative claims such as wrongful death, survival, and loss of consortium.

CHAPTER 10 **CHAPTER 10: STRICT LIABILITY FOR ANIMALS AND FOR ABNORMALLY DANGEROUS ACTIVITIES**

I. **ANIMALS**

A. **Trespassing Livestock:** An owner of livestock is generally strictly liable (liable without fault) for damage caused by their trespass.

1. *Exceptions:* animals straying when being driven on the highway; jurisdictions where fences are required to be maintained to keep the livestock out; the escape of livestock brought about by unforeseeable events.

B. Domestic Animals: The general rule is that there is no strict liability — except possibly for trespass — for harm done by domestic animals, unless the owner knows or has reason to know that the animal is abnormally dangerous.

C. Wild Animals: The owner or possessor of a wild animal may be strictly liable for harm done by the animal, whether or not the harm is foreseeable.

    1. *Possible exceptions to strict liability:* Harm done after escape of the animal and capture by another or return of the animal to its natural habitat; harm to trespassers; harm done by animals possessed by a public officer or common carrier.

        a. There is a division of authority as to whether zoo keepers are strictly liable for harm caused by their animals.

        b. The traditional rule has been that contributory negligence is no defense, but that assumption of the risk is a defense. This rule may change with the widespread adoption of comparative fault.

II. ABNORMALLY DANGEROUS ACTIVITIES

A. Origin and Development of the Doctrine: These are activities that involve abnormal danger, considering the degree and likelihood of risk, the actor's inability to eliminate the risk by the exercise of care, the uncommonness and inappropriateness of the activity to the area where it is carried on, and the extent to which the value of the activity is outweighed by its danger. No single factor and no combination of these factors must be present in order to impose strict liability for damages caused by one engaged in an abnormally dangerous activity.

    1. Typical activities giving rise to strict liability are activities causing damage from the escape of large quantities of stored water (*Rylands v. Fletcher*), from blasting, crop-dusting, and the like.

B. Defenses: There is a division of authority as to whether the harm must be foreseeable and whether there is liability for harm caused by an activity carried on pursuant to a public duty.

    1. The Restatement takes the position that contributory negligence is no defense and that assumption of the risk is a bar to recovery. These rules may no longer be applied with the widespread adoption of comparative fault.

CHAPTER 11: PRODUCTS LIABILITY

I. THEORIES OF RECOVERY

A. Tort and Warranty: Claims are typically brought in negligence, strict tort, and warranty (which is also strict liability). Usually, in order to hold a person strictly liable for the sale or supply of a defective product, the person must be in the business of selling or supplying the product. A claim in strict liability can, however, be brought against a non–business-seller for breach of an express warranty or breach of an implied warranty of fitness for a particular purpose.

    1. Rules pertaining to notice of breach, disclaimer, and sometimes a requirement of privity of contract, and other special warranty rules may apply to claims for breach of warranty. Strict tort and negligence are not governed by such rules, and typically any foreseeable plaintiff may recover for any foreseeable physical injury.

    2. If the defendant supplier engages in intentional, willful, or reckless misconduct, she may be held

CO

liable for injury resulting from such conduct as well, and typically punitive damages are recoverable in this situation.

3. In cases involving defective design or failure to warn, many courts say that an implied strict liability action in warranty or tort is essentially the same as a suit in negligence. Most courts will recognize a true strict liability action, however, for misrepresentation. If the product — especially a prescription drug — is considered unavoidably unsafe (cannot be made safe by the exercise of due care), many courts will refuse to apply strict liability.

II. BASES OF RECOVERY

A. **Types of Defect:** The defective conditions are typically described as: manufacturing defects, design defects, and warning defects (failure to warn, or failure to warn adequately). In addition, a misrepresentation may also be viewed as a defective condition regarding the product.

III. DEFINITIONS OF DEFECTIVENESS

A. **Multiple Definitions:** A widely used definition of defectiveness is that of ordinary consumer expectations: a product is defective if it fails to meet ordinary consumer expectations. Other courts presume seller knowledge of the product's condition and then ask whether a reasonable seller would put the product on the market with that knowledge. Perhaps the most widely used test, particularly for design and warning, is a risk-benefit analysis; the product will be considered defective if the risk outweighs its utility or outweighs the burden of eliminating or avoiding the risk.

IV. THE PARTIES

A. **Possible Plaintiffs and Defendants:** Any foreseeable plaintiff and any defendant in the business of selling, leasing or supplying a product may be involved in a products claim. Products liability has also been extended by many courts to one in the business of building and selling houses.

V. TRANSACTIONS COVERED BY PRODUCTS LIABILITY

A. **The Product:** Products liability applies to the sale or supply of tangible products. At the fringes, there is uncertainty as to what constitutes a product — as opposed to a service or intangible items. Products liability has often been applied to the sale of residential real estate and to leases of personal property.

B. **Solely Economic Loss:** Where the plaintiff suffers only economic loss (*e.g.,* loss of bargain or lost profits), many courts hold that the plaintiff must sue in warranty and cannot sue in negligence or strict tort. Additionally, these courts may require privity of contract, at least in the absence of a breached express warranty by the seller or supplier.

C. **Successor Corporation Liability:** If one corporation buys all the assets of another corporation and continues the same business of the other corporation, which later dissolves, using many of the same officers and employees of the selling corporation, then the buying corporation may be held liable for harm caused by the seller's defective products sold prior to the sale of assets to the buying corporation.

VI. DEFENSES

A. **In General:** Defenses generally available in any tort or warranty action — such as statute of limitations, lack of jurisdiction, etc. — apply to products liability.

B. **Defenses Typical of Products Liability:** In addition, there are some defenses typical of products liability.

1. If a manufacturer manufactures a product according to government specifications for purchase by the federal government and warns the government of any dangers of which the manufacturer knows and the government does not know, the manufacturer will not be liable for defective design of the product.

2. A number of courts have held that compliance with federal safety regulations preempts any claim for product injuries resulting from compliance with such regulations.

3. There is a division of authority regarding whether obviousness of danger is a bar to recovery.

CHAPTER 12: NONDISCLOSURE AND MISREPRESENTATION CAUSING ONLY PECUNIARY (OR PURE ECONOMIC) LOSS

I. NONDISCLOSURE

A. **The Traditional Rule:** The traditional rule is that a person has no duty to disclose a matter known to him that would adversely affect the pecuniary interests of another in a transaction with the person, unless the person was in a fiduciary relation with the other, actively prevented discovery of the matter, or made misleading statements or half-truths about the matter.

   1. The modern rule is that such a person must disclose known facts basic to the transaction that would materially affect the outcome thereof.

      a. The cases speak in terms of "known" facts and of disclosure to "parties" to a "business" transaction. However, the duty may extend to facts of which the person had reason to know or should have known, to those other than the immediate parties to the transaction, and to nonbusiness transactions.

II. DECEIT OR FRAUDULENT MISREPRESENTATION

A. **Liability to Foreseeable Plaintiffs:** One is liable to foreseeable plaintiffs for pecuniary loss caused by a deceitful or fraudulent misrepresentation. Such a misrepresentation is one made knowingly, recklessly, or without belief in the truth of the statement.

III. NEGLIGENT MISREPRESENTATION

A. **Scope of Permissible Plaintiffs:** Recovery of pecuniary loss resulting from negligent misrepresentation is generally permitted, the major question being the scope of permissible plaintiffs.

   1. One rule restricts recovery to those in privity with the defendant and to third party beneficiaries.

      a. A slightly broader rule allows recovery by a "limited group" of third persons for whose benefit the statement is intended, even though those persons are not "specifically identified or known."

      b. There is a trend to extend liability for negligent misrepresentation resulting in pecuniary loss occurring as "reasonably foreseeable consequences" of the statement.

IV. INNOCENT MISREPRESENTATION

A. **Business Misrepresentation:** One who innocently misrepresents to another a business matter of which he has special means of knowledge may be strictly liable to the other for resulting pecuniary loss.

V.   DEFENSES

    A.   Reliance: A plaintiff must generally prove that she relied on the misstatement to her detriment, although that reliance need not be the sole inducement to act as long as it is a substantial factor. Promises to act or to refrain from acting in the future are actionable in tort only if the promise is fraudulently or deceitfully made. The First Amendment to the U.S. Constitution may require proof of knowing or reckless falsity where the plaintiff is a public figure and the matter is one of public interest.

VI.   DAMAGES

    A.   Fraud, Negligence, and Strict Liability.

        1.   In fraud, one may recover out-of-pocket losses or loss of bargain.

        2.   In negligence or strict liability, recovery may be limited to out-of-pocket loss (the difference between the price and value received).

        3.   The plaintiff in any case can recover reasonably foreseeable incidental and consequential damages.

CHAPTER 13   **CHAPTER 13: BUSINESS TORTS**

I.   PRODUCTS DISPARAGEMENT OR INJURIOUS FALSEHOOD

    A.   Definition: This tort consists of the publication of a false statement that is intended or reasonably understood to cast doubt on the quality of another's land, chattels, or intangible things, or on the existence or extent of the other's property interest therein.

        1.   Such a statement may reflect on the other's character as well, in which event it can also constitute defamation.

    B.   Damages: Unlike defamation, the plaintiff can recover for product disparagement only if she can show she has suffered pecuniary loss.

    C.   Privileges: The privileges in defamation also apply to product disparagement. In addition, a person is permitted to make an unfavorable comparison of his product with that of a competitor, as long as the comparison contains no false statement of fact.

        1.   Proof of knowledge or reckless disregard of falsity will be required if the plaintiff is a public person and the matter one of public interest or concern.

II.   INTERFERENCE WITH CONTRACT OR WITH PROSPECTIVE ECONOMIC ADVANTAGE

    A.   Definition: One who intentionally and improperly interferes with another's contract or prospective economic advantage may be liable for resulting pecuniary loss to the other. A determination of the impropriety of the interference takes into account the nature of the actor's conduct, his motive, the interests interfered with and the interests sought to be advanced, the relation of the parties, and proximate cause.

        1.   One cannot interfere with an existing, valid contract solely for purposes of competition. One can interfere with a prospective economic advantage for purposes of competition, unless wrongful means are employed or other, wrongful purposes are a substantial factor in the interference.

III. NEGLIGENT INTERFERENCE

    A. General Rule: The general rule is that there is no tort liability for solely pecuniary loss resulting from the negligent interference by a noncontracting party with a contract or prospective economic advantage. There are exceptions to this rule, where the plaintiff (such as a fisherman) stands in a legally favored position or resembles a third party beneficiary of a contract.

CHAPTER 14: NUISANCE

I. THE RATIONALE FOR NUISANCE

    A. Purpose: Unlike trespass to land in some jurisdictions, an action for private nuisance will lie for a nonphysical invasion such as by sight, sound, or odor, as well as for physical invasion.

        1. The general rule is that nuisance requires proof of significant harm, as judged by a standard of the normal or reasonable person.

    B. Standards of Liability: An intentional nuisance occurs if the actor intended to do the act. A negligent nuisance results from the unreasonable failure to discover and prevent the nuisance. Strict liability for nuisance may be imposed if the act involves abnormally dangerous conduct.

    C. The Balancing Test: There is a division of authority as to whether the utility of the defendant's conduct should be balanced against the harm caused in determining whether liability for nuisance should be imposed.

        1. Another approach is to determine whether the harm caused by defendant's conduct is serious and whether liability would prevent continuation of the conduct. If the harm is serious and liability would not prevent continuation of the conduct, nuisance may be found.

        2. In all events, if defendant's conduct is sufficiently reprehensible, nuisance liability will be found.

II. DAMAGES

    A. Types: Damages may be either temporary or permanent, depending on whether defendant's conduct is sporadic or continuous. In addition, punitive damages can be imposed for reckless or callous misconduct.

    B. Limitations on Recoverable Damages: If plaintiff "comes to" the nuisance (the defendant was there first), this may limit or bar recovery. Also plaintiff will be unable to recover for damages resulting from his extrasensitivity.

CHAPTER 15: CIVIL RIGHTS (OR CONSTITUTIONAL) TORTS

I. ACTIONS AGAINST STATE OFFICIALS: § 1983

    A. 42 U.S.C. § 1983 provides a remedy for persons who have been deprived, under color of state law, of rights secured by the Constitution and laws of the United States. The Court has held that state officials who are acting in clear violation of state law can, nevertheless, be acting under color of state law so as to be subject to suit in federal court under § 1983.

        1. The Court has held that municipalities can be held liable under § 1983 for the acts of their employees in execution of official policy and for actions of senior officials who could be said to make the policy of the municipality.

2. The Court has held that Congress did not intend § 1983 to permit suit against the state itself in the federal courts.

3. The Court has also held that § 1983 covers all federal law and not just those federal statutes concerned with equal rights.

B. Under 42 U.S.C. § 1988, attorney fees can be granted to the prevailing parties in this type of litigation.

C. Punitive damages are available in § 1983 actions against individuals upon the showing that the defendant's conduct was motivated by evil motives or when the defendant's conduct involves reckless or callous indifference to federally protected rights.

1. Punitive damages are not available in § 1983 actions against municipalities.

D. There can be no recovery of presumed damages for abstract deprivation of rights although the Court has left open the possibility that, where compensatory damages for actual injuries are too difficult to measure, resort might be had to something like presumed damages.

E. Actions under § 1983 can be brought in state courts as well as in federal courts.

F. Congress has provided that, where federal law is not suitable to achieve the purposes of the various civil rights statutes or is deficient in the provision of remedies, federal courts may refer to the common law, as modified by the constitution and statutes of the state in which the federal court having jurisdiction over the case is sitting, in so far as so doing would not be inconsistent with the Constitution and laws of the United States.

1. The Court has held that § 1983 actions are to be classified as personal injury actions, and if the state has more than one statute of limitations for personal injury actions, § 1983 actions are to be governed by the residual or general personal injury statute of limitations.

G. The Court has held that resort to § 1983 does not require exhaustion of available state remedies but has also been reluctant to allow § 1983 to become a substitute for state tort law when the defendant is a state official. The Court has held that defamation actions cannot be brought under § 1983.

H. After much wrestling with the problem, the Court has ruled that a § 1983 action will not lie for merely negligent conduct. It has left open whether something less than intentional conduct, such as recklessness or gross negligence, might be enough to give rise to a § 1983 action.

II. ACTIONS AGAINST FEDERAL OFFICIALS

A. In the *Bivens* case, the Court decided that an action could be brought in federal court for an improper arrest and consequent search by federal officials.

1. The Court in *Bivens* left open the question as to what, if any, defenses might be available to federal officials in civil rights actions brought against them in federal courts.

2. As a result of the creation of the *Bivens*-type action, Congress amended the Federal Tort Claims Act in 1974 to provide that, with regard "to acts or omissions of investigative or law enforcement officers of the United States," claims "arising out of . . . assault, battery, false imprisonment, false arrest, abuse of process, or malicious prosecution" could be brought against the United States under the Tort Claims Act. This provision does not, however, prevent an action from also being brought under *Bivens* against federal officials who have violated the constitutional rights of the plaintiff.

3. Many of the doctrines developed in § 1983 actions have been carried over to *Bivens*-type actions against federal officials.

III. IMMUNITIES FROM CIVIL RIGHTS ACTIONS

A. Legislators and persons engaged in performing judicial functions or engaged in performing the functions of a prosecutor have been held to enjoy an absolute immunity from a civil rights action.

   1. The Court has held that the President of the United States is absolutely immune for any activities "within the outer perimeter" of his official responsibilities.

      a. Cabinet officers, presidential assistants, and other executive officers have been held only to enjoy a qualified privilege, namely an immunity from suit when they can show that they have acted in good faith.

   2. In a § 1983 action brought against a municipality, the municipality itself cannot take advantage of any qualified immunity based on the good faith and absence of malice of the officials for whose conduct the municipality is responsible. Any such qualified immunity only applies in actions against the individual officials.

CHAPTER 16: DEFAMATION

I. THE COMMON LAW ACTION FOR DEFAMATION

CHAPTER 16

A. Defamation consists of the publication to third parties of matter which is false and defamatory, that is, of material whose tendency is to harm a person's reputation so as to lower that person in the estimation of the community or to deter third persons from associating or dealing with him.

B. For historical reasons, the tort of defamation has two forms. Slander concerns oral communications, and libel concerns written communications.

C. Slander is a false and defamatory oral communication. To bring an action for slander, the plaintiff is required to show either special damages or that the slanderous statement falls into the category of slander that has been denominated slander per se.

   1. Special damages are damages that have been suffered as a direct result of the plaintiff's loss of reputation in the community. Foreseeable pecuniary harm, such as the medical expenses incurred for a nervous breakdown, is not enough, but loss of employment would constitute special damages.

   2. There are now four categories of slander per se.

      a. Statements imputing criminal conduct.

      b. Statements imputing infection with a loathsome or infectious disease, a category generally restricted to venereal diseases and leprosy.

      c. Statements imputing a lack of chastity to a woman. Some modern authorities suggest that this should extend to all charges of serious sexual misconduct by men and of homosexuality.

      d. Statements directly affecting a person's office, profession, trade, or business.

CO

D. At common law, libel was actionable without proof of actual damages, and this is still the law in England and probably in the majority of American jurisdictions.

   1. A significant number of jurisdictions in the United States distinguish between libel per se, which is actionable without proof of special damages, and libel per quod, which, like slander, requires the allegation and proof of special damages.

   a. The distinction between libel per se and libel per quod may be made on the basis of whether the libel is clear on its face or whether the libel falls into one of the four slander per se categories.

E. It is customary in an action for defamation for the plaintiff to include in the complaint: (1) a verbatim description of the defamatory statement; (2) an allegation of publication to third parties; (3) an explanation of how the statement relates to the plaintiff and why the statement is defamatory; and (4) a claim for damages. If the defamation is of a kind that requires proof of special damages, these must be described in the complaint, and if proof of malice is required, as it sometimes is in order to recover punitive damages or to defeat a claim of privilege, an allegation of such malice must also be included.

   1. When the defamatory character of the alleged defamatory statement or the statement's connection to the plaintiff is not apparent from its actual words, the plaintiff will have to allege the facts necessary to support his claims in a part of the complaint known as the *inducement.*

   2. The *colloquium* is the part of complaint in which the plaintiff, making use where necessary of facts contained in the inducement, asserts that the defamatory statement was made about him.

   3. The *innuendo* is the portion of the complaint in which the plaintiff explains why the statement defames him.

F. Criminal libel, an indictable offense at common law, was aimed at suppressing sedition and extended to reach written material likely to lead to breaches of the peace. Although at one time truth was not a defense to criminal libel, truth is now an absolute defense to such a prosecution.

G. To be actionable, the defamatory statement must be published to third parties.

   1. The publication must be either intentional or the result of negligent conduct. Purely innocent publication is not sufficient, but all that is necessary is that the publication be intended. It is not necessary that the publisher know the statement is defamatory.

   2. One exception to the common law rule imposing absolute liability upon those who intentionally or negligently publish defamatory material arose with regard to libraries, newsstands, book shops, and newspaper and magazine distributors. In actions against such persons, the plaintiff must, at the very least, show that they had some knowledge of the defamatory content of the publication in question.

   3. At common law, each copy of a book containing defamatory material was a separate publication, but most American jurisdictions now follow the "single publication rule," under which any one edition of a book, newspaper, or any one radio or television broadcast is considered a single publication for which only one action will lie.

   4. One who republishes defamatory statements made by another is held to be a publisher of defamatory material.

   5. Someone who fails to remove a defamatory statement affixed to his property by third parties, within a reasonable time after receiving notice of the defamatory nature of the statement, is liable for publishing defamatory material.

H. Movies, television, and — in most American jurisdictions — radio have been classified as libel. A number of states have passed statutes absolving broadcasters from liability for innocent defamation or limiting plaintiffs, in actions against broadcasters, to recovery of only actual damages.

I. A statement of opinion that implies the existence of facts that support the opinion can be defamatory. Where the opinion is based on known facts or does not suggest the existence of undisclosed, defamatory facts that provide the basis for the opinion, it is not actionable.

    1. Determining what is a statement of fact and what is a statement of opinion is very difficult. There are no hard and fast rules that may be used to decide the issue.

J. Because the plaintiff must show that someone to whom a defamatory statement is published would understand that the plaintiff is the person referred to, serious problems arise when the plaintiff is a member of a group that has been defamed.

    1. As the size of the group increases, the likelihood that the courts will allow a jury to conclude that a statement defamatory of a group defames the plaintiff decreases.

K. In almost all states, there can be no defamation of the dead. Moreover, in about half the states, an action for defamation will not survive the death of either the plaintiff or the defendant.

L. From time to time, attempts have been made to provide alternative remedies for defamation that are less complex and easier to utilize. Among the suggestions have been proceedings seeking retraction and proceedings in which the only issue is the falsity of the defamatory statement in which the successful plaintiff will recover attorney fees but no damages.

II. **COMMON LAW DEFENSES TO AN ACTION FOR DEFAMATION**

A. At common law, truth was generally an absolute defense to an action of defamation. The few exceptions concerned statements such as opinions or parodies which were not capable of being true or false but which were nevertheless thought to be actionable because they were unfair or excessive. The Supreme Court has now made it clear that to be actionable an opinion must carry with it a false implication of fact.

    1. At common law, truth was an affirmative defense that had to be raised and proved by the defendant but, at least in those areas of the law of defamation that are affected by the First Amendment, the burden of persuasion on this issue is now on the plaintiff.

B. There are a number of absolute privileges.

    1. Communications between spouses.

    2. Reports of official proceedings, if accurate. This privilege has been extended to cover reports of "public meetings" and now probably includes such things as the shareholders' meeting of a publicly held corporation.

    3. Certain public officials have an absolute privilege for any statement made while they are acting in their official capacity. Such officials include legislators, judges, prosecutors, and other participants in judicial proceedings, and at least some executive officials. At the federal level, the absolute privilege seems to extend to all federal officials acting within "the outer perimeter" of their duties. Many states, however, have distinguished between major executive officers, such as governors and the state equivalents of federal cabinet officers who are granted an absolute privilege, and lesser officials, who are only granted a qualified privilege.

C. In contrast to an absolute privilege, a qualified privilege may be defeated by a showing of "malice."

    1. Statements made in defense of the speaker's interest enjoy a qualified privilege.

        a. One also has a qualified privilege to defend one's self against the defamatory remarks of others.

    2. Members of a group, such as the members of a church, labor union, or business entity, may claim a qualified privilege for statements made to other members of the group in order to protect a common interest.

    3. A qualified privilege sometimes arises with regard to statements made for the purpose of protecting the interests of third parties. Whether the privilege will be recognized depends upon a variety of factors.

        a. When life or serious bodily harm is thought to be at risk, even a third party with no interest in the matter enjoys a qualified privilege to come forward with information.

        b. A member of the immediate family of the person whose interests are involved will have a qualified privilege in circumstances where a friend or mere busybody will not.

        c. A defamatory communication that has been solicited by the person whose interests are at stake or an immediate family member of that person may enjoy a qualified privilege even though the statement would not have been qualifiedly privileged if it had been volunteered.

    4. A claim of qualified privilege may be defeated by a showing of malice. At common law, malice could be shown by demonstrating that the person making the defamatory statement was motivated not by a desire to protect the interests for the protection of which the privilege was granted, but rather merely by the desire to hurt the plaintiff. Another way of defeating the privilege was by showing excessive publication, that is, publication to a class larger than the class for whose protection the privilege is granted.

        a. At one time in the United States, many courts held that a defendant's lack of reasonable grounds for believing in the truth of the statement would defeat a claim of qualified privilege. In contrast, under English common law an honest belief in the truth of the statement, even if the belief were unreasonable, would be enough to sustain a claim of privilege. Given the constitutional developments that we shall examine next, it would seem that most American jurisdictions have now adopted something analogous to the English position.

        b. Given these constitutional developments, it remains to be seen whether a claim of conditional privilege can still be defeated by a showing of common law malice, that is, publication solely from spite, hatred, ill will, or a desire to hurt the plaintiff.

III. CONSTITUTIONAL DEVELOPMENTS

A. Since 1964, the Supreme Court of the United States has superimposed a number of restrictions upon the common law of defamation. These restrictions turn in large part upon the status of the plaintiff. The Court has also, at times, suggested that whether the defendant is one of the news media is an important consideration. In addition, the Court has on some occasions indicated that whether the statement in question concerns matters of "public interest" is relevant. Because the Court has not always been consistent, the law is not completely clear.

B. The Court has held that a public official cannot recover damages for defamatory falsehood relating to that person's official conduct without proof that the statement was made either with knowledge of

CO

its falsity or with reckless disregard of whether the statement was false. This requirement is sometimes known as "actual malice" and sometimes as "constitutional malice."

    1.   The requirement of a showing of actual malice has been applied in cases involving relatively low ranking officials, at least when the defamatory statement concerns the public duties of the officials.

C.   The Court has made clear that to prevail on the issue of constitutional malice the plaintiff must prove knowledge or reckless indifference to truth or falsity by "clear and convincing evidence," rather than the preponderance-of-the-evidence standard that is normally used in civil litigation.

    1.   The Court has held that recklessness can only be proved by the showing of conscious indifference to truth; a mere failure to investigate is not by itself enough.

    2.   The question of actual or constitutional malice has been made into a question of "constitutional fact." A constitutional fact is one as to which the trial court is unable merely to accept the jury determination when there is adequate evidence to support that determination but must itself be convinced that the jury's determination is correct. The appellate courts must likewise review the record and make their own independent determination of the issue.

    3.   Because the question of actual or constitutional malice requires an examination of the defendant's state of mind, the Court has recognized that the plaintiff is entitled to a relatively wide-ranging discovery into the thought processes of the defendant.

D.   The Court has held that, at least with regard to the nonprivate aspects of their lives, public figures who bring actions for defamation are also required to show constitutional malice.

    1.   A person can, at least for a time, become a public figure involuntarily by being involved in important public events, although the Court has made it clear that it is reluctant to take an expansive view of the notion of an "involuntary public figure."

    2.   The Court has repeatedly stated that the question of who is considered a public figure is a question of law to be decided by the courts; it is not a jury question.

E.   In *Gertz v. Robert Welch, Inc.,* the Court declared that defamation actions brought by private persons were not subject to the requirement of showing actual or constitutional malice. The plaintiff in such an action could succeed by showing some lesser level of fault, such as mere negligence, with regard to the truth or falsity of the statements involved. The *Gertz* case involved an action against one of the media, but it does not appear that the holding of the case can be confined merely to actions against media defendants.

F.   In *Gertz*, the Court declared that there can be no recovery of either punitive or presumed damages in actions for defamation unless the plaintiff is able to show constitutional malice. When the action is brought on the basis of any lesser degree of fault, the plaintiff is only entitled to actual damages, but these damages may include intangible items, such as humiliation, embarrassment, etc.

    1.   In *Dunn & Bradstreet, Inc. v. Greenmoss Builders, Inc.,* the Court held that in actions brought by a private figure about matters which are not matters of public concern, that is, about matters that are not "newsworthy," the plaintiff may recover punitive or actual damages, if permitted under state law, on a lesser showing of fault than is necessary to meet the actual or constitutional malice standard.

    2.   The resurrection in *Greenmoss Builders* of the distinction between newsworthy and nonnewsworthy material — a distinction previously rejected in the *Gertz* case — has injected a great deal of uncertainty in the law of defamation. After *Greenmoss Builders,* it is even possible that the Court might hold that the First Amendment does not apply to some types of defamation.

CO

CHAPTER 17

CHAPTER 17: PRIVACY

I.   INTRODUCTION

    A.   The tort of privacy is of relatively recent origin. It has four aspects.

II.   FALSE-LIGHT INVASION OF PRIVACY

    A.   False-light invasion of privacy concerns actions for damages against those who have made false and personally embarrassing but nondefamatory remarks about the plaintiff. Because the action bears so many analogies to defamation, many of the restrictions that are applied in defamation actions have been applied to plaintiffs in false-light invasion of privacy actions.

        1.   In *Time, Inc. v. Hill,* the Court held that before a plaintiff could recover in a false-light privacy action, the plaintiff had to show that the defendant published the material in question either with knowledge of falsity or with a reckless disregard of the truth or falsity of the material.

            a.   Now that the Court has held that a private person may succeed in a defamation action merely by showing negligence, it is unclear whether a false-light invasion of privacy action may also be brought by a private person who can only show negligence with regard to the truth or falsity of the statement. Most courts continue to require all plaintiffs in false-light invasion of privacy actions to show constitutional malice.

        2.   In recent years, a few courts have held that no recovery should be permitted for false-light invasions of privacy and that the remedy for the dissemination of false information about a person is confined to actions for libel or slander.

III.   INTRUSION UPON THE PLAINTIFF'S SOLITUDE

    A.   This aspect of the invasion of privacy tort principally reaches conduct that is quite analogous to conduct that would constitute trespass at common law but which, for technical reasons, cannot be remedied through the traditional action for trespass. Examples include unlawful tapping of telephone lines and gaining entry into a person's home or office under false pretenses.

        1.   It is not tortious, however, to photograph someone in public, so long as the physical safety of the person being photographed is not endangered.

        2.   It has likewise been held that it is not tortious to continue to follow a person when that person is traveling on public streets, as long as that person's physical safety is not put in danger and the person is not subject to some sort of physical intimidation.

IV.   PUBLIC DISCLOSURE OF EMBARRASSING FACTS

    A.   When information has been obtained in the course of a confidential relationship, the law has always provided some legal protection. The difficult question arises when the information has not been obtained in the course of a confidential relationship or by illegal means.

        1.   There have been some cases in which actions were allowed for the public disclosure of embarrassing facts about the plaintiff. Many courts, however, have refused to recognize such actions.

2. Courts that have recognized such actions have tried to circumscribe them by focusing upon whether the intrusion into the plaintiff's personal life would be "grossly offensive to most people" and whether the plaintiff had "voluntarily acceded to a position of public notoriety." It is not clear that even with these qualifications, such actions can survive constitutional challenge.

B. In a series of cases, the Court has struck down statutes making it a crime to publish the names of the victims of sexual offenses. While the Court has not categorically stated that no one can ever be punished for publishing truthful information which has been lawfully obtained, it has indicated that if any such punishment in the form of criminal penalties or a civil action were to be upheld, it would have to be because "a state interest of the highest order" was involved.

1. This is not to say that court files involving the victims of sexual offenses may not be made confidential nor that the custodians of these files may not be forbidden from disclosing these reports to other persons.

V. COMMERCIAL APPROPRIATION

A. This aspect of the invasion of privacy tort concerns the use of a person's name, portrait, or picture without that person's consent for advertising or trade purposes. The appearance of a person's picture and name in a newspaper sold for profit does not of itself constitute the use of a person's picture or name for advertising or trade purposes.

1. Even in an advertisement, the use of a background photograph of a major public event would not necessarily involve an invasion of privacy as long as the advertisement did not draw special attention to the plaintiff.

2. While a person may be photographed in public, particularly when participating in a public event, a commercial appropriation may arise if that person is singled out for more extended coverage, that is, if that person is, in a manner of speaking, made into an actor.

B. There are a number of recent cases on whether the right of commercial appropriation of a person's name or likeness is descendible to that person's heirs or otherwise survives that person's death. Some courts have required that, in order for the right of appropriation to survive a person's death, that person must have commercially exploited his name and likeness in his lifetime. In other states, either by judicial decision or statute, the right of commercial appropriation is descendible even if the person whose name or likeness is involved had not commercially exploited it before his death.

CHAPTER 18: MISUSE OF PROCESS   *CHAPTER 18*

I. MALICIOUS PROSECUTION

A. An action for malicious prosecution may be brought by a person who is not guilty of a criminal offense for which he had been charged against a private person who initiated or procured the institution of those criminal proceedings. The action will not lie against a public prosecutor or a judge.

1. The action is predicated upon the innocence of the plaintiff, but the fact that the plaintiff has been acquitted in a criminal prosecution does not prevent the defendant from relitigating the question of the plaintiff's guilt or innocence of the underlying criminal charge.

2. Criminal proceedings encompass any proceeding in which a governmental body seeks to prosecute a person for an offense and to impose upon that person a penalty of a criminal character.

a. A criminal proceeding is instituted when any process has been issued for the purpose of bringing the person accused of a criminal offense before an official or tribunal whose function is to determine either the guilt or innocence of the accused or whether the accused shall be held for a later determination of guilt or innocence.

3. An action for malicious prosecution may not be brought unless the criminal proceedings have terminated in the plaintiff's favor. A favorable termination includes: acquittal; discharge by a magistrate; refusal of a grand jury to indict; formal abandonment of the proceedings by the prosecutor; and the quashing of an indictment or information.

4. The plaintiff must show that the defendant acted without probable cause. In the absence of other evidence, the discharge of the accused by a magistrate during a preliminary hearing is conclusive evidence of the lack of probable cause, as is the refusal of a grand jury to indict the accused.

   a. The conviction of the accused, even if reversed by an appellate tribunal, conclusively establishes the existence of probable cause unless the conviction was obtained by fraud or some other illegal means.

   b. Liability may be avoided if the prosecution was initiated in good faith in reliance upon the advice of an attorney.

   c. Termination of the proceedings against the accused at the instance of the person who initiated them or the termination of those proceedings because of the initiator's failure to press the prosecution is evidence of a lack of probable cause. Abandonment of the proceedings by the prosecutor is not, however, evidence that the accuser acted without probable cause because there are many reasons not related to guilt or innocence that the prosecutor might refuse to continue with a particular prosecution.

5. It is generally said that the plaintiff must allege and prove that the prosecution was instituted by the accuser primarily for a purpose other than that of bringing the accused to justice, a requirement generally referred to as the need to allege and prove malice.

   a. If a person has probable cause for making a criminal charge, an action for malicious prosecution may not be brought against that person, regardless of the impropriety of the motives that activated him.

6. In an action for malicious prosecution, a number of what are normally thought of as factual issues have traditionally been treated as questions of law to be decided by the court. These include whether the prior proceedings were criminal in nature, whether those proceedings were terminated in favor of the plaintiff, and whether the defendant had probable cause.

II. MISUSE OF CIVIL PROCESS

A. An action may, under certain conditions, be brought against someone who took an active part in the wrongful initiation, continuation, or procurement of civil proceedings against another. This action has many analogies to the action for malicious prosecution, such as lack of probable cause and the bringing of proceedings for a purpose other than that of securing the proper adjudication of the claim upon which the proceedings were based. The proceedings must also have been terminated in favor of the plaintiff. The tort encompasses wrongfully instituted administrative proceedings as well.

   1. The plaintiff must show that the defendant acted without probable cause.

      a. One who acts in reliance upon the advice of disinterested counsel, whose advice has been sought in good faith and after a full disclosure of all the known relevant facts, will establish probable cause.

2. The court, in an action for misuse of civil process, will decide whether a civil proceeding has been initiated, whether any such civil proceeding was terminated in favor of the plaintiff, whether the defendant had probable cause, and whether, in those jurisdictions requiring proof of special damages, the plaintiff has made a sufficient allegation of such damages.

B. American courts are split on the issue of whether the plaintiff must be able to show some kind of special damages in order to bring an action for misuse of civil process.

1. A minority of American jurisdictions hold that no action will lie for misuse of civil process unless the plaintiff can show some sort of interference with the plaintiff's person or property or some other analogous form of special damages. This is often called the English rule.

    a. Some jurisdictions that otherwise follow the English rule will permit an action for misuse of civil process by someone who brings repetitious civil proceedings for the purpose of harassment.

2. The majority of jurisdictions in the United States have now abandoned the requirement that the plaintiff must show special damages in order to bring an action for misuse of civil process.

C. There have been a number of attempts in recent years to bring actions for the misuse of civil process against attorneys and others who have instituted actions with little chance of success. Thus far, the courts have refused to allow any liability to lie against an attorney for negligently instituting civil proceedings.

1. A number of states now provide for the assessment of litigation costs and attorney fees against parties and attorneys who bring "frivolous actions or assert frivolous defenses."

III. ABUSE OF PROCESS

A. An action for abuse of process will lie against a person who, in a previous criminal or civil proceeding against the plaintiff, misused that proceeding in order to accomplish some ulterior purpose (*i.e.,* for some purpose other than to obtain a judgment on the merits). The situations giving rise to an action for abuse of process are often analogous to some form of extortion. This tort does not require a showing that the plaintiff would not have been liable in the prior proceeding. An example would be the issuance of a notice to depose a party in a proceeding in order to execute process against that person in a different proceeding.

CHAPTER 19: WRONGFUL DEATH AND LOSS OF CONSORTIUM

CHAPTER 19

I. WRONGFUL DEATH

A. The common law did not recognize an action for the wrongful death of an individual. In 1846, Parliament responded by passing Lord Campbell's Act, which provided that if the party injured would have had an action had he not died, then an action would lie for the benefit of the wife, husband, parent, and child of the deceased, with the jury to give such damages as they thought proportioned to the injuries resulting from the death to those parties for whose benefit the action was brought.

1. Although Lord Campbell's Act did not by its terms restrict damages to "pecuniary loss," it was soon so construed by the courts.

B. Survival statutes are to be distinguished from wrongful death statutes. In the very earliest days of the common law, what are now called tort actions did not survive the death of either the plaintiff or the defendant. In almost all states, however, most tort actions now survive the death of either the plaintiff

CO

or the defendant and become potential assets or liabilities of the deceased's estate. The most important exception is defamation actions which, in about half of the states, still do not survive the death of either the plaintiff or the defendant.

    1. The action for wrongful death established by Lord Campbell's Act is a new cause of action that arises upon the death of the deceased. It is not an action of the deceased that survives to the deceased's estate. When the person injured does not die immediately, the deceased's cause of action for the damage incurred up to and until the time of death will survive to the deceased's estate. The losses suffered by the deceased's survivors will then, in most states, be recovered in a Lord Campbell's-type action brought by the survivors.

  C. Following the adoption by Parliament of Lord Campbell's Act, similar statutes were enacted in most American jurisdictions. In these statutory schemes, the action is brought primarily for the benefit of the survivors. The survivors are limited either to certain named relatives of the deceased, as in Lord Campbell's Act itself, or to the class of persons who would take if the deceased had died intestate.

    1. A second, much smaller, category of wrongful death statutes provides an action for the loss occasioned by the deceased's death to the estate of the deceased.

    2. A few states have handled the problem of wrongful death by expanding the scope of their survival statutes to include actions for the death of an individual.

  D. The interpretation of Lord Campbell's Act limiting damages to pecuniary loss was carried over into the United States and was often actually inserted into the wrongful death statutes. Although the law recognized that the death of a wife and mother, even one with no outside employment, represented a substantial pecuniary loss to a surviving husband and minor children, it was often difficult to find a basis for awarding damages to surviving parents and siblings of minor children. To meet this problem, the courts in some states started to interpret pecuniary loss to include the loss of society and companionship. In other states, the problem was met by legislative enactments which expressly included these items as elements of damages. There are still, nevertheless, a few states which continue to take a very narrow view of what constitutes "pecuniary loss."

    1. In the minority of jurisdictions that measure damages by the loss suffered by the estate of the deceased, as well as in those few states that have handled the problem of wrongful death by extension of the survival acts, three criteria have been used to determine the loss suffered by the deceased's estate. These are: (1) the present value of the deceased's future accumulations; (2) the present value of the deceased's probable future net earnings; and (3) the present value of the deceased's probable future gross earnings. The last method is the most generous, and the first, the least generous. The second method, which focuses on the present value of the probable future net earnings, is the most common and comes closest to providing a sum equal to the pecuniary loss recoverable under the more typical loss-to-survivor statutes.

      a. The contributory negligence of the deceased, which would have affected his recovery if he had lived, has always been held either to bar a wrongful death action or, in a jurisdiction with comparative negligence, to limit the amount of recovery. The effect of the contributory negligence of a beneficiary is more complicated. In a state where the action is viewed as being for the benefit of the estate, the contributory negligence of someone who will eventually share in the distribution of the estate is normally of no relevance. In the majority of states, in which the wrongful death action is brought for the benefit of the survivors, however, the contributory negligence of one of the survivors will normally reduce the total damages recoverable and bar or reduce — if comparative negligence is in effect — the contributorily negligent survivor's recovery.

  E. In most states, there are special statutes of limitations governing wrongful death actions. Some of the statutes are unclear as to whether they begin to run at the time of injury or at the time of death. Where the statute is unclear, most courts have held that the statute begins to run from the time of death.

    F. Although, at one time, many states had statutory limitations on the amount that could be recovered in a wrongful death action, no state now has any such general limitation. A few states, however, have limitations on the amount of nonpecuniary loss that may be recovered or on the amount that may be recovered by people who are not actually dependents of the deceased.

II.   LOSS OF CONSORTIUM

    A. At common law, a husband had an action for the loss of the consortium of his wife, which was usually joined to the wife's action for her own injuries to which, until the married women's property acts of the nineteenth century, the husband was a necessary party. No action was recognized for a wife's loss of the consortium of her injured husband undoubtedly, in part because at common law, a wife had no separate legal personality apart from that of her husband.

        1. With the passage of the married women's acts in the nineteenth century, some states abolished the husband's loss of consortium action. In recent times, however, most states, including many of those that abolished the husband's action in response to the married women's acts, permit either a husband or a wife to bring an action for the loss of the consortium of an injured spouse.

            a. After some initial cases going the other way, the most recent trend is to deny a loss of consortium action on behalf of cohabiting, unmarried people.

    B. There are a number of jurisdictions that recognize a child's action for the loss of the consortium of a parent, but the great majority refuse to recognize any such action.

    C. A few states recognize a parent's action for the loss of an injured child's consortium. The vast majority, including even states that recognize a child's action for the loss of the consortium of a parent, refuse to recognize such an action.

    D. A few states hold that a loss of consortium action is not barred nor, in a comparative negligence jurisdiction, affected by the negligence of the person whose consortium has been lost. Most courts, however, continue to hold to the contrary.

CHAPTER 20: FETAL INJURIES   *CHAPTER 20*

I.   PHYSICAL INJURY TO THE FETUS

    A. The vast majority of jurisdictions now recognize that a child who is born alive is able to recover for prenatal injuries.

        1. Most states that have considered the question also permit actions by children who were born with defects that were the result of tortious conduct that predated the children's conception.

    B. The majority of jurisdictions now permit a wrongful death action to be brought on behalf of a fetus that is delivered stillborn, provided the fetus was viable at the time of injury.

        1. In a number of jurisdictions, however, it has been held that a fetus is not a "person" within the meaning of that state's wrongful death statute.

CO

II. WRONGFUL BIRTH

A. In these cases, the parents are seeking recovery for a child, usually a healthy child, who was born as a result of a negligently performed sterilization procedure or because of an ineffective birth-control device. A second type of case typically concerns the birth of a child whose conception was intentional but whose parents claim that they would not have conceived the child if they had known of the possibility of genetic defects or that having conceived the child, they would have aborted it if the appropriate tests had been administered or if the risk of producing a defective child had been adequately explained.

1. Almost all courts will permit the parents of a defective child to recover the cost of caring for that child if but for the negligence of the defendant, the parents would either not have conceived the child or not brought the child to term. Some courts expressly limit the damage to the increased costs of raising a defective child over those that would have been incurred for raising a healthy child.

   a. A few states have permitted parents in wrongful birth actions to recover for their emotional injuries, but the majority position is against permitting such recovery.

2. The courts are divided on the question of whether the parents of an unwanted — but healthy — child can recover the cost of rearing that child against someone whose tortious conduct resulted in the child's conception. The trend in the United States is to deny recovery for the cost of rearing a healthy child and only to permit recovery for the cost incurred by the mother in carrying the unwanted pregnancy to term and for the pain and suffering that accompanied the pregnancy and birth.

   a. There are a minority of states that will allow recovery for the cost of raising an unwanted but healthy child. Most of these courts have required that such recovery should be offset by the benefits that the parents derive from the child's aid, society, and comfort.

   b. Perhaps the reason that most jurisdictions do not allow the parents to recover the cost of rearing an unwanted — but healthy — child may be the recognition that parents who do not wish to be saddled with such costs could take steps to mitigate their expenses either by aborting the fetus or putting the child up for adoption after it is born.

      (1) The few actions brought by the siblings of unwanted children claiming that they are deprived of some of their parents' care and attention because of the addition of another child have been uniformly unsuccessful.

III. WRONGFUL LIFE

A. Wrongful life actions are those brought by a child who is born in a defective state, such as a child born a paraplegic or with serious genetic defects. The gist of the action is that the child would rather not have been born and that, but for the defendant's tortious conduct, the child would have not been conceived or would have been aborted. Thus far, such claims have been uniformly rejected.

CHAPTER 21   **CHAPTER 21: DAMAGES**

I. TYPES OF DAMAGES

A. **General and Special Damages:** Special damages are those readily calculable, such as for medical expenses, and they must usually be specially pleaded. General damages, such for as pain and suffering, need not be specially pleaded.

B. **Limiting Rules on Compensatory Damages:** There are a number of restrictions on matters that can be presented to the jury. Damages typically recoverable in tort are those for past lost earnings and loss of future earning capacity, medical expenses, and pain and suffering.

1. Interest on tort claims prior to judgment is usually not recoverable.

2. The general rule is that tort recoveries are not taxable as income.

   a. Also, as a general rule, moneys (such as insurance payments, unemployment benefits, and the like) received from sources other than a tortfeasor are not credited against a tortfeasor's liability. This is called the collateral source rule.

3. Most courts instruct the jury that recovery for future medical expenses and lost earning capacity (but not for pain and suffering) must be reduced to present value. There is a division of authority as to whether inflation should be taken into account in calculating future damages. A few courts have concluded that inflation and present-value determinations cancel each other out, so that neither is taken into account.

4. There is a division of authority regarding whether the plaintiff's attorney can ask the jury to place a monetary value on pain and suffering calculated on the basis of discrete units of time.

5. If the plaintiff has a special susceptibility (*e.g.,* hemophilia), he can recover tort damages precipitated by that special susceptibility. He may not be able to recover, however, for damages resulting from a special sensitivity.

II. DUTIES OF THE PLAINTIFF AND OF THE COURT

A. **Avoidable Consequences:** The plaintiff has a duty to take reasonable steps to minimize his damages.

1. Courts are divided as to whether this duty includes an obligation to wear a seat belt.

B. **Judicial Control of Damages:** Courts have the power to order a new trial if damages are excessively high or low. In addition, many courts have the power to suggest an increase (additur) or a decrease (remittitur) in damages, conditioned on the grant of a new trial if the opponent does not agree.

III. PUNITIVE DAMAGES

A. **Basis of Liability:** Punitive damages are awardable at the discretion of the jury for willful, wanton, or reckless misconduct. In the case of a corporation, some courts require that the conduct be committed by a corporate employee in a managerial capacity. Typically, punitive damages cannot be awarded against a municipality. There is ongoing litigation on the issue of whether an award of punitive damages violates due process of law, at least under some circumstances (*e.g.,* very large awards or multiple awards where tortious conduct injures a number of people).

CHAPTER 22: STATUTORY CHANGES

CHAPTER 22

I. TYPES OF CHANGES

A. **Statutes of Repose:** Such a statute bars a claim after a certain date regardless of whether injury was occured.

B. **Caps on the Amount of Awardable Damages:** A cap fixes a maximum damage recovery.

C. **Elimination of Joint Liability:** Each party is liable only for his own degree of fault.

CO

D. **Implied Statutory Preemption:** A number of courts have found that governmental safety statutes and regulations preempt the field regarding safety standards to which the regulations apply.

II. **CONSTITUTIONAL AND POLICY CONSIDERATIONS**

A. **Constitution:** A number of these statutes have been struck down on various federal and state constitutional grounds.

B. **Policy:** There is ongoing debate on the nature and extent of the tort and insurance "crises," its causes, and whether the types of statutory responses taken are the appropriate ways to meet any such perceived crisis.

CHAPTER 23 **CHAPTER 23: TORT LAW ALTERNATIVES**

I. **PARTIAL ALTERNATIVE SYSTEMS**

A. **Workers' Compensation:** Such compensation provides a limited no-fault recovery for employee workplace injuries.

B. **No-fault Auto Insurance:** Such first-party auto insurance provides limited no-fault recovery to the insured.

C. **Public and Private Health and Unemployment Insurance Schemes:** These include Social Security, Medicare, Medicaid, employer and individual insurance.

II. **TOTAL ALTERNATIVE SYSTEMS**

A. **Alternative Dispute Resolution:** A number of litigants have resorted to nonjudicial, alternative dispute resolution systems, such as informal arbitration and negotiation.

B. **The New Zealand System:** New Zealand has substantially replaced its tort system with a government pay-out scheme for accidental injuries and workplace injuries and diseases.

III. **POLICY CONSIDERATIONS**

A. It remains debatable whether any kind or combination of government compensation and regulatory system will provide adequate compensation and deterrence. An alternative is to retain optional, parallel administrative and tort compensation systems.

CHAPTER 24 **CHAPTER 24: IMMUNITIES**

I. **GOVERNMENTAL IMMUNITIES**

A. Until the enactment of the Federal Tort Claims Act in 1946, the sovereign immunity of the United States, with some minor statutory exceptions, barred all tort actions against the federal government.

1. The Federal Tort Claims Act provides, subject to a number of specific exceptions, that the United States shall be liable in tort in "the same manner and to the same extent as a private individual under like circumstances, but shall not be liable for interest prior to judgment or for punitive damages."

2. One of the exceptions provides that the government is not liable for any act or omission of one of its employees in the "exercise or performance or the failure to exercise or perform a discretionary function or duty."

CO

    a.   It has proved to be very difficult to determine what is a discretionary function. Some courts have distinguished between the planning functions of government, to which the discretionary function exception applies, and the operational functions of government, to which it does not. There is no simple test, and the Supreme Court's decisions have not always been helpful.

3.   As originally enacted, the Tort Claims Act carved out an exception from coverage for claims arising out of "assault, battery, false imprisonment, false arrest, malicious prosecution, abuse of process, libel, slander, misrepresentation, deceit or interference with contract rights." In 1974, this exception was amended to provide that the Tort Claims Act would apply to claims arising from the conduct of investigative or law enforcement officers for assault, battery, false imprisonment, false arrest, abuse of process, and malicious prosecution.

4.   There are a number of other exceptions which include claims arising out of the loss or negligent transmission of postal material, claims arising out of the assessment of taxes, claims arising out of the combatant activities of the military, and claims arising in a foreign country.

    a.   The Court has construed the Act so as not to permit an action against the government by servicemen whose injuries "arise out of or are [incurred] in the course of activity incident to service."

5.   The Court has also construed the Act to exclude the liability of the United States on a strict liability theory.

6.   Since 1988, the remedy against the United States under the Torts Claim Act has remained exclusive with regard to any action based on tort against the employee.

    a.   The provision of the Act making the remedy against the United States the exclusive remedy does not bar actions against government employees arising out of violations of the Constitution or of federal statutes.

7.   All actions under the Act must first be filed with the appropriate federal agency within two years after the claim arises. The statute of limitations is then tolled for a period of six months after the claim is denied by the agency. Actions under the Tort Claims Act are tried by a judge sitting without a jury.

B.   Like the United States, individual states have enjoyed sovereign immunity. At the present time, either by statute or sometimes even by judicial decision, sovereign immunity has been totally abolished or substantially modified in more than three-quarters of the states. States that have not totally abolished sovereign immunity typically recognize liability for motor vehicle accidents, medical malpractice, and accidents caused by the dangerous conditions of state roads and property. Even in a state that has totally abolished the state's sovereign immunity, the courts have recognized on the state level something like the discretionary function exception recognized under the Federal Tort Claims Act. There are a few states that still purport to retain the doctrine of sovereign immunity.

C.   Under the traditional common law, units of local government were not considered to share in the sovereign immunity of the Crown. They were treated as one type of corporate body. In the nineteenth century, however, when private corporations became common and not merely rare entities, the analogy between the municipal corporations and private corporations was no longer readily accepted. By judicial decision or by amendment of a state's constitution, municipal corporations came to be seen as exercising general governmental powers and thus, to some extent, sharing in the immunities of state governments.

1.   Since units of local government do not share in the sovereign immunity of a state, the Eleventh

CO

Amendment of the United States Constitution has never been held to prevent suit in federal court against municipalities.

2. The immunity of municipalities and other units of local government from suit has now either been abolished or substantially limited in most states.

3. Even states that still take a restrictive view of the extent to which governmental immunity has been abolished will often permit an action against a unit of local government if the activity involved is considered to be a proprietary function rather than a governmental function.

II. **CHARITABLE IMMUNITY**

A. The doctrine of charitable immunity arose in the United States during the latter half of the nineteenth century, and the doctrine was soon extended beyond beneficiaries. It has now been totally abolished in at least 80% of the states. In those states where the charitable immunity doctrine continues to have some application, it is usually confined to actions brought by beneficiaries and, in some states, there are statutory limits on damages.

III. **FAMILY IMMUNITIES**

A. Because at common law a wife had no legal personality separate from that of her husband, the possibility of one spouse bringing an action against another could not arise prior to married women's property acts of the nineteenth century. While these acts made it possible for a married woman to sue her husband (or to be sued by him) with regard to disputes over property, most courts refused to construe these acts as affecting actions for personal injuries.

1. With the passage of time, more and more states began to abolish the doctrine either by statute or judicial decision.

2. At the present time, the majority of states has completely abolished inter-spousal immunity.

B. Like charitable immunity, the tort immunity between parent and child has no English counterpart. The modern trend to abolish tort immunities has limited the range of the parent-child immunity but not to the same extent as has been the case with regard to inter-spousal immunity.

1. The parent-child immunity applies between parents of unemancipated minor children.

2. In close to half of the states, the doctrine of parent-child immunity has been completely abolished or abolished with some very slight qualifications. In most of the states that have abolished the doctrine, the conduct of the parent is to be judged according to what "an ordinarily reasonable and prudent parent [would] have done in similar circumstances." In the other states, the doctrine is abolished except when the alleged tortious act involves an exercise of reasonable parental authority over the child or when the act involves the exercise of ordinary parental discretion with regard to such matters as the provision of food, clothing, housing, and medical care.

3. In addition to these jurisdictions, a substantial additional number of states have abolished the doctrine in automobile negligence cases or, in a few instances, in automobile negligence cases in which the parent has liability insurance. A significant minority of states, however, retains the parent-child immunity in something like its former vigor.

INTRODUCTION

▶ **CHAPTER SUMMARY**

INTRODUCTION

Scope of Chapter: We try in this book to cover many of the major points of law, fact, and procedure encountered in a basic torts course. This book, however, should in no way be construed as a substitute for classroom preparation. There is no substitute for a careful reading and analysis of the cases and materials given in class assignments. We hope to provide you with a synthesis and overview that will help you in torts, as well as in other law school courses.

I. THE AMBIGUITY OF THE LAW

AMBIGUITY OF THE LAW

   A. **The Role of Rules:** Many students come to law school expecting to be taught "the law," which they imagine to be a complex set of rules. It is true that there are many rules — some certain, some less certain, and some almost completely open-ended — that govern legal conduct in our society. But no set of rules ever completely governs conduct. Law is a study of life, including economics, psychology, jurisprudence, morality, and what have you.

   1. Many law students appear afraid of forming, or offering, their own opinions in class about legal issues. They seem to think someone else — the teacher? — has the answers. The teacher does not, especially for the larger issues that permeate the life of the law. The teacher is there to engage in a dialogue with the students, and students must enter into that dialogue to make legal education, or any education, meaningful.

   2. The study of law is like the study of any other high art. Take the study of piano playing, for example. To be a good pianist, you must know all the rules well: the scales, timing, meter, and the like. But the successful pianist only begins with this well-learned knowledge. Then comes interpretation. In sports and politics, then comes strategy. And in law, most of all, then comes judgment. Law is about making good judgments.

TAKING A LAW EXAMINATION

II. TAKING A LAW EXAMINATION

   A. **What is expected?** As the period of law exams approaches, students usually ask, "What is the professor looking for?" Often that question takes the form of, "Do you want issue identification or analysis?"

   1. For law professors, that is a false or misleading dichotomy. Issue identification, properly conceived, involves analysis, and analysis can only occur through issue identification.

   2. In reviewing your notes, it is very important to identify the problems the professor has emphasized and wrestled with during the term. By all rules of prediction, those issues will appear in prominent form on the exam.

   B. **Some Do's and Don'ts:** *Do* read the question very carefully, at least twice. Take your time. Read the facts given with the greatest of care. Read the facts stated and, probably more importantly, the facts that are *not stated.*

   1. **Don't** *assume facts.* If there are unstated but important and relevant facts, then ferret out those facts — and assume them both ways, or as many ways as necessary to arrive at a considered judgment. Then answer the question on the basis of all the relevant possibilities. Don't foreclose half or more of your answer by jumping to conclusions. When you interview a client or prepare a case, you must consider all the relevant possibilities — legal, factual, strategic, and procedural. Then, and only then, can you begin to form a judgment as to the possible right answer or answers.

Example: "*A* locked *B* in a room with an open window." Is this false imprisonment? How far is the window from the ground? Is the open window obvious? Did *A* lock *B* in the room intentionally, negligently, or without fault? (False imprisonment is an intentional tort.)

2. **Don't** *simply catalog the possible torts and defenses:* Could *B* perhaps sue for false arrest, false imprisonment, intentional infliction of emotional distress, negligent infliction of emotional distress, etc.? You should also ask how each claim makes a difference, and how the defenses might change depending on the claim asserted.

3. **Do** *read carefully the end of the question to see what you are asked to write about:* Actors *A*, *B, C,* and *D* may be involved in the question; but if the professor asks you to address only the claims of *D* against *A,* then that is all you should answer. You are unlikely to get any credit for discussing the possible claims of *A* against *C,* and so forth. The professor has certain issues she wants you to address and does not want you to write your own question thereby avoiding those issues.

4. Some students carefully outline their answer before they begin to write. If this works for you, do it. While you must answer any specific question your professor has asked, such as, "If you were the trial judge, how would you rule on the defendant's motion for a directed verdict?," do not think the answer has to be in any particular form. You can start anywhere you like, and end anywhere with or without a definite conclusion. The thing the teacher wants to see is that you are thinking throughout the exam, however you choose to approach the issues.

C. **The Essay and Other Exams:** The typical first-year law exam is in the form of an essay question. This type of question allows you to explore the free range of possibilities of the situation. Some professors use multiple-choice questions or other more objective forms of examination. In all cases, the object is to test your ability to read carefully and to think through a problem.

D. **Fairly Implied Inferences:** One of the most difficult problems for law students in taking a *law essay* examination is to determine what issues are fairly implied by the question. The typical *undergraduate essay* question asks, "Tell me what you know" about the causes of the first world war, the development of the nation-state, how a free-market economy differs from a socialist economy, etc. Not so for the law exam. If you stray too far from the issues fairly implied by the question, the professor is likely to conclude that you are trying to create your own question and will not give you credit for irrelevant — although entirely accurate — answers.

1. The best rule to follow is to look for the issues *fairly implied* by the question and answer the matters raised by those issues. There should be more than enough issues fairly implied to keep you occupied throughout the exam without the need to create any other issues.

Example: *X* locked *Y* in a room with an open window. A lion which had escaped from a local zoo jumped through the window and attacked *Y*, severely injuring her. Please discuss *Y's* possible tort claims against *X.*

a. There is an obvious false imprisonment issue. Did *X* lock *Y* in the room intentionally? (If unintentionally, then no false imprisonment, which is an intentional tort.) Where is the window located? (If reasonably accessible to *Y,* no false imprisonment.) The attack by the lion may be unforeseeable, but would the doctrine of transferred intent apply?

b. *Y* may be a minor; the statute of limitations may have run; *X* may be insane; and so on. But these issues are not *fairly implied* by the question, and if you discuss them, you run a substantial risk of receiving no credit for your discussion. Stick to the kinds of issues discussed in subpoint a.

1

2. *General issue identification is not enough:* You should go further and discuss the subissues that are implicated.

    Example: Referring back to the previous example, the general issue of false imprisonment implicates the subissues (or analysis, if you will) of intent, the reasonable possibility of escape, and the like. The issue of transferred intent raises other issues, such as to which torts it applies (false imprisonment and battery?), and whether intent can be transferred from a human to an animal. Here, you need to know the applicable law to answer these questions. Additionally, the issues implicate policy questions (other "issues"): Should the question of *X's* intent turn on whether *X knew* about the open window, or whether *X should have known?* Should the requirement of foreseeability be less demanding in a transferred-intent context, and if so, why? Such policy concerns are as important as any other aspect of the question and should not be overlooked.

3. *Do not discuss the obvious matters that are not in contention:* Get to the issues that present problems of law, fact, procedure, or what have you.

    Example: *D* dislikes *P,* her archrival in the garden club. At a luncheon party attended by socially and politically prominent individuals, *D* maliciously remarked: "*P* likely has AIDS." She based her statement on having observed needle punctures in *P's* arms. In fact, *P* does not have AIDS.

    a. *This is a defamation problem:* It suggests questions as to whether *P* is a public figure, whether the matter is one of public interest, whether there is constitutional malice, and whether the statement is slander *per se* or slander *per quod.*

    b. There does not seem to be much doubt that the statement is defamatory. You might well begin, however, by a brief statement of what constitutes a defamatory remark.

        (1) But do *not* spend time discussing matters that are clearly not in dispute. Do not, for example, waste time discussing the necessity of publication and defining what is a publication. It is obvious that there is a publication, and there can be no dispute about that. You are unlikely to get credit for discussing the obvious, undisputed issues. Get on to the matters that present problems — the matters the professor likely had in mind when drafting the question.

REVIEW

III. REVIEW

A. **The *Sine Qua Non:*** There is no substitute for review, regularly and systematically, throughout the term. The student who waits until the end of the term to review courts disaster. Learning law, like anything else, is a process of absorption which requires deliberation.

THE REAL WORLD

IV. THE REAL WORLD

A. **Law School:** The first-year law exam, as indeed all of law school, tests only a small portion of what you know and of what is important to know. The practice of law is very different from law school itself, as any lawyer will tell you.

B. **Thinking Like a Lawyer:** On the other hand, law schools widely claim that they teach you something very different from other disciplines, something very important, and something you are not likely to learn anywhere else. "Thinking like a lawyer" means being practical, imaginative, careful, diplomatic, and willing to compromise when principled compromise is possible. Good lawyers are ordinary people, thinking as ordinary people think at their best.

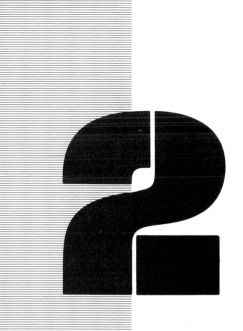

INTENTIONAL TORTS AND DEFENSES

▶ CHAPTER SUMMARY

INTENTIONAL TORTS AND DEFENSES

Scope of Chapter: This chapter deals with the subjects normally dealt with in a chapter in torts casebooks on intentional torts. The subjects typically include assault, battery, false imprisonment, intentional infliction of emotional distress (the tort of outrage), trespass to land, and trespass to and conversion of chattels. In some casebooks there is often a separate chapter (which, in this book, is part of this chapter) dealing with the various defenses of privilege to commit intentional torts.

This chapter does not include all intentional torts. Others will be dealt with in later chapters. For example, a substantial portion of the law of nuisance consists of intentional torts, as does defamation, invasion of privacy, misrepresentation, and various commercial torts such as unfair business practices and the like.

The purpose of presenting the intentional torts given in this chapter is to develop skills in doctrinal categorization. What are the elements of the tort of assault, and how does this tort differ from battery, for example? Later, torts based on negligence are introduced, and they are contrasted with intentional torts. Then, torts of strict liability will be considered. It is often said that tort law is divided into three broad categories: (a) intentional torts, (b) negligence, and (c) strict liability.

Law, like life, cannot be divided into neat categories, however. Some of the intentional torts, such as battery by an incompetent adult, trespass to land, and nuisance, at times more closely resemble strict liability than they do intentional torts. The same is true for negligence. *Res ipsa loquitur* sometimes closely resembles strict liability, for instance. Strict liability, on the other hand, when it imports considerations of risk-benefit analysis and foreseeability of harm, likewise often resembles negligence more than it does true strict liability.

The point to be remembered is that while law consists of a body of rules, those rules are subject to change depending on changing facts and circumstances. Precise legal thinking requires close attention to the rules, to their limitations, and to their potential for development.

ASSAULT

I.   **ASSAULT**

    A. **Definition:** An assault occurs if an actor acts intending to cause harmful or offensive contact to a person, or to cause an apprehension of such contact, and another person is put in apprehension that such a contact will occur imminently. *Restatement (Second) of Torts* § 21.

        1. An intent is defined for this purpose to mean that the actor desires to cause the consequences of her act, or believes that such consequences are substantially certain to occur. *Restatement (Second) of Torts* § 8A.

            a. Note that under this definition the actor need not direct his intent toward the plaintiff. It can be directed toward another person, as long as the plaintiff is put in apprehension of an imminent harmful or offensive contact as a result.

               Example: *X* throws a stone intending to hit *A*, and *B*, who is standing nearby, is put in apprehension that the stone will hit him instead. *X* has assaulted *B*. This is an example of the doctrine of transferred intent, which applies to the tort of assault. *B* also need not actually be hit by the stone for the assault to occur. If he *is* hit, there is a battery as well as an assault.

           b. The apprehension which *B* suffers must be for himself. *Restatement (Second) of Torts* § 26. If *B* is only apprehensive that the stone will hit *A*, then no assault to *B* has occurred — although *B* might have a tort claim against *X* for wrongful infliction of emotional distress.

2. While the *Restatement* indicates that *X* must have intended to cause harm or offensive contact, or the apprehension of such contact, *to a person,* this definition of intent may be too narrow. It may be sufficient that *X* intends to do a wrongful act.

    Example: The doctrine of transferred intent was apparently applied in *Corn v. Sheppard,* 179 Minn. 490, 229 N.W. 869 (1930). The defendant there unlawfully shot at a dog and hit the plaintiff's minor son instead, and was held liable for the child's resulting injuries.

B. **The Nature of the Harm:** The plaintiff must be put in apprehension of an imminent harmful or offensive contact in order for an assault to occur.

    Example: If the defendant merely says, "I will beat you up tomorrow," there is no assault. *See Tuberville v. Savage,* 86 Eng. Rep. 684 (K.B. 1669) (person put his hand on his sword and said, "If it were not assize-time, I would not take such language from you." **Held:** No assault, since it *was* assize time).

    1. There is no apprehension of imminent contact if the plaintiff is not aware of the threatened contact until after the threat has passed.

        Example: *X* points a gun at *Y*'s back intending to shoot *Y* but is prevented form doing so by *Z*, and *Y* learns of *X*'s intent only after *Z*'s successful intervention. There is no assault. *See State v. Barry,* 45 Mont. 598, 124 P. 775 (1912). *Y* might have an action in this situation for wrongful infliction of emotional distress, however. And if *X* had actually shot *Y*, then *Y* would have an action for battery even if *Y* were unconscious at the time and thus had no awareness of the shooting.

        a. On the other hand, if the defendant puts the plaintiff in apprehension of an imminent harmful or offensive contact that will occur unless the plaintiff submits to an unlawful condition — such as unwillingly signing a waiver of her rights — then an assault has occurred. *Trogden v. Terry,* 172 N.C. 540, 90 S.E. 583 (1916). Defendant has no right to impose such an unlawful condition, and the fact that the plaintiff can avoid the apprehended contact by complying with the condition is no defense.

    2. The plaintiff need not be put in fear of the contact, only in apprehension thereof.

        Examples: A scrawny, intoxicated person threatens to strike a heavyweight champion with his fist. This may be an assault because the threat is offensive, even though the champion has no fear for his bodily safety. *Restatement (Second) of Torts* § 24, comm. c, Illus. 1. An unwanted sexual advance, such as an attempted kiss, can also be an assault because it is offensive. *See Samms v. Eccles,* 11 Utah 2d 289, 358 P.2d 344 (1961); *Western Union v. Hill,* 25 Ala. App. 540, 150 So. 709 (1933).

        a. If the plaintiff is extrasensitive and the defendant knows this, then an attempted contact may be an assault even though the contact would not be harmful or offensive to the ordinary person. *See Restatement (Second) of Torts* § 27. The *Restatement* expresses a caveat as to whether a battery would occur, however, in the case of an otherwise reasonable touching of a known extrasensitive person. *Restatement (Second) of Torts* § 19. If there would be no battery in this context, then presumably there would be no assault either. In any event, if the defendant is unaware of the plaintiff's extrasensitive nature, there would be no assault since the defendant would lack the necessary intent.

    3. The apprehension need not be of contact coming from, or caused by, the defendant herself. *Restatement (Second) of Torts* § 25.

Example: Defendant says to the plaintiff, "Watch out for that rattlesnake behind you!" This statement would be sufficient to put the plaintiff in apprehension of imminent harmful or offensive contact, and if knowingly false would therefore be an assault.

C. **The Nature of the Act:** Generally words alone are not sufficient to constitute an assault. The defendant must also normally take some act which puts the plaintiff in apprehension of an imminent harmful or offensive contact. *Cucinotti v. Ortmann,* 399 Pa. 26, 159 A.2d 216 (1960). Words alone may be sufficient, however, if the circumstances are such as to put the hearer in apprehension of such a contact.

Examples: A threat by a highwayman, or a threat to a blind person, could without more be sufficient to give rise to such apprehension. *Restatement (Second) of Torts* § 31. So could the threat of a supposed rattlesnake, given above.

1. It is not the actual ability of the defendant to carry out his act of harmful or offensive contact, but the apparent ability to do so, that determines liability.

   Example: *A* threatens *B* with an unloaded gun. This will be an assault if *B* is put in apprehension of an imminent harmful or offensive contact as a result of the threat. *Allen v. Hannaford,* 138 Wash. 423, 244 P. 700 (1926).

BATTERY   **II.   BATTERY**

A. **Definition:** An actor is subject to liability for a battery if he acts intending to cause a harmful or offensive contact to a person, or an apprehension that such a contact will imminently occur, and that person or another person suffers such a contact as a result. *Restatement (Second) of Torts* § 13.

B. **The Necessary Intent:** The intent here is the same as that for assault, namely, a *desire* to cause a harmful or offensive contact or to cause an apprehension that such a contact is imminent, or a *belief* that such a contact or apprehension is substantially certain to occur. *Restatement (Second) of Torts* § 8A. *Garrett v. Dailey,* 46 Wash. 2d 197, 279 P.2d 1091 (1955). If the intent is to cause either the apprehension or the contact, and the contact results, there is battery; if the same intent causes only the apprehension, then there is an assault. An intentional contact may be sufficient to constitute a battery if the contact is unconsented to, and is either harmful or offensive. *White v. Univ. of Idaho,* 115 Idaho 564, 768 P.2d. 827 (1989)

1. As with assault, the doctrine of transferred intent applies. *Talmage v. Smith,* 101 Mich. 370, 59 N.W. 656 (1894).

   Example: *X* acts intending to cause a harmful or offensive contact or an apprehension thereof to *A*, and *B* suffers the contact as a result. There is a battery to *B*.

   a. The *Restatement* indicates that the intent to commit a battery must be directed at a person. But one case appears to apply the doctrine of transferred intent where the defendant unlawfully shot at a dog and injured the plaintiff's child instead. *Corn v. Sheppard,* 179 Minn. 490, 229 N.W. 869 (1930).

2. It has been held that a mentally incompetent person is capable of forming the necessary intent to commit a battery. *McGuire v. Almy,* 297 Mass. 323, 8 N.E.2d 760 (1937). Likewise, a child of tender years is capable of having such an intent *Baldinger v. Banks,* 26 Misc. 2d 1086, 201 N.Y.S.2d 629 (1960) (six-year-old defendant). The intent does not exist, however, if the defendant acts reflexively or involuntarily. *Restatement (Second) of Torts* § 14.

3. A bodily contact is offensive if it offends a reasonable sense of personal dignity. *Restatement (Second) of Torts* § 19.

Examples: Thus an unwanted kiss from a stranger, a practical joke, or a playful kick may constitute a battery if a reasonable sense of personal dignity would be offended as a result. *Restatement (Second) of Torts* § 16. *Vosburg v. Putney,* 80 Wis. 523, 50 N.W. 403 (1891). Defendant's good intentions and the lack of resulting harm, and indeed an actual beneficial result, will not be a defense if a reasonable sense of personal dignity would be offended. *Clayton v. New Dreamland Roller Skating Rink,* 14 N.J. Super. 390, 82 A.2d 458 (1951); *Mohr v. Williams,* 95 Minn. 261, 104 N.W. 12 (1905).

a. There are certain touchings that should be tolerated in a civilized society, such as a slight jostling in a crowd or touching someone lightly on the arm to ask for directions. *See Cole v. Turner,* 90 Eng. Rep. 958 (K.B. 1704). Even these contacts might give rise to a battery, however, in special circumstances as, for example, if the defendant knew the plaintiff was peculiarly sensitive to such a touching. *Compare Restatement (Second) of Torts* § 27. But the Caveat to *Restatement (Second) of Torts* § 19 states that the "Institute expresses no opinion" on whether a person would be liable for battery if he "inflicts upon another a contact which he knows will be offensive to another's known but abnormally acute sense of personal dignity."

C. **The Nature of the Act:** As stated in the preceding subsection, the act must be volitional, and not reflexive or involuntary. The cases appear to indicate that the act must be an affirmative one, and that mere inaction as, for example, by blocking the entrance to a room will not be a sufficient act for the purpose of committing a battery. *Innes v. Wylie,* 174 Eng. Rep. 800 (Q.B. 1844). The act of battery may be indirect, however, as by setting a dog upon the plaintiff, or daubing with filth a towel which the defendant expects the plaintiff to use. *Restatement (Second) of Torts* § 18, comm. *c.*

D. **The Nature of the Contact:** If the contact would be offensive to a reasonable sense of personal dignity, the plaintiff need not be aware of the contact when it occurs. *Restatement (Second) of Torts* § 18, comm. *d* (example of offensive kissing while the plaintiff is asleep). Indeed, the plaintiff need never be aware of the contact; an intentional killing would constitute a battery, even though the deceased died instantaneously and was never aware of the contact. Battery differs in this regard from assault, which requires an apprehension by the plaintiff of the assault at the time it occurs. This difference is undoubtedly explainable by the fact that battery is generally viewed as a more serious tort than assault.

1. The contact need not be with the actual person of the plaintiff, in order for a battery to occur. It is sufficient if the contact is with something intimately, closely, or customarily associated with the plaintiff's person. *Fisher v. Carrousel Motor Hotel,* 424 S.W.2d 627 (Tex. 1967) (battery committed by angrily touching a plate in plaintiff's hand).

a. The line, says the *Restatement,* between those things closely associated and those things not closely associated with the person is a difficult one to draw and depends on what is customarily regarded as part of the plaintiff's person or personality.

Examples: "Thus, the ordinary man might well regard a horse upon which he is riding as part of his personality, but a passenger in a public omnibus or other conveyance would clearly not be entitled so to regard the vehicle merely because he was seated in it." *Restatement (Second) of Torts* § 18, comm. *c.* Even the *Restatement's* distinguishing examples may be doubtful, depending on the circumstances. If, for example, the "other conveyance" were plaintiff's new Porsche, which the defendant angrily kicked, denting the door while plaintiff sat inside, there might well be a battery to plaintiff. Does not the modern American consider her Porsche as much a part of her personality as the nineteenth-century country gentleman considered his horse to be?

FALSE
IMPRISONMENT

III. FALSE IMPRISONMENT

A. Definition: False imprisonment occurs when one either directly or indirectly intentionally confines another within boundaries fixed by the confiner, without privilege to do so. *Restatement (Second) of Torts* § 35. The intent is the same as that involved for other intentional torts, namely, a desire to cause the consequence of one's act (here, confinement), or a belief that such a consequence is substantially certain to result. *Restatement (Second) of Torts* § 8A.

1. A caveat to *Restatement (Second) of Torts* § 35 states that the "Institute expresses no opinion as to whether the actor may . . . be subject to liability for conduct which involves an unreasonable risk of . . . confinement." The Institute thus declines to say whether there can be a tort of attempted false imprisonment. By analogy to assault (which is the apprehension of a battery), an action for attempted false imprisonment might lie provided the plaintiff suffered damage as a result of the attempt. An alternative action might lie for intentional infliction of emotional distress, although *Restatement (Second) of Torts* § 46 states that for such an action to lie the distress must be severe and the defendant's conduct outrageous.

B. Intent: If one without privilege to do so confines another, there may be false imprisonment even though the actor does not act from hostility or a desire to offend. The comment to *Restatement (Second) of Torts* § 44 states that the actor's motives are immaterial. However, good motives actuated by a reasonable belief could give rise to a privilege.

Examples: Confining someone in reasonable belief of the necessity of the confinement to save the person's life, or for purposes of quarantine, is privileged.

1. The doctrine of transferred intent applies to the tort of false imprisonment. *Restatement (Second) of Torts* § 43 indicates that the scope of the doctrine is limited to a transfer of intent from one *person* to another *person,* and the transferred intent must be that of *false imprisonment.* This definition may be too narrow. The doctrine may also apply to an initial tort of, let us say, trespass to chattel, resulting in the false imprisonment of a person. Compare the discussion of transferred intent in the sections on assault and battery.

   a. The distinction between transferred intent and foreseeability apparently is that for transferred intent it is immaterial whether the defendant either knows or should know of the risk caused to the transferee. In the case of foreseeability, the defendant is liable only for injury caused to those the defendant knows or should know are at risk from her conduct.

C. Plaintiff's Knowledge: *Parvi v. City of Kingston,* 41 N.Y.2d 553, 394 N.Y.S.2d 161, 362 N.E.2d 960 (1977), states that there is a division of authority regarding whether the plaintiff must be aware of his confinement at the time the confinement occurs in order for an action for false imprisonment to lie. The *Parvi* court held that under New York law "false imprisonment, as a dignitary tort, is not suffered unless its victim knows of the dignitary invasion." The court recognized that the *Restatement (Second) of Torts* § 42 has taken the position that there is no liability for intentionally confining another "unless the person physically restrained knows of the confinement *or is harmed by it*" (emphasis added). If the harm is purely dignitary (*i.e.,* offensive to one's feelings), awareness at the time of confinement is required, according to the *Restatement* and to *Parvi.* Some courts, however, would not require such awareness even if the injury is solely dignitary. The *Restatement,* moreover, would allow recovery for postconfinement awareness causing great humiliation and emotional distress "with resulting serious illness." *Restatement (Second) of Torts* § 42, comm. *b,* Illus. 5.

1. The tort of false imprisonment should be compared in this regard to assault and battery. For assault, the hornbook rule is that contemporary awareness is necessary — although it may be doubted whether this would hold true if severe emotional distress and illness resulted from postassault awareness, as in the false imprisonment hypothetical just given. Alternatively, an action for intentional infliction of emotional distress might lie. In the case of battery, contemporary awareness is apparently not required, even though the offense is solely dignitary (*e.g.,* kissing a sleeping woman).

D. **Confinement:** *Restatement (Second) of Torts* § 36(1) states that to make the actor liable for false imprisonment, the confinement within the boundaries fixed by the actor "must be complete." A better statement is that the confinement must reasonably appear to the confined person to be complete.

Example: In *Talcott v. Nat'l Exhibition Co.,* 144 App. Div. 337, 128 N.Y.S. 1059 (1911), plaintiff was admitted to an enclosure where baseball tickets were sold, but was unable to get into the game. Meantime, defendant closed the gates to the enclosure. There was another exit, of which the plaintiff was reasonably unaware. The court held the plaintiff was falsely imprisoned.

1. The concept of complete confinement raises some difficult problems of intent.

   Example: *Restatement (Second) of Torts* § 36, comm. *a,* Illus. 1, states that if *A* locks "*B,* an athletic young man, in a room with an open window" four feet from the floor and from the ground outside, there is no false imprisonment. Is this because *A* did not intend to confine *B*? Presumably there would be an intentional confinement at least until *B* reasonably should have discovered the open window. If *B* has "a disease which makes any considerable exertion dangerous to him," then Illus. 2 of the same section states that there would be a false imprisonment. If, however, *A* neither knew nor should have known of *B*'s diseased condition, it is doubtful whether *A* could be said to have the necessary intent to confine *B* longer than reasonably necessary for *B* to discover the open window.

2. The confinement need not be in a single location.

   Example: In *Whittaker v. Sanford,* 110 Me. 77, 85 A. 399 (1912), plaintiff was unlawfully confined in a vessel at anchor. The confinement would surely have been equally unlawful if the vessel had travelled about.

3. *Restatement (Second) of Torts* § 36, comm. *b,* states that the area of confinement may be "so large that it ceases to be a confinement within the area and becomes an exclusion from some other area." As examples, the *Restatement* says that intentional, wrongful confinement within a large town may be false imprisonment, but that intentional wrongful exclusion from the United States would not be false imprisonment. The principle at work here is not clear. Must the area of confinement be smaller than the area of nonconfinement? In any event, wrongful exclusion from the United States should be actionable — if not as false imprisonment, then as an innominate tort. *See Restatement (Second) of Torts* § 870. *Compare Cullen v. Dickinson,* 33 S.D. 27, 144 N.W. 656 (1913). (unjustified exclusion from dance hall may constitute "wrongful trespass" or "deprivation of liberty").

E. **The Act of Confinement:** The act of confinement can consist of duress other than by physical force or threats of physical force to the plaintiff.

Examples: A threat to shoot a relative of the plaintiff, unless the plaintiff accepts confinement, may be sufficient duress, *Restatement (Second) of Torts* § 40A, comm. *a,* Illus. 1; or a retention of the plaintiff's bag to enforce compliance may constitute sufficient duress. *Griffin v. Clark,* 55 Idaho 364, 42 P.2d 297 (1935).

1. *Restatement (Second) of Torts* § 40, comm. *a,* Illus. 1, indicates that a threat by words alone may be enough to cause unlawful confinement. This rule should be contrasted with that of assault, where it is stated that words alone are generally not sufficient to constitute an assault.

2. *Restatement (Second) of Torts* § 40 also says that the threat must be to apply force "immediately upon the other's going or attempting to go" beyond the area of confinement; but this qualification of immediacy is of doubtful validity.

   Example: *A* says to *B*, "If you leave this room today, I will kill you tomorrow." Surely this threat would constitute sufficient immediate psychological duress to give rise to an action for false imprisonment.

3. A shopkeeper who reasonably believes that one has tortiously taken property of the shopkeeper is entitled to use reasonable force to detain the suspected person, in order to make a reasonable investigation of the facts. *Bonkowski v. Arlan's Dept. Store,* 12 Mich. App. 88, 162 N.W.2d 347 (1968). This shopkeeper's privilege is fraught with difficulties regarding the reasonableness of the suspicion, the length of detention, and the amount of force used to detain.

F. **False Arrest:** A separate body of law exists for the tort of false arrest, which involves the arrest or confinement of a person suspected of committing a criminal offense. A peace officer is privileged to make a reasonable arrest of another under a warrant if the warrant is either valid or fair on its face. *Restatement (Second) of Torts* § 122. Such an officer is entitled to make an arrest without a warrant on reasonable suspicion that a felony has been committed by the arrested person or when "an affray is being or has been committed in the officer's presence," and the officer reasonably suspects the arrested person of participating therein and makes the arrest "at once or on fresh pursuit." *Restatement (Second) of Torts* § 121. An officer is permitted to use deadly force to prevent an escape if the officer has probable cause to believe that the suspect poses a significant threat of death or serious injury to the officer or to others. *State of Tennessee v. Garner,* 471 U.S. 1 (1985). A third person is privileged to assist an officer in making an arrest, unless he is convinced that the officer himself lacks the privilege to arrest. *Restatement (Second) of Torts* § 139(b).

1. Either a private person or a peace officer is entitled to make an arrest for a criminal offense without a warrant:

   a. if the arrested person has committed the felony for which she is arrested;

   b. if a felony has in fact been committed, and the arrester reasonably believes the arrestee committed it;

   c. if the arrestee has attempted to commit a felony in the arrester's presence, and the arrest is made "at once or upon fresh pursuit";

   d. if the arrestee is committing a breach of peace in the arrester's presence or, having committed such a breach, is reasonably believed by the arrester to be about to renew the breach; or

   e. if the arrestee "knowingly" causes the arrester to believe that facts exist to justify an arrest for any of the reasons set forth in this sentence. *Restatement (Second) of Torts* §§ 119, 121(a). A private person is privileged to assist another private person in making an arrest only if the other person "is himself privileged to make the arrest." *Restatement (Second) of Torts* § 139(1).

IV.   INTENTIONAL INFLICTION OF EMOTIONAL DISTRESS

A.   Definition: One who by extreme and outrageous conduct either intentionally or recklessly causes severe emotional distress to another is subject to liability for such distress and for any resulting physical harm. Where emotional distress is thus caused, physical harm is not necessary and the resulting emotional distress alone is a sufficient basis for recovery. *Restatement (Second) of Torts* § 46.

   1.   This tort should be contrasted with that of *negligent* infliction of emotional distress, where it is frequently held that proof of physical injury is a condition to recovery. *See Womack v. Eldridge,* 215 Va. 338, 210 S.E.2d 145 (1974). The physical injury requirement for the negligence tort has been dispensed with by some courts, however, *see St. Elizabeth Hospital v. Garrard,* 730 S.W.2d 649 (Tex. 1987), and when this occurs there may be substantial overlap between the torts of intentional and negligent infliction.

   2.   Indeed, the negligence tort may be broader in scope than the intentional one, since for negligent infliction of emotional distress extreme and outrageous conduct need not be proven nor must it be shown that the resulting mental distress is severe. Typically, punitive damages can be recovered for the intentional tort, although not for the tort of negligent infliction of emotional distress. The tort of negligent infliction of emotional distress will be discussed in Chapter 4, *infra.*

   3.   Where the defendant acts willfully, deliberately or intentionally, plaintiff's burden of proof may be lessened. The court in *Potter v. Firestone Tire & Rubber Co.*, 863 P.2d 795 (Cal. 1993), held that plaintiffs' fear of contracting cancer as a result of defendant's pollution need only be reasonable in order to recover for such fear, if the defendant acted wilfully, deliberately or intentionally; but plaintiffs would have to show it was more likely than not that they would develop cancer in order to recover for such fear, if only negligence of the defendant was shown.

B.   The Necessary Conduct: Unlike the other intentional torts thus far considered, words alone are sufficient to give rise to the tort of intentional infliction of emotional distress where the other elements of the tort are present.

   Example: A threat of future harm unless the plaintiff left the state was held sufficient to give rise to the tort in *Dickens v. Puryear,* 302 N.C. 437, 276 S.E.2d 325 (1981). *See also State Rubbish Collectors Ass'n v. Siliznoff,* 38 Cal. 2d 330, 240 P.2d 282 (1952) (threat of future harm unless the plaintiff paid an extorted sum of money held sufficient).

   1.   The defendant need not actually intend to cause the resulting harm — although such intent will be sufficient for the tort. It is enough if the conduct is reckless.

   Examples: The conduct of the defendant hospital was reckless, giving rise to liability when it failed to properly dispose of plaintiff's miscarried fetus; the shriveled fetus was displayed in a jar of formaldehyde to the plaintiff about six weeks following the miscarriage while plaintiff was visiting the hospital for a checkup and asked what had happened to her baby. *Johnson v. Woman's Hosp.,* 527 S.W. 2d 133 (Tenn. App. 1975). Similarly, in *Blakely v. Shortal's Estate,* 236 Iowa 787, 20 N.W.2d 28 (1945), the defendant estate could be held liable for the act of its deceased, a guest in plaintiff's home, in committing suicide by slashing his throat in plaintiff's kitchen while plaintiff was absent. On plaintiff's return, she suffered severe emotional distress after viewing the grisly sight of the suicide. The conduct of the deceased "evinced a reckless disregard for the safety of others." Other examples of outrageous conduct are threatening to kill plaintiff's pet dog unless defendant's veterinary bill was paid by a certain date, *Lawrence v. Stanford,* 655 S.W.2d 927 (Tenn. 1983); refusal to pay a valid insurance claim, *Fletcher v. West. Nat'l Life Ins. Co.,* 10 Cal. App. 3d 376, 89 Cal. Rptr. 78 (1970); and harassing debt-collection tactics, *Moorhead v. J.C. Penney Co.,* 555 S.W.2d 713 (Tenn. 1977). With regard to debt collection, the Fair Debt Collection Practices Act of 1977 forbids "abusive, deceptive, and unfair debt collection practices" by debt collectors, including communications with the debtor "at any unusual time or place." 15 U.S.C. §§ 1692, 1692c.

   a.   It is often stated that liability does not extend to "mere insults, indignities, threats, annoyances, petty oppressions, or other trivialities." *Restatement (Second) of Torts* § 46, comm. *d.*

       Example: In *Slocum v. Food Fair Stores of Florida,* 100 So. 2d 396 (Fla. 1958), the conduct of an employee of defendant grocery store was held not to be outrageous where the employee refused to assist a customer, saying "you stink to me," even though she suffered a "heart attack and aggravation of preexisting heart disease" as a result.

   b.   There is no bright line in distinguishing between the outrageous and the "mere insult," however, and much depends on the context.

       Example: In *Alcorn v. Anbro Eng'g Inc.,* 2 Cal. 3d 493, 86 Cal. Rptr. 88, 468 P.2d 216 (1970), racial slurs were held to be outrageous and actionable. This case may turn on the known susceptibility or sensitivity of the plaintiff, and may pose free speech problems under the U.S. Constitution. It is widely recognized, moreover, that insults by employees of common carriers and public utilities are actionable, *Slocum, supra, Restatement (Second) of Torts* § 48, and one who intentionally, recklessly, or negligently interferes improperly with the handling or disposal of the body of a dead person may be liable for emotional distress thereby caused to members of the deceased's family. *Restatement (Second) of Torts* § 868; *Meyer v. Nottger,* 241 N.W.2d 911 (Iowa 1976). Outrageousness is an evolving concept.

   c.   It is widely held, moreover, that a person may be held liable for offensive words or conduct directed toward one known to be especially vulnerable or susceptible to emotional distress, such as young children, pregnant women, the ill, or the elderly, even though the same conduct would not be considered outrageous if directed toward an ordinary person.

       Examples: Held, actionable for the defendant to tell a six-year-old girl that her mother was an adulteress who would be punished by God, *Korbin v. Berlin,* 177 So. 2d 551 (Fla. App. 1965); held, actionable to play a practical joke, regarding an alleged hidden pot of gold, on an elderly woman with a history of mental instability where the woman was subjected to embarrassment and humiliation as a result, *Nickerson v. Hodges,* 146 La. 735, 84 So. 37 (1920).

C. The Nature of the Damage: It has been held that not only must defendant's conduct be extreme and outrageous, but plaintiff's resulting emotional distress must be severe in order for an action to lie for intentional infliction of emotional distress. *Harris v. Jones,* 281 Md. 560, 380 A.2d 611 (1977). The severity requirement, like that of outrageousness, is, however, a flexible and evolving concept.

Example: Nominal damages ($750) were allowed in *Browning v. Slenderella Systems,* 54 Wash. 2d 440, 341 P.2d 859 (1959), where the plaintiff suffered embarrassment after being refused service on racial grounds in violation of the state public accommodation law. Recovery for insults of a public utility or common carrier probably does not require proof of severe emotional distress. *See Lipman v. Atl. Coast. R.R. Co.,* 108 S.C. 151, 93 S.E. 713 (1917). Compare the rule for assault and battery, where nominal damages are recoverable for the commission of those torts.

D. Transferred Intent: It is frequently stated that the doctrine of transferred intent does not apply to the tort of intentional infliction of emotional distress.

Example: Thus, in *Taylor v. Vallelunga*, 171 Cal. App. 2d 107, 339 P. 2d 910 (1959), the plaintiff was denied recovery for fright and emotional distress when wshe witnessed the beating of her father by defendants, since there was no allegation that defendants knew of her presence or that "the beating was administered for the purpose of causing her to suffer emotional distress" or that they knew such distress was "substantially certain" to occur. The reason for the rule, say the Restaters, is "justified by the practical necessity of drawing the line somewhere, since the number of persons who may suffer emotional distress at the news of the assassination of the President is virtually unlimited." *Restatement (Second) of Torts* § 46, comm. *l.*

1. The *Restatement* leaves open the question as to whether a plaintiff must actually witness the tortious injury of another by the defendant in order to recover for resulting emotional distress. *Restatement (Second) of Torts* § 46 Caveat. It seems that plaintiff's actual presence would not be necessary, however, where the defendant intends to cause such distress or where it is substantially certain to occur. *See Blakeley v. Shortal's Estate, supra* (the case of the ungrateful guest who slashed his throat in his hostess' absence, causing her severe emotional distress when she later discovered the gruesome body). Of course, the passage of a great amount of time before discovery of the event may present problems of proximate cause, or, as the Restaters say, "the distress of a woman who is informed of her husband's murder ten years afterward may lack the guarantee of genuineness which her presence on the spot would afford." *Restatement (Second) of Torts* § 46, comm. *l.* Compare the rules governing recovery for infliction of emotional distress owing to the negligent injury of another, in Chapter 4, *infra.*

E. The First Amendment Defense: Since speech is frequently involved as the basis for the tort of intentional infliction of emotional distress, there may be a free-speech defense to the tort under the First Amendment of the United States Constitution.

Example: In *Hustler Magazine v. Falwell,* 485 U.S. 46 (1988), plaintiff was constitutionally denied recovery for emotional distress damages caused by a crude lampoon of himself in defendant's magazine. The holding of the case may be limited to situations where the plaintiff is a public figure, and the subject matter is one of public interest.

1. There may also be a First Amendment freedom of religion defense.

Example: A church was constitutionally protected from liability for intentionally inflicting emotional distress by its practice of "shunning" a church member whose conduct was unacceptable to the church. *Paul v. Watchtower Bible and Tract Soc.,* 819 F.2d 875 (9th Cir. 1987). *But see Bear v. Reformed Mennonite Church,* 462 Pa. 330, 341 A.2d 105 (1975) (plaintiff stated claim in tort against church for damages resulting from "shunning").

V. TRESPASS TO LAND

TRESPASS TO LAND

A. Definition: A trespass to land occurs when one voluntarily, intentionally, and without privilege enters or remains on, or causes another person or thing to enter or remain on, the land of a person who is either in actual possession or is entitled to immediate possession of the land. *Restatement (Second) of Torts* §§ 157–158, 160, 164.

1.   Unlike the other intentional torts thus far considered, the intent here need not be to harm or offend, but only to do the act.

Example: *D,* a nine-year-old boy, while swimming at *P's* club, raised a metal cover over a drain in the swimming pool and placed a tennis ball in the drain. *D* did not know there was suction in the drain. The ball was pulled into the drain and caused extensive damage. *D* was held liable in trespass to *P,* regardless of whether he intended or knew that any harm would occur. The issue was whether *D* "possessed the capability to perform the physical act intentionally without regard to knowledge of possible injurious consequences." *Cleveland Park Club v. Perry,* 165 A.2d 485 (D.C. Cir. 1960).

a.   Good-faith mistake is no defense to an action in trespass.

Example: *D* enters Blackacre thinking it is her own, in good faith reliance on a survey done by a reputable surveyor. *D* is liable in trespass to P, owner of Blackacre. *Restatement (Second) of Torts § 164,* Illus. 1 and 3. If, however, P wrongfully caused *D's* mistake, then *D* would have a valid defense in an action by *P* for trespass.

2.   The act must be voluntary in order to constitute trespass, and an involuntary act is not actionable.

Examples: *F* forcibly carries *B* onto *A's* land; *B* without fault slips on a piece of ice on the sidewalk and falls against *A's* building, breaking out a window; *B* suffers a sudden and unforeseeable stroke and loses control of his car which crashes into *A's* property. In each of these examples, *B* is not liable to *A* for trespass; but *F* is liable to *A* for trespass in the first example. *Restatement (Second) of Torts* § 158, Illus. 1, § 166, Illus. 1 and 2.

a.   *The entry need not be direct:* *B* can commit trespass by intentionally causing another person or thing to enter *A's* property.

Examples: *B* drives a stray horse onto *A's* land; *B* builds a dam across a stream on his land, causing the stream to flood *A's* property. In both instances, *B* has trespassed onto *A's* land. *Restatement (Second) of Torts* § 158, Illus. 4 and 5.

3.   A trespass can also be committed by remaining on, or refusing to leave, land after the right or privilege to be there has expired, even though the original entry may have been lawful. *Restatement (Second) of Torts* §§ 158, 160.

Example: Defendant had a license to place a snow fence in decedent's field, under an agreement to remove it at the end of the winter season. Defendant failed to remove an anchor post of the fence, and decedent was killed when his mowing machine struck the post and threw the decedent to the ground. Defendant was held liable in trespass for the wrongful death of the decedent. *Rogers v. Bd. of Road Comm'rs,* 319 Mich. 661, 30 N.W.2d 358 (1948).

4.   Some courts may require that there be a physical entry in order for trespass to occur and may hold that intrusions by vibrations, invisible gases and odors, offensive sounds or sights, and the like do not constitute a trespass. If a court draws this kind of distinction, a plaintiff suffering from such intrusions may be able to bring an action for nuisance which typically does not require physical entry.

B.   **Trespass above and below the Land:** An old legal maxim states, *"Cujus est solum, ejus est usque ad coelum et ad inferos":* The owner of land owns everything above and below it. Thus, it was held a trespass in *Herrin v. Sutherland,* 74 Mont. 587, 241 P. 328 (1925), to shoot across another's land, and in *Edwards v. Sims,* 232 Ky. 791, 24 S.W.2d 619 (1929), the development of a cave under another's land was found to be a trespass.

1. This ancient maxim has given way to modern demands of air flight and underground resource development. In *United States v. Causby,* 328 U.S. 256 (1946), the Supreme Court held that the federal government could establish minimum altitudes for air flight, and any flight above those altitudes would not be a trespass. Cases have held that even flights below those altitudes will not constitute trespass unless they interfere with the actual, as opposed to the potential, use of the land. *Restatement (Second) of Torts* § 159, comm. *k.* The *Restatement* position is that there is no trespass by aircraft unless the plane "enters into the immediate reaches of the air space next to the land, and . . . interferes substantially" with the owner's "use and enjoyment" of the land.

2. Mining, oil drilling, and other underground resource developments may be regulated by statute or by custom. Thus, in *R.R. Comm. v. Manziel,* 361 S.W.2d 560 (Tex. 1962), the court held that a state regulatory agency could authorize the injection of saltwater into oil wells to stimulate the production of oil and gas, and that there would be no trespass if the saltwater penetrated into the wells of adjoining landowners. In many Western states, miners are permitted to follow the vein wherever it leads. State regulation may likewise control slant oil drilling and the withdrawal of oil from any underground pool that extends under the land of more than one owner.

C. **Damages:** The traditional rule is that a plaintiff may sue for trespass and recover at least nominal damages, even though no actual damages have been suffered. *Dougherty v. Stepp,* 18 N.C. 371 (1835). The reason given for this rule is that if it did not exist, the trespasser might acquire a prescriptive right in the land.

1. This nominal-damage rule may likewise give way when larger public interests are involved. Thus, in *Bradley v. Amer. Smelting and Refin. Co.,* 104 Wash. 2d 677, 709 P.2d 782 (1985), the court held that gases and particulate matter emitted from defendant's smelter onto plaintiff's land could constitute a trespass, but only if plaintiff could show he had "suffered actual and substantial damages."

2. When a government agency takes the land of another, this may constitute a taking under the Fifth and Fourteenth Amendments to the United States Constitution. In that event, the Constitution requires that the government provide just compensation for the taking.

D. **Risk-Utility Analysis:** It has been held that the jury should not be instructed in a trespass case to weigh the utility of the defendant's conduct and defendant's efforts to prevent intrusion of gases, odors, and particulates onto plaintiff's land against the harm caused by such intrusion. *Davis v. Georgia-Pacific Corp.,* 251 Or. 239, 445 P.2d 481 (1968). But other courts, in certain situations, do engage in such a weighing process to determine if a trespass has been committed. *R.R. Comm. v. Manziel,* 361 S.W.2d 560 (Tex. 1962) (subsurface invasion from authorized oil recovery operations).

E. **Foreseeability:** As a general proposition, a defendant need not be able to foresee the damages that may result from her trespass. This rule is similar to the thin-skull doctrine of tort law (you take your tort victim as you find him).

Example: Defendant dug a drainage ditch across the property of plaintiff's decedent. When the decedent discovered the trespass, he became so upset he died, apparently from a stroke or heart attack. The court in *Baker v. Shymkiv,* 6 Ohio St. 3d 151, 451 N.E.2d 811 (1983), held that an action in trespass for wrongful death would lie even though the resulting damage may have been unforeseeable.

1. There will be no liability for trespass, however, if the risk itself — as opposed to the resulting damage — is unforeseeable.

   Example: An unprecedented freshet carries away logs from *B's* land and deposits them on the land of *A*. There is no trespass. Similarly, an express company was not liable in trespass for damages resulting from a leaking nitroglycerin container explosion which occurred when the company opened the container, reasonably believing it to contain a harmless oil. *Restatement (Second) of Torts* § 166, Illus. 3 and 5. The latter example resembles the negligence case of *Palsgraf v. L.I. R.R.,* 248 N.Y. 339, 162 N.E. 99 (1928).

2

VI. TRESPASS TO CHATTEL

TRESPASS TO CHATTEL

A. **Definition:** A trespass to chattel may be committed by intentionally dispossessing another of the chattel, or by intentionally using or intermeddling with it. *Restatement (Second) of Torts* § 217. The action lies on behalf of the person who is in possession of the chattel, who is entitled to immediate possession, or who is entitled to future possession, for harm caused to such possessory interest. *Restatement (Second) of Torts* §§ 218–220.

B. **Intent:** The necessary intent is the intent to use or intermeddle with the chattel, or knowledge that such intermeddling will to a substantial certainty occur. *Restatement (Second) of Torts* § 217, comm. *c.*

   1. Reasonable mistake is normally no defense to an action for trespass to chattel, unless the mistake is wrongfully induced by the possessor of the chattel. *Restatement (Second) of Torts* § 244. Thus, abatement of a private nuisance allegedly caused by a chattel is not privileged if the actor is mistaken as to the existence of the nuisance. There are exceptions, however, where the public interest is sufficiently great to justify the mistake. A person is privileged to commit a trespass to chattel in the reasonable but mistaken belief that she has the right to act in self-defense or out of public necessity.

C. **Degree of Harm:** The tort or trespass to chattel is intended to protect against invasions less serious than that of conversion, considered below. To recover for trespass, actual damage must be shown and a harmless interference is not actionable.

   Example: *B* agreed to lodge and feed *A's* horse for a specified period. During that period, B rode the horse for about fifteen miles for pleasure, without *A's* permission. There was no trespass because the horse was not harmed. *Johnson v. Weedman,* 5 Ill. 495 (1843).

   1. The question of actionable harm is a matter of degree, depending on the precise facts involved.

      Examples: Moving *A's* car four feet may not be a trespass, but moving it around the corner may be if *A* is significantly inconvenienced in finding the car. Touching *A's* toothbrush may not be a trespass, but using it to brush one's teeth likely would be. *Restatement (Second) of Torts* § 281, comms. *h* and *i.* Indeed, such use might well constitute a conversion.

CONVERSION ## VII. CONVERSION

A. **Definition:** A conversion is the intentional and unauthorized exercise of dominion or control over the chattel of another which so seriously interferes with the other's right of control that the actor can justly be required to pay the full value of the chattel. In determining the seriousness of the interference and whether the actor should be required to pay full value, the courts look to (1) the extent and duration of the actor's exercise of control, (2) the extent and duration of the interference with the other's right of control, including the harm done to the chattel and inconvenience and expense caused to the other, and (3) the good faith of the actor. *Restatement (Second) of Torts* § 222A.

1. There is no precise rule for determining if a conversion has occurred. According to the *Restatement,* if *B* mistakenly takes *A's* hat from a restaurant for a short time but returns it as soon as the mistake is discovered, there is no conversion; but if the hat is kept for three months before the mistake is discovered, or if *A* is substantially inconvenienced in recovering it, there is a conversion. Even if *B* keeps the hat only for a short time, but does so with the intent to steal it, there is a conversion. If the hat is lost, damaged, or destroyed while in *B's* possession, there is a conversion. *Id.,* comm. *d,* Illus. 1–4, 6, 20. Thus a chattel may be converted if it is retained for a substantial period of time, if the owner is substantially inconvenienced in recovering it, if it is substantially damaged, or if the defendant intends to convert the chattel.

B. Intent: The intent required for conversion is the intent to exercise dominion or control over the chattel. The actor need not intend to interfere with the other's right of control. Thus, the actor may be a converter if she dispossesses another of a chattel in the reasonable belief that it is her own. *Restatement (Second) of Torts* § 224. As noted above, however, good faith is relevant, along with the extent of damage or interference, in determining whether or not a conversion has occurred. As noted below, the presence of good faith is also relevant for purposes of determining damages.

1. Negligent conduct is insufficient to give rise to a claim for conversion.

    Example: *B*, while using *A's* car with *A's* permission, negligently has an accident and destroys the car. There is no conversion, although *B* may be liable to *A* for negligent destruction of property. *Restatement (Second) of Torts* § 224, comm. *b.* If, however, *B* is using the chattel *without authority to do so,* he will be liable to *A* for its substantial damage, loss, or destruction during such use, regardless of whether the mishap occurs as a result of an intentional, negligent, or innocent act of *B*.

C. Stolen goods: The general rule is that one cannot take good title to stolen goods, and the taker commits conversion regardless of the presence or absence of good faith. *Restatement (Second) of Torts* § 229. If, however, the conveyor obtained the goods by fraud or deceit, as opposed to theft, then the conveyee can take good title if she obtains the goods in a good-faith purchase for value. U.C.C. § 2-403.

1. There is a conversion of a negotiable instrument when it is paid on a forged endorsement. *Restatement (Second) of Torts* § 241A. But money or a negotiable instrument payable to bearer can be lawfully transferred to a good faith purchaser for value even though it has been stolen. U.C.C. §§ 3-302, 3-305; *Prosser and Keeton on the Law of Torts* 94 (5th ed. 1984). The reason for this rule is to facilitate commerce. In the case of a forged instrument, the payor is expected to discover the forgery, and she fails to do so at her peril.

D. Bailment: A bailee is typically not strictly liable for keeping or transporting the goods of another. He is liable for conversion only if he refuses to surrender possession after he knows or should know who has the right to possession. *Restatement (Second) of Torts* § 230. He will be liable in conversion, however, if without authority he receives or transfers title to the goods of another, or if he misdelivers such goods. *Restatement (Second) of Torts* §§ 231, 233–234.

E. Damages: The measure of damages for conversion is ordinarily the market value of the goods at the time the conversion occurs, plus interest from that time to the time of payment. *Nephi Process. Plant v. Talbott,* 247 F.2d 771 (10th Cir. 1957). If the goods have a fluctuating value, some courts allow recovery of the highest value within a reasonable time after conversion, during which the plaintiff might have been able to replace the goods. *United States v. Merchants Mut. Bond. Co.,*

242 F. Supp. 465 (N.D. Iowa 1965). If there is no market value, then the cost of replacement is the appropriate measure; if that cannot be determined, then the value to the owner can be used. *Jensen v. C. & W. Ind. R.R.,* 94 Ill. App. 3d 915, 419 N.E.2d 578 (1981).

1. Where converted goods are returned and accepted, recovery will be reduced by the value of the goods as returned. Where the goods have been innocently converted and their value to the owner has not been substantially impaired, the court may in its discretion reduce damages if the converter promptly offers to return the goods to their owner after the conversion is discovered. This reduction can be made even though the tender of return is refused. *Restatement (Second) of Torts* § 922. The amount of the reduction is that which is just and equitable in view of all the surrounding circumstances.

VIII. DEFENSES

DEFENSES

    A. Consent:

1. *Introduction:* The defense of consent extends throughout tort law. One can consent to an intentional, negligent, or strict liability tortious invasion. That invasion may be to one's person, real property, chattels, or intangible interests. Whenever a valid consent is given to any such invasion, there is no tort liability. The situations primarily considered here are consensual intentional invasions of the person, but the applicable principles apply generally.

2. *Definition:* Consent is the willingness for conduct to occur. It can be expressed by words, by conduct, or by inaction, where such expression is reasonably understood to manifest consent. *Restatement (Second) of Torts* § 892.

   Examples: *B* says he wishes to vaccinate *A*, and *A* holds up her arm, apparently indicating consent to the vaccination. *B* is not liable in tort for the vaccination. *O'Brien v. Cunard S.S. Co.,* 154 Mass. 272, 28 N.E. 266 (1891). *B* proposes to kiss *A*, who is *B*'s date. *A* says nothing. The kiss is not actionable as a battery. But if *A* and *B* are quarreling and *B* threatens to punch *A* in the nose and then does so, the punch can be tortious, since consent to physical violence cannot reasonably be implied merely from engaging in a quarrel. *Restatement (Second) of Torts* § 892, comm. *c,* Illus. 3 and 4.

   a. Consent can be implied not just by the plaintiff's conduct, but by law or by custom as well.

      Examples: *B* casually touches *A* on the arm to ask directions. This contact is likely not tortious, since it is customary to make such casual contacts. Contacts ordinarily associated with engaging in a sport are not actionable, *McAdams v. Windham,* 208 Ala. 492, 94 So. 742 (1922)., unless the defendant's conduct is reckless, *Crawn v. Campo,* 136 N.J. 494, 643 A.2d 600 (1994). If *B* acts in an emergency to save *A*, where there is no opportunity to obtain consent and consent may reasonably be implied, there is no tort. *Restatement (Second) of Torts* § 892D.

   b. It should be noted that express and implied consent are closely akin to the defense of assumption of the risk. *See Restatement (Second) of Torts* §§ 496A– 496G. Where the defense of consent applies, recovery is barred entirely and principles of comparative fault do not control.

3. *Scope of Consent:* In order for *A*'s consent to be effective, she must have the capacity to consent. Her consent is effective only as to the particular conduct, or substantially similar conduct, for which it is given, and only on the conditions under which it is given. If the actor exceeds the consent, then that consent is not effective. *Restatement (Second) of Torts* § 892A.

a. Mistake will not invalidate *A*'s consent to *B*'s conduct, unless *B* knows of *A*'s mistake or induces it by misrepresentation, fraud, or duress.

Example: *A* gives *B* permission to cut timber on Blackacre, mistakenly believing the land to be Whiteacre. *B* commits no trespass in cutting the timber on Blackacre. *Restatement (Second) of Torts* § 892B, comm. *c*, Illus. 1. *B* induces *A* to have sexual intercourse without telling *A* that he has a venereal disease. *B* is liable for the resulting harm to *A*. *Id.*, comm. *e*, Illus. 5.

(1) Closely related to the rule of mistaken consent is the doctrine of informed consent, which holds that a consent is not valid unless the consenting party is reasonably informed of the attendant risks involved. The doctrine typically arises in the context of medical malpractice. *See Cobbs v. Grant*, 8 Cal.3d 229, 104 Cal. Rptr. 505, 502 P.2d 1 (1972). But the issue of informed consent is by no means limited to medical malpractice, and it may arise in connection with any professional, fiduciary, or other duty to disclose. The parameters of the doctrine vary, however, depending on the context in which it arises.

(2) If the mistake or fraud on *A* by *B* is not substantial, or is only collateral to the transaction, it may not be sufficient to give rise to an action in tort although it may provide the basis for equitable rescission or restitution.

Example: *B* induces *A* to have intercourse in return for an agreed sum of money, and *B* pays in counterfeit bills. *B* is not liable for battery. *Restatement (Second) of Torts* § 892B, comm. *g*, Illus. 9. *A* could, however, sue *B* for the sum agreed upon, assuming the underlying contract is not illegal. *B* could also be criminally liable for passing counterfeit money.

4. ***Consent to a Crime:*** There are cases holding that one cannot consent to the commission of a crime, *McNeil v. Mullin*, 70 Kan. 634, 79 P. 168 (1905) (unlawful mutual combat, each party may recover against the other in tort). The modern view, expressed in the *Restatement*, is that consent to the commission of a crime is effective to bar recovery in tort, unless the conduct was made criminal in order to protect a certain class of persons without regard to their consent. *Restatement (Second) of Torts* § 892C.

Examples: Consent by a competent adult to the crime of fornication has been held valid, barring a tort claim. *Oberlin v. Upson*, 84 Ohio St. 111, 95 N.E. 511 (1911). But such consent by a minor with an adult has been held to be invalid, not barring the claim. *Bishop v. Liston*, 112 Neb. 559, 199 N.W. 825 (1924).

B. Self-Defense:

1. Defense by use of force not threatening death or serious bodily harm. A person is entitled to use force, not intended or likely to cause death or serious bodily harm, to protect herself against unprivileged harmful or offensive contact which she reasonably believes another is about to inflict *intentionally* upon her. There is no duty to retreat in this situation, or to comply with an unprivileged demand of the other. A mistaken but reasonable belief of the impending contact is sufficient to justify the use of such force. "Serious bodily harm" is harm constituting mayhem, or causing the permanent or prolonged loss of an important bodily organ or member. *Restatement (Second) of Torts* § 63.

a. If the threatened contact is the result of a *negligent,* rather than intentional, act of the other, then the threatened person must act reasonably to retreat or otherwise attempt to avoid the contact.

Example: *A* approaches *B* negligently swinging a cane without keeping a proper lookout ahead. *B* is required to step aside or to alert *A* of the impending danger if it is reasonably possible to do so, instead of using physical force in self-defense. *Restatement (Second) of Torts* § 64, comm. *b,* Illus. 1.

2. Defense by force threatening death or serious bodily harm. A person is entitled to use force causing death or serious body harm to repel what he reasonably believes to be an intentional threat by another of death or serious bodily harm to himself. Some courts hold there *is no duty* of retreat in this situation. The *Restatement* position is that there *is a duty* of retreat if the retreat can be made safely — unless the defender is in his own dwelling, or is making a lawful arrest, in which event there *is no duty* to retreat. *Restatement (Second) of Torts* § 65.

a. The force used must not be excessive, and the defender will be liable for any harm caused by such excessive force. There is no privilege to use force after the threat has terminated. The defender may not use force to resist a lawful arrest, and he will be liable for intentional or negligent injury which he causes to a third person in his own self-defense. *Restatement (Second) of Torts* §§ 72–73.

C. Defense of Others:

1. *Scope of the Privilege:* A person is entitled to use the same force to defend others that she could use to defend herself. This privilege exists regardless of the relationship between the defender and the person defended, *i.e.,* one is entitled to defend a stranger, as well as a friend.

a. A division of authority exists regarding the effect of mistake in this context. Some courts hold that the defender will be liable for resulting injuries if he is mistaken as to the right of self-defense of the person on whose behalf he intervenes, even if the mistake is a reasonable one. This view discourages intervention, and seems contrary to social utility. The better view, embodied in the *Restatement,* is that a mistaken intervention is privileged as long as the mistake is a reasonable one. *Restatement (Second) of Torts* § 76.

b. An arresting officer may not use deadly force to prevent the escape of a suspected criminal unless such force is reasonably required to prevent the escape and the officer has probable cause to believe the suspect poses a significant threat of death or serious injury to herself or others. Use of such force in the absence of the described privilege is a denial of the constitutional rights of the suspect. *Tennessee v. Garner,* 471 U.S. 1 (1985). Assuming a private individual has a right to make an arrest, his use of such unprivileged force would presumably also be actionable as a tort, although not as a constitutional violation if state action were not involved.

D. Defense of Land or Chattels:

1. *General Principles:* One is privileged to use reasonable force, not intended to cause death or serious bodily harm, to prevent the entry onto one's land or the taking of one's chattels, provided the following conditions are met: (1) the defender reasonably believes the entry or taking can be prevented by the use of such force; (2) the defender first requests the other to desist and such request is disregarded, or the defender reasonably believes that the request will be useless or that substantial harm will be done before it can be made; and (3) the entry or taking is unprivileged, or the intruder or taker leads the defender reasonably to believe that the entry or taking is unprivileged. *Restatement (Second) of Torts* § 77.

a.   The defender cannot use force threatening death or serious bodily harm simply to protect his land or chattels. He can use such force only if he would be entitled to do so in self-defense or in defense of others, *i.e.,* where the intruder herself appears to threaten death or serious bodily harm to the defender or others.

Example: A conductor discovers a trespasser on a fast moving train. She is not entitled to eject the trespasser from the moving train. *Restatement (Second) of Torts* § 77, comm. *i,* Illus. 10. She would be entitled to do so, however, if the trespasser threatened her with death or serious bodily harm.

(1)   The defender can use such force as reasonably appears necessary to protect herself or her land or chattels even though the intruder reasonably believes that he is entitled to intrude, unless the defender by her own fault causes the intruder's mistake in this regard. Where both the defender and the intruder are reasonably mistaken, the risk of mistake fails on the intruder. *Restatement (Second) of Torts* § 78.

b.   One can use a mechanical device to protect his land or chattels if the device is reasonably necessary to afford such protection, the use is reasonable under the circumstances, and the device is customarily used for such purpose or reasonable care is taken to make its use known to probable intruders. *Restatement (Second) of Torts* § 84.

Example: One can use barbed wire to protect against intrusion, provided these devices are not concealed from the intruder. *Id.,* comms. *d* and *f.*

(1)   A protective mechanical device that threatens death or serious bodily harm to the intruder can lawfully be used only if the defender himself would be entitled to use such force were he himself present when the intrusion occurred. *Katko v. Briney,* 183 N.W.2d 657 (Iowa 1971). The *Restatement* position is that the use of such force must *in fact* be justified. A reasonable mistake would be a defense if the defender were present, but he uses such a mechanical device at his peril as a substitute for personal intervention. *Restatement (Second) of Torts* § 85, comm. *d.* There is a division of authority as to whether a warning regarding the presence of the mechanical device will be a defense in this regard. A warning may justify a defense of assumption of the risk in some situations. In others, however, as for example with a watchdog that attacks a minor intruder, a warning may well be inadequate.

2. ***Privileges:*** If the intruder is privileged to intrude, then the defender will not be permitted to use force to resist the intrusion unless the intruder reasonably leads the defender to believe there is no such privilege.

Examples: An intruder might otherwise be privileged to enter land to save his own life; but if he leads the defender reasonably to believe that the defender's life is in jeopardy by the intrusion, the privilege may be lost and the defender can use reasonable force to resist the intrusion. Also, an intrusion may be privileged on civil rights grounds, as, for example, the right to use public accommodations under the Civil Rights Act, *Hamm v. City of Rock Hill,* 379 U.S. 306 (1964). One may be privileged to enter land and to destroy property if it reasonably appears necessary to do so in order to prevent an imminent public disaster. *Harrison v. Wisdom,* 54 Tenn. 99 (1872). One may be privileged to enter as a matter of private necessity as well, as, for example, to protect one's own life or property or that of another, but in this event it has been said that the intruder will be liable for any damages which she causes as a result of the intrusion. *Vincent v. Lake Erie Transp. Co.,* 109 Minn. 456, 124 N.W. 221 (1910). An English case, however, indicates that property can be destroyed with impunity in order to save life. *Southport Corp. v. Esso Petrol. Co.,* [1953] 2 All E.R. 1204 (Q.B.), *aff'd* [1956] A.C. 218

(H.L. 1955). There is no bright line between public and private necessity. The difference turns on the magnitude of the danger presented. *See Restatement (Second) of Torts §§ 196–197.*

E. Recapture of Land or Chattels:

1. *Land:* One who has been dispossessed and who has the right to immediate repossession of land is entitled to use reasonable force to regain possession if the dispossession occurred without claim of right or through fraud, duress, or a breaking and entry. *Restatement (Second) of Torts §§ 88–89.* The forcible re-entry must be fairly soon after the dispossession, or otherwise the owner loses the right to use such force and must resort to legal process to regain possession. *Restatement (Second) of Torts § 91.* Before using force the person seeking re-entry must request that the other give up possession, unless such a request appears useless, dangerous, or likely to defeat the exercise of the privilege of re-entry. *Restatement (Second) of Torts § 92.* The force used must be reasonable and not intended or likely to cause death or serious bodily harm. *Restatement (Second) of Torts § 94.* Here again, legal process should be used, rather than excessive force or force likely to cause death or serious bodily harm.

2. *Chattels:* The right to recapture chattels closely parallels the right to recapture land. The recapturer must have the right to immediate repossession. The dispossession or retention must have occurred without claim of right, or by force, fraud, duress, or other tortious conduct. Demand for return must first be made, unless such demand appears useless, dangerous, or likely to defeat the privilege of repossession. Exercise of the privilege must be timely, and excessive force, or force intended or likely to result in death or serious bodily harm, cannot be used. *Restatement (Second) of Torts §§ 101–104, 106, 108. Hodgeden v. Hubbard,* 18 Vt. 504 (1846).

   a. The *Restatement (Second) of Torts* § 110 provides that one is privileged to assist another in the recapture of chattels only if the other

      (1) is privileged to effect the recapture, and

      (2) requests such assistance, or is a member of the assisting person's immediate family or household.

   b. The privilege to assist third parties in the recapture of chattels is substantially narrower than the privilege to defend another person. In the latter instance, one can assist a stranger, and good faith mistake as to the existence of the privilege is, under the better view, a defense. Thus, greater value is placed on the defense of others than on the defense of others' property.

F. Other Privileges:

1. *Discipline:* One may be permitted to use reasonable force to maintain discipline where one is in a position of authority. Thus, reasonable force can be used for such a purpose by parents over their children, or by school teachers over their students — at least where the students are minors. Local school regulations may prevent, or limit, a school teacher's use of force for purposes of discipline. *See Simms v. School Dist. No. 1,* 13 Or. App. 119, 508 P.2d 236 (1973); and a student's parents may be able to put restrictions on the use of such force as well. The United States Supreme Court has held that there is no constitutional right to notice or prior hearing before corporal punishment can be used by a public school teacher. *Ingraham v. Wright,* 430 U.S. 651(1977).

2. *Justification:* One may be permitted to use reasonable force to maintain order, safety, or the preservation of property.

Example: In *Sindle v. N. Y. C. Transit Auth.,* 33 N.Y.2d 293, 352 N.Y.S.2d 183, 307 N.E.2d 245 (1973), a jury would be permitted to find that a city bus driver could reasonably detain school children in the bus and take them to a police station for investigation, where the children were rowdy, refused to calm down on request, and were vandalizing the bus.

CHAPTER 2 – QUESTIONS, ANSWERS, AND TIPS.

1. **Q:** A fell against B. Was this a battery?

   A: No, there was no battery because the contact was not intentional – assuming the word "fell" implies inadvertence.

   Tip: Watch out for ambiguity in questions. While the word "fell" normally implies an unintentional act, it need not do so; so qualify your answer.

2. **Q:** C, seeing B fall against A, suffered emotional shock. Was C assaulted?

   A: No, for two reasons: (a) A had no intent to commit an assault or battery, and (b) C probably did not fear for her own safety unless she was standing close to B when the fall occurred.

   Tip: In question 2 there are two likely answers (no intent and no fear). Give both answers, not just one. When you later study bystander emotional distress, you will note this tort as another possible answer.

3. **Q:** A, a dirty, drunken person, touched B on the arm on a city street and asked, "Hey, buddy, can you spare a dime?" Was this a battery?

   A: Yes, since the touching was probably offensive even if not physically harmful.

   Tip: Sometimes a tort has two or more applications – in question 3, an intentional touching that is either physically harmful *or* offensive. Consider all applications in relation to the facts.

4. **Q:** A yelled at B, "Watch out for that rattlesnake behind you!" Was this an assault of B by A?

   A: Yes, if A knew there was no rattlesnake. If there was a snake, the yell would be a possible life-saving warning.

   Tip: Avoid reading facts into the question. Do not assume the yell in question 4 was false, unless that assumption is fairly suggested by the facts.

5. **Q:** A tortiously kicked a house door closed, thereby unforeseeably confining B within the house. Did A falsely imprison B, even if B suffered no harm from the confinement?

   A: Yes, provided one would reasonably believe there was no safe escape and (in some jurisdictions) provided B was aware of the confinement. Foreseeability of confinement is not required because the tortious intent is transferred from realty trespass to false imprisonment.

   Tip: In question 5, there can be no privilege since the kick was tortious. There must appear to be no safe escape. In some jurisdictions, B's awareness of the requirement is required since he suffered no harm.

6. Q: Owing to his negligent diagnosis, Dr. concluded that W was dying of cancer and so advised H, W's husband. H told W of the diagnosis, and she suffered a heart attack as a result. Can she recover from Dr. for reckless infliction of emotional distress?

A: No. The diagnosis was not reckless, and therefore neither would the advice be, even if it were substantially certain that H would tell W what Dr. said.

Tip: It would not be reckless for Dr. to tell either H or W that W had cancer, even if Dr. mistakenly believed this diagnosis to be true. The statement could be reckless if Dr. knew W was unusually susceptible to emotional distress, but the facts do not indicate such knowledge.

7. Q: A used B's car under the reasonably mistaken belief that A had the authority to do so, and during such use A negligently wrecked the car. Is A liable to B for conversion of the car?

A: Yes. Reasonable mistake is no excuse, and A is liable for conversion whether or not he wrecked the car negligently.

Tip: Negligent wrecking will not prevent an unauthorized taking from being a conversion, although a claim for negligent wrecking may also be available. It may be advantageous to sue in conversion to get the full value of the car, and not just the decrease in market value, or repair costs, from the wreck.

8. Q: A lost control of her car and entered B's property. B mistakenly believed A intended to run him down with the car, so he shot and killed A. Can B avoid liability to A's estate on grounds of self-defense?

A: Yes, if B reasonably believed A intended to run him down.

Tip: B's mistaken belief must be reasonable. If the mistake is negligent, he is liable.

NEGLIGENCE

▶ **CHAPTER SUMMARY**

NEGLIGENCE

Scope of Chapter: In this chapter we shall discuss the subject of negligence. This is a tort that developed during the nineteenth century to embrace a whole range of actions in which the plaintiff sought to recover for injuries caused by the defendant that were unintentional but, nevertheless, attributable to the fault of the defendant. The discussion in this chapter will focus particularly on the criteria by which the fault of the defendant will be judged and the methods by which that fault is proved.

INTRODUCTION

3

I.   INTRODUCTION

    A. Definition and General Principles: Negligence may be defined as an injury to another arising from the failure of the defendant to take reasonable care to avoid a foreseeable risk of injury to that other person. More concisely it can be defined as subjecting a person to an unreasonable risk of injury. It is sometimes said that the tort of negligence consists of the breach of a "duty" of care owed to another. Since in modern law one normally owes a duty to refrain from conduct which unreasonably threatens injury to others, in most cases an analysis based upon a "breach of duty" is just another way of stating that the defendant has subjected the plaintiff to an unreasonable risk of injury. We shall see in subsequent chapters situations in which one sometimes has no obligation to refrain from creating a risk of injury to other persons, even persons whose presence and susceptibility to injury are highly foreseeable. In those situations the concept of duty means something more than an obligation to refrain from subjecting others to a foreseeable and unreasonable risk of injury.

    B. Plaintiff's Prima Facie Case: To recover in an action for negligence, the plaintiff must allege and prove:

        1. Damage *to the plaintiff.* There are no presumed damages in negligence. An action for negligence will not lie unless the plaintiff alleges and proves actual damage.

        2. Fault *on the part of the defendant:* As we have seen, this requirement can be interpreted as the requirement of showing that the plaintiff has been subjected to an unreasonable risk of injury by the defendant (or that the defendant has breached the duty of care that is owed to the plaintiff).

        3. Causation: That is, the plaintiff must show that the defendant's fault was the legal cause of the plaintiff's injuries.

STANDARD OF CARE

II.   STANDARD OF CARE

    A. Objective vs. Subjective: The standard is an *objective* one. The defendant is required to conform to the conduct of the "reasonable person" in like circumstances. In deciding whether the defendant has subjected the plaintiff to an unreasonable risk of injury, the conduct of the defendant will be examined from the objective criterion of this hypothetical "reasonable person."

        1. If the defendant is engaged in an activity that requires special skills, such as those of a physician or an attorney, the defendant will be held to the standard of what would be expected of a reasonable person with those special skills. There may furthermore be some rare cases in which a defendant who holds himself out as possessing some unique, special skills will be held to the higher and somewhat individualized standard which the defendant himself has established.

        2. There are certain facts which it is said that the hypothetical reasonable person is presumed to know or at the very least is under a "duty to find out."

Example: A defendant will be required to know that tires without tread are dangerous, that objects dropped from a height will fall, that water will freeze if the temperature drops sufficiently, etc. *See Delair v. McAdoo,* 324 Pa. 392, 188 A. 181 (1936).

3. ***Children are held to a slightly different standard:*** The standard to which a child is held has been worded in several different ways. The most common wording holds a child to the standard of what it is reasonable to expect of a child of like age, intelligence, and experience. This test opens up the possibility that a particularly precocious child may be held to a higher standard than some other child of the same age, and to that extent includes a personalized feature not normally present in the test governing adults. In some jurisdictions, by analogy to criminal law, a child under seven cannot be guilty of negligence. In most jurisdictions, there is no such absolute restriction, but in all jurisdictions, there is an age below which a child will be held to be incapable of negligent conduct. It would, for example, be surprising to find a case in which a child under four was held to be capable of negligent conduct. When the age of majority was twenty-one, one could occasionally find cases in which nineteen- or even twenty-year-olds were given the benefit of special doctrines governing children, even though there was a tendency to treat minors over eighteen as adults. Now that the age of majority is eighteen, such persons would certainly be characterized as adults.

   a. Special doctrines have evolved for minors engaged in adult activities, such as driving a car or a motor boat. Such minors have been held to an adult standard. *See Dellwo v. Pearson,* 259 Minn. 452, 107 N.W.2d 859 (1961). What is an adult activity is a difficult question when one moves beyond motor vehicles.

      Example: Some courts have held neither bicycle riding nor skiing nor hunting to be an adult activity, while others have held golf, as played by a child who had taken substantial instruction in the sport, to be an adult activity.

   b. It is sometimes said that a child is and should be held to a higher standard when the child is a defendant than when the child is a plaintiff and the issue is the child's contributory negligence. While one can find numerous statements of this position, there are *very* few judicial holdings actually adopting this position. With the advent of comparative negligence, there is both less incentive to use such a double standard — because the child's contributory negligence will not necessarily totally foreclose recovery — and strong logical reasons not to, because the use of two different standards to judge the plaintiff's conduct makes it harder to compare the comparative fault of the plaintiff and defendant.

4. A mentally deficient adult is held to the objective reasonable adult standard when such a person is a defendant in a negligence action. There are, however, a number of cases that have taken account of a mentally deficient person's diminished capacity on the issue of contributory negligence, but almost all of the cases involved a person whose diminished mental capacity was known to the defendant.

5. What is reasonable conduct under the circumstances depends on many factors. One of these factors is whether an emergency situation existed that required some speedy action. Such a person will be judged by what it was reasonable to do in the emergency with which that person was confronted. Such a person will not be required to have exercised the judgment and care of a person who has ample time to reflect upon what to do. The courts sometimes describe this emergency doctrine in terms of "instinctive action," but the doctrine covers more than purely instinctive reaction.

6. A physically handicapped person can only be required to exercise the skill and care of which such a person is physically capable. At the same time, a person with physical handicaps must, in deciding what to do, take into consideration the handicaps from which that person suffers. A person on crutches, unless faced with an emergency, should not attempt to climb a steep flight of stairs when elevator service is available.

    a. A more interesting question arises as to whether or not other people must anticipate the presence of physically handicapped persons. There are a few cases holding that the presence of blind people is sufficiently foreseeable to require defendants to take some precautions to protect them when the precautions involve minimal expense.

        Example: The defendant may be obliged to put a small cheap fence or barrier around a temporary excavation in the road even though a prominently placed notice together with the accumulated dirt from the excavation might be enough care for persons with sight. *See Haley v. London Elec. Bd.,* [1965] A.C. 778 (1964), [1964] 3 W.L.R. 479, 3 All E.R. 185 (H.L.).

7. In recent years a number of courts have held that the standard of care applicable among participants in sporting activities is merely to refrain from intentionally or recklessly injuring other participants. See *Crawn v. Campo,* 136 N.J. 494, 643 A.2d 600 (1994). Whether this standard will actually lead to different results than would the reasonable conduct under the circumstances standard — where the circumstances include participation in an activity that accepts vigorous efforts in quest of victory as the norm — is an question. The adoption of a supposedly lesser duty of care in some states was undoubtedly prompted by the concurrent attempt to abolish assumption of risk as a separate defense. *See* Chapter 5, *infra.*

B. **Calculus of Risk:** The so-called *"calculus of risk"* is used to determine whether a defendant has met the required standard of care. As enunciated by Judge Learned Hand in *United States v. Carroll Towing Co.,* 159 F.2d 169 (2d Cir. 1947), if the defendant's burden of protecting against the injury is less than the loss (L) incurred times the probability (P) of the loss being incurred, that is, if $B < PL$, the defendant is negligent. The same kind of analysis can be applied to determine whether the plaintiff has been guilty of contributory negligence.

    1. The test cannot be taken too literally because it is not only hard to determine antecedently potential losses and the probability of those losses being incurred, but the burdens involved must include matters that are difficult to quantify, such as the social utility of the defendant's conduct, the inconvenience to the defendant, and others, of chances in the defendant's conduct to avoid certain types of accidents, etc. There will of course be easy cases where it is clear that the defendant could have avoided the accident with minimal effort and in which the probability of substantial loss is not insignificant.

C. **Who Decides:** Determining what a defendant should have done in any particular case is usually a question for the trier of fact. Since most negligence cases in the United States are tried to a judge and jury, this means that the question of whether the defendant was negligent is ultimately a jury question. While the determination of whether or not the defendant would have behaved as a reasonable person in like circumstances may be a factual question, it is not the sort of factual question which is answered purely by observation. Whether or not someone has behaved reasonably is ultimately a matter of evaluation. That is the reason why courts will sometimes second-guess a jury and decide that, in the particular case before the court, no rational jury could find the defendant to be negligent. In some states and on rare occasions, the court may decide that no rational jury could find that the defendant was not negligent.

1. This intervention by the courts is usually justified by the expectation that, while questions of fact are for the jury and questions of law are for the judge, the question of whether someone was negligent is a "mixed question of law and fact." Judicial intervention is also sometimes explained by the argument that whether or not something is the case is a question of fact for the jury, but whether there is enough evidence to justify the jury's conclusion is a question of law. Not all people find either of these explanations very convincing. The important thing is that sometimes judges will second-guess the jury and rule that as a matter of law a defendant (or plaintiff if the issue is contributory fault) was or was not guilty of negligence.

D. **Statutory Violations:** Sometimes the standard of care is set by the *legislature.* In some of these instances, certain types of conduct are declared to be unlawful, and a civil cause of action is given to those who might be injured by that type of conduct. More typically, however, the legislature makes certain types of conduct illegal but says nothing about any fight of civil action. While the Supreme Court of the United States has become somewhat cautious in recognizing any implied civil action for violations of federal regulatory legislation, in the state courts an implied cause of action based on a statutory prohibition will typically be recognized. More to the point, proof that the defendant has violated the statute will be held to be "negligence per se," that is to say that, once a violation has been proven, the defendant will be unable to contest the issue of fault.

1. A minority of states uses the statutory violation merely as "evidence of negligence," or as "prima facie evidence of negligence." In addition, some courts that are prepared to hold that the violation of a statute is negligence per se will treat violations of administrative regulations or local ordinances as only evidence of negligence. A great number of courts, however, do not make any distinction among administrative regulations, local ordinances, and statutes, treating violations of all alike as negligence per se.

2. A difficult question arises with regard to what are called "excused violations." Most of the cases involving so-called excused violations are really cases where the statute has not been violated at all. Suppose, for example, that a person, through no fault of his own, suffers a blowout and, as a result of losing control of the vehicle, ends up driving on the wrong side of the yellow highway dividing line. It is hard to believe that any jurisdiction would permit such a person to be prosecuted for "driving on the wrong side of the road." Nevertheless, because when the issue arises in a tort action for damages the courts are very reluctant to make a definitive construction of the criminal law, they will often treat the case as one involving an excused violation. The problem with this analysis is that it suggests that there may be situations where a statute is admittedly violated, and the violator is subject to criminal prosecution, but the violator's conduct is nonetheless not to be considered negligent if the jury concludes that the violator's conduct was reasonable under the circumstances. Such an expansion of the concept of excused violation undermines the whole concept of statutory violations constituting negligence per se. Rather than resulting in the legislature's establishing the standard of conduct, it places that authority back in the hands of the jury with the possible difference that the jury will take into account, when evaluating the reasonableness of the defendant's conduct, the fact that the defendant's conduct was unlawful.

3. In order to be able to take advantage of a statutory violation, the plaintiff must be within the class of persons whom the legislature was trying to protect.

Example: In the famous English case of *Gorris v. Scott,* L.R. 9 Ex. 125 (1874), a statute required that animals being carried as deck cargo should be confined in pens with footholds. The plaintiff's cattle were carried as deck cargo on a ship that had no such pens and were washed overboard in a storm. In the plaintiff's action, the court held that the purpose of the statute was merely to prevent diseased cattle from communicating their disease to other animals. The injuries suffered were thus not of the kind the legislature sought to prevent.

3

4. Some statutes impose *absolute criminal liability* such as statutes prohibiting the sale of adulterated food or, as they are sometimes construed, statutes requiring motorists to have brakes in good operating condition. Whether a statute imposing absolute criminal liability also imposes absolute civil liability often depends on the size of the class of persons upon whom the absolute duty is imposed and the nature and size of the class of people for whose benefit that duty has been imposed. If the purpose of the statute is to protect people from a danger from which it is felt they are unable to protect themselves, the courts will be inclined to impose absolute civil liability for a breach of the statute.

Example: Statutes making unlawful the sale of adulterated food or the serving of alcohol to minors by persons holding licenses to sell alcoholic beverages are likely to be construed as imposing absolute civil liability as well.

F. Custom as Determining the Standard of Care: Sometimes evidence of custom is used to establish whether or not someone has been negligent. Often the custom is presented to the trier of fact through the testimony of an expert. An expert, in the context of an action for personal injury, is someone who, because of special knowledge, is able to testify on matters of fact within that field of knowledge and to express an opinion on a variety of matters within the expert's area of expertise. Normally witnesses who are not experts are only permitted to testify about what they have observed, but there are of course some exceptions.

Example: An ordinary person is usually permitted to testify that someone was "drunk" or to estimate that someone's car before an accident was traveling at, say, fifty miles per hour.

1. In order to use expert testimony, the person presenting the testimony must first be qualified as an expert during a preliminary qualification procedure called the "voir dire." After considering the witness's qualifications, the judge will decide whether the witness is in fact an expert and what it is the witness is an expert on. The jury will usually be present during some portion of the voir dire, and it may be expected to consider the qualifications of the so-called expert in deciding what weight to give to the expert's testimony. Experts are typically used to establish the custom of an industry or even what is considered, say, "good engineering practice."

2. *Effect of Custom:* It is now universally held that evidence of custom, except in certain types of medical and perhaps other professional malpractice actions, is not conclusive. *See The T J. Hooper,* 60 F.2d 737 (2d Cir. 1932). It is thus typically said that neither compliance with an industry-wide custom nor the failure to comply with such a custom is conclusive evidence on the question of negligence. In point of fact, however, it would be very rare to find an instance in which a defendant was found to have failed to conform to customary standards but was nevertheless not found negligent.

3. *Medical Malpractice:* In cases involving medical malpractice, with some very few exceptions such as instances where the physician operates on the wrong leg of the patient or where surgical instruments have been left inside a patient, a physician may not be held liable in a negligence action unless the applicable standard of care is established through the use of expert testimony.

a. *Standard for physicians:* Traditionally a physician was held to the standard of physicians practicing in the same community. In most jurisdictions, this was soon expanded to the "same-or-similar community" test because there were communities in which the defendant physician was the only medical practitioner. There has been considerable dissatisfaction with the traditional test, and it has been changed in many jurisdictions.

(1) Specialists: The majority of jurisdictions have now probably abandoned the same-or-similar communities standards in favor of a national standard where specialists are concerned. The presence of national boards that certify specialists has facilitated the movement to a national standard for specialists.

(2) General practitioners: There is a similar movement toward a national standard with regard to general practitioners, although a majority of states may still be applying the same-or-similar community standard. The courts which have retained the same-or-similar community standards have nevertheless sometimes eased the plaintiff's burden by permitting specialists or physicians who do not practice in the same or similar community to testify as to what the appropriate standard is on the basis of their "familiarity" with the standards of medical practice in the relevant communities. *See Siirila v. Barrios,* 398 Mich. 576, 248 N.W.2d 171 (1976).

(3) Statutory changes: The rising cost of medical malpractice insurance has led to some legislative attempts to regulate malpractice claims by providing for submission of claims to screening panels, for settlement conferences, and sometimes for limits on the amounts that may be recovered in medical malpractice cases. Some of these damage limitations have been upheld; others have been struck down, often on the basis that, under the state constitution, it is improper to distinguish among categories of personal injury actions.

b. As we have seen in the previous chapter, a person normally has the right to refuse medical treatment and to insist that any consent given to medical treatment be based on adequate information. Where no consent at all has been given to medical treatment, the courts have continued to treat the matter as an instance of the intentional tort of battery. Where, on the other hand, the plaintiff has consented to the treatment but complains that the consent given was not fully informed because of the inadequacy of the information provided, the situation becomes more complicated. Traditionally these cases were also treated as cases of battery. The modern trend is to treat the issue of the adequacy of the information given to the patient as a question of negligence. This creates several problems.

(1) Even if the plaintiff establishes that he was not fully informed about the consequences of the treatment, it does not automatically follow, as it would under a battery theory, that the plaintiff should recover. The plaintiff must first show that a reasonable person in the plaintiff's position would have refused the treatment if an adequate disclosure had been made. It is normally not enough, in most jurisdictions, for the plaintiff to claim or even to "establish" that he would not have submitted to the treatment. Even if the plaintiff establishes that a reasonable person, if adequately informed, would not have submitted to the treatment, the plaintiff must then also show that, as a result of being treated, he has been injured.

(2) The second problem presented by the modern tendency to treat the question of informed consent under a negligence theory is the question of from whose perspective the adequacy of the information given is to be judged. Is it from the perspective of the patient, namely what a reasonable patient would want to know, or is it from the perspective of the physician, that is what information a reasonable physician would give? If the question is to be answered from the perspective of a physician, it then becomes not only relevant but possibly dispositive that the physician did or did not follow the custom of the medical profession with regard to disclosures in that particular type of situation. The modern trend in the United States is to answer this question from the perspective of the plaintiff, namely what would a reasonable person in the position of the plaintiff want to know before making a

decision whether to submit to treatment. *See Canterbury v. Spence,* 464 F.2d 772 (D.C. Cir. 1972), *cert. denied,* 409 U.S. 1064. Regardless of what perspective is to be applied, if the patient asks specific questions, the physician is obliged to give honest and accurate answers.

(3) Even if the question of the adequacy of the information being presented is determined from the reasonable plaintiff's perspective, the courts have recognized that there may be some situations in which the need for treatment is very great and the provision of a detailed explanation might confuse and possibly even increase the patient's anxiety so as to make treatment more difficult. The courts have suggested that in these circumstances perhaps a fuller disclosure could be made to the patient's relatives.

3

III.   PROOF OF NEGLIGENCE: The doctrine of res ipsa loquitur.

*PROOF OF
NEGLIGENCE*

A. In the trial of all legal matters, questions of fact are sometimes determined by the use of circumstantial evidence. In the law of torts, a special name has been given for the use of circumstantial evidence in some special instances. In these special instances not only may the parties seek to persuade the trier of fact to reach certain conclusions through the use of circumstantial evidence, but the jury will be specifically told that proof of a certain fact, *A,* can be treated by the jury as proof of another fact, *B.* This is the so-called doctrine of "res ipsa loquitur."

Example: A typical case would be one in which a soda bottle explodes and an action is brought against the bottler. Proof of the bottle's explosion is certainly evidence that the bottle was either improperly constructed by the manufacturer and/or improperly inspected by the bottler or improperly filled by the bottler. Of course, the explosion of the bottle is also consistent with the bottle having been mishandled by the retail store or by others. In the absence of other evidence, most courts would hold that the doctrine of res ipsa loquitur can be invoked on the issue of whether the bottle exploded because the bottler was negligent. *See Escola v. Coca Cola Bottling Co.,* 24 Cal.2d 453, 150 P.2d 436 (1944).

If the doctrine of res ipsa loquitur comes into play, the jury will be specifically told that proof of the bottle's explosion may be considered by them as proof that the bottler improperly inspected the bottle and/or improperly filled the bottle and/or damaged the bottle in the process of delivering it to the retail store at which the plaintiff purchased the bottle.

1. *Requirements for Applying the Doctrine of Res Ipsa Loquitur:* It is said that the doctrine of res ipsa loquitur only becomes applicable if the action is one which does not normally occur in the absence of someone's negligence. In addition, it is usually said that, in order for the doctrine to apply, the defendant must exercise exclusive management or control of the instrumentality that caused the accident. If this requirement is taken literally, res ipsa loquitur could not be invoked when the patron of a restaurant is injured by the unexpected collapse of the stool upon which the patron is sitting. The same might be said of exploding bottles because at the time of the accident it is the plaintiff not the defendant who has "control" of the bottle. Some courts have tried to handle this problem by speaking in terms of "constructive control." It would be more helpful to restate the requirement as being not that the defendant must have exclusive management or control of the instrumentality, but that the defendant have had a sufficiently close connection with the instrumentality that caused the plaintiff's injury so that it is more likely than not that the defendant was negligent, given that an accident happened which normally does not occur in the absence of negligence of someone in the defendant's position.

2. *Effect of Applying the Doctrine:* In most jurisdictions, invocation of the doctrine of res ipsa loquitur does not shift the ultimate burden of persuasion. It is still the plaintiff's task to convince the trier of fact that the plaintiff's version of what happened is more probable than

not. Thus the doctrine of res ipsa loquitur normally does not compel the jury to decide in the plaintiff's favor. It merely represents an explicit authorization that they may do so if they wish.

    a.   In some jurisdictions, it is occasionally held, however, that the invocation of the doctrine of res ipsa loquitur actually requires the defendant to come forward with enough evidence to negate the inference of negligence. Under this view, unless the defendant comes forward with such evidence, a decision must be rendered for the plaintiff. Given that the standard of persuasion in a civil case is merely the preponderance of the evidence, this comes close to placing the burden of persuasion upon the defendant because, in order to negate the inference, the defendant must show that it is not more likely than not that the defendant was negligent.

3.   *Justification for the Doctrine:* Although the doctrine of res ipsa loquitur has a logical basis, its use is justified by a policy justification because, in the cases in which it is invoked, the defendant normally — although not always — has greater access to information as to how the accident occurred. By informing the jury that it may infer negligence from proof of the accident, invocation of the doctrine encourages defendants to come forward with information as to how the accident actually happened in order to exculpate themselves.

    a.   In *Ybarra v. Spangard,* 25 Cal.2d 486, 154 P.2d 687 (1944), the court used this policy justification to invoke the doctrine of res ipsa loquitur when a patient was injured while under general anesthesia, against all the doctors and nurses who had dealt with the patient in the hospital. With regard to some of these personnel, such as the special duty nurse who was in the patient's room when he awoke from the anesthesia, the likelihood that the injury to the plaintiff's shoulder could be traced to any negligence on their part was extremely remote. The case represents a relaxation of the logical requirements of the doctrine of res ipsa loquitur that only a few jurisdictions have been prepared to follow and then almost always only with regard to plaintiffs undergoing general anesthesia. The purpose of invoking the doctrine in these cases, which normally involve multiple defendants, is of course to encourage the defendants to come forward with evidence incriminating each other.

CHAPTER 3 - QUESTIONS, ANSWERS, AND SOME TIPS

1.   **Q:** Allegation and proof of actual damages are an essential element of a modern action for negligence.

    A: True

    Tip: Nominal damages are not recoverable in negligence. Nominal damages are normally only recoverable for intentional torts.

2.   **Q:** If an adult does the best that he can, he has met the reasonable person standard of care.

    A: False

    Tip: The reasonable person standard, especially as applied to adults, is an objective standard, not a subjective one.

3. **Q:** An adult with diminished mental capacity is never required to exercise the level of care that would be required of an adult of normal mental abilities.

A: False

Tip: The standard of reasonable care under the circumstances is not only an objective one but is premised on the assumption that all adults have a certain minimum mental capacity.

4. **Q:** If a child is unusually precocious, that factor will be taken into account in determining whether the child has exercised due care under the circumstances.

A: True

Tip: At first glance this looks as if children are being held to a subjective and not an objective standard of care. Nevertheless, even in this situation, the standard is not strictly speaking subjective, because the jury is asked what would it be reasonable to expect of a child of this child's age, experience, and ability.

5. **Q:** Uncontradicted evidence of failure to comply with customary standards is normally conclusive on the issue of due care.

A: False

Tip: Except for medical malpractice cases, neither compliance with custom nor failure to comply with custom is conclusive on the issue of negligence. As a practical matter, however, a person who has failed to comply with custom is unlikely to avoid a jury finding of negligence unless he can show that compliance with the customary standard would have subjected the plaintiff to a greater risk.

6. **Q:** To avoid tort liability for any injuries he may unintentionally cause to others, a physically handicapped adult must meet the level of skill possessed by an adult with no physical handicaps.

A: False

Tip: The courts make a distinction between the physically handicapped and those with diminished mental capacity probably because physical handicaps are more readily apparent and objectively measurable. A blind person cannot be expected to see whereas it is harder to determine what it is appropriate to expect of a person with diminished mental capacity.

7. **Q:** A jury may never disregard expert medical testimony that a physician accused of malpractice has exercised due care.

A: False

Tip: The word "never" is important here. If there is no expert medical testimony that a physician has failed to conform to customary medical standards, normally a jury may not find the physician negligent. If there is conflicting expert medical testimony, however, the jury may choose to accept the opinion of one expert and to reject the opinion of the expert holding the contrary opinion.

8. **Q:** A physician who fully describes the risks of treatment to a patient is not responsible for any harm that is incurred by the patient if the patient decides to refuse the treatment.

A: False

Tip: It is not just the risks of the proposed treatment that must be conveyed to the patient. To make a fully informed decision on whether to undergo a proposed treatment, the patient must be advised of the risks of refusing treatment.

9. **Q:** The doctrine of *"res ipsa loquitur"* can be applied even when the defendant is in no better position than the plaintiff to explain what caused the accident that injured the plaintiff.

    A: True

    Tip: The doctrine of *res ipsa loquitur* in most jurisdictions is ultimately a doctrine about the logical weight of the evidence. Even if the defendant is in no better position to explain what caused the accident than is the plaintiff, say the steering mechanism of an automobile suddenly ceased to function and the car was completely demolished, if the automobile is a new one and if a reasonable jury could find that new cars do not normally suddenly lose their steering unless the manufacturer has been negligent, the jury can be instructed that the fact of the accident will permit them to conclude that the accident was caused by the defendant manufacturer's negligence.

    Additional Exam Tip: In answering essay questions, remember that, unless there is some doctrine of law that limits a person's liability for negligence, such as in cases involving emotional distress or, in many states, the liability of owners and occupiers of real property, most negligence cases turn on the facts— what dangers could a reasonable person foresee; what could a reasonable person have done to avoid the foreseeable dangers—and this means that they usually present questions that must be resolved by the trier of facts, usually a jury.

SPECIAL SITUATIONS

▶ CHAPTER SUMMARY

SPECIAL SITUATIONS

Scope of Chapter. In this chapter we shall consider those situations in which a person who subjects others to an unreasonable risk of foreseeable injury is nonetheless not necessarily subjected to liability. In these situations, whether one person may be said to have a duty to protect the interests of another cannot be answered merely by exploring whether or not the first person could reasonably foresee that negligent conduct on her part would create an unreasonable risk of injury to the other. Despite the gradual expansion of the foreseeable injury test, there are still a number of situations where the foreseeability of injury is not enough to impose liability. In this chapter we shall discuss three such situations. The first involves the negligent infliction of emotional distress; the second involves the obligations of owners and occupiers of land; and the third involves duties to aid others.

4

NEGLIGENT INFLICTION OF EMOTIONAL DISTRESS

I.   NEGLIGENT INFLICTION OF EMOTIONAL DISTRESS

    A.   General Principle: Practically all states now recognize some liability for the negligent infliction of emotional distress, even in the absence of some kind of physical impact on the plaintiff. There is, however, a major division of authority on the question of whether the plaintiff must have been threatened with physical injury or whether it is enough that the plaintiff witnesses an injury to a close relative. There is also a division of authority as to whether, in order to recover, the plaintiff must show that the emotional distress has manifested itself in some form of physical injury or illness.

        1.   *The Zone of Danger Test:* In place of the now almost universally discarded "impact rule," a number of jurisdictions have substituted the "zone of danger" test. Under this doctrine, if the plaintiff is in the area in which a reasonable person would perceive himself to be in danger of physical impact as a result of the defendant's negligence, even in the absence of any physical impact, the plaintiff may recover for any physical injuries and the resulting pain and suffering that is caused by the emotional trauma that has been experienced by the plaintiff. In some early opinions, there were suggestions that the plaintiff's emotional trauma and resulting injuries must arise out of a fear for the plaintiff's own physical safety and not for the safety of another. In actual practice it is common for plaintiffs to include an allegation that, however much they feared for the safety of others, they also feared for their own safety. It is, however, almost impossible to find a case in which a person who was threatened with physical injuries and who suffered the required injuries has been denied recovery because the plaintiff feared for the safety of another rather than for himself.

        2.   *Beyond the Zone of Danger Test:* In *Dillon v. Legg,* 68 Cal. 2d 728, 69, Cal. Rptr. 72, 441 P.2d 912 (1968), the court held that a mother could recover for physical injuries caused by emotional distress allegedly suffered as a result of witnessing the death of her daughter who was struck by the defendant's negligently driven automobile. The mother was not herself in the zone of danger. In determining whether there should be liability, the court held that the following factors should be taken into account: first, whether the plaintiff was located near the scene of the accident; second, whether shock resulted from a direct emotional impact from the contemporaneous sensory observation of the accident; and third, whether the plaintiff and victim were closely related.

            a.   Some California lower courts were prepared to extend recovery to parents who arrived at the scene of an accident after it had occurred and observed their injured children. In *Thing v. La Chusa,* 48 Cal. 3d 644, 257 Cal. Rptr. 865, 771 P.2d 814 (1989), however, the court ruled that *Dillon* applied only to close relatives who were present at the "injury-producing event" and who were aware that this event was causing the injury to the victim. To recover, furthermore, such persons must suffer "severe emotional distress," that is, reaction beyond that which could be anticipated in a disinterested witness. Some courts in other states, however, have been prepared to extend liability to close relatives who witnessed the immediate aftermath of an accident but not the accident itself. *See Dziokonski v. Babineau,* 375 Mass. 555, 380 N.E.2d 1295 (1978).

    (1) There has, however, been substantial agreement that liability only extends to close relatives. Most courts have been reluctant to allow recovery by people who cohabit with each other and who might be said to have a significant emotional relationship. For example, in *Elden v. Sheldon*, 46 Cal. 3d 367, 250 Cal. Rptr. 254, 758 P.2d 582 (1988), the court declared that, except perhaps for foster parent and child and step-parenting relationships, it was not prepared to extend liability beyond nuclear family relationships. Nevertheless, in *Dunphy v. Gregor*, 136 N.J. 99, 642 A.2d 372 (1994), the court was prepared to recognize a cause of action where the plaintiff had witnessed the accident that soon thereafter led to the death of her fiancé, with whom she had been cohabiting for over two years. Such persons could be said to have had "an intimate familial relationship that is stable, enduring, substantial and mutually supportive [and] . . . cemented by strong emotional bonds."

  b. There is some suggestion in the cases that the recovery of someone who suffers emotional distress as a result of witnessing injury to another will be affected by the contributory negligence, if any, of the victim. In some ways this does not make sense since the plaintiff is suing to recover for the plaintiff's own injuries and not those of the victim. Indeed, with the erosion of intrafamily immunities, the theoretical possibility is open for the plaintiff to bring an action against a relative who negligently subjects himself to the injury which has caused the plaintiff's emotional distress.

  c. In theory it should not matter whether the person for whose safety the plaintiff feared was seriously injured or even injured at all. *See Barnhill v. Davis,* 300 N.W.2d 104 (Iowa 1981). But other courts have insisted that there may be no recovery by one witnessing a threatened accident to a close relative unless the relative is in fact seriously injured or killed.

3. Many jurisdictions have required that, before a plaintiff can recover for severe emotional distress in the absence of a physical impact with the person of the plaintiff, plaintiff must suffer some kind of physical injury or illness. This injury can be rather attenuated — a prolonged inability to function normally has been held to be enough — but a mere inability to sleep or feelings of nausea have been held not to be enough. More recently, however, some courts have been prepared to abandon the requirement that the emotional distress manifest itself in some form of physical injury if the plaintiff can establish that he suffered "severe emotional distress."

4. In *Molien v. Kaiser Foundation Hospitals,* 27 Cal. 3d 916, 167 Cal. Rptr. 831, 616 P.2d 813 (1980), the court held that someone who suffered emotional distress as a result of conduct "directed toward" himself could recover for emotional distress even without showing any physical injury. In *Molien,* the defendant mistakenly told a woman that she had syphilis and advised her to notify her husband of that fact. The woman immediately suspected that she might have contracted the disease from her husband and, even though the mistaken diagnosis was eventually corrected, the marriage could not survive the stress put upon it. The husband thereupon brought an action seeking damages for loss of consortium and the negligent infliction of emotional distress. It was held that he had a cause of action on both counts, and that, because the defendant's conduct was "directed" toward him, he did not have to show any physical illness in order to recover for his emotional distress. It remains to be seen to what if any extent this doctrine will be adopted and how far it will be extended.

Example: In *Cordts v. Boy Scouts of America, Inc.*, 205 Cal. App. 3d 716, 252 Cal. Rptr. 629 (1988), a mother whose two sons were sexually abused by a scoutmaster was held not to be a direct victim of the tortious conduct involved in that case. *See also Frame v. Kothari*, 115 N.J. 638, 560 A.2d 675 (1989). On the other hand, in *Marlene F. v. Affiliated Psychiatric Med. Clinic, Inc.*, 48 Cal. 3d 583, 257 Cal. Rptr. 98, 770 P.2d 278 (1989), a mother whose son was alleged to have been sexually abused by the therapist who had been counseling the mother and the son, was held to be a direct victim and thus to have a cause of action for negligent infliction of emotional distress.

5. Courts have traditionally been prepared to allow close relatives of a deceased person to bring an action for emotional distress for the mishandling of the corpse of the deceased on the ground that if the action were not permitted to lie, corpses could be abused with impunity. In *Christensen v. Superior Court*, 54 Cal. 3d 868, 2 Cal. Rptr. 2d 79, 820 P.2d 181 (1991), which involved the improper handling of the cremation of corpses, the court extended the right to recovery beyond those relatives who had the statutory right to control the disposition of the deceased's corpse to relatives of the deceased who were aware that the defendants were performing funeral-related services at the time the corpse was abused. The court refused, however, to extend liability to close friends of the deceased.

LIABILITY OF **II.** **THE LIABILITY OF POSSESSORS OF LAND**
POSSESSORS
OF LAND

A. **Definitions:** A possessor of land is someone who occupies the land with the intention to control it or, in the absence of any such person, someone who is entitled to immediate possession of the land. The liability of a possessor to persons injured on the land is still greatly influenced by the status of the person injured. People who enter (or remain on) the land of others have traditionally been placed in one of three categories. These categories are as follows:

1. *Trespassers:* Persons who enter or remain on land without the consent of the person in possession of the land or who enter or remain on the land without some legally recognized privilege.

2. *Licensees:* Persons who enter or remain on land with the consent of the person in possession of the land but who are not invitees. People who enter land by virtue of a legally recognized privilege have received the same legal protection as is afforded to licensees.

   Example: Firemen and policemen who enter land in pursuance of their duties have traditionally been classified as licensees.

3. *Invitees:* Principally people who are invited to enter or remain on land for a purpose that directly or indirectly involves some kind of business dealing with the possessor. These people are often called "business invitees," although in recent years there has been an increasing recognition, following the *Restatement (Second) of Torts* § 332, of a class of "public invitees," that is, persons who, as members of the public, are "invited to enter or remain on land that has been held open to the public."

   Example: People who enter a shopping mall not to shop but to admire Christmas decorations would probably fall within the class of public invitees.

B. At common law, the extent of the duty owed by a possessor of land to those who are injured on the land depended upon the status of the person injured, namely upon whether the person injured was a trespasser, licensee, or invitee. In recent years there has been some movement away from the strict application of the common law doctrine. About ten states have now completely rejected the dispositive effect of the traditional categories and extend to all those injured on land the benefits of the general negligence doctrine, namely the ability to bring an action when the possessor has created or maintained land in a condition that presents an unreasonable risk of injury to the plaintiff.

1. **Duty to Trespassers:** At common law, the only duty owed to trespassers was to refrain from intentionally or negligently injuring known trespassers as a result of activity carried on upon the land and to warn known trespassers of highly dangerous artificial conditions which the trespasser was unlikely to appreciate, such as an abandoned mine shaft. The possessor had no responsibility even to known trespassers for injuries arising from natural conditions. This limited responsibility to known trespassers was gradually extended to constant trespassers who might be injured as a result of highly dangerous activities carried on in a limited area of the defendant's land.

   a. *Children.* Although at one time the law made no distinction between children and adults — and this is probably still the law in a small number of jurisdictions — the duty of possessors of land to child trespassers has been extended. The early extensions were based on the premise that someone who left dangerous equipment lying unprotected on his land was "enticing" or "inviting" children to enter the land and therefore should be responsible for the unfortunate consequences of this invitation. This was the so-called doctrine of *"attractive nuisance."* The law, however, has gone beyond this. In most jurisdictions, the possessor of land will be liable for harm caused to trespassing children from highly dangerous artificial conditions if the possessor knows or has reason to know that children are likely to trespass on the land and if there is a failure to exercise reasonable care to protect the children.

2. **Duty to Licensees:** Under the traditional common law doctrine, the possessor of land owes licensees all the duties owed to trespassers together with a duty to warn licensees of any highly dangerous artificial conditions and to warn them of any activities being carried on upon the land or of any natural or artificial conditions on the land that are dangerous and which licensees would be unlikely to discover on their own. The duty to warn of dangerous conditions, however, only extends to those conditions of which the landowner is aware or has reason to be aware. There is no affirmative duty to discover dangerous conditions on the land. If the danger is obvious, the possessor has no duty to warn, and this is true even if the licensee's failure to discover the peril is not due to the licensee's own carelessness.

   Example: A social guest driving on a private road fails to see a pothole because his attention has been distracted by the screams of a child who has been bitten by an insect. There is no liability on the part of the possessor of the land to the guest for any injuries suffered as a result of driving into the pothole.

3. **Duty to Invitees:** Under the traditional common law doctrine, a possessor of land not only owes invitees all the duties of care that are owed to trespassers and licensees but the further duty to use reasonable care to discover any dangerous conditions on the land that the possessor should expect that invitees will not discover on their own and to protect invitees from any such dangers that invitees will be unable to protect themselves.

C. In *Rowland v. Christian,* 69 Cal. 2d 108, 70 Cal. Rptr. 97, 443 P.2d 561 (1968), the court abandoned the common law distinctions and ruled that the liability of the possessor of land should be based upon the reasonable person standard, namely, given the totality of the circumstances, whether the possessor has exercised reasonable care. The only relevance of characterizing the injured person as a trespasser lies in the degree to which the presence of that person could reasonably be foreseen. As noted above, perhaps as many as ten jurisdictions have completely adopted this doctrine.

D.   A number of American jurisdictions have abandoned the common law distinction between licensees and invitees, but not the special doctrines affecting trespassers. As to trespassers, most jurisdictions have thus far refused to abandon the common law doctrine.

E.   A number of states have enacted statutes limiting the liability of owners of land that is used for recreational purposes. These statutes typically provide that there is no liability for negligence unless an entrance fee is charged. Cal. Civil Code § 846. Where no fee is charged, there is no liability unless the landowner has "unlawfully or maliciously" failed to guard against or warn of dangerous conditions.

F.   A possessor of land is responsible for taking whatever measures are reasonably necessary to prevent excavations, structures, and other artificial conditions on the land from endangering persons outside of the land. This is particularly true if the land adjoins a public highway.

G.   Unless a landowner was actually in possession of land, at common law the landowner's principal duties were to warn a tenant of hidden dangers of which the tenant was not aware and to maintain in proper repair portions of the premises that remained under the landowner's control, such as common stairways and halls. In addition, the landowner was under a duty of care to those who used premises leased for immediate public use, such as theaters or sports arenas and, of course, to carry out with reasonable care repairs made by the landlord on premises owned by the landowner but leased to others. In *Sargent v. Ross,* 113 N.H. 388, 308 A.2d 528 (1973), the court rejected the common law doctrine and extended to landowners not in possession (typically lessors) the duty of reasonable care under the circumstances. A few other jurisdictions have followed this lead.

H.   **Duty to Prevent Harms Arising From the Acts of Others:** The *Restatement (Second) of Torts* § 344 (1965) states that a possessor of land is subject to liability to business invitees "for physical harm caused by the accidental, negligent, or intentionally harmful *acts of third persons or animals,* and by the failure of the possessor to exercise reasonable care to (a) discover that such acts are being done, or are likely to be done, or (b) give a warning adequate to enable the visitors to avoid the harm, or otherwise to protect them against it" (emphasis supplied). Not all courts follow this guidance. In *Williams v. Cunningham Drug Stores, Inc.,* 429 Mich. 495, 418 N.W.2d 381 (Mich. 1988), the court refused to find that a storeowner had a duty to provide security guards to prevent injuries to customers from the criminal acts of third parties inside the store. The court said that the owner did not have a suffcient degree of control over the community at large to impose such a duty, the requirements of such a duty would be too vague, the owner was not the insurer of the safety of his invitees, and that imposing such a duty would be advocating self-help by occupiers of land. Subsequently, a lower court in the same state held that liability could arise if a store owner failed either to eject unruly patrons or to call the police. See *Jackson v. White Castle System, Inc.,* 205 Mich. App. 137, 517 N.W.2d 286 (1994). Another court found a duty where the nature of the neighborhood and the history of the specific location made the grave danger sufficiently foreseeable. See *Taco Bell, Inc. v. Lannon,* 744 P.2d 43 (Colo.1987).

1.   A number of jurisdictions have now read into leases of residential property an implied warranty of habitability. Under such a warranty the lessor is strictly liable for any unsafe condition existing in the premises at the time they are leased.

FAILURE TO AID

III.   **FAILURE TO AID — AFFIRMATIVE DUTIES**

A.   **General Principle:** At common law one had no duty to help another person unless one had some special relationship to that person. To some extent this is still the law, but the range of special relationships has been materially extended.

Example: Teachers and other custodians of young children have traditionally been held to have the requisite special relationship to their charges and are under an obligation to take reasonable steps to come to their assistance while they are in the custody of their teachers or other guardians. So, too, have employers an obligation to come to the assistance of their employees who are injured, sick, or otherwise become helpless while on the job.

1. The common law also recognized a special relationship between a tortfeasor and his victim. Thus, a person who negligently runs over another will be under a legal obligation to take measures to assist an injured victim.

   a. In recent years this obligation of coming to the assistance of others has been extended to all those who injure other people, even if the injury was not tortious and thus not one for which the injurer was legally responsible. This development was undoubtedly influenced by the "hit-and-run" statutes that require the person involved in an accident to remain on the scene, to give his name and other pertinent information to persons injured in the accident, aid to the police, and to render what assistance he can. In the case of a motorist who has negligently injured or killed someone, these statutes present constitutional problems concerning the privilege against self-incrimination that have not yet been fully addressed.

   b. The law seems to be moving in the direction of recognizing some duty to aid business invitees, such as department store customers who become ill and faint in the store.

   c. Vermont, by statute (Vt. Stat. Ann., tit. 12, § 519), imposes a general duty upon a person to help when doing so can be done "without danger or peril to himself or without interference with important duties owed to others" whenever a person "knows that another is exposed to grave physical harm." A few other states have statutes imposing a duty to help upon those witnessing certain emergencies or a duty to report certain crimes that they have witnessed to the authorities.

      (1) Courts have also found a duty not to interfere with rescue efforts. Relying on this doctrine, in *Soldano v. O'Daniels,* 141 Cal. App. 3d 443, 190 Cal. Rptr. 310 (1983), the court held a restaurant liable to a man killed in the bar across the street when a restaurant employee refused to allow a third party to call the police to alert them that the man in the bar was being threatened.

2. There are a growing number of cases imposing some duty on psychiatrists and others to warn individuals whom they have reason to believe will be threatened with physical injury by a patient released from a mental institution or by an inmate released from a public institution.

3. Once a person has come to the assistance of another, at common law the rescuer had the full obligation of exercising reasonable care under the circumstances. In order to encourage rescuers, the *Restatement (Second) of Torts* §§ 323–324 has proposed that rescuers should only be liable for discontinuing their aid if by so doing they increase the danger of injury to the rescued person. For the same reason of encouraging the rendition of assistance to injured persons, all jurisdictions have now enacted some form of "good samaritan statute." Such statutes relieve either physicians or, more typically, all those who come to the assistance of accident victims from either all liability or, more commonly, all liability for merely negligent behavior. Whether these statutes have increased the propensity of potential providers of assistance actually to provide such assistance is another matter.

4. ***Other Special Relationships Creating a Duty to Aid:*** Common carriers have a duty to their passengers to take reasonable action to (a) protect them against unreasonable risk of physical

harm, and (b) to give them first aid when their injuries are known or should be known and to care for them until they can be cared for by others. Innkeepers have the same duty to their guests, as do possessors of land, who hold that land open to the public, to those who enter in response to that invitation. A person who takes custody of others so as to deprive them of their normal ability and capacity to protect themselves likewise assumes a similar duty to protect and assist those who are in his custody. *See Restatement (Second) of Torts* § 314A (1965).

5. ***Duty to Control the Conduct of Others:*** There is no duty to control the conduct of a third person so as to prevent him from causing physical harm to another unless (a) a special relation exists *between the actor and the third person* which imposes a duty upon the actor to control the third person's conduct, or (b) a special relation exists *between the actor and the other* which gives to the other a right to protection. *See Restatement (Second) of Torts* § 315 (1965). See *also id.* §§ 316-320.

6. ***Liability Premised on a Common Undertaking:*** In *Farwell v. Keaton,* 396 Mich. 281, 240 N.W.2d 217 (1976), the court recognized a duty between companions on a social venture. If one of the companions knows or should know of the other's peril, he is required to render reasonable care under the circumstances. The reasoning in this case, however, has not been followed by other courts.

CHAPTER 4 - QUESTIONS, ANSWERS, AND SOME TIPS

1. **Q:** A volunteer who, without an affirmative duty to do so, comes to the rescue of a person endangered by someone's negligence is usually held to have assumed the risk of injury to himself.

   A: False

   Tip: The mere fact that a person is under no duty to come to the aid of an endangered person does not mean that the volunteer rescuer losses the benefit of the doctrine that "danger invites rescue."

2. **Q:** At common law a possessor of land owned no duty of care to trespassers.

   A: False. Although the duty of care was limited, a possessor of land owed some duties of care, such as the duty not to negligently injure known trespassers as a result of activities carried out upon the land.

3. **Q:** In most jurisdictions at the present day a child trespasser may not recover damages against the possessor of land if the child is injured as a result of the highly dangerous natural condition on that land.

   A: True

   Tip: The key term here is "natural condition." There is generally still no duty towardstrespassers on the part of possessors of unimproved land. But once a possessor of land has in anyway tinkered with the natural condition, say by putting in drainage pipes or landscaping the property, the land begins to lose the quality of being in its "natural condition."

4. **Q:** At common law a social guest was treated as an invitee.

   A: False. This is still the law in many jurisdictions

5. **Q:** In some jurisdictions persons who have witnessed a serious bodily injury to a friend can recover for the negligent inflections of emotional distress even if they were not themselves physically threatened.

    A: False. In the United States, only a limited category of family members of the primary victim can recover for negligent inflection of emotional distress from witnessing serious injury to another when they themselves are not threatened with bodily injury. Even co-habitating adults are denied recovery in these circumstances in most jurisdictions.

    Additional Exam Tip: The three areas of tort law discussed in this Chapter are undergoing change which entails that there will be many variations among the various jurisdictions. For this reason, if you are asked an essay question about present day law, it is best to preface your answer with phrases such as " in some jurisdictions" or "in many jurisdictions," etc.

4

NOTES

PLAINTIFF MISCONDUCT

▶ **CHAPTER SUMMARY**

PLAINTIFF MISCONDUCT

Scope of Chapter: In this chapter we shall consider what effect if any the plaintiff's misconduct will have on the plaintiff's recovery. Traditionally the two main doctrines that served to bar the plaintiff's recovery were contributory negligence and assumption of the risk. The effect of both these doctrines has been affected by a number of modern developments, the most important of which has been the adoption by most American jurisdictions of some form of comparative negligence or, as it is sometimes more generally called, comparative fault. In the following discussion, we shall consider in turn contributory negligence, assumption of risk, and comparative fault.

5

CONTRIBUTORY NEGLIGENCE

I.   CONTRIBUTORY NEGLIGENCE

A. **In General:** At common law, the plaintiff's *contributory negligence* was a complete bar to an action seeking recovery from a negligent defendant. At the present time, the vast majority of states have adopted some general form of comparative negligence. Nevertheless, the common law rule has thus far not been changed in a small number of jurisdictions: Alabama, Maryland, North Carolina, Virginia, and the District of Columbia. In this section, we will consider the rule as it existed at common law and still exists in a few jurisdictions.

1. *Burden of Proof:* In the nineteenth century, contributory negligence was generally not treated as a defense, but rather the absence of contributory fault was something that the plaintiff had to allege and prove. In most jurisdictions the burden of raising the issue of contributory fault and of carrying the burden of persuasion on the issue is now on the defendant.

2. *Necessity of Causal Relationship:* At common law, the plaintiff's contributory negligence completely barred the plaintiff's recovery if the plaintiff's negligence was causally related to the plaintiff's injury. If the plaintiff's fault bore no causal relationship to the plaintiff's injury, it had no effect on the plaintiff's recovery.

    Example: The plaintiff has been driving a car while under the influence of alcohol. While waiting for a red traffic light to turn green, the plaintiff's car is struck in the rear by an approaching car that was unable to stop in time owing to the negligent inattention of the driver. Although the plaintiff was certainly at fault in operating a motor vehicle while under the influence of alcohol, this fault on the part of the plaintiff will have no legal effect on his recovery because it had no causal relationship to the injury. A vehicle driven by a sober person would have suffered the same consequences.

B. To ameliorate the harshness of the common law rule, a number of doctrines were evolved which permitted even a contributorily negligent plaintiff whose fault was causally related to his injuries to recover.

1. *Defendant's Aggravated Fault:* If the defendant's condition could be considered reckless (and *a fortiori* if intentional), the plaintiff was not barred by contributory negligence. In order to preclude the plaintiff's action, the plaintiff's misconduct had to be of the same order of magnitude, *i.e.,* if the defendant was found to have behaved recklessly, only reckless conduct on the part of the plaintiff would bar the plaintiff's action. In many jurisdictions which have adopted comparative negligence, the plaintiff's contributory negligence will still not diminish the plaintiff's recovery if the plaintiff was merely negligent and the defendant was reckless. In other jurisdictions, the plaintiff's contributory negligence will be taken into account in weighing the comparative fault of the defendant and the plaintiff if the defendant was reckless, but not in almost all jurisdictions if the defendant's fault was intentional.

2. ***The Doctrine of Last Clear Chance:*** At common law, the plaintiff's contributory negligence was no bar to an action if the defendant was found to have had the "last clear chance" to avoid the accident. It was generally held that if the plaintiff through her own fault had been rendered helpless and thus no longer able to avoid the accident by the exercise of reasonable care, a negligent defendant would be liable for failing to use with reasonable care his then-existing opportunity to avoid the harm when the defendant *knew* of the plaintiff's situation and thus realized or had reason to realize the plaintiff's peril.

Many jurisdictions, following *Restatement (Second) of Torts* § 479(b)(ii), would also apply the doctrine in favor of a helpless plaintiff if the defendant would have discovered the plaintiff's situation and thus have had reason to realize the plaintiff's peril, had the defendant exercised the duty of care which the defendant owed to the plaintiff. In all these situations, it could be said that the defendant's negligence was *the* cause of the plaintiff's injury.

Example: A drunk plaintiff has gone to sleep in the middle of a city street. An approaching motorist fails to keep his eyes on the road because he is fiddling with the dials of his car's radio, which is not working properly. Because the defendant motorist is inattentive, he does not notice the helpless plaintiff, but of course the defendant would have noticed the plaintiff if the defendant had been keeping a proper lookout. Under *Restatement (Second)* § 479(b)(ii), the plaintiff's contributory negligence in lying down on the street will not bar the plaintiff's recovery. Note that if the defendant saw the helpless plaintiff but was unable to stop because of the defendant's antecedent negligence in failing to have the brakes of his vehicle repaired, in most American jurisdictions the last clear chance doctrine would not apply because, at the time the plaintiff's peril was discovered or should have been discovered, the defendant had no existing opportunity to avoid the accident.

a. In a number of jurisdictions, the doctrine of last clear chance was extended, as described in *Restatement (Second) of Torts* § 480, to give protection to an "inattentive plaintiff" but only if the defendant actually knew of the plaintiff's situation and thus realized or had reason to realize that the plaintiff was inattentive, and thereafter the defendant was negligent in failing to use his then-existing opportunity to avoid the harm.

b. Most jurisdictions that have adopted comparative fault have now ostensibly abolished the doctrine of last clear chance, particularly when the plaintiff was merely inattentive. The plaintiff's fault in placing herself in a situation in which she might be hurt would be one factor to be taken into account in weighing the negligence of the parties. In a jurisdiction with a so-called modified form of comparative negligence, in which a plaintiff who is more negligent than the defendant is still completely barred from recovery, there are strong, logical reasons for preserving the doctrine of last clear chance in those situations where the plaintiff's recovery would otherwise be completely barred. It is not clear, however, what the courts would do in such situations.

II. ASSUMPTION OF RISK

ASSUMPTION OF RISK

A. At common law *assumption of risk* was also a complete defense to a negligence action. The theory underlying this doctrine was that a plaintiff who consciously subjected herself to a particular risk of injury could not complain if the injury ensued. In recent years there has been a great deal of criticism of the doctrine, and a number of jurisdictions have attempted to incorporate much of the doctrine of assumption of risk into the doctrine of contributory negligence. Assumption of risk is often classified as being either express or implied.

1. *Express* assumption of risk typically arises in situations in which the plaintiff has signed a release acknowledging knowledge of the risk involved and absolving the defendant from any

legal liability if injury ensues. The courts have sometimes struck down these releases as contrary to public policy in situations where the defendant is providing what might be considered a necessary public service and, because of the disparity in bargaining power, the plaintiff has no option but to sign if the plaintiff wishes to receive the service involved. Thus, in *Tunkl v. Regents of the University of California,* 60 Cal. 2d 92, 32 Cal. Rptr. 33, 383 P.2d 441 (1963), a release signed by a patient that exculpated the defendant hospital from liability on account of any negligence on the part of the hospital's employees, if the defendant exercised due care in selecting those employees, was struck down. Releases signed by race car drivers and others competing in sporting events have, on the other hand, generally been upheld. Even with the adoption of comparative negligence, the courts continue to recognize express assumption of risk as a complete defense to a negligence action.

    a.   The concept of express assumption of risk has been extended by analogy to cover certain situations in which there was no actual formal agreement to assume the risk of injury. There are several cases, for example, holding that jockeys "consent" that the duty of care owed to them by the organizers and other participants of horse races does not "tend beyond a duty to avoid reckless or intentionally harmful conduct." *See Turcotte v. Fell,* 68 N.Y.2d 432, 510 N.Y.S.2d 49, 502 N.E.2d 964 (1986). Because of the absence of a formal written agreement, these are probably instances of *implied* assumption of risk. Unlike the other types of implied assumptions of risk to be discussed below, however, these situations have not, in most jurisdictions, been merged with the doctrines of contributory negligence or comparative fault.

    2.   *Implied* assumption of risk is the term used to describe the other situations in which a plaintiff, who might be said to have consciously accepted a risk, is barred from recovery. The doctrine owed much of its origin to employment situations in which the employee was said to have assumed the ordinary risks of employment. Determining what is a conscious appreciation of a risk has sometimes proved to be difficult, particularly in situations in which the plaintiff, as a practical matter, may have had no real choice.

        Example: A worker is ordered by his employer to use a machine which the worker thinks may be defective and dangerous. Fearing the loss of his job, the worker uses the machine and is injured. Although barred by worker's compensation from bringing a tort action against his employer, the worker brings such an action against the manufacturer of the machine. Unless the employee's use of the machine bordered on the foolhardy, few modern courts would hold that the employee has assumed the risk. While the doctrine of implied assumption of risk owes much of its origin to employment situations in which, during the nineteenth century, the employee was said to have assumed the ordinary risks of employment, the employment situation is nowadays one in which the courts are extremely reluctant to apply the doctrine.

        Because of dissatisfaction with the doctrine of implied assumption of risk, many courts, even before the advent of comparative negligence, merged the doctrine of implied assumption of risk with that of contributory negligence. In the process of merging the doctrine of implied assumption of risk with contributory negligence or comparative negligence, the courts have distinguished between two types of situations that were grouped together under the rubric of implied assumption of risk.

    a.   Implied assumption of risk is sometimes used to describe a situation in which the courts would be inclined to hold that the defendant had *no duty* to the plaintiff. Typical of these situations are cases in which a spectator at a baseball game is struck by a batted ball. In these situations, the defendant ball park is usually absolved of liability even toward persons unfamiliar with baseball and the risks it entails, although, if a spectator is hit by a thrown bat or trampled by an inadequately policed crowd, liability has been imposed upon the ball park on the ground that the spectator had no reason to believe that exposure to these risks was an ordinary incident to watching a baseball game. In the batted-ball context, earlier judicial declarations that the plaintiff had assumed the risk have been interpreted by modern courts to mean that the defendant was not negligent towards the plaintiff, *i.e.*, that the defendant had no duty to the plaintiff. *See Jones v. Three Rivers Management Corp.*, 483 Pa. 75, 394 A.2d 546 (1978). Under this analysis, the question of assumption of risk or contributory negligence as a defense to a negligence action does not arise because the defendant has breached no duty to the plaintiff. The same no-duty analysis has been used to deny recovery to participants in informal sporting events. *See Crawn v. Campo*, 136 N.J. 494, 643 A.2d 600 (1994).

b.   Implied assumption of risk has also been used to describe situations in which the defendant was clearly negligent toward the plaintiff but in which it was felt that the plaintiff was aware of the risk that had been created. It is these situations which many courts have been inclined to merge with the doctrines of contributory and comparative negligence. In a state which has adopted comparative negligence, this will mean a great deal of difference because, while assumption of the risk is a complete bar to an action, comparative negligence or fault only diminishes but does not completely eliminate the plaintiff's recovery, except in those comparative fault jurisdictions in which, as will be seen below, the plaintiff is completely barred if his contributory negligence is greater than that of the defendant.

III.   COMPARATIVE FAULT

A.   As already noted, most jurisdictions have now adopted some form of comparative fault. In the late nineteenth and early twentieth centuries, a number of jurisdictions adopted comparative fault statutes applicable to railroad workers, of which the most famous is the Federal Employer's Liability Act of 1908, 45 U.S.C. §§ 51 *et seq.* These employer liability acts are usually of the so-called "pure" form, namely schemes in which, at least theoretically, a worker can recover a portion of his damages even if the plaintiff-worker is much more negligent than the defendant-employer. The "pure" type of comparative fault is distinguished from what are sometimes called "modified" comparative fault schemes, under which particularly negligent plaintiffs are still totally barred from recovery. Under a "pure" scheme, even a worker who is 99% at fault would be entitled to recover damages representing 1% of the worker's injury. Beginning with Mississippi in 1910, perhaps a half-dozen states had adopted by statute some general form of comparative negligence by 1960. In the last thirty years, however, there has been an overwhelming movement toward comparative negligence including a number of states, beginning with *Hoffman v. Jones,* 280 So. 2d 431 (Fla. 1973), that have adopted comparative negligence through judicial decision.

B.   Generally, comparative fault schemes are of three basic types.

1.   The first is the so-called "pure" type, described above, adopted, for example, by New York by statute and in Florida and California by judicial decision. The Uniform Comparative Fault Act, which has been adopted by a few states, is likewise of the "pure" form.

2.   The second type of comparative fault scheme permits plaintiffs to recover at least some of their damages in situations in which the plaintiff's negligence was "less than" that of the defendant. Arkansas and Colorado are jurisdictions that have adopted such "modified" schemes.

3.   The third and most popular form of comparative negligence scheme is that in which plaintiffs can recover at least some of their damages in situations in which the plaintiff's fault is "not greater than" that of the defendant, that is, plaintiffs may recover a portion of their damages if their fault is less than or equal to that of the defendants. Under this type of "modified" scheme, if the defendant counterclaims and if the trier of fact finds the parties to be equally at fault, both

parties can recover against each other. Wisconsin, New Jersey, and Texas are jurisdictions that have adopted such schemes.

C. In jurisdictions which have adopted the so-called pure form of comparative fault, when the plaintiff and the defendant have both been injured in an accident, it frequently happens that the plaintiff and the defendant will each get a judgment against each other. Under traditional notions, these judgments should be set off against each other and one judgment entered for the balance due against one of the parties. In a case in which plaintiff and defendant are each seriously injured in an automobile accident and the plaintiff has a judgment for $200,000 after factoring in the plaintiff's fault and the defendant has a judgment of $225,000 after factoring in the defendant's fault, the net effect would be that the plaintiff owed the defendant $25,000 on the defendant's counterclaim. Florida by judicial decision has now declared that setoffs are only to be made when the parties are either uninsured or the amounts awarded exceed policy limits. A number of states by statute have likewise prohibited setoffs. Section 3 of the Uniform Comparative Fault Act provides that claims and counterclaims shall not be set off against each other except by agreement of both parties or in situations in which the obligation of either party is likely to be uncollectible.

D. In jurisdictions that have adopted one of the so-called "modified" comparative fault schemes, there is a division of authority, in cases involving more than one defendant, as to whether the plaintiff's fault must be compared to the fault of each defendant separately or to the combined fault of all the defendants.

Example: Plaintiff is found to be 40% at fault and each of two defendants 30% at fault. If the plaintiff's fault is compared with the combined fault of the defendants, the plaintiff's fault is less than that of the defendants and the plaintiff's recovery will be reduced but not barred. If the plaintiff's fault is compared with the fault of each defendant separately, the plaintiff's fault will be greater than that of each of the defendants and the plaintiff's recovery will be bared.

SO-CALLED SEAT BELT DEFENSE **IV. THE SO-CALLED SEAT BELT DEFENSE**

A. In about ten jurisdictions, either by statute or judicial decision, some reduction in damages is possible for a plaintiff's failure to wear an automobile seat belt. In about half the states, either by judicial decision or statute, no reduction of damages is made because of the plaintiff's failure to wear a seat belt. In the remaining states, the law is unclear. In the analogous situation involving motorcycle helmets, there are a few cases permitting the failure of the plaintiff to wear a helmet to be admitted in evidence on the issue of damages.

CHAPTER 5 - QUESTIONS, ANSWERS, AND SOME TIPS

1. Q: If A is vicariously liable for the torts of B, B's contributory negligence will always be imputed to A in an action by A against a third party C for injuries suffered by A as a result of the combined negligence of B and C.

A: False. Even when A is B's employer there are some circumstances in a few states in which B's contributory negligence will not be imputed to A. In non-employment situations, there is a greater likelihood that B's contributory negligence will not be imputed to A, particularly when the basis for imputing B's negligence to A is an owner-responsibility motor vehicle statue.

2. **Q:** Contributory negligence can, depending on the jurisdiction, be either a complete or partial defense, to an action based on a statutory violation.

    A: True. Unless the statue was aimed at protecting a limited class, such as children or workers, from the effect of their own negligence, the normal doctrines applicable to all negligence actions apply to actions based upon a violation of a statutory duty.

3. **Q:** Most jurisdictions that have adopted comparative negligence can be expected to treat conduct that would previously have been considered to amount to an "assumption of the risk" as a possible instance of contributory negligence.

    A: True

4. **Q:** Even in a jurisdiction that has completely abolished the common law doctrine of contributory negligence and has opted for the pure form of comparative negligence, is unlikely to allow the plaintiff's contributory fault to reduce his recovery against an intentional tortfeasor.

    A: True

5. **Q:** Most jurisdiction that have adopted comparative negligence have abolished express assumptions of the risk.

    A: False

    Tip: The key word here is "express." Express assumption of risk normally refers to situations in which the injured person has, prior to his injury, signed a release acknowledging the risk and absolving the defendant from any legal liability if injury ensues. Unless the court is prepared to hold that such contractual provisions are against public policy because they condition the plaintiff's access to essential services such as medical care or transportation, courts will generally uphold such provisions if executed by knowledgeable adults.

NOTES

MULTIPLE DEFENDANTS, CONTRIBUTION, AND INDEMNITY

▶ **CHAPTER SUMMARY**

MULTIPLE DEFENDANTS, CONTRIBUTION, AND INDEMNITY

Scope of Chapter: It is quite common for there to be more than one defendant, or potential defendant, in a lawsuit. This can occur, for example, where: (1) an employee is negligent and her employer is vicariously liable for that negligence; (2) two or more tortfeasors act in concert in injuring the plaintiff; or (3) the acts of two or more tortfeasors concur in bringing about a single, indivisible injury. In these situations, the plaintiff is typically permitted to sue all of the potential defendants and to recover a judgment for her full compensatory damages against each of them. She can then collect all or part of her compensatory damages against any one of the defendants. She can recover her full compensatory damages only once, however, although each defendant may be separately liable for punitive damages.

Example: The tortious acts of *X, Y,* and *Z* concur to injure *A* in the amount of $50,000. *Y* and *Z* are also found liable to *A* for punitive damages in the amounts of $10,000 and $15,000, respectively. *A* can only collect a total of $50,000 in compensatory damages, although she can collect all or any part of that sum from *X, Y,* or *Z.* In addition, she can collect $10,000 in punitive damages from *Y,* and $15,000 in punitive damages from *Z.*

X, Y, and *Z* may be jointly liable to *A* even though the grounds of their liability differ.

Example: The tortious acts of *X, Y,* and *Z* concur to injure *A.* These actors may be jointly liable, even though *X* acted negligently, *Y* acted intentionally, and *Z* is strictly liable.

JOINT LIABILITY

I. JOINT LIABILITY

A. Typical Situations: As already noted, vicarious liability, concert of activity, and concurrent activity can give rise to joint liability (typically referred to as joint and several liability). Where tortious acts, or failures to act, concur, some courts impose liability on the basis that the injury would not have occurred *but for* the act or inaction of each defendant. Some courts will also impose joint liability if the tortious act or inaction of each defendant is a *substantial contributing cause* of the injury, even though it is possible that the injury might have occurred as a result of the action or inaction of any one of the defendants. *See Anderson v. Minneapolis, St. Paul, & Sault Ste. Marie Ry.,* 146 Minn. 430, 179 N.W. 45 (1920).

1. Some courts think that joint liability is inappropriate where the conduct of two or more defendants independently cause successive rather than concurrent injuries, or where the conduct of a tortfeasor does not cause the accident but only increases the plaintiff's injuries. In these situations, the plaintiff may be required to prove the proportion that each defendant contributed to her damages and to collect from each defendant only the proportion of damages caused by that defendant.

   Examples: Plaintiff is injured by defendants in successive, independent or unrelated collisions. It is her duty to show what portion of her damages was caused by each defendant, and she can collect only the portion of damages caused by each defendant from that defendant. *Bruckman v. Pena,* 29 Colo. App. 357, 487 P.2d 566 (1971). Plaintiff is involved in an automobile accident in which his injuries are increased by defendant's defective design of the automobile. The defendant designer is liable only for the increased injuries caused by the design, which plaintiff must show. *Huddell v. Levin,* 537 F.2d 726 (3d Cir. 1976).

   The better rule in these situations is that the defendants should be jointly liable (i.e., each liable for the entire damages) if the damages are theoretically or practically indivisible. *See Glick v. Ballentine Produce,* 396 S.W.2d 609 (Mo. 1965) (successive torts); *Chrysler Corp. v. Todorovitch,* 580 P.2d 1123 (Wyo. 1978) (increased injuries). A principal rationale for imposing joint liability for concurrent acts is that the damages are practically indivisible, and the rationale should apply to successive acts and injuries as well.

II. SEVERAL LIABILITY

A. **Abolition of Joint Liability:** A number of jurisdictions, by case law or statute, have abolished the traditional rule of joint liability for cotortfeasors, in favor of several liability — which means that each defendant is liable only for the damages caused by her own fault. Joint liability may be abolished in its entirety or retained only in limited situations. In this connection, see the discussion of the issue in Chapter 22 on statutory changes.

1. With the widespread adoption of comparative fault in almost all jurisdictions, some courts and legislatures have felt that the retention of joint liability is no longer justified. Under the traditional contributory negligence rule, the plaintiff could recover only if she were free of fault. As between an innocent plaintiff and a faulty defendant, the courts reasoned, the latter should bear the risk of nonrecovery against a potential codefendant. But under comparative fault, the plaintiff is permitted to recover at least part of her damages even though both she and the defendant are at fault; so as between two wrongdoers, there is no reason, some feel, why the defendant, any more than the plaintiff, should bear the risk of nonrecovery against a potential codefendant.

   a. Other courts have retained joint liability even with the adoption of comparative fault. The reasons for doing so are that: (1) each defendant (under a "but-for" rule) causes the entire damages; (2) in many cases the plaintiff may be free of fault; (3) even if the plaintiff is at fault, her contributory (self-directed) fault is less culpable than the defendant's fault which is directed toward others; and (4) elimination of joint liability would have an undesirable effect on the plaintiff's ability to collect full compensation. *Coney v. J.L.G. Industries,* 97 Ill. 2d 104, 454 N.E.2d 197 (1983). In addition, cotortfeasors who stand in a master-servant or concerted-action relationship resemble a single actor more than separate actors; since in these situations each acts for the other, it is reasonable to make each liable for the other's acts.

III. CONTRIBUTION

A. **Types of Contribution:** Where cotortfeasors are held severally rather than jointly liable, there is no need for contribution since each tortfeasor is responsible only for his own share of liability. Where joint liability is retained, however, one tortfeasor may end up paying more than his fair share of liability and in that event he may seek to recover the amount he has paid over his fair share from another cotortfeasor. This right of recovery over between tortfeasors is called a right of contribution.

1. At the early common law, contribution between cotortfeasors was not permitted. *See Merryweather v. Nixan,* (K.B. 1779) 101 Eng. Rep. 1337. The rationale for this rule of no contribution as it developed may have been much the same as that which barred recovery by a plaintiff guilty of contributory negligence — namely, that an at-fault party should not be permitted to recover. Today, the no-contribution rule has been generally abolished either by statute or court decision, but it is frequently retained to bar contribution where the person seeking contribution was guilty of intentional misconduct.

   a. Where contribution is allowed, apportionment is usually made on one of two bases: relative degrees of fault, and/or relative degrees of causation. Where one defendant is held strictly liable, it would seem that his contribution would have to be made on the basis of cause, or else on some concept of constructive fault. *See Safeway Stores v. Nest-Kart,* 21 Cal.3d 322, 579 P.2d 441 (1978).

(1) Another approach, followed by the Uniform Contribution Among Tortfeasors Act, is to apportion liability equally among the available cotortfeasors. Thus, if there are two cotortfeasors, each would be liable for one half of the liability; if three, each would be liable for one third; and so on. This method of division commends itself for ease of application but seems unfair to those concerned with relative degrees of fault or causation.

2. Some jurisdictions require that codefendants be held liable in a joint judgment before contribution can be obtained. *See Dole v. Dow Chem. Co.,* 30 N.Y.2d 143, 331 N.Y.S.2d 382, 282 N.E.2d 288 (1972). The reason for this rule is probably to prevent relitigation of the underlying issues, but it works a hardship on the defendant who must depend on the plaintiff's willingness or ability to sue a codefendant in the same action in which the defendant is sued, before contribution is available.

3. Many jurisdictions do not allow contribution by one person against another person who is immune from liability to the original claimant. The rationale for denying contribution here is that the persons are not cotortfeasors.

    Example: *A* and *B* are involved in a two-car collision in which both *A* and *B* as drivers are negligent. *B's* spouse, *C,* who is a passenger in *B's* car, is injured in the accident and sues *A. A* cannot seek contribution from *B,* because *B* at that time was not liable to *C* owing to spousal immunity. *Yellow Cab Co. v. Dreslin,* 181 F.2d 626 (D.C. Cir. 1950).

    Other courts allow contribution in this situation. *Dole v. Dow Chem. Co., supra* (product manufacturer allowed to sue plaintiff's employer for contribution, even though the employer was immune from liability in tort to the plaintiff owing to the exclusive-remedy rule of workers' compensation).

    a. The situations dealt with here are those where one tortfeasor is immune from liability *to the plaintiff,* and not where the tortfeasor is immune from liability to *anyone, e.g.,* as a result of charitable immunity. In the latter situation, contribution cannot be obtained because the charitable tortfeasor enjoys total immunity.

B. **Settlement:** The traditional position is that the release of one tortfeasor automatically releases any cotortfeasor. Some courts distinguish between a release and a covenant not to sue, holding that the former is a complete release while the latter only releases the covenantee. The modern trend is not to distinguish between a release and a covenant not to sue, since the distinction is based only on semantics, but instead to provide that the release of one tortfeasor does not release another unless the intent to do so is clearly expressed in the release. Unif. Contribut. among Tort. Act § 4(a).

1. A settlement should be distinguished from the satisfaction of a judgment, which is generally treated as releasing any cotortfeasor from liability to the plaintiff. The reason for the latter rule is that a judgment is deemed to represent the full amount of compensation due, while a settlement is frequently for less than the full amount of compensation due.

2. If a settlement is intended to be for the full *amount* of liability to the plaintiff, or if the plaintiff satisfies a judgment which is deemed to be for the full amount of such liability, then the settler or judgment-payer may be able to seek contribution against a cotortfeasor depending on the rules of the jurisdiction.

3. If settlement is for *less than the full amount* of plaintiff's damages, then the rules regarding the effect of such a settlement vary.

a. One approach is to leave the settler liable for contribution to a cotortfeasor who pays more than his fair share of liability.

b. The more common approach is to immunize the settler from liability for contribution, but to grant any cotortfeasor a credit for the settlement against any liability the cotortfeasor has to the plaintiff. The credit is typically computed in one of two ways: (i) a credit is given for the amount actually paid, or (ii) a credit is given for the amount of liability attributable to the settler. The first method encourages settlement more than the second, but the second is fairer to the nonsettling tortfeasor than the first since the amount of settlement is usually less than the amount of liability of the settler.

Example: *A* and *B* are each 50% responsible for *P's* damages, which are computed at $100,000. *A* settles with *P* for $10,000. Under the first method of credit, *B* remains liable to *P* for $90,000; under the second method, he is liable for only $50,000.

Where tortfeasors are severally (rather than jointly) liable there is no settlement credit, just as there is no right of contribution, since each tortfeasor is responsible only for her share of liability.

IV. **INDEMNITY**

A. **Basis and Effect:** Where one tortfeasor is vicariously liable for the tort of another, that tortfeasor may be able to obtain indemnity or full recovery over against the other. Indemnity is also typically allowed by the buyer of a product against his seller, for injuries caused by the buyer of a product to a victim to whom the buyer is liable. Some courts allow indemnity between two tortfeasors, one of whom (the indemnitee) is found to be only "passively" or "secondarily" at fault while the other (the indemnitor) is found to be "actively" or "primarily" at fault.

1. The trend is to abolish indemnity (full recovery over) in favor of contribution (apportionment of liability) in the active-passive situation, in part because of the difficulty of distinguishing between active and passive fault. *See Dole v. Dow Chem. Co., supra.* There is some indication that contribution, rather than indemnity, will also be adopted between a product buyer and seller for injuries caused to a third person by the product. *See Casey v. Westinghouse Elevator Co.,* 651 F. Supp. 258 (S.D. Ill. 1986).

B. **Settlement:** Some courts hold that settlement with an indemnitor automatically releases the indemnitee. *See Craven v. Lawson,* 534 S.W.2d 653 (Tenn. 1976). *Contra Harris v. Aluminum Co.,* 550 F. Supp. 1024 (W.D. Va. 1982). The *Craven* rule can be very treacherous, *e.g.,* in the active-passive indemnity situation, where the settlor thinks he is dealing with a cotortfeasor in a contribution context but is actually dealing with an indemnitor because the latter is an active or primary tortfeasor.

CHAPTER 6 – QUESTIONS, ANSWERS AND TIPS

1. **Q:** Multiple tortfeasors can be held jointly liable on different theories, e.g., negligence and strict liability, but not on different causes of action, e.g., defamation and misrepresentation.

A: False.

Tip: Multiple tortfeasors can be held jointly liable both on different theories and on different causes of action. Indeed, different causes of action may be based on different theories, e.g., defamation may be brought in negligence and misrepresentation in strict liability.

6

2. **Q:** Where defendant's conduct need only be shown by the plaintiff to have been a substantial, rather that a but-for, cause, plaintiff need not show such cause by a preponderance of the evidence.

   A: False.

   Tip: Unless the burden of proof on causation is shifted to the defendant, the plaintiff must prove causation at least by a preponderance of the evidence (i.e., more likely than not).

3. **Q:** Defendant negligently ran over plaintiff leaving plaintiff lying injured in the road. An ambulance, sent to the scene of the accident, failed to see plaintiff and ran over and injured him further. Defendant is liable for the damages he caused in running over plaintiff, and also for the damages caused by the ambulance.

   A: True.

   Tip: A predecessor tortfeasor may not be liable for independent, unrelated damages caused by a successor tortfeasor, but the predecessor will be liable for successive damages foreseeably and proximately caused by the predecessor, as here.

4. **Q:** Where joint liability has been abolished, the right of contribution by a tortfeasor held judicially liable is also abolished.

   A: True.

   Tip: In a several liability situation the right of contribution by a tortfeasor held judicially liable is abolished because the tortfeasor will be found liable only for his own share. The result could be different if the tortfeasor settled and, as part of the settlement agreement, took an assignment of the claimant's rights against a co-tortfeasor.

5. **Q:** If A and B concurrently injure C tortiously, and B settles with C, A as a jointly liable co-tortfeasor with B will typically receive a credit against its liability to C based either on the amount of the settlement or the amount of fault attributable to B.

   A: True.

   Tip: One approach is to leave the settler liable for contribution to the non-settler, but the more common approach is to give the non-settler a credit for the dollar amount of the settlement, or the dollar value of the settler's fault. Settlement should be distinguished from contribution sought by one held judicially liable, where the contribution is usually based on relative degrees of fault or on an equal division of liability between or among co-tortfeasors.

6. **Q:** Release of one tortfeasor by the plaintiff does not automatically release a co-tortfeasor from liability to the plaintiff unless the co-tortfeasor is an indemnitee.

   A: False.

   Tip: Release (as opposed to a covenant not to sue) may automatically release both tortfeasors in some jurisdictions. Conversely, in some jurisdictions release of the indemnitor does not automatically release the indemnitee. There is a division of authority on both issues. In any event, release of one party may release another if the settling parties expressly so agree.

ACTUAL CAUSE

 CHAPTER SUMMARY

7

ACTUAL CAUSE

Scope of Chapter: As part of establishing a prima facie case, the plaintiff must prove that the defendant's negligence "caused" the plaintiff's injuries. The search for the legal cause of the plaintiff's injuries usually involves two elements: first, establishing that the defendant's conduct was the *actual cause* or *cause in fact* of the plaintiff's injuries; and, second, establishing that the defendant's conduct was the *proximate cause* of the plaintiff's injuries. The reason for this further inquiry, which we shall explore in the next chapter, is because the mere fact that the defendant's negligent conduct may have been the actual cause of the plaintiff's injuries does not necessarily mean that the defendant will be liable to the plaintiff. In this chapter, we shall explore the first of these inquiries, the search for an actual cause of the plaintiff's injury. Nominally a defendant's conduct cannot be a proximate cause of the plaintiff's injuries if the defendant's conduct was not an actual cause of the plaintiff's injuries. As we shall see, however, there are a few unusual situations in which defendants will be held liable to plaintiffs even though it is difficult to maintain that it is more likely than not that the defendant's negligent conduct was the actual cause of the plaintiff's injuries.

IN GENERAL   **I.   IN GENERAL**

    A.   Theoretical Background: To say that one event, such as the defendant's negligent conduct, is the cause of another event, such as the plaintiff's injuries, raises many philosophically difficult questions which the law has tried, not always successfully, to avoid. Ascriptions of a causal relationship between two events are used as part of our attempt to understand these events and the extent of the relationship between them. If we are unable to discover any causal relationship between two events, those events are random with respect to each other. If we could fully comprehend the cause of a particular event, we should, in theory at least, be capable of recreating that event by bringing into existence all the precedent events which lead to the event in question.

        1.   It is often the case, however, that it is impossible to completely recreate an event, even in theory. Under such circumstances, we look for some prior event which could have been part of the cause of the event in question. We then try to eliminate all other possible causes so that by a process of elimination the prior event, say the defendant's negligence, becomes the most likely cause of the event in which we are interested, say the plaintiff's injuries. By this process we seek to establish that the defendant's negligent conduct was more likely than not part of the causal chain that has led up to the plaintiff's injuries. In summary, one event will be established as the cause in fact of another if there is a sufficiently high statistical correlation between the occurrence of these types of events and if, in the particular case under consideration, there is no other plausible explanation of the occurrence of the second event.

        2.   The inquiry is not purely an objective one because the causal inquiry will be affected by the level of generality at which the inquiry takes place.

            Example: Driving a convertible down a straight highway at a 100 miles per hour does not appear to have any statistical correlation with the car's being hit by lightning. The two events, driving the car and the hitting of the car by lightning, seem random with regard to each other. If, however, one were to describe the events in greater detail so as to include precise time, atmospheric and wind conditions, etc., we would eventually reach a description of the two events in which there was indeed a correlation between the act of driving in excess of the speed limit and the striking of the vehicle by lightning. The appropriate level of generality with which the events should be described depends largely on common sense as reflected in legal precedent.

    B.   Anomalous Situations and the Notion of "Substantial Cause": Sometimes courts will find a causal connection between the defendant's negligence and the plaintiff's injuries when, as a matter of strict logic, it would be difficult to conclude that the proof permits the inference that it is more likely than not that the defendant's negligence caused the plaintiff's injuries.

Example: Take a case in which the defendant has started a forest fire and the fire joins up with a forest fire caused by lightning. The combined fire then destroys the plaintiff's property. A strong argument could be made that the plaintiff's property would have been destroyed by the naturally caused fire regardless of whether the defendant had negligently started a forest fire. Nevertheless, in such circumstances most courts will allow recovery against the defendant on the ground that the fire caused by the defendant was a *substantial cause* or a *substantial contributing cause* of the plaintiff's injuries.

1. The notion of substantial cause is also sometimes used to describe the situation in which the defendant's negligent conduct initially appears to have had only a low probability of causing the plaintiff's injuries, but the plaintiff has succeeded in eliminating other possible causal explanations.

    Example: In *Daly v. Bergstedt,* 267 Minn. 244, 126 N.W.2d 242 (1964), the plaintiff was allowed to get to the jury on the question of causation when she showed that the defendant's conduct had resulted in physical injury to her, that a cancer eventually developed at the spot of the trauma, that, through medical testimony based on a physical examination shortly before the accident the affected area was noncancerous prior to the infliction of the trauma, and that, based on competent medical testimony, the cancer could have been induced by the trauma inflicted by the defendant's negligent conduct.

    Presumably if the plaintiff has eliminated all other possible causes of the injuries, it could be said that the plaintiff has established that the trauma inflicted by the defendant was more probably than not the cause of the cancer. The use of the term "substantial cause" by the *Daly* court indicates that, in these circumstances, some courts are prepared to allow the plaintiff to recover despite having some lingering doubts as to whether the plaintiff has shown that the defendant's conduct was in point of fact more likely than not the cause of the cancer. Whether the plaintiff, in *Daly*, had in fact eliminated all other possible causes of her cancer is another question.

C. **Multiple Causation:** *Actual cause* or *cause in fact* has also successfully been established in circumstances in which the plaintiff has shown that there are several possible causes, each of which alone is sufficient to account for the plaintiff's injuries, but the plaintiff is unable to establish which particular cause actually caused the injuries.

    Example: The most famous such instance is *Summers v. Tice,* 33 Cal. 2d 80, 199 P.2d 1 (1948). In that case, the plaintiff was a member of a hunting party which included two other hunters. Both of the other hunters fired their shotguns at some quail. The plaintiff was hit in the eye. It was found that both of the other hunters were negligent. It proved impossible, however, to determine from which gun the shot that injured the plaintiff had come. The plaintiff was permitted to recover against both defendants. The case can be explained on one of two grounds.

    1. One explanation of *Summers v. Tice* is that the conduct of both of the defendants was the "substantial cause" of the plaintiff's injuries despite the fact that it is clear that the shot which injured the plaintiff could only have come from the gun of one of the defendants. As a matter of strict logic, this explanation leaves much to be desired.

    2. The other and perhaps more satisfactory explanation is that, in such situations, once it is shown that both defendants are negligent, and the plaintiff is unable to show which of the negligent defendants actually caused the injury, the burden of persuasion on the issue of causation shifts to the defendants. This is the position adopted by *Restatement (Second) of Torts* § 433B(3). The purpose of this doctrine of course is to encourage defendants to come forward with

evidence that will help to establish that one of the other defendants is the responsible party. In many situations, however, such proof is unavailable, and the effect of shifting the burden of persuasion to the defendants will be to impose liability upon all the defendants, even though it is clear that all of them did not cause the injury. As the number of defendants increases in number beyond the two defendants involved in *Summers v. Tice,* the imposition of liability upon all the defendants becomes more questionable both on considerations of logic and of fairness.

    a.   If the two defendants in *Summers v. Tice* were considered part of a joint venture whose activities injured a third party, the case would present little difficulty because each of the defendants would be vicariously liable for the tortious acts of the other. The court, however, treated as crucial the fact that both the defendants negligently fired their guns, not the fact that they were members of the same hunting party, a hunting party which of course also included the plaintiff.

    b.   In cases involving liability for injuries caused by DES, plaintiffs were unable to establish which, of the many manufacturers of DES, produced the DES that actually caused their injuries. A number of courts have imposed liability upon all the manufacturers apportioned on a market-share basis, sometimes, as in *Hymowitz, infra,* even in the face of evidence that a particular manufacturer could not have produced the DES in question. *See Hymowitz v. Eli Lilly & Co.,* 73 N.Y.2d 487, 539 N.E.2d 1069, 541 N.Y. S.2d 941 (N.Y. 1989) (national market share); *Sindell v. Abbott Laboratories,* 26 Cal. 3d 588, 163 Cal. Rptr. 132, 607 P.2d 924 (1980) (market share in California). While a few courts have extended market share liability to other truly fungible products, most courts have thus far refused to extend this type of liability to products other than DES, such as asbestos or vaccines.

D.   A difficult problem that has arisen in recent years is whether the plaintiff can bring an action because the negligent conduct of the defendant has resulted in the plaintiff's *loss of a chance* to avoid some particular risk. An important recent case is *Herskovits v. Group Heath Co-Op. of Puget Sound,* 99 Wash. 2d 609, 664 P.2d 474 (1983), in which the personal representative of a person who died from lung cancer was accepted as having established that, owing to the defendant's negligence, the deceased's 39% chance of survival from lung cancer was reduced to a 25% chance. Summary judgment for the defendant was reversed. In remanding the case for trial, the court did not expressly state what damages, if any, were recoverable on the assumed facts. It thus left open the possibility that, if the defendant physician's negligence was found by the jury to have been a substantial factor in reducing the deceased's chances of obtaining a better result, the personal representative might recover the full range of damages suffered from the failure to achieve this better result.

    1.   To deal with this problem, a few courts have permitted plaintiffs to recover only a portion of their eventual injuries by instructing the jury to evaluate the monetary value of the chance of recovery, the loss of which was incurred by the plaintiff. Because of the difficulty of evaluating the value of the loss of a chance, most courts are inclined to deny recovery in such situations. Where the probability of the chance of which the plaintiff has been deprived as a result of the defendant's negligence increases toward and beyond 50%, the courts of course would be more inclined to find, using the more conventional analysis, that the defendant's negligent conduct was a substantial cause, or even more likely than not *the* cause in fact or actual cause, of the plaintiff's injury.

CHAPTER 7 - QUESTIONS, ANSWERS, AND TIPS

1. **Q:** A runs a red light. Once past the intersection, a tree falls on the car. The tree would not have fallen on the car if A had observed the traffic signal. B, a passenger in the car who has been injured by the falling tree, can rely on A's violation of the traffic laws to establish that A's negligence has "caused" B's injuries.

   A: False. It is not the case that running traffic lights increases the risk of a car being hit by a falling tree.

2. **Q:** A plaintiff who eliminates all other possible causal explanations of his injuries, can sometimes prevail on the issue of actual cause, even if the evidence pointing to the defendant's causal responsibility is otherwise of a low order of probability.

   A: True

3. **Q:** The actions of A, B, and C have combined to produce P's injuries under circumstances in which it is fairly certain that the actions of A, B, or C, taken alone, would each by themselves have produced P's injuries. In an action against A, P may not recover.

   A: False. As long as a defendant's negligence has contributed to a final result it is no defense for the defendant to maintain that the plaintiff's injuries would have ensued even if the defendant had no involvement in the events in question.

   Additional Exam Tip: The situation in question 3, *supra*, is sometimes described as an instance of the "substantial cause" doctrine. The doctrine that the plaintiff is only required to show that the defendant's conduct was a substantial cause of his injury is largely reserved for those joint injury situations in which a strict reliance upon the doctrine of actual cause would absolve from liability all persons whose combined conduct resulted in the plaintiff's injuries.

NOTES

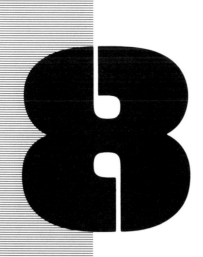

PROXIMATE CAUSE

▶ **CHAPTER SUMMARY**

PROXIMATE CAUSE

Scope of Chapter: The term "proximate cause" has traditionally been used to describe the ultimate conclusion of whether the defendant will be held legally responsible for the plaintiff's injuries. The term is used because the mere fact that the defendant may be said, in some factual sense, to have caused the plaintiff's injuries is not always enough to establish the plaintiff's legal liability. The *Restatement (Second) of Torts* uses the term "legal cause" in place of the traditional terminology of proximate cause. The cases, however, sometimes use the notion of legal cause in a more extended sense that encompasses not only what is traditionally known as proximate cause but also the antecedent inquiry as to whether or not a defendant's conduct has been an actual cause or cause in fact of the plaintiff's injury. We shall therefore use the less ambiguous traditional terminology in this outline.

8

THE DIRECT CAUSE TEST

I.   THE DIRECT CAUSE TEST

A.   The older cases have generally spoken in terms of the defendants being liable to the plaintiff when the defendant's negligent conduct was the *direct cause* of the plaintiff's injuries. The most famous articulation of this standard is contained in an English case, *In re Polemis*, [1921] 3 K.B. 560 (C.A.). In that case, a fire that ultimately destroyed a cargo ship was started when some stevedores negligently dislodged a plank which fell into the lower hold of the ship and caused some sparks which then ignited gasoline vapor that had escaped from containers of gasoline being carried by the ship. It was found as a fact, probably mistakenly to the modern eye, that the causing of the fire and subsequent loss of the ship was not a foreseeable consequence of the stevedore's negligence. Nevertheless, the defendants were held liable because their conduct had threatened some damage to the ship and its cargo and was the direct cause of the injury.

1.   Although the direct cause test has some support in common sense, its actual application is difficult. It suggests that there are some results which are not direct results because they are "too remote," without explaining how remoteness is to be determined. It also suggests that a cause might not be a "direct cause" if there are sufficient other "intervening causes," without adequately explaining what is a sufficient intervening cause.

II.   THE REASONABLE FORESEEABILITY TEST

THE REASONABLE FORESEEABILITY TEST

A.   Courts applying the "direct cause" test to determine whether the defendant's conduct is the proximate cause of the plaintiff's injuries have, following the *Polemis case, supra,* usually declared that the foreseeability of the defendant's conduct injuring the plaintiff is relevant to the question of whether or not the defendant's conduct was negligent with regard to the plaintiff, but is not relevant to the question of causation. The modern trend, in contrast, accepts that the reasonable foreseeability of the defendant's conduct resulting in injury to the plaintiff is not only relevant to the question of whether the defendant was negligent toward the plaintiff, but is also relevant to the question of the extent of the defendant's liability.

1.   The most important cases on the reasonable foreseeability test are two British cases that were decided by the Privy Council. *Overseas Tankship (U.K.) Ltd. v. Morts Dock & Eng. Co., Ltd. (the Wagon Mound),* [1961] A.C. 388, 2 W.L.R. 126, 1 All E.R. 404, and *Overseas Tankship (U.K.) Ltd. v. The Miller Steamship Co. Pty. (the Wagon Mound No. 2),* [1967] 1 A.C. 617 (1966), [1966] 3 W.L.R. 498, 2 All E.R. 709. These cases involved litigation arising out of the spillage of a substantial amount of bunkering oil into the harbor of Sydney, Australia. In the first case, it was accepted that the spilled oil posed a foreseeable risk of fouling the slipways of the plaintiff dock owners, but that it was not reasonably foreseeable that the oil would be ignited while it was floating on the water and would destroy the property of the plaintiff dock owners. The plaintiffs were consequently unable to recover for the loss of their property. In the *Wagon Mound No. 2,* the plaintiffs were the owners of ships damaged in the resulting fire.

The trial judge had again found that the fire was not reasonably foreseeable. The Privy Council, however, latching on to some subsidiary findings of the trial judge that a reasonable person in the position of the defendant's engineers would foresee a fire as only a remote possibility, concluded that the possibility of fire was sufficiently foreseeable to impose liability, given that it would have taken very little effort to prevent the bunkering oil from spilling and that the potential damage from allowing the oil to spill could be very great indeed, as in point of fact was the case.

a. Most of the recent American cases seem to adopt the reasonable foreseeability test. Although adopted ostensibly to limit a defendant's liability, if the foreseeability of a slight chance that the defendant's conduct will cause injury is sufficient to satisfy the reasonable foreseeability test, it does not seem to offer defendants much comfort. Indeed, in actual practice, the reasonable foreseeability test will lead to much the same results as the earlier direct cause test.

b. In the English cases, there was a suggestion that conduct which is negligent with regard to some particular interest of the plaintiff may not be negligent with regard to some other interest of the plaintiff because, while there is a foreseeable risk of injury to the first interest, there is not a foreseeable risk of injury to the second interest. This was the position taken in 1935 by *Restatement of Torts* § 281. In 1965, however, the *Restatement (Second) of Torts* § 281 took the position that if the actor is negligent with respect to another person, the actor would be liable for an invasion of a legally protected interest of that other person. It dropped the express requirement that the interest injured must be the interest that was actually threatened. The reasonable foreseeability test thus allows a potentially wide range of liability.

c. To the question, how foreseeable must an injury be in order to be "reasonably foreseeable," there can be no certain answer. Courts will be guided by common sense and precedent and their perception of the importance of the interests involved. Moreover, as under the direct cause test, the question arises as to when some independent intervening cause will be held to be a "superseding cause" of the plaintiff's injuries. The question of intervening superseding cause will be discussed below in section III of this chapter.

2. ***Is proximate cause ultimately a policy question?*** In his dissenting opinion in *Palsgraf v. Long Island Railroad Co.,* 248 N.Y. 339, 162 N.E. 99 (1928), Judge Andrews suggested that, in the last analysis, the question of whether the defendant's conduct was the proximate cause of the plaintiff's injuries must be decided on policy grounds. While superficially attractive, the courts have been reluctant to accept openly that the ascription of causation in an action for damages is ultimately a political question. The courts instead will stress the foreseeability or lack of foreseeability of the ultimate result, the remoteness in time between the defendant's conduct and the plaintiff's injury, the number, if any, of intervening causes (to be discussed below), etc. As a reflection of this uncertainty, the *Restatement (Second) of Torts* § 435(2) states that "the actor's conduct may be held not to be a legal cause of harm to another where after the event and looking back from the harm to the actor's negligent conduct, it appears to the court highly extraordinary that it should have brought about the harm." In so doing, the *Restatement (Second)* seems to adopt a foreseeability approach, although in other provisions it espouses a direct cause approach. It also appears, perhaps giving voice to Judge Andrews's concerns, to be providing an escape valve for courts to refuse to permit liability for so-called bizarre accidents.

3. ***What has to be foreseen?*** Accepting that the foreseeability of a result is a crucial component in determining whether one event is the "proximate cause" of another event, exactly what has to be foreseen?

8

a. It is universally held that if damage of a certain type is foreseeable as a result of the defendant's negligent conduct, the defendant is legally responsible for all the damage of that type suffered by the plaintiff even if the extent of the damage actually inflicted cannot be said to be reasonably foreseeable. This is the basis for the old saw that "the defendant takes the plaintiff as he finds him."

Example: The defendant negligently bumps into someone and knocks him against a sharp object. As a result, this person suffers some minor cuts, a clearly foreseeable result, but, owing to the fact that the person is a hemophiliac, he bleeds to death, a highly unforeseeable result. The defendant will be legally responsible in tort for the death of the injured person.

b. As in our discussion of actual cause (p. 7-2, *supra*), the causal inquiry will be affected by the manner in which we describe the events in question.

Example: In *Chase v. Washington Power Co.,* 62 Idaho 298, 111 P.2d 872 (1941), a high tension electrical line came into sufficient proximity with a guy wire that the wingtips of two sparring hawks joined the two lines with the result that a fire was started that destroyed the plaintiff's barn. The plaintiff was allowed to recover. If what had to be foreseen was the action of the hawks, the accident was clearly unforeseeable. If, on the other hand, the situation is characterized as one where the wires were placed in sufficient proximity that some natural event could result in the two wires coming in contact with each other, the result that actually ensued is not particularly unforeseeable.

INTERVENING CAUSE

III. INTERVENING CAUSE

A. **General Principle:** Even where the defendant's conduct is held to be a direct cause or a foreseeable cause of the plaintiff's injury, the defendant may still escape liability if there are any *superseding intervening causes* of the plaintiff's injuries.

1. *Acts of God and of innocent or negligent third parties:* If the intervening cause is an act of nature or the innocent or merely negligent act of a third party, the universal rule is to hold the defendant liable if the intervening act of nature or of a third party can be said to have been "reasonably foreseeable."

   a. *The aggravation of injuries:* A special application of the rule about the effect of intervening causes concerns a plaintiff who has been negligently injured by the defendant and whose injuries are subsequently aggravated through the negligence of the treating physician. It is universally held that the plaintiff may recover from the defendant not only the damages resulting from the initial injury, but also the damages resulting from the enhancement of those injuries in the course of subsequent medical treatment. One theoretical justification for this result is that, by injuring the plaintiff, the defendant has exposed the plaintiff to a foreseeable risk of injury by health care professionals.

2. *Intentional or reckless acts of third persons:* A difficult question arises when the defendant has exposed the plaintiff to a foreseeable risk of injury, but the injuries suffered by the plaintiff would not have occurred without the intervening reckless or intentional acts of third persons. Some of the earlier cases took the position that if the intervening act was the intentional criminal act of a third person, there could be no recovery against the defendant. But then cases arose in which the defendant's negligent conduct was what clearly made the intervening criminal conduct possible.

Example: A negligently driven automobile disables the guard whom the plaintiff has employed to protect the plaintiff's property. As a result, the guard is unable to prevent the theft of the property which he was guarding. Almost all courts would permit recovery for the stolen property against the negligent motorist.

a. The modern tendency therefore is to permit recovery in some situations in which the plaintiff would not have been injured but for the intervening reckless or intentional conduct of a third person. In considering whether liability will lie against a negligent defendant whose negligence started the causal chain, the courts will consider the culpability of the intervening act — the more culpable it is, the less likely it is that the original defendant will be held liable — and, perhaps more importantly, the foreseeability of the intervening act. The more foreseeable the intervening acts of the third party are, the more likely it is that the courts will hold a negligent defendant responsible for the ultimate result.

b. Traditionally, a defendant was not held responsible for the plaintiff's subsequent *suicide* on the ground either that the suicide was "unforeseeable" or was the result of the plaintiff's own intentional misconduct. More recently, courts have sometimes allowed plaintiffs to recover in such situations on the theory that the original injuries caused by the defendant's negligent conduct had rendered the plaintiff emotionally unstable.

IV. LIABILITY TO RESCUERS

LIABILITY TO RESCUERS

A. **General Principle:** On the theory that "danger invites rescue," one who injures another or subjects another to a serious risk of injury will be held to have caused the injuries incurred by someone making a reasonable rescue attempt.

1. This principle has been qualified in many jurisdictions by a doctrine that precludes recovery by persons who might be described as "professional rescuers." The theory underlying these cases is that persons who accept jobs as policemen or firemen or paramedics assume such risks as part of their employment.

CHAPTER 8 - QUESTIONS, ANSWERS, AND TIPS

1. **Q:** Most modern cases require that a defendant should have been able to foresee the actual manner by which the plaintiff was injured before the defendant's negligent conduct will be said to be the proximate cause of the injury.

    A: False

    Tip: The way or manner in which an event is described will influence our conclusion as to whether the defendant's conduct was causally related to the plaintiff's injuries—see the example on p. 8-4, *supra*— but, once it is accepted that there is a foreseeable causal relationship between the defendant's conduct and the plaintiff's injury, the fact that the actual manner in which the defendant's conduct caused the injury was unforeseeable will not prevent a court from concluding that the defendant's conduct was the proximate cause of the plaintiff's injuries.

2. **Q:** If some damage to the plaintiff was foreseeable most modern courts will hold a negligent defendant liable for the full amount of the plaintiff's injuries even if the extent of the plaintiff's injuries was not foreseeable.

    A: True

8

3. **Q:** Under the approach of the *Restatement (Second) of Torts*, a negligent defendant may escape liability by establishing that the injuries sustained by the plaintiff were of a different type than could be reasonably foreseen by the defendant. For example, the defendant could reasonably foresee that his conduct might damage the plaintiff's property interests, but could not reasonably foresee that his conduct might damage the plaintiff's person.

   A: False. See p. 8-3, *supra*.

4. **Q:** The more culpable the defendant's actions, the less likely is it that an intervening act will be held to cut off his liability.

   A: True

5. **Q:** A child on a school outing falls into a pond. An observer rescues the child from drowning but sustains injuries in the course of carrying out the rescue. If the school authorities were negligent in supervising the child, they will be subject to liability for the rescuer's injuries.

   A: True

   Additional Exam Tip: After the event, with the benefit of hindsight, almost anything that in point of fact actually happened can appear, in retrospect, to have been foreseeable. The question the courts must decide is what was reasonably foreseeable before the event. The difficult question is not so much what was foreseeable—with enough imagination almost anything is foreseeable—but what was *reasonably* foreseeable. Questions of reasonableness are uniquely questions of judgment and thus almost always, in the first instance, questions for the jury or other trier of fact.

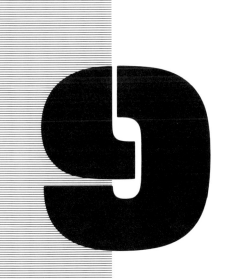

VICARIOUS ABILITY

▶ CHAPTER SUMMARY

VICARIOUS LIABILITY

Scope of Chapter: Vicarious liability is a doctrine used to impose liability on one person for the acts of another, who for this purpose is viewed as the agent of that person or as one acting for that person. The doctrine, particularly in the employer-employee context, is often referred to as *respondeat superior,* "let the master answer" (for the acts of his servant or employee).

Where the doctrine applies, it can be used to impute the tortious acts of an agent to the agent's principal, whether the tort be one of intentional misconduct, negligence, or strict liability. The vicarious liability of the principal is strict, in that no fault on the part of the principal need be shown.

The agent must be guilty of some tortious conduct, in order for the principal to be held liable. *Louie Queriolo Trucking v. Superior Court,* 252 Cal. App. 2d 194, 60 Cal. Rptr. 389 (1967). The fact that the agent is immune from liability to the plaintiff does not necessarily mean, however, that the principal will be discharged from liability.

Example: Where a husband tortiously injures his wife while driving a company car in the scope of employment, he may be immune from liability by virtue of spousal immunity but the company can, nevertheless, be found liable to the wife under the doctrine of *respondeat superior. Fields v. Synthetic Ropes,* 59 Del. 135, 215 A.2d 427 (1965).

The doctrine of vicarious liability must be distinguished from liability based on actual fault of the principal. If the principal is actually at fault, then the doctrine of *respondeat superior* is unnecessary as a basis of liability and indeed may even be inapplicable to the facts.

Example: An employer fails to exercise due care in hiring an employee. The employer may be liable for the resultant tortious acts of the employee, even though those acts are committed outside the scope of employment *Di Cosala v. Kay,* 91 N.J. 159, 450 A.2d 508 (1982). Of course, the acts must be employment-related, however, or otherwise there will be no proximate cause for holding the employer liable.

RATIONALE
FOR THE RULE

I. THE RATIONALE FOR THE RULE

A. ***Quit Facit Per Alium FacitPer Se:*** "He who acts through another acts himself," according to the Latin maxim. If the principal authorizes or ratifies the agent's tortious conduct, the basis for imposing vicarious liability is easy to understand. Indeed, such conduct on the part of the principal may itself be negligent. Where there is no such authorization or ratification, several explanations have been offered for imposing vicarious liability, none of which is entirely satisfactory. One is that the principal should be liable for the acts of the agent, since the principal has the right of control over those acts. The right of control does not mean actual control, however, since if the principal actually controlled the agent, she would either prevent the tort or would likely be at fault for not doing so. A right of control that cannot be effectively exercised is of little value. Another explanation is that the principal should be liable for her agent's acts which are performed in furtherance of the interests of the principal. *See Fruit v. Schreiner,* 502 P.2d 133 (Alaska 1972). This explanation is also unsatisfactory, since the commission of a tort by an agent can hardly be considered to be in furtherance of the principal's interests.

1. Probably the best explanation is that offered in *Ira S. Bushey & Sons, Inc. v. United States,* 398 F.2d 167 (2d Cir. 1968). The court there held that the principal should be liable for an agent's acts that are fairly characteristic of the principal's enterprise or activity. This test provides no bright-line rule.

Example: In the *Ira S. Bushey* case, the court held that the United States could be found liable for the drunken misconduct of a seaman in damaging the plaintiff's drydock, where the seaman's ship was berthed for repairs. The court said by way of dictum that the United States would not be liable if the seaman "upon returning to the drydock, recognized the Bushey security guard as his wife's lover and shot him." Such an act would be "related to the seaman's domestic life, not to his seafaring activity."

Another rationale for vicarious liability was given in *Mary M. v. City of Los Angeles*, 54 Cal.3d. 202, 814 P.2d 1341 (1991), where the city was held liable for a rape committed by its policeman during the course of employment. Police officers exercise "the most awesome and dangerous power that a democratic state possesses with respect to its residents," and the "cost resulting from misuse of that power should be borne by the community, because of the substantial benefits that the community derives from the lawful exercise of police power."

II.   TYPICAL SITUATIONS OF VICARIOUS LIABILITY

A.   The Employment Relationship: As already indicated, an employer can be liable for the tortious acts of an employee — provided those acts are committed within the scope of employment. There is considerable litigation regarding what acts are within, and what acts are outside, the scope of employment. It is widely held that driving to and from the place of employment is not within the scope of employment. But an exception to this rule occurs where the employee uses his car to perform his actual work, *e.g.,* as a salesperson. *Lundberg v. State,* 25 N.Y.2d 467, 306 N.Y.S.2d 947, 255 N.E.2d 177 (1969). It is often held that willful or intentional misconduct is not within the scope of employment, but there are exceptions here as well where the use of force is an integral part of the employment as, for example, in the case of a bodyguard or a bouncer. It has even been held that the use of illegal force in an agent's attempt to collect a debt for the principal is within the scope of employment since such acts are done in an attempt to further the principal's interests.

Example: A gasoline station owner was held liable for the act of an attendant who shot a customer when the latter refused to pay cash. *Jefferson v. Rose Oil Co.,* 232 So.2d 895 (La. App. 1970).

1.   The fact that the employee violates express rules of the employer will not necessarily relieve the employer of liability.

Example: The employer was held liable for the act of a store attendant who shot a person engaged in a holdup prank, in spite of the fact that the employer had expressly instructed its employees never to resist a holdup attempt. *Frederick v. Collins,* 378 S.W.2d 617 (Ky. 1964). This rule makes good sense, since otherwise the employer could insulate herself from vicarious liability simply by expressly forbidding all tortious acts of her employees.

B.   Partners and Joint Venturers: Partners are liable for the partnership-related torts of each other. So are joint venturers — two or more persons engaged in a joint enterprise, with mutual rights of control and a common business purpose. The purpose has to be one of business.

Example: Thus it has been held — although there is a division of authority where there has been something like a mutual right of control — that sharing expenses on a vacation or pleasure trip is not a joint enterprise. *See Edlebeck v. Hooten,* 20 Wis.2d 83, 121 N.W.2d 240 (1963).

C.   The Independent Contractor: As a general rule, a principal is not liable for the torts of an agent who acts as an independent contractor. The reason for this rule is that the principal lacks control over the work details of the independent contractor. *Murrell v. Goertz,* 597 P.2d 1223 (Okla. App. 1979).

1.   There are a number of exceptions to this rule, usually described as activities involving nondelegable duties. Where a nondelegable duty is involved, the principal is liable for the tortious performance of that duty by an independent contractor.

9

Examples: Violation of an automobile safety statute may be considered a nondelegable duty, even though the violation results from defective repairs by an independent contractor. *Maloney v. Rath,* 69 Cal.2d 442, 71 Cal. Rptr. 897, 445 P.2d 513 (1968) (auto brakes); *contra Hackett v. Perron,* 119 N.H. 419, 402 A.2d 193 (1979). A lessor may owe a nondelegable duty to keep public premises, such as a shopping center, safe for use by the public. *Misiulis v. Milbrand Maint. Corp.,* 52 Mich. App. 494, 218 N.W.2d 68 (1974). An employer may have a nondelegable duty to provide a safe workplace; a carrier to provide safe carriage; a landlord to provide for the safety of common passageways; and a neighbor to provide lateral ground support. *See Restatement (Second) of Torts §§ 416–429.* Risks associated with work involving abnormally dangerous activities are normally nondelegable. *Restatement (Second) of Torts § 427A.*

    a.   If the negligence of the independent contractor is considered collateral, the principal may not be liable even though the activity is one that would otherwise involve a nondelegable duty.

        Example: Routine safety precautions were held in *Clausen v. R. W. Gilbert Construc. Co.,* 309 N.W.2d 462 (Iowa 1981), not to be part of the peculiar risk of a highly dangerous activity.

2.   A principal can be liable for the torts of an independent contractor acting with the apparent authority of the principal.

    Example: A hospital was held liable for the negligence of an emergency room doctor, even though the latter was an independent contractor, since the patient did not select and had no control over the doctor. *Paintsville Hosp. Co. v. Rose,* 683 S.W.2d 255 (Ky. 1985). Similarly, a hospital was held liable for the negligence of an independent-contractor radiologist, selected by the hospital to read X-ray films. *Marek v. Professional Health Serv.,* 179 N.J. Super 433, 432 A.2d 538 (1981).

3.   The label attached to the agent in her contract with the principal will not be determinative of that agent's status vis-à-vis third parties. The court will make its own determination of liability, based on the facts of the case. *Hardy v. Brantley,* 471 So.2d 358 (Miss. 1985) (hospital emergency room doctor). The agreement between the principal and agent may provide for indemnity of the principal by the agent for tortious acts of the latter. Such an agreement may have effect between the principal and agent, but it will not affect the rights of noncontractual third parties against the principal for tortious acts of that agent. *Van Arsdale v. Hollinger,* 68 Cal.2d 245, 66 Cal. Rptr. 20, 437 P.2d 508 (1968).

D. Bailors Including Automobile Owners: The general rule is that a gratuitous bailor is not vicariously liable for the negligence of her bailee. The bailor will of course be liable for her own negligence, however, as, for example, in negligently entrusting a chattel into the hands of an incompetent bailee.

1.   A number of jurisdictions make an exception to the bailment rule for automobiles. One exception is the family-purpose doctrine, by which the head of a household who is a car owner is vicariously liable for torts committed by family members using the car with the owner's consent. This doctrine may exist by common law, *Sale v. Atkins,* 206 Ky. 224, 267 S.W. 223 (1924), or by statute, *White v. Yup,* 85 Nev. 527, 458 P.2d 617 (1969). Other jurisdictions hold the car owner vicariously liable for torts committed with the car by anyone using the car with the owner's permission, even though the use may go beyond the scope of that permission as, for example, by the permittee allowing a subpermittee to drive the car. This vicarious liability is typically imposed by statute, *Shuck v. Means,* 302 Minn. 93, 226 N.W.2d 285 (1974). The

statute may create a presumption of consent by the owner, based on proof of ownership of the car.

a. A jurisdiction may have a consent statute and may apply the family purpose doctrine as well. The number of permittees included under a consent statute is broader than that of the family purpose doctrine.

E. **Liability of Parents for the Torts of Children:** As a general rule parents are not vicariously liable at common law for the torts of their children. This rule has been partially abrogated by statute in a number of jurisdictions, typically by making parents vicariously liable in limited amounts for the intentional torts of their children.

Example: Cal. Civ. Code § 1714.1 makes parents liable up to $10,000 for torts resulting from "willful misconduct" of their children. Louisiana by court decision has abolished the common law rule entirely, making parents liable generally for the tortious misconduct of their children. *Turner v. Bucher,* 308 So.2d 270 (La. 1975).

1. As in other situations, parents may be liable for their own negligence in failing to properly supervise their children. This liability is based on the primary negligence of the parent, rather than on vicarious liability.

    Examples: A parent may be liable in failing to protect other children from a dangerous characteristic of his child, such as bullying. *Linder v. Bidner,* 50 Misc. 2d 320, 270 N.Y.S.2d 427 (1966). He may have a duty to warn others, such as a babysitter, of a known dangerous characteristic of the child. *Ellis v. D'Angelo,* 116 Cal. App. 2d 310, 253 P.2d 675 (1953). He may be negligent in entrusting a dangerous instrument, such as a car, into the hands of a child known to be a reckless driver, *Kahlenberg v. Goldstein,* 290 Md. 477, 431 A.2d 76 (1981), or in leaving a dangerous weapon such as a loaded gun in an unlocked dresser readily accessible to a young child, *Kuhns v. Brugger,* 390 Pa. 331, 135 A.2d 395 (1957).

III. IMPUTED CONTRIBUTORY NEGLIGENCE

IMPUTED CONTRIBUTORY NEGLIGENCE

A. **The "Both-Ways" Rule:** Some courts impute an agent's negligence to the principal when the principal is a plaintiff, rather than a defendant. This imputation is sometimes described as the "both-ways" rule, based on the mechanistic reasoning that whenever the agent's negligence would be imputed to the principal as a defendant, it should also be imputed to the principal as a plaintiff. The imputation is typically made in the employer-employee and joint-enterprise contexts, and some courts also apply the rule in the context of automobile accident claims by the owner-principal against a negligent third party where the driver-agent was also negligent. *See Smalich v. Westfall,* 440 Pa. 409, 269 A.2d 476 (1970). The imputation can also be made in the context of torts of willful misconduct or strict liability.

1. A special situation exists when the plaintiff's claim is considered to be derivative, as in the case of wrongful death or survival claims. Courts in this situation generally impute the negligence of the deceased to the person claiming on behalf of the deceased. The same sort of imputation is typically made in claims for loss of consortium. *Pioneer Constr. Co. v. Bergeron,* 170 Colo. 474, 462 P.2d 589 (1969).

2. If the principal, as defendant, is held vicariously liable to a third party for a tort of her agent, then, typically, the principal can sue the agent in indemnity to recover for the amount of the third-party liability. In such an indemnity claim, the negligence or other tortious misconduct of the agent is not imputed to the principal. *Brown v. Poritzky,* 30 N.Y.2d 289, 332, N.Y.S.2d 872, 283 N.E.2d 751 (1972).

CHAPTER 9 – QUESTIONS, ANSWERS AND TIPS

1. **Q:** Bank hired a security guard without checking his background. The guard had an employment history of violence. The guard shot and killed a Bank customer whom the guard mistakenly suspected of being a Bank robber. Bank is probably liable to customer's estate: (1) vicariously; (2) for negligently hiring the guard; (3) for both negligence and vicarious liability; (4) for neither negligence nor vicarious liability.

    A: (3) for both negligence and vicarious liability.

    Tip: Both (1) and (2) are correct, but only partially so: (3) is the best answer, since the Bank was negligent in hiring and was also vicariously liable for a tort committed by the guard in the scope of his employment, i.e., while acing as a guard and in presumed (though mistaken) furtherance of the Bank's interest.

2. **Q:** The principle of vicarious liability is based on: (1) the employer's right to control the employee; (2) employee acts in furtherance of the employer's interests: (3) employee acts fairly characteristic of the employer's enterprise or activity; (4) all of the above.

    A: (4) all of the above.

    Tip: Look for the most inclusive answer as the best one, as long as that answer does not include irrelevant or wrong information.

3. **Q:** An employer cannot be held vicariously liable for employee acts: (1) committed in violation of an express rule; (2) committed outside the scope of employment; (3) involving the use of deadly force; (4) consisting of the use of employee's automobile as a salesperson.

    A: (2) acts committed outside the scope of employment.

    Tip: There is no clear agreement of what kinds of acts are within or outside the scope of employment. But once an employee's act is labeled outside the scope of employment, there is no employer vicarious liability.

4. **Q:** A principal is not liable for the acts of an independent contractor where those acts involve: (1) a nondelegable duty of the principal; (2) acts of an independent contractor acting with apparent authority of the principal; (3) acts of an independent contractor for which the principal has disclaimed liability by agreement with the contractor; (4) collateral negligence of the contractor.

    A: (4) collateral negligence of the contractor.

    Tip: Read the question carefully. A principal *is* liable for acts (1) through (3), but the questions asks you to identify the type of activities for which the principal is *not* liable.

5. **Q:** In which of the following situations can a person not be found vicariously liable: (1) acts of the person's child; (2) use of the person's car by another with consent of the person; (3) both (1) and (2) above; (4) a person's negligent entrustment of a chattel into the hands of an incompetent gratuitous bailee.

    A: (4) a person's negligent entrustment of a chattel into the hands of an incompetent gratuitous bailee.

Tip: In (1) through (3) there *can* be vicarious liability, dependent on the law of the jurisdiction. But there *cannot* be vicarious liability of a person for her own negligent conduct. Such liability, by definition, is based on negligence and not vicarious liability.

6. **Q:**   The contributory negligence of an agent is usually not imputed to the principal (1) when the principal is sued for the negligence of an agent acting within the scope of her employment; (2) when a wife sues a third party for loss of consortium resulting from injuries to her husband, whose negligence contributed to the injuries; (3) when a principal sues her agent in indemnity for liability vicariously incurred by the principal to a third party as a result of the agent's negligence; (4) when an employer sues a third party for damages to the employer caused by the concurrent negligence of the third party and of the employee acting within the scope of her employment.

   A: (3) when a principal sues her agent in indemnity for liability vicariously incurred by the principal to a third party as a result of the agent's negligence.

   Tip: Fault of an employee or of a spouse is usually, although not always, attributed to the employer where the principal sues, or is sued, for the fault of an employee, and where a spouse sues for loss of consortium. Be aware however that, even if fault of an agent is not attributed to the principal as plaintiff, the plaintiff's recovery may nevertheless be reduced by the fault of the agent in a jurisdiction applying several, as opposed to joint and several, liability.

9

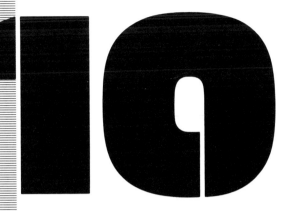

LIABLITY FOR ANIMALS AND FOR ABNORMALLY DANGEROUS ACTIVITIES

▶ **CHAPTER SUMMARY**

STRICT LIABILITY FOR ANIMALS AND FOR ABNORMALLY DANGEROUS ACTIVITIES

Scope of Chapter: Typically strict liability for animals and strict liability for abnormally dangerous activities are treated together in a torts course. This is probably because the holding in the seminal case in this area, *Rylands v. Fletcher,* [1868] L.R. 3 E. & I. App. 330 (H.L.), involving strict liability for escaping waters from a reservoir, is based in part on the longstanding strict liability for harm caused by trespassing animals and by wild animals. It should be borne in mind, however, that the rules applicable to strict liability for animals are not the same as those for abnormally dangerous activities. The liability in each situation is fact-specific.

10

ANIMALS

I. ANIMALS

A. **Trespassing Livestock:** The general rule is that the possessor of livestock is strictly liable for foreseeable damages caused by the trespass of such animals onto the land of another. Exceptions to this rule are: (1) harm done by animals straying onto *abutting* land while being driven on the highway; and (2) harm done by trespassing animals where the applicable common law or statute requires the person whose land is intruded upon to erect and maintain a fence to prevent the intrusion of livestock. In the first instance, the livestock owner will be liable only if she is *at fault* in not preventing the intrusion onto the land abutting the highway, but she will be *strictly liable* if such straying livestock continue beyond the abutting land to more remote land.

Example: *D's* cattle, while being driven along the highway, inadvertently stray onto the land of *A,* and from thence onto the land of *B. D* is strictly liable for damage done to *B's* land by the cattle, since *D* must retrieve the cattle with all reasonable speed and if he fails to do so it is at his peril.

In the case where a fencing statute applies, the landowner cannot be heard to complain if she fails to erect or maintain adequate fences. If the livestock break through an adequately maintained fence, however, then their owner may be liable for resulting damage. *Restatement (Second) of Torts* § 504, comm. *l.*

1. The term "livestock" is used for purposes of this rule to "denote those kinds of domestic animals and fowls normally susceptible of confinement within boundaries without seriously impairing their utility and the intrusion of which on the land of others normally causes harm to the land or to crops thereon." The term includes "horses, cattle, pigs and sheep and also poultry, unless by custom poultry are permitted to run at large." It does not include "dogs and cats, which are difficult to restrain and unlikely to do any substantial harm by their intrusion." *Restatement (Second) of Torts* § 504, comm. *b.* There may be liability for harm caused by dogs or cats, however, under principles hereafter considered, as, for example, if the animal is known to be vicious or if a statute imposes liability for harm done by such animals.

2. *Restatement (Second) of Torts* § 504(3)(c) states that there is no liability for harm caused by trespassing livestock "brought about by the unexpectable operation of a force of nature, action of another animal or intentional, reckless or negligent conduct of a third person."

   Examples: *B's* cattle escape onto *A's* land because lightning strikes the fence and destroys part of it, or because the fence is destroyed by an automobile negligently driven by *C.* In neither situation is *B* strictly liable for harm done to *A. Id.,* comm. *i, illus.* 3-4.

   This rule is superseding cause for trespassing livestock should be compared with the rule as applied to wild animals and abnormally dangerous activities. The position of the *Restatement* is that unforeseeability is no defense in the latter two situations. *Restatement (Second) of Torts* §§ 510, 522. Some cases, however, impose a foreseeability requirement for abnormally dangerous activities.

B. Domestic Animals: The traditional rule, except for trespassing livestock, is that one who owns or harbors a domestic animal, including birds and insects, is not strictly liable for damage done by such an animal. He can be held strictly liable, however, for harm caused by such an animal if he knows or has reason to know that the animal is "abnormally dangerous" and the harm results from such an abnormally dangerous characteristic. *Restatement (Second) of Torts* § 518. An animal is abnormally dangerous if it is "vicious," or "has a tendency to attack human beings or other animals that is abnormal in animals of its class. *Restatement (Second) of Torts* § 509, comm. *c.*" A domestic animal for this purpose is termed as one "that is by custom devoted to the service of mankind at the time and in the place in which it is kept." The fact that the animal, bird, or insect "is incapable of effective control does not affect its classification as a domestic animal. Thus, bees are not wild animals although it is impossible to confine them to the land on which their hives are situated." *Restatement (Second) of Torts* § 506(2) and comm. *b* thereto. Nor should they be considered trespassers, since by custom they are free to roam as they like.

1. The rule stated in *Restatement (Second) of Torts* § 518 may be varied by statute. In some jurisdictions, for example, the owner of a dog is held strictly liable for damage caused by the dog, regardless of whether the owner knows or has reason to know of the dog's abnormally dangerous propensity. *See, e.g., Henry v. Brown,* 495 A.2d 324 (Maine 1985).

C. Wild Animals: The general rule is that one who owns or harbors a wild animal is strictly liable for harm done by the animal resulting from "a dangerous propensity that is characteristic of wild animals of the particular class" or resulting from a dangerous characteristic "of which the possessor knows or has reason to know." *Restatement (Second) of Torts* § 507. A wild animal for this purpose is defined as one "that is not by custom devoted to the service of mankind at the time and in the place in which it is kept." *Id.* § 506(1). This liability continues for harm done even after the animal escapes from its possessor, "no matter how long after its escape" the harm occurs, unless (1) someone else takes possession of the animal, or (2) the animal returns "to its natural state as a wild animal indigenous to the locality." *Restatement (Second) of Torts* § 507, comm. *d,* § 508.

1. *Restatement (Second) of Torts* § 510 says that the possessor of a wild animal may be held strictly liable for harm caused by the animal even though the harm would not have occurred "but for the unexpectable (a) innocent, negligent or reckless conduct of a third person, or (b) action of another animal, or (c) operation of a force of nature." This rule should be compared with that concerning superseding cause with regard to domestic animals, given above, and abnormally dangerous activities, given below.

2. There are special rules given in the *Restatement* regarding the liability of wild animal possessors toward trespassers and towards persons guilty of contributory fault or assumption of risk and of possessors of wild animals pursuant to a duty imposed upon the possessor as a public officer or employee or as a common carrier. These rules may not, however, be followed by courts today.

   a. The *Restatement* says that the wild-animal possessor is not subject to strict liability for damage done by the animal to one who intentionally or negligently trespasses upon the land of the possessor. He is, however, liable to the trespasser for *negligence,* to the same extent as he is "for other artificial conditions or for activities on the land." *Restatement (Second) of Torts* §§ 511, 512. He may also be liable in negligence to frequent trespassers of whom he knows or should know and to small children in the vicinity. *Id.* § 512, comm. *c.* He can be held strictly liable to licensees and invitees. *Id.* § 513. He is privileged to employ a watchdog only to the extent that he is privileged "to use a mechanical protective device." *Id.* § 516. *See* in this connection Chapter 2 on Intentional Torts, dealing with spring guns. Moreover, with the breakdown of the distinctions among trespassers, licensees, and invitees for purposes of determining the landowner's duty of care, there may be a similar breakdown for purposes of determining the strict liability of a possessor of wild animals.

b. In *Restatement (Second) of Torts* § 515, it is stated that ordinary contributory negligence of a plaintiff is no defense to the strict liability of the possessor of a wild animal or of an abnormally dangerous domestic animal, but that plaintiff's contributory negligence "in knowingly and unreasonably subjecting himself to the risk" is a defense. Likewise, the knowing and *reasonable* assumption of a risk may be a defense.

Example: "Thus an employee may quite reasonably agree to work with a slightly unreliable horse, whose characteristics are known to the owner; and if he is injured as a result, he may be barred from recovery by his assumption of the risk." *Restatement (Second) of Torts* § 515, comm. *e.*

With the widespread adoption of comparative fault or comparative responsibility for negligence and for strict products liability, including comparison of plaintiff's ordinary contributory negligence and unreasonable assumption of the risk, it seems likely that such a comparative approach will also be adopted for strict liability for animals — as well as for abnormally dangerous activities, considered below. In a case of true consent, however, whether reasonable or unreasonable, the courts are likely even under comparative fault to consider such consent as a complete bar to liability.

c. *Restatement (Second) of Torts* § 517 states that the rules of strict liability for dangerous animals "do not apply when the possession of the animal is in pursuance of a duty imposed upon the possessor as a public officer or employee or as a common carrier." As will be seen below, this rule is not uniformly followed with regard to abnormally dangerous activities, and it seems likely, therefore, that it may not be uniformly followed with regard to abnormally dangerous animals. Similarly, there is a division of authority as to whether zoo keepers and the like are strictly liable for harm caused by the zoo animals. *See Isaacs v. Powell,* 267 So. 2d 864 (Fla. App. 1972).

II. ABNORMALLY DANGEROUS ACTIVITIES

ABNORMALLY DANGEROUS ACTIVITIES

A. **Origin and Development of the Doctrine:** The doctrine of strict liability for abnormally dangerous activities derives from *Rylands v. Fletcher,* discussed at the beginning of this chapter. There the court based strict liability on the concept of a "nonnatural use" of one's land. This concept was picked up by the first *Restatement of Torts* § 520 and described in terms of an "ultrahazardous activity" that "necessarily involves a risk of serious harm" which "cannot be eliminated by the exercise of the utmost care" and which is "not a matter of common usage." The *Restatement (Second)* changed the concept to one of "abnormal danger," which takes into account the degree and likelihood of risk, the actor's inability to eliminate the risk by the exercise of reasonable care, whether or not the activity is a matter of common usage, and also the "inappropriateness of the activity to the place where it is carried on" and the extent to which the value of the activity to the community "is outweighed by its dangerous attributes." *Restatement (Second) of Torts* § 520. If the activity is found to be appropriate to its location and its value to the community outweighs its danger, then a court may find the activity not abnormally dangerous. *New Meadows Hold. Co. v. Wash. Water Power Co.,* 102 Wash. 2d 495, 687 P.2d 212 (1984) (no liability of natural gas company for escape of gas caused by telephone company damage to gas pipeline). See the comparison, at the beginning of the products liability chapter, of strict products liability with strict liability for abnormally dangerous activities.

1. The prototypical activities giving rise to strict liability for abnormal danger are blasting and storage of explosives. Beyond these activities, there is no consensus on what kinds of harmful conduct will give rise to strict liability. Some, but not all, courts impose strict liability for damage caused by crop-spraying. Similarly, there is a division of authority as to strict liability

for the storage of flammable liquids, the use of flammable gases, and land damage from falling aircraft.

    a.   The courts are almost uniform in holding that there is no strict liability for the manufacture and sale of handguns. *Burkett v. Freedom Arms, Inc.,* 299 Or. 551, 704 P.2d 118 (1985). A Maryland court imposed strict liability for handguns described as "Saturday Night Specials," *Kelley v. R. G. Indus., Inc.,* 304 Md. 124, 497 A.2d 1143 (1985), but that decision was reversed by statute. Md. Code Annot. Art. 27, § 36F (1988). There seems to be a consensus that regulation of the manufacture and sale of handguns is a matter peculiarly appropriate for the legislature.

10

2.   It is not necessary that each of the factors enumerated in the *Restatement* be present in order for strict liability to be imposed, "especially if others weigh heavily." *Restatement (Second) of Torts* § 520, comm. *f.* The court in *Clark-Aiken Co. v. Cromwell-Wright Co.,* 367 Mass. 70, 323 N.E. 2d 876 (1975) (escaping waters caused by collapsed wall) held, for example, that the plaintiff could sue in strict liability even though the facts would also support a claim in negligence.

    a.   The court in *Luthringer v. Moore,* 31 Cal. 2d 489, 190 P.2d 1 (1948), dealt with the issue of defining an uncommon activity. Strict liability was imposed there for injury resulting from fumigation of a building with hydrocyanic gas for pest control. The court found such fumigations to be an uncommon usage. "[I]t may be commonly used by fumigators, but they are relatively few in number and are engaged in a specialized activity," the court said. Other courts impose strict liability even though the activity is considered to be a common activity.

        Example: Strict liability was imposed for damages resulting from the common activity of crop-dusting in *Loe v. Lenhardt,* 227 Or. 242, 362 P.2d 312 (1961).

    b.   Appropriateness of the activity to its location is used by some courts to deny the application of strict liability, as in *New Meadows v. Wash. Water Power,* considered above. Conversely, if the location of the activity is inappropriate, the court may impose strict liability. *Yommer v. McKenzie,* 255 Md. 220, 257 A.2d 138 (1969) (strict liability for gasoline station storage-tank leakage in residential area contaminating drinking water). Still other courts impose strict liability even if the activity is considered appropriate to the location. For these courts, the dangerousness of the activity is the most important factor.

        Examples: Strict liability was imposed for damages resulting from hauling explosives in *Chavez v. So. Pacific Transp. Co.,* 413 F. Supp. 1203 (E.D. Cal. 1976), and for damages resulting from escaping fire of a field-burning in *Koos v. Roth,* 293 Or. 670, 652 P.2d 1255 (1982), even though both activities were considered appropriate to the location.

B. Defenses: There is a division of authority as to whether unforeseeable acts of third parties or of nature constitute a defense.

Examples: In *Golden v. Amory,* 329 Mass. 484, 109 N.E.2d 131 (1952), the court refused to impose strict liability for water damage from a dike overflow caused by an unforeseeable hurricane. By contrast, the *Restatement (Second) of Torts* § 522 provides strict liability for harm from abnormally dangerous activity even though the harm is caused by an unexpectable act of a third person or animal or force of nature. Pursuant to the Price-Anderson Act, 42 U.S.C. § 2210, the Nuclear Regulatory Commission provides strict liability for harm resulting from a nuclear-reactor accident even though the accident is caused by unforeseeable intervening causes "whether involving the conduct of a third person, or an act of God." 10 C.F.R. § 140.91.

10

1. *Restatement (Second) of Torts* § 524A states that there is no strict liability for abnormally dangerous activity if the harm results from "the abnormally sensitive character of the plaintiff's activity."

   Examples: There was no liability for damages from blasting, the vibration from which caused plaintiff's abnormally sensitive mother mink to kill their whelp. *Foster v. Preston Mill Co.,* 44 Wash.2d 440, 268 P.2d 645 (1954). But compare *MacGibbon v. Robinson,* [1953] 2 D.L.R. 689, where liability was imposed on the defendant for firing a stumping blast on his land during the whelping season of plaintiff's mink on a neighboring farm, resulting in damages as in *Foster v. Preston Mill Co.* The *MacGibbon* court found that the defendant well knew the probable consequences to plaintiff's mink from the blasting, and that the defendant had no need to fire the blast at that particular time.

3. The *Restatement* takes the position that as a general rule there is no strict liability for harm caused to unforeseen trespassers by abnormally dangerous activity. *Restatement (Second) of Torts* § 520B. As discussed above with regard to wild animals, this rule may change with the breakdown of distinctions among trespassers, licensees, and invitees. On the other hand, to the extent that strict liability for abnormally dangerous activity turns on the escape of a dangerous instrumentality from the defendant's property, the defendant might not be strictly liable to entrants on the property. *See Read v. J. Lyons & Co.,* [1947] A.C. 156 (H.L. 1946) (no strict liability imposed for explosion in defendant's munitions plant injuring a government inspector, since nothing "escaped" from defendant's land).

4. The *Restatement* takes the same position regarding plaintiff's contributory negligence and assumption of the risk for abnormally dangerous activity as it does for the possession of wild animals. *See Restatement (Second) of Torts* §§ 523–524. The same reservations about this position apply here as in the case of wild animals, as discussed above.

5. *Restatement (Second) of Torts* § 521 states that there is no strict liability for harm by an abnormally dangerous activity "if the activity is carried on in pursuance of a public duty imposed upon the actor as a public officer or employee or as a common carrier." Not all courts follow this rule, however.

   Example: Strict liability was imposed on a common carrier for resulting damage when eighteen bomb-loaded boxcars exploded in defendant's railway yard. The court saw no reason to create a common-carrier or public-duty exception to strict liability, since the defendant was capable of distributing the loss to the public. Moreover, whether the carrier was "free to reject or bound to take the explosive cargo, the plaintiffs are equally defenseless." *Chavez v. So. Pacif. Transp. Co.,* 413 F. Supp. 1203 (E.D. Cal. 1976).

6. The term "foreseeability" is used in two senses: (1) foreseeability of external events, and (2) foreseeability of harm involved in the activity itself. The courts divide on whether foreseeability in the second sense is required to impose strict liability for abnormally dangerous activities.

CHAPTER 10 – QUESTIONS, ANSWERS AND TIPS

1. **Q:** Owner kept in her house a pet boa constrictor, which escaped from its pen. Owner was unable to find the animal. She sold her house to buyer six months after the snake's escape. After buyer moved in, the boa, which had been hiding in the walls of the house, came out and choked buyer's baby. Does baby, or her guardian or estate, have a good strict liability claim against owner?

   A: Yes, the snakes's escape and the subsequent lapse of time will not excuse owner from strict liability for the harm caused by her wild animal, which still belonged to her since it had not returned to its natural habitat and no one else had taken possession of it.

   Tip: The snake is not a domestic animal, because it is not devoted to the service of mankind. Buyer was not the possessor of the animal, since knowing possession is required for purposes of the strict liability of an owner or harborer of a wild animal.

2. **Q:** John, unbeknownst to a municipal zoo, entered the zoo's lion cage and was mauled by the lion. Is zoo strictly liable to John?

   A: Zoo may only owe a duty of care, either because it is a zoo or because John is a trespasser. There is a division of authority on both issues. John may be barred from recovery by consent, or his recovery may be reduced by assumption of the risk under comparative fault.

   Tip: There is no clear line between consent and assumption of the risk, so you can point out that a court might find either to exist. Comparative fault has been widely adopted and will likely apply in strict liability.

3. **Q:** A hurricane caused water to escape from owner's abandoned well into the nearby aquifer. The water, unbeknownst to and through no fault of owner, had become contaminated with poisonous chemicals and as a result neighbor's water supply became contaminated. Is owner strictly liable to neighbor for the water contamination?

   A: There is a division of authority (a) whether intervening events must be foreseeable and (b) whether the abnormally dangerous nature of an activity must be foreseeable. A court might require foreseeability for (a) but not for (b), or vice versa. Unlike *Rylands*, involving a large storage of water, the maintenance of a well would probably not be considered an abnormal or unnatural activity. A hurricane might be foreseeable, depending on the time and location, while the breakage of the well by the hurricane might not be.

   Tip: Foreseeability of use, and foreseeability of danger of an activity, are not always distinguished by the courts although they are clearly different concepts. In products liability, for example, foreseeability of danger of a product is often not required while foreseeability of use normally is. Note that the occurrence of a hurricane might be foreseeable, while the type of damage caused might not be.

10

NOTES

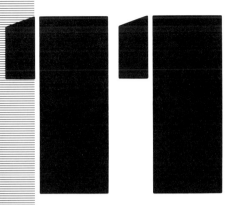

PRODUCTS LIABILITY

▶ **CHAPTER SUMMARY**

PRODUCTS LIABILITY

Scope of Chapter: The law of products liability applies to the sale, lease, or supply of defective products that cause damage. If the seller, lessor, or supplier is in the business of providing the product, he can be sued in strict liability (tort or warranty) and also for fault (negligence or intentional misconduct). If he is only a casual (not a regular) seller of the product, then strict liability does not apply unless the plaintiff suffers injury or damage as a result of the breach of an express warranty or of an implied warranty of fitness. The express warranty and the implied warranty of fitness provisions of the Uniform Commercial Code, §§ 2-313 and 2-315, do not require the warranter to be a business supplier of the product.

11

Strict products liability should be distinguished from strict liability for abnormally dangerous conduct, as set forth in *Restatement (Second) of Torts* § 519 *et seq.* Abnormally dangerous conduct involves activities such as blasting, crop-spraying, water storage (*Rylands v. Fletcher,* [1868] L.R. 3 E. & I. App. 330 (H.L.)), keeping wild animals, and the like, where the actor is held strictly liable for damages resulting from his activity; abnormally dangerous conduct may be an uncommon activity, one inappropriate to the location, or not socially useful, and it may involve a high degree of risk that generally cannot be eliminated by the exercise of due care. *Restatement (Second) of Torts* § 520. Products liability, on the other hand, focuses on the manufacture and sale of products that are in some way defective or that do not match the defendant's representations. *Restatement (Second) of Torts* §§ 402A– 402B; U.C.C. §§ 2-313 through 2-315.

These two bodies of strict liability law may occasionally overlap.

Example: In *Perez v. Southern Pacific Transp. Co.*, 180 Ariz. 187, 883 P. 2d 424 (1993), the court held that the activity of distributing asbestos could be an abnormally dangerous activity, and that marketing the asbestos product could be a basis for imposing products liability. The product may have been defective because of failure to warn, or because the risk outweighed the utility of the product, *O'Brien v. Muskin Corp.*, 94 N.J. 169, 463 A.2d. 298 (1993). The activity may have been abnormally dangerous because of its high degree of risk.

THEORIES OF RECOVERY

I.   THEORIES OF RECOVERY

A.   **Tort and Warranty:** A suit in products liability can typically be brought in both negligence and strict liability. *MacPherson v. Buick Motor Co.,* 217 N.Y. 382, 111 N.E. 1050 (1916); *Greenman v. Yuba Power Products Inc.,* 59 Cal.2d 57, 27 Cal. Rptr. 697, 377 P.2d 897 (1963). In many jurisdictions, the strict liability claim can be brought in either tort, *Greenman supra*, or warranty which is normally considered a remedy for breach of contract. *Henningsen v. Bloomfield Motors, Inc.,* 32 N.J. 358, 161 A.2d 69 (1960).

1.   If the defendant's injurious conduct is reckless, willful, or wanton, or in callous disregard of the interests of the public, the defendant can be held liable for punitive as well as compensatory damages.

Example: In *Grimshaw v. Ford Motor Co.,* 119 Cal. App. 3d 757, 174 Cal. Rptr. 348 (1981), the defendant was held liable for $2.5 million compensatory and $3.5 million punitive damages for knowingly manufacturing an automobile with inadequate fuel tank protection against rear-end collisions.

2.   In a negligence action, the plaintiff must prove that the defendant failed to exercise reasonable care in its production or marketing of the product or in its representations concerning the product. A products liability negligence action is not significantly different from any other type of negligence action. The hallmark of modern products litigation is the action in strict liability, whether in warranty or tort.

3. If a claim is brought for breach of warranty, various contractual or warranty restrictions may be imposed on the claim. These include privity of contract (particularly where pure economic loss is sought), notice of breach, the warranty statute of limitations, and the enforceability of disclaimers and limitations of remedy. There are three basic warranty theories: (1) the implied warranty of merchantability, or of fitness for the ordinary purposes for which such goods are used, made by a seller engaged in the business of selling a product, U.C.C. § 2-314(2)(c); (2) the implied warranty of fitness for a particular purpose, where the seller has reason to know that the buyer is relying on the seller's skill or judgment to select or furnish goods suitable for a particular purpose, U.C.C. § 2-315; and (3) an express warranty, that is, an affirmation of fact or a promise made by a seller which relates to the goods and which is made a part of the basis of the bargain, U.C.C. § 2-313.

4. A claim in strict tort can be viewed as grounded on either an implied or an express representation of safety. The doctrinal foundation often used for *implied* strict tort liability is *Restatement (Second) of Torts* § 402A, which states that a seller engaged in the business of selling a product is strictly liable for physical harm to person or property caused by his sale of the product in an unreasonably dangerous and defective condition. *Restatement (Second) of Torts* § 402B is used to impose *express* strict tort liability. That section states that a seller engaged in the business of selling a product is strictly liable for personal harm caused by justifiable reliance on a public misrepresentation made by the seller concerning the character or quality of the product. Under Restatement (Third) of Torts: Products Liability *§* 9 a business seller can be held strictly liable in tort for a misrepresentation resulting in harm to either person or property, without regard to whether the misrepresentation is made to the public.

II. BASES OF RECOVERY

A. **Types of Defect:** There are basically four types of product failures that can give rise to an action in products liability. They are: (1) a manufacturing or production defect or flaw, where a product randomly fails to meet manufacturing or production standards, *e.g.,* a burr in a can of peas; (2) a design defect; (3) a failure to warn or an inadequate warning; and (4) a misrepresentation regarding the character or quality of a product.

1. A production flaw can occur as the result of negligence.

   Examples: Res ipsa loquitur was applied in *Escola v. Coca Cola Bottl. Co.,* 24 Cal.2d 453, 150 P.2d 436 (1944), to the manufacturer's failure to discover a defect in the bottle or the bottling process of a Coca Cola. In *MacPherson v. Buick Motor Co.,* 217 N.Y. 382, 111 N.E. 1050 (1916), the assembler of an automobile was found negligent in failing to discover defective wood in the spokes of one of the automobile wheels.

   a. Strict liability, in tort or warranty, can also be imposed for a production flaw.

      Example: The seller of baby chickens infected with scientifically undetectable avian leukosis was held strictly liable in *Vlases v. Montgomery Ward & Co.,* 377 F.2d 846 (3d Cir. 1967). Some courts may, however, allow a defense in strict liability for production defects, as well as for defects in warning or design, if the product as manufactured complies with the state of the art or is unavoidably unsafe. State of the art is frequently defined as "the state of scientific and technological knowledge available to the manufacturer or seller at the time the product was placed on the market." Tenn. Code Annot. § 29-28-105(b). A product is unavoidably unsafe, according to comment *k* to *Restatement (Second) of Torts* § 402A, if, given "the present state of human knowledge," a useful product is "incapable of being made safe" for its intended and ordinary use and is "properly prepared, and accompanied by proper directions and warnings." California allows the unavoidably-unsafe defense to be asserted with regard to all prescription drug products. *Brown v. The Superior Court (Abbot Laboratories),* 44 Cal.3d 1049, 245 Cal. Rptr. 412, 751 P.2d 470 (1988).

2. A design defect arises when a whole line of products is unacceptably unsafe. Unsafeness for this purpose can be measured by a standard of whether a safer product could have been designed so as to avoid the accident, without excessive cost or excessive sacrifice of product utility. *See Wilson v. Piper Aircraft Corp.,* 282 Or. 61, 577 P.2d 1322 (1978): Restatement (Third) of Torts: Products Liability § 2(b). Some courts indicate, however, that a product may be considered defectively designed if the risk of harm outweighs the utility of the product, without regard to whether a safer alternative design is feasible or practical. *See O'Brien v. Muskin Corp.,* 94 N.J. 169, 463 A.2d 298 (1983). The New York Court of Appeals in *Denny v. Ford Motor Co.*, 662 N.E.2d 730 (N.Y. App. 1995), held that a design claim could be brought on the basis of both risk-utility and consumer expectations.

   a. Many courts say that a design defect case, at least when brought against the product manufacturer, is essentially a suit in negligence whether or not strict liability in tort or warranty is alleged. Since "the unreasonableness of the danger must be determined by the potential available to the designer at the time of design, it is apparent that the strict liability and negligence claims merge." *Balido v. Improved Machinery, Inc.,* 29 Cal. App. 3d 633, 105 Cal. Rptr. 890 (1972). Such a merger need not occur, however, since a safer design may be available even though the designer had no reason to know and in the exercise of reasonable care should not have known of its availability at the time of manufacture. In addition, a number of courts permit evidence of postsale improvements in the design of a product, in order to show the "feasibility of precautionary measures, if controverted." Fed. R. Evid. 407; *Ault v. Internat'l Harv. Co.,* 13 Cal.3d 113, 117 Cal. Rptr. 812, 528 P.2d 1148 (1974). The admission of such knowable or available *at the time of manufacture.* Moreover, in a design claim brought against a nonmanufacturing seller, such as a wholesaler or retailer, it normally would not be contended that such a defendant had reason to know or should have known of a safer design at the time that defendant marketed the product. Some courts, as in *Dart v. Wiebe Mfg., Inc.,* 147 Ariz. 242, 709 P.2d 876 (1985), hold that a design claim can be brought in strict tort liability.

3. A product may be safely designed and may contain no production defect and still be defective because it carries no warning, or carries an inadequate warning, of the dangers associated with use of the product.

   Example: Defendant was held liable in *Boyl v. Cal. Chem. Co.,* 221 F. Supp. 669 (D. Or. 1963), for failure to warn of the long-lasting effects of its highly toxic chemical weed killer, where plaintiff poured the residue of the chemical on her grass and was severely burned by the chemical while sunbathing on the grass five days later.

   a. Claims of failure to warn, or failure to warn adequately, are not limited to situations where the product is safely designed. It is very common for the plaintiff to allege defective design and inadequate warning as alternative bases for recovery in the same lawsuit.

   Example: In *Phillips v. Kimwood Mach. Co.,* 269 Or. 485, 525 P.2d 1033 (1974), plaintiff alleged that defendant's sanding machine was defective because it lacked a safety device to prevent regurgitation of boards that were being sanded, and also because the defendant failed to warn of the danger involved in feeding boards into the machine manually.

b. Product defectiveness based on the absence or inadequacy of a warning resembles a design defect, since in either case a whole product line is usually affected. For the same reasons given in the design cases, many courts assert that a product claim based on failure to warn is essentially one in negligence, regardless of whether the claim is made in warranty or strict tort liability. *See Borel v. Fibreboard Paper Products Corp.,* 493 F.2d 1076 (5th Cir. 1973). Other courts, as in *Sternhagan v. Dow Co.,* 935 P.2d 1139 (Mont. 1997), hold that a claim for failure to warn can be brought in strict tort liability.

c. On the other hand, if a product is defectively designed, a manufacturer may not be able to discharge its duty merely by warning of the danger. *Rogers v. Ingersoll-Rand Co.,* 144 F.3d 841 (D. C. Cir. 1998). The reason for this rule is that a consumer may foreseeably disregard a warning of an unreasonable danger, which a redesign of the product could eliminate.

d. A product can be defective because of the defendant's failure to warn of dangers which it discovered or should have discovered after the product has been marketed. *Braniff Airways, Inc. v. Curtiss-Wright Corp.,* 411 F.2d 451 (2d Cir. 1969). This postsale duty to warn is widely characterized as one in negligence. If such a warning is likely to be insufficient, then the defendant may have an additional duty to recall or repair the product. *Gracyalny v. Westinghouse Elec. Corp.,* 723 F.2d 1311 (7th Cir. 1983). A duty of recall may be imposed by statute, as under the Nat'l Traffic and Motor Vehicle Safety Act.

4. Whether or not a product is defectively manufactured or designed, or lacks an adequate warning, a defendant product supplier may also be liable for resulting injuries if it misrepresents a quality or characteristic of its product. This liability for misrepresentation can be based on deceit, negligence, express warranty, or strict tort.

a. In a strict liability claim based on breach of express warranty, U.C.C. § 2-313, or on tortious misrepresentation, *Restatement (Second) of Torts* § 402B, it is widely held that defendant's knowledge or reason to know of the danger is irrelevant. *See Crocker v. Winthrop Labs,* 514 S.W.2d 429 (Tex. 1974). Whatever may be said about other bases of recovery in products liability, misrepresentation provides a basis of strict liability recovery for which evidence of due care and even of compliance with the state of the art should be no defense. There need be no defect, other than the misrepresentation which provides the basis for plaintiff's expectations with regard to the product. In this respect, strict products liability for misrepresentation resembles strict liability for a seller's breach of the implied warranty of fitness for a particular purpose, as set forth in U.C.C. § 2-315.

b. There is a divergence of authority as to whether, and to what extent, the plaintiff must prove reliance in order to recover for misrepresentation. The court in *Cunningham v. C.R. Pease House Furn. Co.,* 74 N.H. 435, 69 A. 120 (1908), indicated that a negligent misrepresentation must be shown to induce plaintiff's purchase of the goods in order to be actionable. Other courts indicate that the misrepresentation must induce the use of the goods. *Amer. Safety Equip. Corp. v. Winkler,* 640 P. 2d 216 (Colo. 1982) [*Restatement (Second) of Torts* § 402B]. Comm. *j* to *Restatement (Second) of Torts* § 402B states that the reliance required under that section "need not necessarily be that of the consumer who is injured," but "may be that of the ultimate purchaser" who because of such reliance passes the product on to the consumer that is injured. U.C.C. § 2-313 states only that the express warranty must be a part of the "basis of the bargain" in order to be actionable. One court has interpreted this phrase to mean that the plaintiff must show that she had "read, seen or heard" the express warranty, with the defendant then being permitted to show by way of defense that the plaintiff "did not believe the safety assurances contained therein." *Cipollone v. Liggett Group, Inc.,* 893 F.2d 541 (3d Cir. 1990) (cigarette case).

III. DEFINITIONS OF DEFECTIVENESS

A. **Multiple Definitions:** One of the most widely used definitions of product defectiveness is that based on ordinary consumer expectations. As stated in comm. *i* to *Restatement (Second) of Torts* § 402A: "The article sold must be dangerous to an extent beyond that which would be contemplated by the ordinary consumer who purchases it, with the ordinary knowledge common to the community as to its characteristics." This definition works reasonably well in some cases, such as those involving ordinary production flaws and warnings that are inadequate as a matter of common knowledge. *Soule v. General Motors. Corp.,* 882 P.2d 298 (Cal. 1994). In other, more complex cases expert testimony may be required to establish consumer expectations. *Karns v. Emerson Elec. Co.,* 817 F.2d 1452 (10th Cir. 1987).

1. Other courts have used a definition of *presumed* seller knowledge. A product under this definition is considered defective or unreasonably dangerous if a reasonably prudent manufacturer or seller would not put it on the market, assuming he knew of its dangerous condition. One court has said that this definition is essentially the same as that based on ordinary consumer expectations "because a seller acting reasonably would be selling the same product which a reasonable consumer believes he is purchasing." *Phillips v. Kimwood Mach. Co.,* 269 Or. 485, 525 P.2d 1033 (1974).

2. A definition of defectiveness widely used in design litigation is that of risk-utility analysis. The usefulness of the product is weighed against the risk of danger it creates. In determining usefulness, the availability of substitute products, the manufacturer's ability to eliminate the risk without undue cost or sacrifice of utility, and his ability to spread the loss through pricing or insurance, are considered. In determining risk, the user's anticipated awareness of, and ability to avoid, the danger are considered. *Roach v. Kononen,* 269 Or. 457, 525 P.2d 125 (1974).

3. If the defendant represents his product to be of a certain character or quality, then the plaintiff may recover for injuries proximately resulting from the failure of the product to comply with that representation. The representation itself sets the standard by which the product is judged. *Huebert v. Fed. Pacif. Elec. Co.,* 208 Kan. 720, 494 P.2d 1210 (1972).

IV. THE PARTIES

A. **Possible Plaintiffs and Defendants:** One of the areas of substantial and continuing growth in products liability is that of possible plaintiffs and defendants. The growth here parallels that regarding the variety of transactions covered by products liability, considered in the next section.

1. For many years, privity of contract was generally required between plaintiff and defendant as a condition to recovering for injuries resulting from the sale of a defective product. This requirement was eliminated for an action in negligence in the landmark case of *MacPherson v. Buick Motor Co., supra;* it was eliminated for warranty actions in *Henningsen v. Bloomfield Motors, supra;* and a hallmark of strict tort liability, as established in *Greenman v. Yuba Power Products, supra,* is the elimination of the privity requirement. Today, except in cases involving economic loss for which privity of contract may still be required, typically any foreseeable plaintiff can recover for damages caused by a defective product.

2. Any supplier of a defective product, or of a defective part of a product, may be liable for damages caused by the defect in the product or part, provided that defect was present in the

product or part when it left the supplier's hands and was not unforeseeably altered or changed before the injury occurred. In addition, certifiers of product safety and franchisers of product use can be held liable for injuries traceable to the certification or to the franchiser's control of the product. *Hanberry v. Hearst Corp.,* 276 Cal. App. 2d 680, 81 Cal. Rptr. 519 (1969) (negligent certification); *City of Hartford v. Assoc. Constr. Co.,* 34 Conn. Supp. 204, 384 A.2d 390 (1978) (franchiser strict liability).

    a.   Some courts may relieve nonmanufacturing sellers from strict liability. Auctioneers are typically not held strictly liable. Retailers and wholesalers may also be relieved from strict liability or they may be relieved from such liability where the manufacturer is solvent and subject to suit.

    3.   Principles of products liability, including strict liability, have been widely extended to persons in the business of leasing products, *Cintrone v. Hertz Truck Leasing & Rental Serv.,* 45 N.J. 434, 212 A.2d 769 (1965), and even to business licensors or bailers of products, *Garcia v. Halsett,* 3 Cal. App. 3d 319, 82 Cal. Rptr. 420 (1970). There is a division of authority here, however, with some courts unwilling to extend strict liability to small businesses or to situations typically covered by negligence for premises liability.

V.   TRANSACTIONS COVERED BY PRODUCTS LIABILITY

TRANSACTIONS COVERED BY PRODUCTS LIABILITY

    A.   The Product: The core area of products liability has been for damages caused by tangible personal property that is defective or unsafe. The tendency, however, has been to extend products liability law, including strict liability, to injuries resulting from the sale of defective residential real estate by a business seller, *Schipper v. Levitt & Sons, Inc.,* 44 N.J. 70, 207 A.2d 314 (1965). There is some tendency to extend strict liability to the business supplier of intangible property, such as electricity. One court extended strict liability to the supplier of a defective navigational map. *Saloomey v. Jeppesen & Co.,* 707 F.2d 671 (2d Cir. 1983). Courts are reluctant to impose strict liability, or even negligence liability, on publishers of books, magazines and the like, for erroneous information contained therein, in part because of freedom of speech concerns. Courts are likewise reluctant to impose strict liability on the professional provider of services, in part because of the difficulties of defining defectiveness of services except in terms of a departure from the standard of reasonable care.

    B.   Pure Economic Loss: The tendency has been to deny liability in tort, whether in negligence or strict liability, for pure economic loss, and to relegate the plaintiff to his remedies in contract or warranty, with some courts requiring privity of contract in this situation at least in the absence of the breach of an express warranty. *Seely v. White Motor Co.,* 63 Cal.2d 9, 45 Cal. Rptr. 17, 403 P.2d 145 (1965). Economic loss for this purpose is typically defined as loss in value of the product and lost profits. Where there is physical injury to person or property, recovery in tort for all damages, including economic loss, is normally allowed, *Seely, supra;* although in the case of physical damage to property, some courts require that the damage be to property other than the product sold by the defendant before tort law will apply. *East River Steamship Corp. v. TransAmerica Delaval,* 476 U.S. 858, 106 S. Ct. 2295, 90 L. Ed. 2d 865 (1986).

    1.   The rationale for the pure-economic-loss rule seems to be that the loss is commercial in nature and related only to the contractual expectations of the parties. Other courts concentrate on the safety goals of tort law and conclude that tort rather than warranty law should be applied whenever a product defect presents a safety hazard, regardless of whether the hazard results in physical injury to person or property. *Wash. Water Power Co. v. Graybar Elec. Co.,* 112 Wash.2d 847, 774 P.2d 1199 (1989). Still other courts think that the commercial status of the plaintiff, rather than the nature of the damages, should be the focus of inquiry. Under this analysis, tort law applies when the plaintiff is a nonbusiness consumer, but warranty law applies when the plaintiff is a business entity. *Spring Motors Distrib. v. Ford Motor Co.,* 98

N.J. 555, 489 A.2d 660 (1985). Still other courts apply tort principles where the product supplier is guilty of negligence that causes loss, whether physical or purely economic. *Berg v. General Motors Corp.*, 555 P.2d 818 (Wash. 1976).

C. **Successor Corporation Liability:** Some jurisdictions hold corporation *B* liable for injuries resulting from defective products sold by corporation *A*, where, after the sale but before the injury, *B* buys substantially all of the assets, good will, patents, trade name and the like of corporation *A*, *A* dissolves, and then *B* continues essentially the same business as *A* was engaged in before the asset sale and purchase. Courts used to require continuity of stock ownership between *A* and *B*, i.e., *B* had to purchase the assets of *A* in substantial part with stock of *B*, before successor liability would be imposed on *B*. The modern tendency is to impose successor liability on *B* even where the exchange is solely for cash. *Ray v. Alad Corp.*, 19 Cal.3d 22, 136 Cal. Rptr. 574, 560 P.2d 3 (1977). Most courts do require, however, that there be continuity of officers, directors, or key personnel between *A* and *B* before successor liability will be imposed on *B*.

VI. **DEFENSES**

A. **In General:** There are many defenses in products liability actions that are typical of tort law in general. These include defenses such as the running of the statute of limitations, contributory negligence, assumption of risk, misuse, comparative fault, lack of foreseeability, lack of proximate cause or of cause in fact, and the like. This section focuses on defenses that are unique to or characteristic of products liability actions in particular.

B. **Defenses Typical of Products Litigation:** There are defenses peculiar to warranty, such as notice of breach and the like. There are other limitations on tort recovery, notably the pure-economic-loss rules. In addition, there are defenses that are typical of products litigation, whether brought in tort or warranty.

   1. If a product has been designed and made according to government specifications, the manufacturer will not be liable for defective design as long as it warns the government of any dangers in the product of which the manufacturer is aware and the government is not. *Boyle v. United Tech. Corp.*, 487 U.S. 500, 108 S. Ct. 2510, 101 L. Ed. 2d 442 (1988). The cases divide on whether the government contract defense applies only to military procurement contracts, *Nielsen v. Geo. Diamond Vogel Paint Co.*, 892 F.2d 1450 (9th Cir. 1990), or to all government contracts, *Garner v. Santoro*, 865 F.2d 629 (5th Cir. 1989).

   2. A number of courts hold that federal safety-regulation statutes impliedly preempt a common law cause of action. Such preemption has been found in the case of claims based on failure to warn of the dangers of smoking, the absence of air bags in cars, and FDA or other federal regulation of warnings and the like. *See, e.g., Palmer v. Liggett Group, Inc.*, 825 F.2d 620 (1st Cir. 1987). The more typical rule, however, is that statutory compliance, like compliance with industry standards and customs, is some evidence of due care and nondefectiveness but is not a complete bar to recovery. *Medtronic, Inc. v. Lohr*, 518 U.S. 470 (1996).

   3. There is no need to warn of an obvious danger, since the obviousness of the danger serves the same purpose as a warning — to alert the plaintiff of the danger. A number of courts, however, permit recovery based on defect in design, even though the danger is obvious. *Micallef v. Miehle Co.*, 39 N.Y.2d 376, 384 N.Y.S.2d 115, 348 N.E.2d 571 (1976). The rationale for permitting recovery here is that consumer accidents from mistake and inadvertence are readily foreseeable, and liability should be imposed where grave injury from such accidents can practically be avoided by a needed change in design.

11

DEFENSES

CHAPTER 11 – QUESTIONS, ANSWERS AND TIPS

1. **Q:** Fumigator sprayed apt. A, and the fumes penetrated into apt. B causing damage owing to a defective fire wall between the apartments. Can the fumigator and the manufacturer of the fire wall be held strictly liable for the damage?

   A: Yes, on grounds of abnormal danger and strict products liability, respectively.

   Tip: For purposes of abnormal-danger liability the activity (fumigating) must be abnormally dangerous, and for strict products liability the product (the firewall) must be defective.

2. **Q:** A products liability suit can be brought against the business supplier of a defective product in both negligence and strict liability.

   A: True.

   Tip: In some situations theories of recovery are exclusive, and in others they overlap. For example, an intentional tort and a negligent tort are thought to be mutually exclusive, e.g., an action for battery cannot be based on both intent and negligence: a negligent touching is not a battery, but negligence. In products liability, on the other hand, there is a great deal of overlap; for example, typically a products liability claim can be brought in both negligence and strict liability and the strict liability claim can be brought in both warranty and strict tort.

3. **Q:** A product must have a manufacturing design, warning, or representational defect in order to give rise to a products liability claim.

   A: True. Stated another way, the product must have a defect in order for there to be a products liability claim.

   Tip: Contrast abnormally dangerous activity, where there need be nothing wrong with, or defective about, a product (e.g., dynamite). There can be negligent entrustment of a perfectly good product, e.g., supplying a gun to a minor, but this situation would be more aptly described as one involving ordinary negligence rather than a products liability claim.

4. **Q:** A product design defect can be shown by proof: (1) of a reasonable alternative design; (2) that the risk of injury from a product outweighed its utility; (3) that the product failed to meet ordinary consumer expectations; (4) all of the above.

   A: (4) all of the above.

   Tip: Not every jurisdiction allows proof of design defect by (1), (2), and (3). But all three of these methods of proof are allowed in different jurisdictions: some use (1), some (2), some a combination of (2) and (3), and so forth.

5. **Q:** How does negligence differ from state of the art?

   A: Negligence is that which one should know and do, or refrain from doing, while state of the art is that which is knowable and capable of being done.

Tip: That which is knowable and doable at time of trial was likely knowable and doable at the time of manufacture (state of the art), although the manufacturer at the time of manufacture may not have actually known and should not have known and done (negligence) that which may have been knowable and doable at that time. Since manufacturers are held to the standard of an expert in their trade, courts tend to think that that which is knowable should be known. But in fact, what one is able to know is not the same as what one should know.

6. **Q:** Plaintiff's fault is never used to reduce her recovery in a strict products liability action, since fault cannot be compared with strict liability.

   A: False.

   Tip: Although there is a division of authority, the majority of courts apply comparative fault in strict liability. Insofar as strict liability is simply another name for negligence, such a comparison presents no problem. Where true strict liability is applied (e.g., production or manufacturing defect, innocent misrepresentation), a comparison of fault is not possible and the jury must make an allocation based on some broader principle of comparative responsibility.

7. **Q:** Only product manufacturers are held strictly liable for damages caused by the supply of a defective product.

   A: False.

   Tip: While there are various exceptions (e.g., for pharmacists, for retailers), as a general rule any business supplier of a defective product can be held strictly liable for such damages. Likewise, any supplier who misrepresents a product can be held strictly liable for damages caused by such a misrepresentation.

8. **Q:** Why are remedies often limited to warranty law, where a product causes only economic loss?

   A: Because the resulting damages are considered commercial, because the parties are commercial entities, because the product is not considered dangerous, or because the product supplier was not negligent in supplying the product.

   Tip: In the area of pure economic loss, as in many areas of products law and indeed tort law in general, there are divergent rationales which result in a division or divisions of authority.

NONDISCLOSURE AND MISREPRESENTATION CAUSING PURE ECONOMIC LOSS

▶ CHAPTER SUMMARY

NONDISCLOSURE AND MISREPRESENTATION
CAUSING PURE ECONOMIC LOSS

Scope of Chapter. Misrepresentation, express and implied, permeates the law of torts. Special treatment is given here to misrepresentation resulting only in pure economic loss because the rules, especially with regard to the extent of liability, may differ markedly from those where physical injury to person or property is involved. It will be recalled that in products liability (Chapter 11) many courts restrict the claimant's remedy to warranty where only economic loss (no physical injury) is involved. Outside the products area, no such restriction exists for misrepresentation, and claims are widely brought in negligence, with less inclination to allow recovery.

12

NONDISCLOSURE

I. NONDISCLOSURE

A. **The Traditional Rule:** The traditional, or older, rule was that a party to a transaction acting at arm's length had no duty to disclose matters actually known to him that would adversely affect the interests of another party to the transaction. The only duty was not to actively prevent the other party from discovering those adverse matters, and not to speak half-truths or make misleading statements. If, however, the party stood in a fiduciary or confidential (as opposed to an arm's-length) relationship with the other party, then a duty to disclose such known adverse matters could arise. *Swinton v. Whitinsville Savings Bank,* 311 Mass. 677, 42 N.E.2d 808 (1942).

    1. The modern rule, and perhaps the majority position today, is that there is a duty to disclose such known matters not only in the situations mentioned above but in other situations as well. There may be a duty to correct prior misleading statements, once the speaker learns that the statements are false or learns that the other party is relying on those statements. In addition, according to *Restatement (Second) of Torts* § 551(2)(e), a party to a "business transaction" is under a duty to disclose "facts basic to the transaction" if he "knows" that the other is about to enter into the transaction under a mistake as to such facts and that the other, "because of the relationship between them, the customs of the trade or other objective circumstances, would reasonably expect a disclosure of those facts." The *Restatement* and the case law give no bright-line rule as to what are "facts basic to the transaction" about which, under the circumstances, disclosure would reasonably be expected. It is unclear whether this duty of disclosure might extend beyond business transactions to include, say, social or other transactions.

        a. The duty to disclose is widely couched in terms of a duty to disclose facts of which one "knows," as opposed to facts of which one has reason to know or should know. However, a duty to disclose facts of which one has reason to know or should know may arise in special circumstances.

        Example: In California, a real estate broker is required to make a reasonable investigation of property she has listed for sale in order to discover defects for the benefit of the buyer. *Easton v. Strassburger,* 152 Cal. App. 3d 90, 199 Cal. Rptr. 383 (1984).

        b. It is unclear to whom the duty to disclose facts, especially known facts, may extend. The *Restatement* talks in terms of "parties to a transaction," suggesting something approaching a privity or contractual relationship. The duty may extend beyond such a relationship, however.

        Example: In *Griffith v. Byers Construc. Co.,* 212 Kan. 65, 510 P.2d 198 (1973), the developer of property was found to have a duty to disclose its saline condition for the benefit of purchasers who acquired the property from an intervening builder.

II. DECEIT OR FRAUDULENT MISREPRESENTATION

A. **Liability to Foreseeable Plaintiffs:** One is liable to foreseeable plaintiffs for pecuniary loss resulting from a deceitful or fraudulent misrepresentation. *Ultramares Corp. v. Touche, Niven & Co.,* 255 N.Y. 170, 174 N.E. 441 (1931). A deceitful or fraudulent misrepresentation is a false statement made knowingly, recklessly, or without belief in the truth of the statement. *Derry v. Peek,* [1889] 14 App. Cas. 337 (H.L.). In addition, a statement is actionable as fraudulent or deceitful if a party represents a fact to be true of her own personal knowledge when she lacks such personal knowledge. *Sovereign Pocohontas Co. v. Bond,* 120 F.2d 39 (D.C. Cir. 1941).

12

1. Foreseeability of plaintiffs, according to the *Restatement,* is defined in terms of those persons whom the maker of the misstatement "intends or has reason to expect" to be influenced by the misstatement in the "type of transaction involved." "Reason to expect" is defined as a *"special reason to expect"* that the misstatement "win be communicated to others, and will influence their conduct." *Restatement (Second) of Torts* § 533, and comm. *d.*

    Example: If *A* makes a fraudulent misstatement to *B* regarding Blackacre, intending to induce *B* to buy Blackacre but with no intent or reason to expect that *C* will rely on the statement in later purchasing Blackacre from another person, *A* is not liable to *C. Westcliff Co. v. Wall,* 153 Tex. 271, 267 S.W.2d 544 (1954).

    Comment *d* to Caveat to *Restatement (Second) of Torts* § 533 states that a "developing trend toward extending the scope of liability in this area of the law may eventually extend beyond the rule stated in this Section." In other words, one who makes a fraudulent or deceitful misstatement may be liable to any foreseeable plaintiff of which one either has reason to know *or should know.*

2. A foreseeable plaintiff can typically recover in products liability for fraudulent misrepresentation resulting in pure economic loss. *St. Jos. Hosp. v. Corbetta Construe. Co.,* 21 Ill. App. 3d 925, 316 N.E. 2d 51 (1974).

III. NEGLIGENT MISREPRESENTATION

A. **Scope of Permissible Plaintiffs:** The early rule was that there was no liability in damages for pecuniary loss resulting from negligent misrepresentation, although the aggrieved party might have a claim for rescission of a contract induced by the negligent misrepresentation. *Derry v. Peek, supra.* This decision was for all practical purposes overruled in England by *Headley Byrne & Co. v. Hellar & Partners,* [1964] A.C. 465 (H.L. 1963), and today a damage action for negligent misrepresentation causing pecuniary loss is widely allowed in this country. *See Internat'l Products Co. v. Erie R.R. Co.,* 244 N.Y. 331, 155 N.E. 662 (1927).

1. The problem for recovery in negligent misrepresentation is in determining who are permissible plaintiffs. To use a standard of foreseeability, said Judge Cardozo, would subject a person making a negligent misstatement to "liability in an indeterminate amount for an indeterminate time to an indeterminate class." *Ultramares v. Touche, supra.*

    a. One rule restricts liability to situations closely resembling that of privity, or of third party beneficiaries, under a contractual theory. According to this rule, in order to be liable one who negligently makes a misstatement must be aware of the purpose for which the statement will be used and of the party who will rely upon the statement, and there must be some conduct linking the one who makes the misstatement with the party relying on the statement *Credit Alliance Corp. v. Arthur Andersen & Co.,* 65 N.Y.2d 536, 493 N.Y.S.2d 435, 483 N.E.2d 110 (1985).

Example: *A* employs *B* to weigh a quantity of beans and to send a certificate of the weight to *C* who is buying the beans. *B* will be liable to *C* for negligent certification of the weight of the beans. *Glanzer v. Shepard,* 233 N.Y. 236, 135 N.E. 275 (1922).

b. The *Restatement* position is that the person making the negligent misstatement must intend or know the person, or "limited group of persons," for whose benefit the statement is to be used and must intend or know the type of transaction or "substantially similar transaction" in which the statement will be used. It is not required that the person or persons who will rely on the statement be specifically identified or known. It is enough "that the maker of the representation intends to reach and influence either a particular person or persons known to him, or a group or class of persons, distinct from the much larger class who might reasonably be expected sooner or later to have access to the information and foreseeably to take some action in reliance on it." *Restatement (Second) of Torts* § 552, and comm. *h.* There is no requirement that there be conduct linking the one making the statement with the party relying on it. Section 552 does state, however, that the rule applies only to statements made in the course of one's business, profession, or employment, or in a transaction in which one has a "pecuniary interest."

(1) A special rule is given in the *Restatement* for one who is under a "public duty" to give information. In that situation, the liability of the person giving the information "extends to loss suffered by any of the class of persons for whose benefit the duty is created, in any of the transactions in which it is intended to protect them." *Restatement (Second) of Torts* § 552(3).

Example: A notary public negligently acknowledges a signature on a deed as that of *B.* In fact, the signature is not that of *B,* but is a forgery. *C* in reliance on the acknowledgment purchases the land from *D* and suffers pecuniary loss as a result. The notary is liable to *C* for the loss. *Restatement (Second) of Torts* § 552, comm. *k,* illus. 16.

c. Some courts have held that, in the case of negligent misrepresentation, the person making the representation will be liable for the "reasonably foreseeable consequences" of the statement. *H. Rosenblum, Inc. v. Adler,* 93 N.J. 324, 461 A.2d 138 (1983). Considerations of policy may limit liability here, however, as for example where the "injury is too remote," "wholly out of proportion to the culpability," "highly extraordinary," and the like. *Citizens State Bank v. Timm, Schmidt & Co.,* 113 Wis.2d 376, 335 N.W.2d 361 (1983).

2. Courts generally deny recovery in products liability for pure economic loss resulting from negligent misrepresentation. *Coastal Group, Inc. v. Dryvit Systems, Inc.,* 274 N.J. Super. 171, 643 A.2d 649 (1994). Such holdings reflect the unwillingness of courts to allow recovery in tort for products liability that results in pure economic loss, the preference being to restrict recovery for such loss to warranty.

INNOCENT MIS-REPRESEN- TATION

IV. **INNOCENT MISREPRESENTATION**

A. **Business Misrepresentation:** One who innocently misrepresents a business matter of which he has special means of knowledge may be liable in tort to another who suffers pecuniary loss in justifiable reliance on the misrepresentation. *Richard v. A. Waldman & Sons, Inc.,* 155 Conn. 343, 232 A.2d 307 (1967). *Restatement (Second) of Torts* § 552C states that liability arises for such a misrepresentation made "in a sale, rental or exchange transaction with another." In a caveat, the *Restatement* says the American Law Institute "expresses no opinion" as to whether such strict liability may arise in business transactions other than those involving a sale, rental, or exchange.

1. Comment *d* to *Restatement (Second) of Torts* § 552C states that the rule given therein "is limited to the immediate parties to the sale, rental, or exchange transaction itself."

2. Courts allow recovery of pure economic loss in products liability for breach of express warranty. *Randy Knitwear, Inc. v. Amer. Cyanamid Co.,* 181 N.E.2d 399 (N.Y. App. 1962). Products liability recovery for tortious innocent misrepresentation is normally restricted to cases involving physical injury to persons or property. *Crocker v. Winthrop Labs*, 514 S. W.2d 429 (Tex. 1974); Seely v. White Motor Co., 403 P.2d 145 (Cal. 1965).

   Example: A product manufacturer was held strictly liable in tort for economic loss resulting to the purchaser of a tractor from misrepresentations about the tractor in the manufacturer's sales brochure. *Ford Motor Co. v. Lonon,* 217 Term. 400, 398 S.W.2d 240 (1966). This case was subsequently overruled, *First Nat. Bank v. Brooks Farms,* 821 S.W. 2d 925 (1991), as being out of line with the general rule denying recovery in strict tort for pure economic loss.

12

DEFENSES

V. DEFENSES

A. **Reliance:** A plaintiff must have justifiably relied on a misrepresentation in order to recover. For the reliance to be justified, the misrepresentation must be material and not known to be obviously false. *Restatement (Second) of Torts* §§ 538, 541. Reliance on the defendant's statement need not be the sole inducement to action, however, as long as it is a substantial factor.

   Example: *A, B,* and *C* each makes the same misrepresentation to *D* to induce *D* to buy Blackacre. *A, B,* and *C* are all liable for economic loss to *D* resulting from his reliance on their statements, although the statement of any one of them would have been sufficient to induce *D* to buy Blackacre. *See Restatement (Second) of Torts* § 546, comm. *b,* Illus. 1.

   One who acts in reliance on his own investigation cannot recover for misrepresentation, unless the misrepresentation prevented the investigation from being effective. *Restatement (Second) of Torts* § 547; *Sippy v. Cristich,* 4 Kan. App. 2d 511, 609 P.2d 204 (1980).

   1. It is often stated that one is not entitled to rely on statements of opinion by another. *Vulcan Metals Co. v. Simmons Mfg. Co.,* 248 F. 853 (2d Cir. 1918). A better statement of the rule is that one is not entitled to rely on the opinion of another *unless* the other reasonably appears to have special knowledge or information regarding the subject matter of the opinion. *See Hanberry v. Hearst Corp.,* 276 Cal. App. 2d 680, 81 Cal. Rptr. 519 (1969).

B. **Promises:** If one promises to act or refrain from acting in the future, the promisor is not liable in tort unless the promise is fraudulently or deceitfully made, *i.e.,* unless the promisor has no intention, at the time the promise is made, of keeping the promise. *See Adams v. Gillig,* 199 N.Y. 314, 92 N.E. 670 (1910). One who fails to carry out a promise owing to negligence, or owing to any reason other than deceit or fraud in the inducement, is liable, if at all, for breach of contract. A misrepresentation of present fact or opinion, however, can give rise to liability for negligent or tortious innocent misrepresentation.

   Example: If *A* negligently misrepresents to *B* that goods are stored at Dock *D, A* can be liable to *B* for pecuniary loss resulting from the misrepresentation. *Internat'l Prods. Co. v. Erie R.R. Co.,* 244 N.Y. 331, 155 N.E. 662 (1927). But if *A* promises *B* that *A* will pay off a mortgage on Blackacre sometime in the future, *A* will be liable to *B* in tort for resulting pecuniary loss only if *A* has no intention at the time of making the promise of carrying it out. *Burgdorfer v. Thielemann,* 153 Or. 354, 55 P.2d 1122 (1936).

C. **Constitutional Free Speech:** The First Amendment of the United States Constitution may impose constitutional limits on tort liability resulting from misrepresentation. The U.S. Supreme Court has indicated that constitutional malice is required for recovery by a public figure for economic loss resulting from product disparagement. *Bose Corp. v. Consumers Union,* 466 U.S. 485, 104 S. Ct. 1949, 80 L. Ed. 2d 502 (1984). The First Amendment may not apply at all, on the other hand, to defamation of a private person concerning a matter not of public interest. *Dun & Bradstreet, Inc. v. Greenmoss Builders, Inc.,* 472 U.S. 749, 105 S. Ct. 2939, 86 L. Ed. 2d 593 (1985). It is unclear to what extent, if any, the First Amendment applies to the tort of misrepresentation, as opposed to defamation or product disparagement.

VI. **DAMAGES**

A. **Fraud:** The victim of fraudulent misrepresentation can recover for the difference between the value of what he has received and what he paid, plus any consequential damages. In many jurisdictions, such a victim in a business transaction with another can also recover from the other "damages sufficient to give him the benefit of his contract with the maker, if these damages are proved with reasonable certainty." *Restatement (Second) of Torts* § 549; *Hinkle v. Rockville Motor Co.,* 262 Md. 502, 278 A.2d 42 (1971).

Example: Buyer buys Blackacre from Seller for $10,000 as a result of a fraudulent misrepresentation by Seller. The land is actually worth only $5,000. Buyer can recover $5,000 damages, plus any other consequential damages (*e.g.,* expenses for improvements) she may have incurred. Also, if she can prove with reasonable certainty that Blackacre should have been worth $15,000 if it had been as represented, she can recover an additional $5,000.

B. **Negligent and Innocent Tortious Misrepresentation:** The *Restatement* provides that the plaintiff can recover only the difference between value given and value received, plus consequential damages, for negligent or innocent tortious misrepresentation but cannot recover for loss of benefit of the contract (*i.e.,* that additional value, over and above value given, if the representation had been true). *Restatement (Second) of Torts* §§ 552B–C.

CHAPTER 12 – QUESTIONS, ANSWERS, AND TIPS

1. **Q:** A party to a business transaction has a duty to disclose to the other party facts that are basic to the transaction and that are known by the party but not by the other party.

   A: This is the general rule.

   Tip: There may, however, be exceptional situations where the duty to disclose extends to non-parties in a non-business context. Such a duty exists where there is physical injury or damage, and it may extend to economic loss cases in view of the difficulty of distinguishing between physical damage and economic loss.

2. **Q:** One who makes a fraudulent misrepresentation can be liable to anyone the maker knows or has reason to expect will rely on the misrepresentation to their harm.

   A: This is the general rule.

   Tip: The duty may develop so as to extend to anyone the misrepresenter should foresee as likely to rely on the misrepresentation. Note that deceit or fraud can arise if a person represents a fact to be true of her own personal knowledge when she lacks such personal knowledge.

3. **Q:** Why is recovery for negligent misrepresentation often restricted to an intended plaintiff, or to a class of intended plaintiffs, involving an intended business transaction or a transaction that is substantially similar to the intended one?

    A: Courts are concerned that, without such restrictions, one who negligently misrepresents facts could be liable for an indefinite period of time and to an unlimited number of persons in unlimited amounts.

    Tip: The indeterminate liability problem is usually not present in the case of personal injuries, but he problem can arise where there is a mass tort. Compare *Enright v. Eli Lilly & Co.*, 570 N.E. 2d 198 (N.Y. 1991), where the court refused to allow a plaintiff to recover for injuries resulting from her grandmother's ingestion of DES because, the court said, the line had to be drawn somewhere in order to prevent unlimited liability.

4. **Q:** Recovery in strict tort for innocent misrepresentation resulting in pure economic is normally allowed.

    A: False.

    Tip: Strict tort recovery for misrepresentation is generally allowed when there is physical damage to person or property. When the loss is purely economic, the Restatement restricts strict tort recovery for misrepresentation to sale, rental or exchange transactions involving parties in privity.

5. **Q:** A negligently promises B that he will sell B his horse at the end of the following month. Is A liable to B for negligent misrepresentation in failing to fulfill the promise?

    A: No.

    Tip: If the statement were fraudulent or deceitful, A would be liable in tort. But A is only liable in breach of contract for a promise that is negligently made.

6. **Q:** Reliance on a misrepresentation must be a but-for cause of plaintiff's injury in order to recover for pure economic loss.

    A: False.

    Tip: There may be several causes, as long as the actionable cause is a substantial factor in causing plaintiff's injury.

12

NOTES

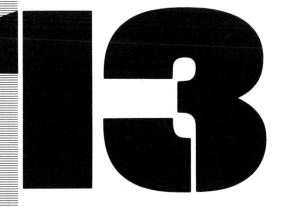

BUSINESS TORTS

▶ # CHAPTER SUMMARY

BUSINESS TORTS

Scope of Chapter: Business torts cover a broad range of activities, including bad faith insurance practices, violation of trade secrets and covenants not to compete, wrongful discharge, defamation, and misrepresentation. These topics are dealt with or referred to either expressly or by implication elsewhere in this book. Other business torts, such as patent, copyright and trademark infringement, unfair pricing, monopolistic activities, and unfair labor practices, are typically dealt with in other courses.

I. PRODUCT DISPARAGEMENT OR INJURIOUS FALSEHOOD

13

*PRODUCT
DISPARAGEMENT*

A. Definition: Product disparagement, or injurious falsehood, consists of the publication of a false statement that is intended or reasonably understood to cast doubt on the quality of another's land, chattels, or intangible things, or upon the existence or extent of the other's property interest therein. *Restatement (Second) of Torts* §§ 629, 634.

Example: *B* falsely publishes the statement that *A* has gone out of business. *A* has an action for resulting damages against *B* for injurious falsehood. *Ratcliffe v. Evans,* [1892] 2 Q.B. 524 (C.A.).

1. There is a close relationship between injurious falsehood and defamation. The former disparages one's property, while the latter disparages one's reputation. The two may, however, overlap.

    Example: An allegation that plaintiff's milk is "rotten" may be product disparagement and may also be defamation injuring plaintiff's reputation in its trade or business. *Waechter v. Carnation Co.,* 5 Wash. App. 121, 485 P.2d 1000 (1971).

B. Damages: Unlike defamation, there can be recovery for product disparagement or injurious falsehood *only* if the plaintiff suffers pecuniary loss. *Ratcliffe v. Evans, supra.* When the damage consists of loss of custom, some courts require the plaintiff to prove loss of particular customers as a result of the falsehood. A modern approach allows the plaintiff to recover, however, if she can show a resulting general business loss.

Example: *B* publishes an untrue statement about *A*'s product. Prior to the publication, *A* had annual sales at a constant volume of $500,000 a year. Immediately after the publication, *A*'s sales began to decline, and in the following year, sales amounted to only $200,000. *A* can show that the market for the product in general remained steady, there was no change in competition or in the *A's* sales methods, and *A*'s product itself remained unchanged. On proof of these facts, *A* can recover from *B* the loss of profits he would have made on sales of $300,000. *Restatement (Second) of Torts* § 633, comm. *h,* Illus. 1.

C. Privileges: The absolute and conditional privileges applicable to defamation generally apply to product disparagement as well. *Restatement (Second) of Torts* §§ 635, 646A. In addition, a person is privileged to make a comparison of his product with that of a competitor, presenting the competitor's product in an unfavorable light by comparison, as long as the comparison does not contain false assertions of fact regarding the competitor's product. *Restatement (Second) of Torts* § 649.

1. The United States Supreme Court in *Bose Corp. v. Consumers Union,* 466 U.S. 485, 104 S. Ct. 1949, 80 L. Ed. 2d 502 (1984), sustained the lower court's finding that a product disparagement must be shown to have been made with knowledge or reckless disregard of its falsity by the defendant in order for the plaintiff as a public figure to recover. It is unclear whether there are any constitutional restrictions on the tort if the plaintiff is a private figure, or if the subject matter of the disparagement is not of public interest or concern.

II. **INTENTIONAL INTERFERENCE WITH CONTRACT OR WITH PROSPECTIVE ECONOMIC ADVANTAGE**

A. **Definition:** One who intentionally and improperly interferes with a contract or prospective contract of another can be liable for pecuniary loss resulting to the other from such interference. In determining whether or not the interference is improper, according to the *Restatement,* consideration is given to the following factors: (1) the nature of the actor's conduct; (2) her motive; (3) the nature of the interests interfered with; (4) the interests sought to be advanced by the interference; (5) the social interests involved; (6) the proximity of the actor's conduct to the interference; and (7) the relation of the parties. *Restatement (Second) of Torts* §§ 766, 766A, 766B, 767.

13

1. It is clear that one cannot interfere with an existing, valid contract solely for purposes of competition. *Lumley v. Gye,* 118 Eng. Rep. 749 (Q.B. 1853). One can interfere with another's prospective economic relations or with another's contract terminable at will for purposes of competition unless the interference is accomplished by wrongful means or with wrongful motives. *Restatement (Second) of Torts* § 768.

   Example: A lawyer who left the plaintiff law firm was enjoined for a period of time from soliciting clients of the firm, in part because of the confidential relationship existing between the lawyer and the firm. *Adler, Barish , etc. v. Epstein,* 482 Pa. 416, 393 A.2d 11 75 (1978).

   a. It may be difficult to distinguish what are proper, and what are improper, means or motives for interference. The determination turns on all the facts and circumstances, as well as current mores.

      Examples: It seems clearly improper today to interfere with a contract to purchase realty on grounds of racial prejudice. *Duff v. Engelberg,* 237 Cal. App. 2d 505, 47 Cal. Rptr. 114 (1965). It is less clear whether one should be able to interfere for other reasons of dislike or disapproval of the plaintiff. In one case, the defendant franchiser was held to have improperly interfered with a franchisee's at-will employment of the plaintiff as franchise manager, where the interference was based on the grounds that the manager was a member of a trade organization, which did not adversely affect plaintiff 's job performance. *Smith v. Ford Motor Co.,* 289 N.C. 71, 221 S.E.2d 282 (1976). In *Brimelow v. Casson,* [1924] 1 Ch. 302 (1923), a union organizer was permitted to interfere with plaintiff 's theater performance contracts in an attempt to force the plaintiff to pay higher wages to his chorus girls. A different result than that in *Brimelow* might be reached in a jurisdiction more fully committed to a free market economy, and less concerned with the private lives of the girls who allegedly sought to supplement their income by engaging in immoral sexual activities.

B. **Contract and Tort Remedies:** A person whose contract is interfered with may have a tort action against the interferer, as well as an action against the other party to the contract for breach of contract, although the same damages can be recovered only once. *Duff v. Engelberg, supra.* Typically, damages for mental suffering and punitive damages are recoverable in tort, although not for breach of contract.

C. **Causation:** If it appears that the contract or prospective economic advantage would have been terminated anyway, for valid reasons, then a wrongful interference may be noncausal. An interference for an improper purpose may be actionable if that purpose is a *substantial cause* of the interference, even though there may also be proper purposes for the interference.

NEGLIGENT
INTERFERENCE

III.   NEGLIGENT INTERFERENCE

A.   **General Rule:** The general rule is that there is no liability for pure pecuniary loss (no physical harm to the other or to his property) resulting from the negligent interference with a contract or prospective economic advantage. *Restatement (Second) of Torts* § 766C. The reason for this rule is to prevent unlimited liability. *Robins Dry Dock & Repair Co. v. Flint,* 275 U.S. 303, 48 S. Ct. 134, 72 L. Ed. 290 (1927).

1.   There are exceptions to this rule, as for example in the case of commercial fishermen who are favorites in the eyes of the law, so that they may be able to recover for loss of livelihood as the result of a negligent oil spill by the defendant in their fishing areas. *Union Oil Co. v. Oppen,* 501 F.2d 558 (9th Cir. 1974). A tort action does not lie in admiralty, however, when a commercial buyer suing the seller of a defective product alleges injury only to the product itself. *East River Steamship Corp. v. TransAmerica Delaval, Inc.,* 476 U.S. 858, 106 S. Ct. 2295, 90 L. Ed. 2d 865 (1986). It has been held there can be recovery where the plaintiff stands in a relationship resembling that of a third party beneficiary of a person who negligently fails to perform a contract with another to the plaintiff's pecuniary loss. *See J'Aire v. Gregory,* 24 Cal.3d 799, 157 Cal. Rptr. 407, 598 P.2d 60 (1979).

2.   To the extent that interference occurs through statements of the defendant, it is unclear to what extent, if any, constitutional free speech considerations may apply. In that connection, *see* the discussion of *Bose Corp. v. Consumers Union,* in the first part of this chapter.

APPROPRIATION
OF INTANGIBLE
PROPERTY RIGHTS

IV.   APPROPRIATION OF INTANGIBLE PROPERTY RIGHTS

A.   *Trade Secrets.* Some businesses have intellectual property rights which are not patentable, or not copyrightable, or which the business for its own reasons chooses not to patent or copyright. In those situations the business may prefer to protect such a right as a trade secret.

1.   The key to trade secret protection is secrecy. Obviously total secrecy is not practical, since some employees and sometimes customers must have access to the secret information in order for that information to be useful. The law requires only that reasonable efforts be made to keep the information secret. If such efforts are not made, trade secret protection will be lost. *Rockwell Graphic Systems v. DEV Industries,* 925 F.2d 124 (7th Cir. 1991).

a.   Trade secrecy protection is not lost if the information is obtained by another through improper methods, such as theft, fraud, unauthorized interception, or breach of confidence. *Restatement of the Law (Third): Unfair Competition* § 43. Employees who have access to the information can be required to sign a confidentiality agreement. *Pepsi Co. Inc. v. Redmond,* 54 F.3d 1262 (7th Cir. 1995). Reverse engineering of a product by a third party competitor is a proper means of acquiring trade secret information, since such engineering involves the use of technical skills that the law seeks to encourage. *Rockwell Graphic Systems v. DEV Industries, supra.*

WRONGFUL
DISCHARGE

III.   WRONGFUL DISCHARGE

A.   *General Rule.* The common law rule is that an employee-at-will can be discharged for good cause, bad cause, or no cause at all. *Harney v. Meadowbrook Nursing Center,* 784 S.W.2d 921 (Tenn. 1990).

B. *Exceptions to the General Rule.* Discharge of an employee-at-will is tortious if the discharge violates public policy. Such a violation occurs if an employee is discharged for refusing to participate in an illegal activity, for performing an important public obligation, exercising a legal right or interest, or exposing a wrongdoing. *Groce v. Foster*, 880 P.2d 902 (Okl. 1994).

1. There are federal and state statutes prohibiting the discharge of an employee for "whistle-blowing," e.g., 42 U.S.C. § 5851 (nuclear industry); *Tenn Code Annot.* § 50-1-304 (discharge of an employee for refusal to participate in, or refusal to remain silent about, illegal activities).

2. An employee may be a contractual, or tenured, employee rather than an employee-at-will, and in that event she can be lawfully discharged only for breach of contract or for good cause. *K-Mart Corp v. Ponsock*, 732 P.2d 1364 (Nev. 1987). The contract may be express, or implied-in-fact. Foley v. Interactive Data Corp., 765 P.2d 373 (Cal. 1988).

3. If the employee is a public employee, i.e., employed by federal, state or local government, then a discharge may violate the employee's constitutional rights. *Pickering v. United States,* 391 U.S. 563 (1968). The employer has wide latitude, however, in employment discharge decisions over matters of only personal interest, as opposed to matters of public concern that may implicate constitutional rights such as freedom of speech. *Connick v. Myers,* 461 U.S. 138 (1983).

VI. CIVIL RICO   *CIVIL RICO*

A. *General Rule.* The Racketeer Influenced and Corrupt Organizations Act (RICO), 18 U.S.C. § 1961 et seq., provides a civil remedy to recover treble damages plus attorney fees for any violation of its substantive provisions. These provisions are violated if the defendant engages in a pattern of criminal activity to invest in, acquire, establish, maintain or conduct any enterprise. A pattern consists of two or more related criminal activities, with a threat of continuing criminal activity. *H.J., Inc. v. Nw. Bell Tel. Co.*, 492 U.S. 229 (1989). RICO specifies the criminal activities, prominent among which are extortion, bribery, wire fraud, mail fraud, and fraud in the sale of securities. 18 U.S.C. § 1961. RICO was amended in 1995 to provide that fraud in the purchase or sale of securities does not constitute a basis for a civil RICO actions unless there has been a criminal conviction. A plaintiff who suffers injury to his business or property as a result of a pattern of RICO violations can recover therefore under the RICO statute.

CHAPTER 13 – QUESTIONS, ANSWERS, AND TIPS

1. **Q:** Bob wrote a letter to the newspaper editor falsely stating that Grocer's fresh products were often rotten. The letter was published by the newspaper. As a result, Grocer suffered mental distress and incurred considerable expense in refuting Bob's statement. Can Grocer recover against Bob for product disparagement?

   A: The expense incurred in refuting Bob's statement may be recoverable as pecuniary loss if reasonably incurred.

   Tip: The mental distress claim could be brought in defamation. It may be necessary to prove constitutional malice in both cases, if the plaintiff is a public person and the matter is one of public interest. Presumably the public would have considerable interest in the quality of Grocer's fresh products.

2. **Q:** What is a principal difference between intentional interference with contract and intentional interference with prospective economic advantage?

A: Interference with contract for competitive reasons is unlawful, but interference with prospective economic advantage for competitive reasons is lawful.

Tip: The Restatement of Torts 2d §768 comm. *i* states that a competitor is free to interfere with a contract at will for competitive purposes, since the future hopes of the party to such a contract is only an expectancy and when it is terminated by the other party there is no breach.

13

3. **Q:** A negligently damaged a bridge so that the river under the bridge was closed to traffic. Can the people who would have used the river for commercial traffic recover against A for their loss of business as a result of the closure? Why or why not?

   A: No, they cannot recover because they have suffered no physical damage and the interference was negligent, not intentional.

   Tip: If the interference had caused physical damage to the boat of a river user, that user could recover at least for the damage to the boat.

4. **Q:** Corp. A has a unique way of making plastic containers that are used generally in the food industry. If an employee of A steals one of the molds for making the containers, and sells the mold to Corp. B which then reverse-engineers construction of the container from the mold, is B guilty of wrongfully appropriating A's trade secret?

   A: If A made a reasonable effort to keep the method of constructing the mold secret, there would be such an appropriation.

   Tip: B did not reverse-engineer construction of the container, which was available generally. The fact that B might have been able to do so does not validate the illegal appropriation, nor does the reverse-engineering of the illegally appropriated mold validate the appropriation.

5. **Q:** Give an example of a discharge for a bad cause that is probably not against public policy.

   A: Discharge of an at-will employee because other employees do not like him may not be actionable if the discharge is not made on grounds of race, ethnicity, religion or gender and does not violate a statutory right. See *Rinehimer v. Luzerne County Community College*, 539 A.2d 1298 (Pa. Super. 1988).

   Tip: Rinehimer was a public employee, but the court there did not discuss any possible constitutional violation. Federal constitutional rights may be implicated where the federal government or a state entity is the employer since the federal constitution is primarily designed to protect against government activities. State constitutions often protect against private as well as government activities.

6. **Q:** Can a RICO plaintiff recover for personal injuries as well as property damage resulting from a pattern of RICO violations by the defendant?

   A: The answer depends on whether the damage provision of the RICO statute is interpreted as exclusive, or merely as a threshold requirement for recovering all damages proximately caused by the defendant.

   Tip: The issue can be argued either way. The statutorily enumerated damages are arguably the exclusive civil remedy under the statute, since if Congress had meant for property or business damage to be merely a trigger for recovering all damages it could have expressly said so. On the other hand, if it meant for the enumeration of damages to be exclusive, it could have expressly said that also.

NUISANCE

► CHAPTER SUMMARY

NUISANCE

Scope of Chapter: Nuisances are divided into two basic categories: public nuisances and private nuisances. A public nuisance is an unreasonable interference with a right common to the general public. *Restatement (Second) of Torts* § 821B. A private nuisance is an unprivileged invasion of another's interest in the private use and enjoyment of land. *Restatement (Second) of Torts* § 821D.

A public nuisance often involves conduct proscribed by statute. *State ex rel. Swann v. Pack,* 527 S.W.2d 99 (Tenn. 1975) (religious snake-handling). The *Restatement* says that a public nuisance may also consist of conduct involving a significant interference with the public health, safety, peace, comfort or convenience, conduct of a continuing nature, or conduct having a permanent or long-lasting effect of which the actor knows or has reason to know. *Restatement (Second) of Torts* § 821B.

In the case of a public nuisance, the private plaintiff must generally suffer some damage different from the public in general in order to be able to recover.

Examples: If *D* blocks a road to the public in general, no single member of the public can sue to stop the blockage since all members using the road suffer essentially the same injury. *Restatement (Second) of Torts* § 821C, comm. *g,* Illus. 8. But if *D* builds a dam whose waters block *P's* sole means of access to his land, *P* can successfully sue. *Pilgrim Plywood Corp. v. Melendy,* 110 Vt. 12, 1 A.2d 700 (1938). Commercial fishermen may have an interest different from other public-water users and, thus, may be able to sue a water polluter. *Burgess v. M/V Tamano,* 370 F. Supp. 247 (D. Me. 1973). And, of course, landowners may be able to sue for a private nuisance for injuries arising out of what is otherwise a public nuisance, *e.g.,* riparian landowners suffering from water pollution.

The *Restatement* and a growing number of cases recognize that a private person can sue to prevent a public nuisance where the person sues as a representative of the general public, as in a class action. *Restatement (Second) of Torts* § 821C(2)(c); *Armory Park Neigh'd Ass'n v. Epis. Comm. Services,* 148 Ariz. 1, 712 P.2d 914 (1985) (neighborhood residential association sued to enjoin public nuisance created by defendant's service of meals to indigents who created a nuisance). Otherwise, a public official with authority to do so can bring the suit. *See State ex rel. Swann v. Pack, supra* (suit brought by the state attorney general to enjoin religious snake-handling).

A private nuisance can be brought by the possessor of the land, an owner of an easement in the land, or an owner of a nonpossessory estate in the land who is detrimentally affected in her use or enjoyment of the estate. *Restatement (Second) of Torts* § 821E. Comm. *d* to § 821E says family members who share occupancy with the possessor may also have standing to sue. *But see Page v. Niagara Chem. Div.,* 68 So.2d 382 (1953), holding that employees of a business lacked standing *to enjoin* the emission of dangerous chemicals from a neighboring plant.

*RATIONALE
FOR
NUISANCE*

I. THE RATIONALE FOR NUISANCE

   A. Purpose: One of the major reasons for bringing an action in nuisance is to seek an injunction to prohibit the defendant from continuing his conduct, where that conduct is of a continuous nature. Put another way, when a plaintiff seeks the equitable remedy of preventing or enjoining another from a continuing course of conduct, particularly where that conduct involves the invasion of plaintiff's interest in the use and enjoyment of her land, the court is likely to describe the suit as one in nuisance with all the attendant rules applicable thereto.

      1. The private nuisance action closely parallels that of trespass to land. While *Restatement (Second) of Torts* § 821D describes the private nuisance as "a nontrespassory invasion," comm. *e* to this section and the case law recognize that there may be substantial overlapping of the two torts. *Bradley v. American Smelting and Refining Co.,* 104 Wash.2d 677, 709 P.2d 782 (1985) (intrusion onto plaintiff's land of copper-smelting particulates from defendant's plant treated as both trespass and nuisance, with proof of actual and substantial damages required for both).

    a.   Some courts, however, may distinguish between trespass and private nuisance by holding that the former involves a physical and the latter may involve a nonphysical invasion.

        Examples: In *Martin v. Reynolds Metals Co.,* 221 Or. 86, 342 P.2d 790 (1959), the invasion of microscopic particulates was treated as a trespass and not a nuisance for statute of limitations purposes; while in *Wilson v. Interlake Steel Co.,* 32 Cal.3d 229, 185 Cal. Rptr. 280, 649 P.2d 922 (1982), the court said: "All intangible intrusions, such as noise, odor, or light alone, are dealt with as nuisance cases, not trespass."

    b.   The general rule is that nuisance requires proof of significant harm, as judged by a nominal-person standard. *Restatement (Second) of Torts* § 821F. An action for trespass to land can generally be brought without proof of actual damage; but proof of actual damages may well be required when the two torts overlap, as in *Bradley v. American Smelting, supra.*

    c.   If a court requires physical invasion of land in order to sustain an action in trespass, nuisance may be the plaintiff's only available remedy for a nonphysical invasion.

B. **Standards of Liability:** A nuisance action can be brought on the basis of negligence, intentional conduct, or strict liability. *Restatement (Second) of Torts* § 822. A failure to act can also give rise to an action for nuisance, where the defendant is under a duty to act. *Restatement (Second) of Torts* § 824.

    1.   A good deal of confusion has resulted from attempts to distinguish between negligent and intentional nuisance. Some courts find that a nuisance is intentional (or "absolute," as it is sometimes described) if the actor intends to do the act, whether or not he intends the harmful consequences. The necessary intent is particularly likely to be found here if the act is in violation of a regulatory statute.

        Examples: In *Jacko v. City of Bridgeport,* 26 Conn. Supp. 73, 213 A.2d 452 (1965), maintaining a cracked, raised sidewalk could be viewed as an absolute nuisance to which ordinary contributory negligence would be no defense. The court defined an absolute nuisance as "intentional in the sense that its creator intended to bring about the conditions found to constitute a nuisance." *Contrast Deane v. Johnston,* 104 So.2d 3 (Fla. 1958) (keeping a sidewalk weighing-machine was not an intentional nuisance, but it might be a negligent nuisance if improperly maintained).

        a.   The distinction between negligence and intent is often drawn for purposes of determining whether the defense of contributory negligence applies. The hornbook law is that ordinary contributory negligence (in the sense of careless failure to discover or to avoid a danger) is a defense to a negligent, but not to an intentional or a strict-liability, nuisance. *Restatement (Second) of Torts* § 840B. No distinction should, however, be drawn between negligence and intent in the absence of willful or wanton misconduct, particularly where comparative fault has been adopted as is the case in most jurisdictions. Comparative fault has been widely applied in strict products liability actions, and this application may well be extended to strict liability nuisances and to intentional nuisances not involving malice, recklessness, wantonness, or the like.

    2.   The *Restatement* says a nuisance action based on strict liability can be brought when the defendant's conduct is abnormally dangerous (blasting, keeping wild animals, and so forth). The definition of intent as used in intentional nuisance is broad enough, however, to cover some types of activity that is reasonable, so that the liability for intentional nuisance may resemble strict liability. The intent required is to invade another's interest for the purpose of causing the invasion, that is, acting or failing to act with knowledge that the invasion is substantially certain to result, or with knowledge "that it is resulting." *Restatement (Second) of Torts* § 825. One may be engaged in a lawful activity that is conducted with care and yet be liable for an intentional invasion of another's interest in land, as long as the actor knows the invasion is occurring. *Morgan v. High Penn Oil Co.,* 238 N.C. 185, 77 S.E.2d 682 (1953) (gases and odors from a nearby refinery invading plaintiff's land).

3. A distinction is made between a continuing and a permanent nuisnace. A continuing, or temporary, nuisance is one that is subject to remediation or cleanup at a reasonable cost, while a permanent nuisance is not subject to such remediation. The statute of limitations begins to run on a permanent nuisance as soon as the plaintiff has reasonable notice of its existence, while the limitations period for a continuing or temporary nuisance begins anew each day the nuisance continues. *Mangini v. Aeroget-Gen'l Corp.,* 912P.2d 1220 (Cal. 1996). In the case of a permanent nuisance only a single lawsuit can be brought, but successive actions can be brought for each new invasion of the plaintiff's interest in the case of a continuing nuisance. *Hoffman v. United Iron and Metal Co.,* 671 A. 2d 55 (Md. App. 1996).

C. **The Balancing Test:** Some courts say the utility of the defendant's conduct should be balanced against the risk of harm created, in determining nuisance, with no liability imposed if the utility outweighs the risk. *Carpenter v. Double R Cattle Co.,* 108 Idaho 602, 701 P.2d 222 (1985). Others say no such balancing should be undertaken, and the defendant should be liable if he causes significant harm to the plaintiff. *Jost v. Dairyland Power Coop.,* 45 Wis.2d 164, 172 N.W.2d 647 (1970).

1. The *Restatement* approach to intentional nuisance is to balance the social value and suitability of the defendant's conduct and the practicality of his avoiding injury to the plaintiff against the social value and utility of the plaintiff's conduct and the extent and character of the harm suffered by the plaintiff. *Restatement (Second) of Torts* §§ 827–828. If the harm is significant and could be avoided without undue hardship, the defendant may be liable. *Restatement (Second) of Torts* § 830. Furthermore, if the harm is great, the defendant may be liable even if the cost of avoidance would make her operation unprofitable. *Id.,* comm. *c,* Illus. 2. Similarly, the defendant may be liable if its conduct is unsuitable to the location. *Restatement (Second) of Torts* § 831. Compliance with zoning ordinances will usually establish suitability of location, although not necessarily of use. *Winget v. Winn-Dixie Stores,* 242 S.C. 152, 130 S.E.2d 363 (1963). Presumably, also, indecent or malicious conduct, *see Restatement (Second) of Torts* § 829, will be actionable with no balancing required.

a. *Restatement (Second) of Torts* § 826(b) states, as an alternative to the risk-utility test, that an intentional invasion is unreasonable if "the harm caused by the conduct is serious and the financial burden of compensating for this and similar harm to others would not make the continuation of the conduct not feasible." Even if liability would render continuation of the conduct infeasible, however, liability may still be imposed for the reasons noted above. *Restatement (Second) of Torts* § 829A states that an invasion is unreasonable if the resulting harm "is severe and greater than the other should be required to bear without compensation."

b. Comment *i* to *Restatement (Second) of Torts* § 821B, dealing with public nuisance, distinguishes between an action in nuisance for damages and one for an injunction. "In an action for injunction the question is whether the activity itself is so unreasonable that it must be stopped. It may be reasonable to continue an important activity if payment is made for the harm it is causing, but unreasonable to continue it without paying." This approach has been taken toward a private nuisance. *Boomer v. Atl. Cement Co.,* 26 N.Y.2d 219, 309 N.Y.S.2d 312, 257 N.E.2d 870 (1970) (injunction to issue unless damages paid). Moreover, an injunction may be less drastic and more likely available where it partially, rather than totally, restricts an activity. *Boudinot v. State ex rel. Cannon,* 340 P.2d 268 (Okla. 1959) (noise and odors from forty cats held a public nuisance; defendant required to keep no more than four cats).

2. Where two competing interests are involved, the court may be required to weigh which interest is of greater value, either to the individuals involved, *Hendricks v. Stalnaker,* 380 S.E. 2d 198 (W. Va. 1989), or to the state, *Miller v. Schoene,* 276 U.S. 272 (1928). The lesser interest can be abated as a nuisance.

14

II.   DAMAGES

DAMAGES

A. **Types:** Damages may be either temporary or permanent. Temporary damages result if the injury "is not continuous but is sporadic and contingent upon some irregular force such as rain." *Atlas Chem. Indus. v. Anderson,* 524 S.W.2d 681 (Tex. 1975). When damages are permanent, the plaintiff may be required to seek all his damages in one action, rather than in successive actions as when damages are temporary; and the statute of limitations problems may be different for the two types of damages. A court may give the plaintiff her choice of whether to sue for temporary or permanent damages. *Baker v. Burbank, etc. Airport Authority,* 39 Cal.3d 862, 218 Cal. Rptr. 293, 705 P.2d 866 (1985).

1. If the defendant's conduct is wilful or callously indifferent to the interests of others, an award of punitive damages will be appropriate.

    Examples: In the *Atlas Chemical* case, given above, punitive damages were appropriate for defendant's continual discharging of black sediment into a creek with no apparent efforts to correct the problem. Punitive damages were also held appropriate in *Reynolds Metals Co. v. Lampert,* 324 F.2d 465 (9th Cir. 1963), where gladiolus growers sued an aluminum plant for harmful emissions. One of the defendant's managing officers had said that it was "cheaper to pay claims than it is to control fluorides."

B. **Limitations on Recoverable Damages:** If the plaintiff "comes to" the nuisance, *i.e.,* if the defendant was there first, this is a relevant factor but will not necessarily bar recovery. *McQuade v. Tucson Tiller Apts., Ltd.,* 25 Ariz. App. 312, 543 P.2d 150 (1975). If the coming-to amounts to consent, it can bar recovery entirely.

    Examples: Plaintiff sold defendant a portion of her land knowing that defendant intended to use it to construct a carbon-black plant. She could not recover for smoke and soot damages caused by the plant to the remainder of her property. *Crawford v. Magnolia Petrol. Co.,* 62 S.W.2d 264 (Tex. 1933). But a different result was reached in *Kellogg v. Village of Viola,* 67 Wis.2d 345, 227 N.W.2d 55 (1975), where the problem (smoke from trash burning) became much worse after the plaintiff mink farmer moved to the area. In *Spur Indus. v. Del E. Webb Dev. Co.,* 108 Ariz. 178, 494 P.2d 700 (1972), the court required the plaintiff, who moved to the nuisance, to pay for the costs of abatement of the nuisance.

1. Plaintiff is not entitled to damages if his injury results from his unusual sensitivity. The cases divide on the issue of what is unusual sensitivity or an idiosyncratic or unreasonable fear.

    Examples: Running a funeral home in a residential area was held to constitute a nuisance in *Travis v. Moore,* 377 So.2d 609 (Miss. 1979). But the plaintiffs were not entitled to an injunction based on decreased land values, resulting from speculative fears about the dangers of a half-way house for prison parolees, in *Nicholson v. Conn. Half-Way House, Inc.,* 153 Conn. 507, 218 A.2d 383 (1966).

2. If the government takes property, it may be constitutinally required to furnish just compensation unless the taking is permissible under the government's police power. The cases are divided on whether the damage or destruction of a building by the government to apprehend a fugitive is a taking for which compensation must be made. Annot., 23 A.L.R. 5th 834 (1994).

14

CHAPTER 14 – QUESTIONS, ANSWERS, AND TIPS

1. **Q:** Defendant tortiously destroyed a bridge which provided the only practical route for the residents of a village to reach their places of employment. Does each resident have an action in nuisance against the defendant?

   A: Each resident can recover if the destruction is a private nuisance as to each of them. Arguably the destruction is such a private nuisance, since each resident suffers damage different from the public in general, i.e., different from all users of the bridge other than the residents of the village. If the destruction is viewed as a public nuisance as to the residents, then perhaps they could seek relief in a class action.

   Tip: The problem with the public-private nuisance distinction is that it is unclear what is the obverse of "the public in general." The same problem is presented with the concept of false imprisonment where it involves a locking out rather than a locking in, and with distinguishing between public necessity and private necessity.

2. **Q:** A nuisance consists of an intangible invasion, while a trespass consists of a tangible invasion.

   A: False.

   Tip: Either tort can involve either type of intrusion, although some jurisdictions restrict trespass to a physical invasion.

3. **Q:** Plaintiff's contributory or comparative fault is no defense to an intentional nuisance action.

   A: The hornbook rule is that contributory or comparative fault is no defense in a case of intentional or reckless misconduct.

   Tip: Perhaps the hornbook rule should be restricted to intentional torts defined in terms of intent to cause the harm, rather than intent to do the act. The latter definition resembles strict liability, where plaintiff's fault has typically been a defense. *Cf.* the intentional torts of trespass to land and conversion, which are treated in some jurisdictions as including strict liability claims.

4. **Q:** A continuing nuisance is one subject to remediation at a reasonable cost, while a permanent nuisance is not subject to such remediation. What are the legal effects of this distinction?

   A: The statute of limitations for a single cause of action begins to run on reasonable discovery of a permanent nuisance, but the statute begins to run anew with each new invasion of a continuous nuisance so successive actions can be brought.

Tip: While successive actions can be brought for a continuing nuisance, only one action should be maintainable for all invasions occurring prior to filing that action and the statute will run on such invasions that occur after the statutory period has run on those invasions. In other words, a suit can be brought for all damages suffered within the statutory period before the suit was filed.

Note in the following section on damages it is stated that some courts give the plaintiff a choice to sue for temporary or permanent damages. That choice should determine the applicable statute of limitations and res judicata rules.

5. **Q:** Is the balancing test for determining negligence the same as that for determining nuisance?

   A: Yes, except that in nuisance, according to Rest. 2d of Torts §829A, a nuisance invasion is unreasonable if the harm caused is severe, and greater than the victim should be required to bear without compensation.

   Tip: Rest. 2d of Torts §829A recognizes a basic tension in the risk-benefit analysis: why should a party be allowed to take the property of another with impunity, even if the taking is for the greater public good? While the burden of correction may be impractical, the burden of paying for harm done may not be. Compare eminent domain, and public and private necessity, where the taker may be required to pay even though the taking is for the greater public good.

6. **Q:** If the government destroys plaintiff's premises in order to apprehend a fugitive, must it pay plaintiff for the damage caused by the destruction?

   A: The cases divide on the issue.

   Tip: The better rule seems to be that the government should have to pay, just as a private person should be required to pay if she destroyed property for the greater good. If the destruction resulted in personal injury or death, payment should be required; property damage should receive no less protection.

NOTES

CIVIL RIGHTS (OR CONSTITUTIONAL) TORTS

▶ CHAPTER SUMMARY

15

CIVIL RIGHTS (OR CONSTITUTIONAL) TORTS

Scope of Chapter: At English common law a government official who injured someone while acting beyond the scope of his authority was subject to suit by the injured person in the ordinary courts of law in the same way that a private person would be subject to such suit. Public officials were thus held liable for assault and battery, false imprisonment, etc. Some officials, judges, legislators, prosecutors, and cabinet officers, etc., enjoyed certain immunities from suit, particularly from actions for defamation, but in general, public officials were as much responsible for their torts as were private individuals. This aspect of the common law was carried over to what is now the United States. Over the years, the traditional common law remedies have been thought to be less effective in resolving official misconduct in the United States than they have been in England. State court juries were felt to be biased in favor of local officials, such as policemen, particularly in actions brought by members of minority groups. There thus arose substantial pressure to create federal remedies for what are sometimes called civil rights torts and at various other times constitutional torts. This chapter will outline these developments.

ACTIONS AGAINST STATE OFFICIALS

I. ACTIONS AGAINST STATE OFFICIALS: SECTION 1983

A. In General: First enacted in 1871, as part of the "Ku Klux" Act, 42 U.S.C. c 1983 provides that:

Every person who, under color of statute, ordinance, regulation, custom, or usage, of any State or Territory or the District of Columbia, subjects, or causes to be subjected, any citizen of the United States or other person within the jurisdiction thereof to the deprivation of any rights, privileges, or immunities secured by the Constitution and laws, shall be liable to the party injured in an action at law, suit in equity, or proper proceeding for redress.

In *Monroe v. Pape,* 365 U.S. 167, 81 S. Ct. 473, 5 L.Ed.2d 492 (1961), the Court held that police officers who, in making an arrest, were clearly acting in violation of the constitution and laws of Illinois and, consequently, could have been subject to suit in the Illinois state courts, were nevertheless acting under color of state law so as to be also subject to suit in federal court under § 1983.

A plaintiff seeking § 1983 redress must assert a violation of a federal *right*, not merely a failure to observe federal law. A plaintiff has such a right when (1) the Constitution (and interpretations of it) so requires or (2) a federal statute creates the right. A federal statutory provision creates such a right when the plaintiff is an intended beneficiary of the statute in question, his interests are not vague and amorphous, and the statute imposes a binding obligation on a State official.

1. **Municipalities:** The Court in *Monroe* initially held that § 1983 did not impose liability on a municipal corporation for the acts of its employees. The Court has since overruled that portion of *Monroe* and has held that municipalities can be held liable under § 1983 for the acts of their employees when the actions in question were done in execution of official policy or were the actions of senior officials who could be said to make the policy of the municipality. Municipalities are thus not themselves liable under § 1983 for all torts committed by their employees while the employees are acting in the course of their employment. To hold a municipality liable, a plaintiff must identify a municipal *policy or custom* that caused the injury; that is, the employee must have been following the policy or custom of the municipality when he caused the plaintiff's injury. This ensures that the injury results from the *policy maker's* acts, not merely the independent tortious acts of the employee. The plaintiff must then demonstrate that the policy maker acted with the intent to deprive the plaintiff of a federally protected right, acted in violation of federal law, or was deliberately indifferent to the known or obvious consequences of its actions. The plaintiff must of course also show a direct causal link between his injury and the policy maker's action. *See Board of the County Commissioners of Bryan County, Oklahoma v. Brown*, 520 U.S. 397, 117 S. Ct. 1382, 137 L.E.2d 626 (1997).

2. ***States:*** The Court has continued to hold, however, that Congress did not provide the specific authorization in § 1983 that is required by the Court's reading of the Eleventh Amendment in order to permit suit against the state itself in the federal courts.

3. ***Range of Rights Protected:*** The Court has also held that the reference in § 1983 to deprivation of rights, etc., "secured by the . . . laws" covers all federal law and not just those federal statutes concerned with equal rights. The Court has furthermore ruled that actions for violations of the Commerce Clause may also be brought under § 1983. *See Dennis v. Higgins,* 498 U.S. 439, 111 S. Ct. 865, 112 L.Ed.2d. 969 (1991). The dissenters in *Dennis* argued that the Commerce Clause is only concerned with delimiting the regulatory power of state and federal governments and not the creation of "rights," as is required by the language of § 1983.

15

B. **Attorney Fees:** Under an amendment to 42 U.S.C. § 1988 enacted in 1976, attorney fees can be granted to the prevailing parties in this type of litigation. In actions brought under § 1983 and related statutes, attorney fees are almost always granted to prevailing plaintiffs, but defendants can only recover attorney fees when the plaintiff's action is frivolous.

C. **Punitive Damages:** The Court has held that punitive damages are available in § 1983 actions against individuals upon a showing that the defendant's conduct was motivated by evil motives, or when the defendant's conduct involved reckless or callous indifference to federally protected rights.

1. Punitive damages are not available, however, in actions against municipalities.

D. **Recovery:** The Court has held that § 1983 only permits the recovery of actual damages. There can be no recovery of presumed damages for the abstract deprivation of rights. The Court has, however, left open the possibility that where compensatory damages for actual injuries are difficult to measure, resort might be had to presumed damages.

E. **Where Can Suit Be Brought?:** Actions under § 1983 can be brought in state courts as well as in the federal courts. Where the action is brought in the state courts the states may not apply provisions of state law which impose restrictions upon the plaintiff that would not be applicable if the action had been brought in the federal courts.

F. **Reference to State Law:** In 42 U.S.C. § 1988, in provisions which date from 1866, Congress has provided that, where federal law is not suitable to achieve the purposes of the various civil rights statutes or are deficient in the provision of remedies, the federal courts may refer to the common law as modified and changed by the constitution and statutes of the state in which the federal court having jurisdiction over the case is sitting, so far as so doing would not be inconsistent with the Constitution and laws of the United States.

1. ***Limitation Periods:*** Relying on § 1988, the Court has held that the characterization of § 1983 actions for purposes of applying a statute of limitations would be governed by federal law, but state law would provide the appropriate limitation. The Court has furthermore held that there should be a single statute of limitations for all § 1983 claims regardless of their nature and that all § 1983 claims should be characterized as "personal injury actions" for the purpose of applying state statutes of limitations. If the state has more than one statute of limitations for personal injury actions, § 1983 actions are to be governed by the residual or general personal injury statute of limitations rather than the statute of limitations for enumerated intentional torts.

G. **Relationship to State Remedies:** In *Monroe v. Pape, supra,* the Court held that resort to § 1983 does not require exhaustion of available state remedies. The Court has, however, been reluctant to

15

allow § 1983 actions to become substitutes for state law when the defendant is a state official whose actions are alleged to have injured the plaintiff. In *Paul v. Davis,* 424 U.S. 693, 96 S. Ct. 1155, 47 L.Ed.2d 405 (1976), the Court held that what was in essence a defamation action against the defendant police chiefs for libeling the plaintiff in a flyer about shoplifters could not be brought under § 1983. Similarly, the Court has held, in *Ingraham v. Wright,* 430 U.S. 651, 97 S. Ct. 1401, 51 L.Ed.2d 711 (1977), that the paddling of students in a public school did not give rise to a claim under the Eighth Amendment's Cruel and Unusual Punishment Clause because the students were not being punished for the commission of a crime and that, whatever due process claims the students might have because of the manner in which the paddlings were administered could be redressed under Florida statutory and common law.

H. **Types of Conduct That Can Give Rise to an Action:** After wrestling with the question for a substantial period of time, the Court has ruled that a § 1983 action will not lie for merely negligent conduct. The Court has expressly left open whether something less than intentional conduct, such as recklessness or gross negligence, might be enough to give rise to a § 1983 action. In a recent case, the Supreme Court held that prison officials would be liable for harm to an inmate only when they knew that the prisoner faced a substantial risk of serious harm and exhibited deliberate indifference to that risk. *See Farmer v. Brennan,* 511 U.S. 825, 114 S.Ct. 1970, 128 L.Ed.2d 811 (1994).

I. **Civil Rights Actions Against States and Their Officials under State Law:** Some State courts allow civil actions for violations of provisions of their State Constitutions. In *Binette v. Sabo,* 244 Conn. 23, 710 A.2d 688 (1998), the court grounded its creation of such an action against state and local officials on provisions of the *Restatement (Second) of Torts* and *Bivens v. Six Unknown Named Agents of Federal Bureau of Narcotics,* 403 U.S. 388, 91 S. Ct. 1999, 29 L.Ed.2d 619 (1971), which recognized the possibility of actions against federal officials for conduct that violated the United States Constitution. The *Restatement (Second)* states that when a "legislative [or constitutional] provision protects a class of persons by proscribing or requiring certain conduct but does not provide a civil remedy for the violation, the court may, if it determines that the remedy is appropriate in furtherance of the purpose of the legislation and needed to assure the effectiveness of the provision, accord to an injured member of the class a right of action." Restatement (Second) of Torts § 874A cmt. a (1979). The reasoning underlying *Bivens* also provides a rationale for allowing such actions, namely deterring state officials who "possess a far greater capacity for harm than an individual trespasser exercising no authority other than his own."

1. One court has even allowed such actions against the State itself for civil rights violations perpetrated by its employees. The court in *Brown v. New York,* 89 N.Y.2d 172, 674 N.E.2d 1129, 652 N.Y.S.2d 233 (1996), found that the state should be held vicariously liable for its employees' acts because it could avoid such misconduct by properly training and supervising its employees and disciplining and discharging offenders.

ACTIONS   II.   **ACTIONS AGAINST FEDERAL OFFICIALS**
AGAINST
FEDERAL
OFFICIALS   A. **In General:** In *Bivens v. Six Unknown Named Agents of Federal Bureau of Narcotics,* 403 U.S. 388, 91 S. Ct. 1999, 29 L.Ed.2d 619 (1971), the Court finally decided that an action could be brought in federal court for an improper arrest and consequent search by federal officers. The majority of the Court declared that the interests protected by state laws regulating trespass and invasions of privacy and the interests protected by the Fourth Amendment's protection against unreasonable searches and seizures might be inconsistent or even hostile.

1. The Court in *Bivens* left open the question as to what if any defenses might be available to federal officials in civil rights actions brought against them in the federal courts. Almost

immediately, the lower courts held that law enforcement officials had no absolute privilege but would be protected if they could show good faith and reasonable grounds for believing that they were acting properly. This question will be discussed more fully in Section III, *infra,* devoted to the broader question of immunities.

2. ***Relation to Actions Brought against the United States:*** As a result of the creation of the *Bivens*-type action against federal officials, in 1974 the Federal Tort Claims Act was amended to provide that with regard "to acts or omissions of investigative or law enforcement officers of the United States," claims "arising out of . . . assault, battery, false imprisonment, false arrest, abuse of process, or malicious prosecution" could be brought against the United States. The Court has held that the availability of an action against the United States under the Federal Tort Claims Act does not prevent an action from also being brought under *Bivens* against federal officials. The availability of a civil rights action against federal officials has been preserved even after the Congress in 1988 made the remedy available under the Federal Tort Claims Act the exclusive remedy for torts committed under state law by federal officials acting in the course of their employment. *See* 28 U.S.C. § 2679(b)(2).

3. Many of the doctrines developed in § 1983 actions have been carried over to *Bivens*-type actions against federal officials. One of the most important common features relates to the question of the immunities that might be possessed by the defendants in such actions, and it is to this question that we now turn.

III. IMMUNITIES FROM CIVIL RIGHTS ACTIONS

IMMUNITIES
FROM CIVIL
RIGHTS ACTIONS

A. Immunities can be absolute or qualified. Relying on common law analogues, the Court has held that legislators are absolutely immune from civil rights actions, at least with regard to any activities that might be considered part of their legislative functions. The same absolute immunity has been granted to persons performing a judicial function and to those persons engaged in performing the functions of a prosecutor. *See Butz v. Economou,* 438 U.S. 478, 98 S. Ct. 2894, 57 L.Ed.2d 895 (1978). That is not to say that a judge may not be the subject of a civil rights action for conduct engaged in by the judge when not acting in a judicial capacity.

Example: Judges have been subject to suits by judicial administrative employees on the ground of sex discrimination in employment.

1. Although the Court had at one time ruled to the contrary, it has now held that the President of the United States is absolutely immune for any activities within the "outer perimeter" of his official responsibilities. *Nixon v. Fitzgerald,* 457 U.S. 731, 102 S. Ct. 2690, 73 L.Ed.2d 349 (1982). The President is not entitled to immunity, however, for his unofficial acts and is not automatically entitled to have all civil actions stayed until the conclusion of his term of office. *See Clinton v. Jones,* 117 S. Ct. 1636, 137 L.Ed.2d 945 (1997).

    a. Cabinet officers, presidential assistants, and other executive officers, however, have been held only to enjoy a qualified privilege, namely an immunity from suit when they can show that they have acted in good faith. The qualified privilege thus shields these and subordinate public officials from liability unless their actions "violate 'clearly established statutory or constitutional rights of which a reasonable person would have known.'" *Mitchell v. Forsyth,* 472 U.S. 511, 524, 105 S. Ct. 2806, 2814, 86 L.Ed.2d 411 (1985). If the claim of constitutional violation is based simply on what the Court termed a "substantive due process" violation of the plaintiff's rights, rather than on the violation of some more specific constitutional provision, the conduct in question must "shock the conscience." *City of Sacramento v. Lewis,* 188 S. Ct. 1708 (1998) (police office not liable to person injured in high-speed chase.)

    b.   While § 1983 can impose liability upon private individuals acting under color of State law, such private individuals cannot take advantage of the immunities available to state employees even if, like private prison guards, they are performing a function normally performed by state employees. *See Richaardsoon v. McKnight,* 117 S. Ct. 2100, 138 L..Ed.2d 540 (1997).

    2.   When a § 1983 action is brought against a municipality, the municipality itself cannot take advantage of any qualified immunity based upon the good faith and absence of malice of the officials for whose conduct the municipality is responsible. Qualified immunity only applies in actions against individual officials.

15

CHAPTER 15 - QUESTIONS, ANSWERS, AND SOME TIPS

1. **Q:** If the actions of a state government official are clearly illegal under state law, his actions will not be considered as being "under color of state law" for purposes of a civil rights action brought under 42 U.S.C. § 1983.

  A: False

2. **Q:** A plaintiff who prevails in a § 1983 action has a good chance of receiving, in addition, an award of attorneys fees.

  A: True. Note, however, that the statutory authorization (42 U.S.C. § 1988) for attorneys fees in these actions does not apply to Bivens-type civil rights actions against federal officials.

3. **Q:** A defendant who prevails in a § 1983 action brought against him has a good chance of receiving an award of attorneys fees against the unsuccessful plaintiff.

  A: False. Unlike a prevailing plaintiff a prevailing defendant can only obtain an award of attorneys fees if the plaintiff's action is found to have been frivolous.

  Tip: Section 1983 actions have been regarded as designed to free the plaintiff from procedural obstacles that would otherwise discourage plaintiffs from seeking to vindicate their civil rights. Routinely awarding attorneys fees to prevailing defendants would discourage potential plaintiffs.

4. **Q:** Since Congress has now made a Federal Tort Claims action against the United States, the exclusive remedy for torts under state law committed by federal employees acting in the course of their employment, Bivens-type civil-rights actions can no longer be brought against federal officials acting in the course of their employment for conduct that would be tortious under state law.

  A: False. One reason why a plaintiff might want to pursue a Bivens-type civil-rights action against a federal official, rather than an action against the United States under the Federal Tort Claims Act, is that under a Bivens-type action the plaintiff can secure a jury trial and, in some circumstances, also secure an award of punitive damages, neither of which would be possible under the Tort Claims Act.

5. Q: A § 1983 action may be brought against a state when state officials acting under color of state law violate a person's federally protected civil rights.

A: False. Section 1983 has been held not to authorize actions against the states.

6. Q: Municipalities can, under some circumstances, be subject to a § 1983 action for invasion of a person's federally protected civil rights by municipal employees.

A: True. If the actions of the municipal employees are performed in execution of official municipal policy or are the actions of senior officials with policy-making responsibilities and authority, an action will lie against the municipalities.

Tip: While municipalities are treated differently from states, they still enjoy some protection not accorded to individual defendants. For example, municipalities are not liable for punitive damages. The presence of a governmental entity as a defendant should always make you ask whether that circumstance makes a difference.

7. Q: A state or federal judge only enjoys a qualified immunity from civil-rights actions for anything the judge might say or do in the exercise of his judicial functions.

A: False. Judges enjoy an absolute immunity for anything said or done in the performance of their judicial duties.

Tip: When issues of immunity are raised, a good starting point is to consider whether the governmental official would enjoy any immunity under state common law, as for example in state-law defamation actions or actions for malicious prosecution.

8. Q: A state or federal official may be liable in a civil-rights action for unintentional harm caused by the official's negligent conduct.

A: False. The Supreme Court has even left open the question whether recklessness or gross negligence will be enough to provide a basis for a civil-rights action.

NOTES

DEFAMATION

▶ CHAPTER SUMMARY

DEFAMATION

Scope of Chapter: Defamation is a tort that is still characterized by a great many technical considerations that in other areas of tort law would have been discarded as anachronisms. Undoubtedly, the common law's retention of most of these technical features has been influenced by the desire to give greater protection to freedom of speech. Since 1964, the Supreme Court of the United States has engrafted additional restrictions on a plaintiff's ability to bring defamation actions on the ground that these additional restrictions are needed in order to realize the purposes of the First Amendment. In this chapter, we will first discuss the common law development of defamation, a development which includes the historic distinction between slander and libel, and the various defenses to an action for defamation which evolved at common law. We shall then turn to the constitutional considerations which the Supreme Court has superimposed upon this basic common law structure.

16

COMMON LAW ACTION

I. THE COMMON LAW ACTION FOR DEFAMATION

A. Definition: Defamation consists of the publication to third parties of matter which is false and defamatory. The material will be defamatory if its tendency is to harm the reputation of another person so as to lower that person in the estimation of the community or to deter third persons from associating or dealing with that person. Some courts have preferred an alternate definition: namely, false statements about another to that person's discredit.

B. The Distinction between Slander and Libel: For historical reasons, the tort of defamation has two forms. The first, *slander,* concerns oral communications. The second, *libel,* concerns written communications. Jurisdiction over what is now called slander was, before the Protestant Reformation, primarily exercised by the ecclesiastical courts. With the decline of the ecclesiastical courts after the Reformation, plaintiffs turned to the common law courts. Many of the restrictions on the tort of slander are therefore explained as reflecting the desire of the common law courts to discourage the bringing of such actions. Libel, which concerns written matter, was viewed differently by the Crown and its ministers. With the advent of printing, the Court of Star Chamber, a prerogative court which served as a judicial arm of the Privy Council, became most interested in prosecuting criminal libel in which the defendant was accused of undermining public confidence and authority; but Star Chamber also provided remedies for aggrieved private persons. With the abolishment of Star Chamber in 1641, the exercise of this jurisdiction, too, was taken on by the common law courts.

C. Slander: Slander may be defined as a false and defamatory oral communication. In order to bring an action for slander, the plaintiff is required to show either special damages or that the slanderous statement falls into the category of slander that has been denominated *slander* per se.

1. Special damages: These are damages that have been suffered by a plaintiff as the direct result of the plaintiff's reputation having been lowered in the eyes of the community. It is not enough that the plaintiff has suffered some kind of foreseeable pecuniary harm as a result of the slanderous statement; the harm must flow directly from the plaintiff's loss of reputation. The plaintiff's loss must flow from the reaction to the defamatory remark by third parties, not from any reaction to the defamation by the plaintiff himself, such as his suffering emotional distress.

Example: In the course of a speech, *B* states that *A*, a prominent retired lawyer, has held himself out as an ex–major league baseball player when in fact *A*, who was once a noted college athlete, was never a major league baseball player. The statement by *B* is false. *A* has never held himself out to be an ex–major league player. As a result of *B*'s statement, which was heard by a great many people, *A* suffers severe embarrassment and humiliation. He is obliged to seek medical treatment and has expended a considerable amount of money for medical treatment. *A* has not suffered any special damages. *Cf. Terwilliger v. Wands,* 17 N.Y. 54, 72 Am. Dec. 520 (1858). Although mental distress and the attendant expenses do not constitute special damages, once special damage is shown, the plaintiff's recovery can also include compensation for these items.

Example: In a speech, *B* states that *A* was disciplined in college for cheating on an examination. *A* is a teacher at a private school. The statement is repeated to the headmaster of the school, and *A* is discharged. *A* has suffered special damages. Unlike the illness suffered in the first example, the loss of his position is a direct consequence of *A*'s lowered reputation in the community.

At common law, in addition to the loss of employment, the loss of a favorable marriage and the denial of membership in a club were also considered examples of special damages.

2. Certain categories of slander were characterized as slander per se, namely as instances of slander in which recovery might be had without allegation and proof of special damages. In actions involving instances of slander per se, some damage as a result of the defamatory statement was presumed. Statements that are slanderous per se fall into the following four categories:

    a. *Statements imputing criminal conduct:* The older cases indicate that the crime must be one involving moral turpitude or an indictable offense. More recent authority holds that the imputation of any criminal conduct is enough, whether the conduct is punishable by imprisonment or fine. *Restatement (Second) of Torts* § 571 adopts the intermediate position that the conduct charged must be punishable by imprisonment or involve moral turpitude.

    b. *Statements imputing infection with a loathsome or infectious disease:* This category is generally restricted to venereal diseases and leprosy. Presumably AIDS would come within this category as well.

    c. *Statements imputing a lack of chastity to a woman:* At common law such statements were not actionable without proof of special damages but, following the British Slander of Women Act of 1891, 54 & 55 Vict. c. 51, the law was changed by statute or judicial decision in America as well. *Restatement (Second) of Torts* § 574 extends this category of slander per se to all "serious sexual misconduct," including lack of chastity in men and homosexuality. It is unclear whether all courts will follow this extension.

    d. *Statements directly affecting a person's office, profession, or trade or business:* Most cases of slander per se fall into this category which is the most expandable of all the slander per se categories.

        Example: *B* makes an oral statement falsely alleging that *A*, a lawyer, has misused the funds of clients. The statement would be actionable as an instance of slander per se by *A*. A charge that a lawyer misuses funds entrusted to his care by a client will affect *A* in his business or professional capacity.

    e. The four slander per se catergories remain fixed, although there has been at least one unsuccessful recent attempt to create a new catergory to cover charges of social and ethnic bigotry. *See Ward v. Zelinovsky,* 136 N.J. 516, 643 A.2d. 972 (N.J. 1994).

D. Libel: At common law libel was actionable without proof of special damages. This is still the law in England and is probably the law in the majority of American jurisdictions. *See Restatement (Second) of Torts* § 569; *Hinsdale v. Orange County Publications, Inc.,* 17 N.Y.2d 284, 270 N.Y.S. 592, 217 N.E.2d 650 (1966).

16

1. A significant number of jurisdictions in the United States distinguish between libel per se, which is actionable without proof of special damages, and libel per quod, which, like slander, requires the allegation and proof of special damages.

   a. *Basis for the distinction:* The jurisdictions that distinguish between libel per se and libel per quod may do so on several possible bases.

      (1) If a libel is clear on its face, that is, if to make out the libel the plaintiff does not have to allege any extrinsic facts, the libel will be considered per se. If, in order to make out the libel, the plaintiff must allege the existence of extrinsic facts, that is, facts which are not apparent from the statement in question, the libel will be considered per quod.

      Example: A newspaper reports that *X* and *Y* are engaged to marry. It turns out that not only are *X* and *Y* not engaged to marry, but each is currently married to another person. These were essentially the facts in the *Hinsdale* case, *supra,* in which the New York Court of Appeals reaffirmed the traditional common law rule and refused to distinguish between so-called libel per se and libel per quod, holding that all libel is actionable without allegation and proof of special damages. In a jurisdiction that did distinguish between libel per se and libel per quod, this statement would probably not be actionable without allegation and proof of special damages because, to make out the libel, the plaintiffs must allege and prove certain extrinsic facts, namely that they are presently married to other people.

      (2) Libel per se and libel per quod may be distinguished on the basis of whether the libel falls into one of the four slander per se categories.

         (a) Some of the courts distinguishing libel per se and libel per quod on this basis will also insist that the libel not only fall into one of the slander per se categories but also that the libel appear on the face of the statement and not require the allegation and proof of extrinsic facts. Other jurisdictions that distinguish between libel per se and libel per quod only insist that the libel fall into one of the slander per se categories.

E. **Pleading an Action for Defamation:** It is customary for a plaintiff to include in the complaint a verbatim description of the defamatory statement. The complaint will also, of course, allege publication to third persons and explain how the statement relates to the plaintiff and why the statement is defamatory. It will finally include a claim for damages. If the defamation is of a kind that requires proof of special damages, these must be described in the complaint, and if proof of malice is required — as we shall see it sometimes is — in order to recover punitive damages or to defeat a claim of privilege, an allegation of such malice must also be included in the complaint. There are technical terms that are given to certain portions of the complaint. These are:

   1. *The inducement:* When neither the defamatory character of an alleged defamatory statement nor the statement's connection to the plaintiff is apparent from its actual words, the plaintiff will have to allege the facts necessary to support the claim that the statement is defamatory and that it refers to him in a portion of the complaint known as the *inducement.* It is sometimes said that these so-called extrinsic facts are "alleged by way of inducement."

   2. *The colloquium:* The part of the complaint in which the plaintiff, making use where necessary of facts contained in the inducement, asserts that the defamatory statement was made about him is called the *colloquium.*

16

3. ***The innuendo:*** The portion of the complaint in which the plaintiff explains why the statement defames him is called the *innuendo.* When courts wish to describe the method by which the plaintiff derives the defamatory meaning rather than some discrete portion of the complaint, the courts will speak of the plaintiff showing the defamatory nature of the statement "by way of innuendo." The meaning which the plaintiff wishes to derive from the statement in question must be a reasonable one. The trial judge will rule on whether reasonable people could so construe the statement. If the judge decides they could, the jury will then decide whether, in point of fact, the people to whom the statement was addressed did so understand the statement.

F. **Criminal Libel:** Criminal libel was an indictable offense at common law. As noted above, it was aimed at suppressing sedition and later extended to reach written material likely to lead to breaches of the peace. There never was any criminal slander. At one time, in contrast to the civil action for libel, truth was *not* a defense to criminal libel. This state of the law was altered in England by statute in 1843, and eventually in most American jurisdictions, to make truth a defense, at least if the matter was published for a "proper motive." In *Garrison v. Louisiana,* 379 U.S. 64, 85 S. Ct. 209, 13 L. Ed. 2d 125 (1964), the Court held that truth is an absolute defense to a prosecution for criminal libel.

G. **Publication:** In order for an action for defamation to lie, the defamatory statement must be published to third parties, that is, to someone other than to the person defamed. Publication to third parties must be either intentional or the result of negligent conduct on the part of the publisher. Purely innocent publication is not sufficient.

1. It is not necessary that a person realize that the statement made is defamatory in order for there to be publication. So long as the person intends to publish some particular statement or allows the statement to be published on account of negligence, the defamatory material is considered to have been published.

    Example: *A* makes the statement to third parties that "Robert F. Jones, 27 Pleasant Drive," etc., was convicted of tax fraud. The statement is true of a Robert G. Jones, 319 Summit Avenue. *A* thought he was referring to the correct Jones but owing to a mistake made either by himself or others — it makes no difference in this regard — has identified the wrong Jones. *A* has published matter defamatory of Robert F. Jones. *Cf. Michaels v. Gannett Co.,* 10 A.D.2d 417, 199 N.Y.S.2d 778 (1960).

    Example: *A* makes diary entries concerning people whom he meets during the course of his day. Many of these entries are highly unflattering and even defamatory of the persons named. Through no fault of *A*, the diary is stolen by a burglar and eventually finds its way to a sensationalist newspaper which publishes some of the defamatory extracts contained in the diary. *A* has not published the defamatory material and therefore will not be liable in any defamation action brought by the persons whom he has defamed. The magazine publisher, on the other hand, has published the material and is potentially liable to the persons defamed.

2. ***Distributors:*** Although the common law imposed what might be called an absolute liability upon those who intentionally or negligently published defamatory material, exceptions arose with regard to libraries, newsstands, book shops, and newspaper and magazine distributors. In actions against persons in these categories, the plaintiff must, at the very least, show that they had some knowledge of the defamatory content of the publication in question.

    a. The courts have reached inconsistent results as to whether internet providers are distributors. *In Cubby, Inc. v. CompuServe, Inc.,* 776 F.Supp. 135 (S.D.N.Y. 1991), for example, the court held that the defendant was merely a distributor and had no editorial control what was said over a discussion forum. In *Stratton Oakmont, Inc. v. Prodigy Services Co.,* 1995 WL 323710, 23 Media L.Rep. 1794 (N.Y.Sup. 1995), however, the court found that the defendant was a publisher, not a mere distributor, because it represented itself as exercising and had the capability of exercising *editorial control* over its bulletin board and could therefore be held liable for defamatory publications on that board.

3. At common law, each copy of a book containing defamatory material was a separate publication. Most American jurisdictions now follow what is called the "single publication rule." *See Restatement (Second) of Torts* § 577A. Under the single publication rule, any one edition of a book, newspaper, or any one radio or television broadcast is considered a single publication for which only one action will lie.

4. One who republishes defamatory statements made by third parties is held to be a publisher of defamatory material and is subject to liability as if he had originally published that material.

    Example: A newspaper feature syndicate supplies a defamatory column to a large number of subscribing newspapers. Each paper that prints the column has published a libel for which it may be subject to liability. The columnist who wrote the column would, under the single publication rule, most probably only be liable for the first publication of the column. This is important for statute of limitations purposes if the column is published, as is commonly the case, on different days in different newspapers. *See Givens v. Quinn*, 877 F. Supp. 485 (W.D. Mo. 1994).

5. Someone who fails to remove a defamatory statement affixed to his property by third parties within a reasonable time after receiving notice of the defamatory nature of the statement is himself liable for publishing the defamatory material. *See Hellar v. Bianco*, 111 Cal. App. 2d 424, 244 P.2d 757 (1952).

H. **Classification of Movies, Television, etc.:** The courts initially had some difficulty in classifying nontraditional methods of communication. Some of the early cases held that radio broadcasts were a type of slander because the publication was oral. On the other hand, phonograph records were analogized to libel because the defamatory statement had a permanent form. Television and motion pictures have now all been classified as libel and so, in most jurisdictions, has radio either because the defamatory material was read from a text or, more often, because radio can reach a vast audience and is thus capable of causing the same kind of damage as a written statement.

1. In the United States, a number of states have passed statutes absolving broadcasters from liability for innocent defamation. Even where the defendant is unable to show a lack of fault in publishing the defamatory material, some of these statutes limit the plaintiff to the recovery of only actual damages, that is, they do not permit recovery of "presumed damages."

I. **Opinion:** The *Restatement of Torts* § 566 took the position that defamation might consist of a statement of opinion even if the underlying facts were known or assumed by the parties to the communication. There was some limited common law support for this position, but not much. The greater problem was that the *Restatement's* position contradicted its own requirement that no defamation action could lie unless the matter in question was false. There were also some cases imposing liability for defamation upon those who engaged in parody for what were considered to be unfair parodies of others. The Court has now made it clear in *Gertz v. Robert Welch, Inc.*, 418 U.S. 323, 94 S. Ct. 2997, 41 L. Ed. 2d 789 (1974) (dictum) and *Old Dominion Branch No. 496, Nat'l Ass'n of Letter Carriers v. Austin*, 418 U.S. 264, 94 S. Ct. 2770, 41 L. Ed. 2d 745 (1974) (alternative holding) that the mere expression of opinion cannot be the subject of an action for defamation. For this reason the *Restatement (Second)* has dropped any provisions dealing with defamatory opinions or parodies. An expression of opinion (or a parody) is actionable only if it implies that there are undisclosed defamatory facts which provide the basis for the opinion. *See Restatement (Second) of Torts* § 566. But, if there is such a factual implication, couching a statement in the form of an opinion will prevent liability. *See Milkovich v. Lorain Journal Co.,* 477 U.S. 1, 110 S. Ct. 2695, 111 L. Ed. 2d 1 (1990), where the Court rejected the suggestion that, under *Gertz,* an opinion was not actionable even if it carried with it a defamatory factual implication. When an author outlines the facts available to him, however, and makes it clear that the challenged statements represent his own interpretation of those facts and leaves the reader free to draw his own conclusions, his statements are generally protected by the First Amendment. *See e.g., Partington v. Bugliosi,* 56 F.3d 1147 (9th Cir. 1995). As already noted, however, if the stated or implied facts underlying an opinion are defamatory in nature, and if it can be shown that the plaintiff had the necessary scienter regarding the possible falsity of those facts, an action for defamation may lie.

Example: *A* and *B* are discussing a wealthy neighbor *C* whom *A* and *B* both know to be an ardent supporter of abortion rights. After adverting to *C's* position on the issue of abortion, *A* tells *B* that "in my opinion, *C* is an abettor of murder." *A*'s statement, as the expression of an opinion, is not actionable. Even if *A* had omitted the words "in my opinion," in this context the statement would still, most probably, be held to be the protected expression of an opinion.

Example: *A* and *B* are discussing a wealthy neighbor *C* whom *A* purports to know well, but with whom *B* has only a passing acquaintance. *A* tells *B,* "I've known *C* for thirty years, and in my opinion, the reason *C* has become so rich is that he's been embezzling money from the company at which he works." Although couched as an opinion, to someone like *B* who does not know *C* well, *A's* statement implies that *A* is aware of specific facts that provide the basis for *A's* opinion. *A's* statement about *C* is defamatory and, if false, actionable.

1. In many cases, deciding what is a statement of fact and what is a statement of opinion will be very difficult. There are no hard and fast rules that can be used to decide the issue. The courts have considered how specific a statement is, the degree of its verifiability, the textual context, such as the entire article or speech in which the statement appeared, and finally, the social context or setting in which, say, the article appeared or the speech was made. A leading case on the subject is *Ollman v. Evans,* 750 F.2d 970 (D.C. Cir. 1984) (en banc).

2. A defamatory charge may be made by inference, implication or insinuation. In a recent case, a doctor told patients that he would not want a physician with AIDS treating him were he a patient. The court ruled that the doctor had falsely implied that a cardiologist with AIDS was placing his patients at inappropriate risk and insinuated that he was unfit to perform his job. *See Tolman v. Doe,* 988 F.Supp. 582 (E.D. Va. 1997).

J. **Group Defamation:** In order to recover, the plaintiff must show that someone to whom the defamatory statement was published would understand that the plaintiff is the person referred to. This has become a difficult question when the plaintiff is a member of a group that has been defamed.

Example: In *Fawcett Publications, Inc. v. Morris,* 377 P.2d 42 (Okla. 1962), *cert. denied,* 376 U.S. 513 (1964), the defendant magazine published an article which a reasonable person could interpret as stating that the members of a championship college football team took amphetamines to enhance their athletic performance. The statement was false. The plaintiff was one of about twenty-five players who played regularly on that team. It was held that a reasonable jury could conclude that the plaintiff, as one of the regular players on the team, was using amphetamines. The total number of players on the team approached seventy. It is unclear whether one of the players who seldom appeared in a game would have been able to succeed in an action for defamation.

1. Certainly as the class of which the plaintiff is a member increases in size the likelihood that the courts will allow a jury to conclude that the statement defamed the plaintiff decreases. Furthermore, in *Morris, supra,* if the statement in question had been interpreted as saying only that some of the football players on the team took amphetamines, it becomes more doubtful

that even a regular player, such as the plaintiff, would have been held to have been defamed by the statement in question.

    a.   There have been some intermittent attempts to make group defamation of racial or religious minorities prosecutable as some sort of criminal libel. In recent years, such attempts have been largely unsuccessful. The subject is more appropriately covered in a course on constitutional law.

K. Miscellaneous Matters: As the student has by now already observed, the law of defamation has many special features. In this subsection, we discuss a few of the additional special features of which a student should be aware.

    1.   Although a few states by statute have provided otherwise, the general rule is that there can be no defamation of the dead. That is not to say that there cannot be defamation by the dead. There are a number of cases in which defamatory statements made in a will about living persons have been held to give rise to a defamation action brought against the estate of the deceased.

    2.   Defamation is one of the actions which, in at least half the states, does not survive the death of either the plaintiff or the defendant.

L. Alternative Remedies: From time to time, suggestions have been made with regard to the provision of alternative remedies which are less complex and easier to utilize by those who feel that false things have been said about them than the traditional common law of defamation.

    1.   *Retraction:* A timely retraction has always been considered relevant to the issue of damages. A few states by statute provide that unless a retraction is demanded and refused, the plaintiff may not recover any general damages from a media defendant; such a plaintiff is limited to his "special damages."

        a.   In *Miami Herald Publishing Co. v. Tornillo,* 418 U.S. 241, 94 S. Ct. 2831, 41 L. Ed. 2d 730 (1974), a unanimous Court struck down a Florida statute requiring newspapers to publish a reply by any candidate for public office whom the newspaper had attacked. This does not mean that a state may not make a request for a retraction a condition for bringing an action.

    2.   In recent years, particularly in response to the constitutional developments that will be discussed later in this chapter, there have been a number of suggestions that the plaintiff should be given an action in which the principal issue is only the falsity of the defamatory statement that has been made about the plaintiff. The plaintiff would not have to introduce any proof about the defendant's state of mind but would recover no damages. Some of these proposed statutes are limited only to media defendants. These proposals usually provide for the award of attorney fees to the prevailing parties. Thus far, none of these suggestions has been adopted.

M. Circumstances Mitigating Damages: A defendant may also offer proof that, prior to the publication of the defamatory statements, the plaintiff had a poor general reputation. Proof of a poor reputation can reduce the value of the injured interest. The defendant may not reduce this value, however, by alleging that the plaintiff has performed specific unsavory acts with no connection to the defamation in question. *See Crane v. New York World Telegram Corp.,* 308 N.Y. 470, 126 N.E.2d 753 (N.Y. 1955).

COMMON LAW   **II.**   **COMMON LAW DEFENSES TO AN ACTION FOR DEFAMATION**
DEFENSES

    A. Truth: At common law, truth was generally an absolute defense to an action for defamation. The few exceptions concern statements such as opinions or parodies which were not capable of being true or false, but which, as indicated above, were nevertheless thought actionable because they were unfair or excessive.

1. At common law, truth was an affirmative defense which had to be raised and proved by the defendant. It now seems clear that, at least in those areas of the law of defamation that are affected by the constitutional considerations to which we shall turn in section III of this chapter, the burden of persuasion on the issue of truth or falsity is on the plaintiff. *See Philadelphia Newspapers, Inc. v. Hepps,* 475 U.S. 767, 106 S. Ct. 1558, 89 L. Ed. 2d 783 (1986). That is, rather than the defendant having to show that the statement was true, the plaintiff will be obliged to show that the statement in question was false.

B. Absolute Privileges: In addition to truth, the common law recognized other absolute defenses to an action for defamation, but unlike truth — which was always known as an absolute *defense* — these other absolute defenses are normally described as absolute *privileges.* The absolute privileges include:

1. ***Spousal communications:*** Communications between spouses are absolutely privileged. Although a statement by one spouse to another about someone else constitutes publication, the publication is privileged and cannot form the basis of an action for defamation.

2. ***The reporting privilege:*** Reports of official proceedings, if accurate, are absolutely privileged. This common law privilege has been extended to cover "public meetings" and now probably includes the shareholders' meeting of a public corporation. An open question is whether the reporting privilege will permit a newspaper to claim absolute privilege for accurately reporting a public dispute between two public figures.

    Example: A newspaper publishes an accurate report of the charges and counter-charges made by contending scientists on the issue of whether the use of some insecticide is affecting bird life. Many of these charges are false and defamatory. In *Edwards v. National Audubon Soc'y, Inc.,* 556 F.2d 113 (2d Cir.), *cert. denied,* 434 U.S. 1002 (1977), such a news report by the *New York Times* was held entitled to the reporting privilege. It remains to be seen whether *Edwards* represents the wave of the future. It has been rejected by some other federal circuits and state courts and accepted by a few state courts.

3. ***Privileges of public officials and participants in public proceedings:*** Certain public officials have an absolute privilege for any statements made while they are acting in their official capacity. An absolute privilege has also been extended to private persons who participate in certain types of public proceedings.

    a. *Legislators:* Statements made by legislators acting in a legislative capacity are absolutely privileged. With regard to Congress, the Court has held that the privilege extends to committee meetings and the insertion of material in the *Congressional Record.* The privilege also protects legislative staff members insofar as the latter are assisting a legislator in the performance of what might be called a "legislative act." Some states distinguish between state legislators who are granted an absolute privilege and the members of subordinate legislatures, such as city councils and school boards, who are only granted a qualified privilege, a subject which will be discussed below. Most jurisdictions, however, grant an absolute privilege to members of all legislative bodies, including subordinate legislatures. Witnesses before legislative bodies, at least if their remarks are germane to the issue under legislative consideration, will be granted the same privilege as is granted to the members of those bodies.

    b. *Judicial Privileges:* Judges and prosecutors enjoy an absolute privilege with regard to statements made while they are acting in their official capacity. This absolute privilege also extends to statements made by parties, witnesses, jurors, and attorneys in the course of judicial proceedings, although with regard to these persons there is some uncertainty as to whether the absolute privilege extends to all statements they might make in the course of the judicial proceedings or whether the absolute privilege only extends to statements that have some relevance to the judicial proceeding in question.

    (1) In most jurisdictions, statements made to prosecuting authorities about suspected criminal conduct are absolutely privileged. This privilege has been extended to cover complaints to entities such as bar grievance committees. If the plaintiff has any redress in such situations, the remedy would be an action for malicious prosecution, which will be discussed in Chapter 18, *infra.*

    c. *Executive Officials:* In *Barr v. Matteo,* 360 U.S. 564, 79 S. Ct. 1335, 3 L. Ed. 2d 1434 (1959), the Court held that federal officials enjoy an absolute privilege with regard to all statements made within "the outer perimeter" of their duties. Although, as noted in Chapter 15, *supra,* subsequent cases have made it clear that most federal officials have no absolute privilege protecting them against civil rights actions or most common law tort actions, the Court has given no indication that it is prepared to cut back on the absolute privilege of federal officials acting within the scope of their authority from state-law defamation actions that was recognized in *Barr v. Matteo.* Most states have traditionally distinguished between major executive officers, such as governors and the state equivalents of federal cabinet officers, who are granted an absolute privilege, and lesser officials, who are only granted a qualified privilege, a subject that will be discussed below. The trend in many states appears to be to enlarge the class of officials who are granted an absolute privilege.

    d. *Witness Statements:* There is normally an absolute privilege for a witness's statements in judicial proceedings. The *Restatement (Second) of Torts* § 590A (1977) accords an absolute privilege to a witness's statements made as part of a legislative proceeding so long as they bear some relation to the proceeding. At least one state court, however, has declined to follow the Restatement's guidance in some circumstances. In *Vultaggio v. Yasko,* 572 N.W. 2d 450, 215 Wis.2d 325 (1998), the court ruled that witnesses giving voluntary, *unsworn* testimony in legislative proceedings enjoy only a qualified privilege.

4. ***Publications consented to:*** A defendant normally enjoys an absolute privilege for publications consented to by the plaintiff provided that the plaintiff knows the exact language of the publication or has reason to know that the publication will be unflattering. *See Lee v. Paulson,* 273 Or. 103, 539 P.2d. 1079 (1975); *see also Christensen v. Marvin,* 273 Or. 97, 539 P.2d. 1082 (1975). A recent English case, however, has held that although a defendant who gave an unfavorable employment reference had a "qualified privilege" against a defamation action, the plaintiff could nevertheless bring an action based on the theory of negligent misrepresentation. *See Spring v. Guardian Assurance Plc.,* [1995] 2 A.C. 296, 3 W.L.R. 354, 3 All E.R. 129. It is doubtful that this decision will be followed in the United States.

C. Qualified Privilege: In contrast to an absolute privilege, a qualified privilege may be defeated by a showing of "malice." We shall first set forth the various qualified privileges and then discuss how a claim of privilege may be defeated by a showing of malice.

1. ***Statements made in the defense of the speaker's interests:*** False and defamatory statements made in order to protect one's own interests enjoy a qualified privilege.

Example: In *Faber v. Byrle,* 171 Kan. 38, 229 P.2d 718 (1951), one of the defendant's statements to the plaintiff's brother was that the plaintiff was stealing the defendant's gasoline and that the defendant had feared for his life if he should say anything to the plaintiff. This statement was held to be qualifiedly privileged.

    a.   *Self-defense:* One has a qualified privilege to defend oneself against the defamatory remarks of others. This privilege is somewhat analogous to the defense of consent — one who defames others consents to be defamed in turn — as well as to the qualified privilege that arises when one makes statements in defense of one's own personal interests.

2.   ***Statements made to protect a common interest:*** Members of a group may claim a qualified privilege for statements made to other members of the group in furtherance of the group's common interests. This privilege, for example, covers statements made by one employee of a company to another regarding matters of concern to the company. The privilege also extends to communications between members of labor unions and members of religious bodies concerning matters of concern to the group of which they are members even though the class of which they are members is very large.

    Example: A is a shareholder of a publicly held corporation with over one million shareholders. A, believing that the officers and directors of the corporation are paying themselves huge salaries and neglecting the interests of the shareholders, sends a letter in which he makes false and defamatory remarks about some of the officers to all the other shareholders of the corporation. A's remarks enjoy a qualified privilege.

3.   ***Statements made to protect the interests of third parties:*** A qualified privilege sometimes arises with regard to statements made for the purpose of protecting the interests of third parties, that is, of people who are not members of the same organization as the defendant and who are not members of the defendant's close nuclear or "immediate" family. Whether a privilege will be recognized depends upon a variety of factors.

    a.   The first factor is the importance of the interests involved. When life or serious bodily harm is thought to be at risk, even a third party with no interest of her own in the matter enjoys a qualified privilege to come forward with information. The privilege has also been recognized when significant property interests have been involved.

        Example: *A,* a member of the public, believes that an employee of a clothing store is embezzling the employer's money. *A* writes a letter containing false and defamatory statements about the employee to the owner of the store. *A* will be entitled to claim a qualified privilege. *See Doyle v. Clauss,* 190 A.D. 838, 180 N.Y.S. 671 (1920).

    b.   The second factor is the relationship between the person making the defamatory statement and the person whose interest the statement was intended to protect. A member of the immediate family of the person whose interests are involved will have a privilege in circumstances where a friend or mere busybody will not. Teachers and others who may be said to be in some fiduciary relationship to the person whose interests are sought to be protected may also, in some circumstances, claim a privilege when other people will not be able to do so.

    c.   A third and final factor is whether the defamatory communication has been solicited by the person whose interests are at stake or an immediate family member of that person.

        Example: In *Rude v. Nass,* 79 Wis. 321, 48 N.W. 555 (1891), defendant's defamatory letter had been solicited on behalf of the father of a girl whom the plaintiff had been charged with seducing. The letter was held to enjoy a qualified privilege.

4.   ***Defeat of a claim of qualified privilege:*** As has already been noted, a claim of qualified privilege may be defeated by a showing of malice. One way of showing malice at common law

16

would be by demonstrating that the person making the defamatory statement was motivated not by a desire to protect the interests, for the protection of which the privilege was granted, but rather by a desire to hurt the plaintiff. Another way of defeating the privilege would be by showing excessive publication, that is, publication to a class larger than the class for whose protection the privilege is granted.

Example: A union newsletter that is sent to several hundred thousand members of the union accuses *X* of engaging in strike-breaking against the union. A few copies of the newsletter are routinely sent to university libraries that have asked to receive copies of the union's publications. If the number of copies routinely sent to nonunion members is small in relation to the number of copies sent to union members, the statements made in the newsletter will be privileged. *See Bereman v. Power Pub. Co.,* 93 Colo. 581, 27 P.2d 749 (1933). Note, however, that if the union were to send copies of the particular newsletter in question to third parties who did not routinely receive the newsletter, this purposeful distribution to third parties would not be privileged.

a. *Restatement of Torts* § 601 took the position that a defendant's lack of reasonable grounds for believing in the truth of a defamatory statement made would defeat a claim of qualified privilege. English common law was more favorable to the defendant. A belief in the truth of the statement, even if the belief were unreasonable, would be enough to sustain a claim of privilege. Given the constitutional developments to which we shall shortly turn, it would seem that most American jurisdictions have now adopted something analogous to the English position. *See Restatement (Second) of Torts* § 600, which states that a claim of qualified privilege can be defeated only if the person making the defamatory statement in question knew that the statement was false or acted in reckless disregard of the truth or falsity of the statement.

b. As indicated above, at common law a claim of conditional privilege could be defeated by a claim of *malice* in the sense of publication not for the purpose of protecting the interest giving rise to the privilege but solely from spite, hatred, ill will, or a desire merely to hurt the plaintiff. In the light of the constitutional developments to which we shall now turn, it remains to be seen whether a claim of qualified privilege can be defeated by a showing of common law malice, particularly in those situations in which the defendant can show that there was a reasonable basis for his belief in the truth of the defamatory statement.

III. **CONSTITUTIONAL DEVELOPMENTS**

CONSTITUTIONAL DEVELOPMENTS

A. Since 1964, the Supreme Court of the United States has, in the interest of protecting the freedom of speech guaranteed by the First Amendment (and made applicable to the states by the Fourteenth Amendment), superimposed a number of restrictions on the common law of defamation that has been described above. The restrictions turn in large part upon the status of the plaintiff, namely whether the plaintiff is a public official, public figure, or merely a so-called "private" person. At various times, the Court has suggested that the status of the defendant, namely whether the defendant is one of the news media, is also important. The Court has also, on some occasions, indicated that the subject matter involved, namely whether the speech in question concerns matters of "public interest," is relevant. Although the main outlines of this development are clear, the Court has not been completely consistent with regard to many secondary but nevertheless important issues. The succeeding discussion will set forth these developments and point out the areas in which the Court's decisions have left, or sometimes more accurately have even created, a substantial amount of uncertainty.

B. **Public Officials:** In a landmark case, *New York Times Co. v. Sullivan,* 376 U.S. 254, 84 S. Ct. 710, 11 L. Ed. 2d 686 (1964), the Court held that a public official could not recover damages for defamatory falsehood relating to his official conduct unless he could prove that the statement was made either with knowledge of its falsity or with reckless disregard of whether or not the statement was false. This requirement is sometimes known as "actual malice" and sometimes as "constitutional malice." It differs from common law malice as to which, as described above, evidence of ill will against the person defamed could support a conclusion of malice as could, in many jurisdictions, evidence that the defamatory statement was made without a reasonable basis for believing that the statement was true.

1. In *Rosenblatt v. Baer,* 383 U.S. 75, 86 S. Ct. 669, 15 L. Ed. 2d 597 (1966), the requirement of showing actual malice was applied in an action for defamation brought by the former supervisor of a county recreational facility against a person who had criticized the management of this facility during the period in which the plaintiff had been the supervisor. The *Baer* case suggests that if the criticism relates to the official's performance of his duties, even minor officials will be required to show constitutional malice before they may successfully bring a defamation action. At the same time, it is becoming increasingly evident that the public regards the private life of at least high government officials as materially affecting their ability and capacity to perform their official duties. As a consequence, the higher the office held by the plaintiff, the more likely it is that almost anything said about the official will be held to be relevant to the performance of the official's public duties. Moreover, many high-ranking officials would probably also qualify as public figures and would be faced with the restrictions placed on the ability of public figures to bring actions for defamation that will be discussed below.

C. **Constitutional Malice:** The Court has made clear, in a number of cases, that in order to prevail on the issue of constitutional malice the plaintiff must prove knowledge or reckless indifference to truth or falsity by "clear and convincing evidence," rather than the preponderance-of-the-evidence standard that normally prevails in civil litigation.

1. In several cases, the Court has held that recklessness can only be proved by some showing of *conscious* indifference to truth. A mere failure to investigate is not enough.

   a. In *Masson v. New Yorker Magazine, Inc.*, 501 U.S. 496, 111 S. Ct. 2419, 115 L. Ed.2d 447 (1991), a majority of the Court held that misquoting a person did not amount to intentional falsehood unless the misquotation materially changed the meaning of the actual statement.

2. The question of actual or constitutional malice has now been definitely made into a question of "constitutional fact." *See Bose Corp. v. Consumers' Union of the United States, Inc.,* 466 U.S. 485, 104 S. Ct. 1949, 80 L. Ed. 2d 502 (1984). By making the issue one of constitutional fact, the Court has made the issue one as to which the trial court is unable merely to accept a jury determination when there is adequate evidence to support that determination, but must itself be convinced that the jury's determination is correct. Appellate courts must likewise review the record and make their own independent determination of the issue.

3. Because the question of actual or constitutional malice requires an examination of the defendant's state of mind, the Court has recognized that the plaintiff is entitled to relatively wide-ranging discovery into the thought processes of the defendant. *See Herbert v. Lando,* 441 U.S. 153, 99 S. Ct. 1635, 60 L. Ed. 2d 115 (1979), in which the Court upheld fairly wide-ranging inquiry into the editorial processes of CBS News and the *Atlantic Monthly.*

D. **Public Figures:** In *Curtis Publishing Co. v. Butts,* 388 U.S. 130, 87 S. Ct. 1975, 18 L. Ed. 2d 1094 (1967), the Court held that, at least with regard to the nonprivate aspects of their lives, public figures who brought actions for defamation were also required to show constitutional malice. Since it is hard to find cases holding that any aspect of a public figure's life is "private," it is probably safe to conclude that public figures, such as movie stars and other public celebrities, must be prepared to show constitutional malice before they can succeed in bringing any action for defamation.

1. A person can, at least for a time, become a public figure involuntarily by being involved in important public events, as for example, being the witness to an attempt to assassinate the President. Nevertheless, in *Gertz v. Robert Welch, Inc.,* 418 U.S. 323, 94 S. Ct. 2997, 41 L. Ed. 2d 789 (1974), which is an important restatement by the Court of the doctrines it had previously enunciated, the Court made clear that it is reluctant to take an expansive view of the notion of an "involuntary public figure."

Example: In *Time, Inc. v. Firestone,* 424 U.S. 448, 96 S. Ct. 958, 47 L. Ed. 2d 154 (1976), the Court held that a woman who had married into the Firestone family and who was involved in a messy divorce proceeding during the course of which she even made some statements to the press in response to reporters' inquiries was not a public figure for purposes of the application of the *New York Times Co. v. Sullivan* requirement of showing constitutional malice. The Court noted that plaintiff's resort to the divorce courts could not be considered a voluntary injection of herself into the public eye because the state's regulation of the marriage relationship left her no choice but to resort to the courts in order to end her marriage. While there may be a public interest in accurate reports of judicial proceedings, there was no such interest in the inaccurate report which formed the basis of the plaintiff's action.

2. The Court has repeatedly stated that the question of who is a public figure is a question of law to be decided by the courts. It is not a jury question.

E. Private Figures: In *Gertz v. Robert Welch, Inc., supra,* the Court declared that defamation actions brought by what might be considered private persons were not subject to the requirement of showing actual or constitutional malice. Rather, in such actions, the plaintiff could succeed by showing some lesser level of fault, such as mere negligence, with regard to the truth or falsity of the statements involved.

1. The *Gertz* case involved an article published in *American Opinion,* a monthly magazine of the John Birch Society. There are a number of statements in Justice Powell's opinion for the Court in the *Gertz* case which can be taken to suggest that the Court's decision was limited to actions brought against media defendants, that is, newspapers, magazines, and radio and television broadcasters. Statements of the majority of the members of the present Court that have been made in a variety of cases suggest, however, that the Court will not accept this distinction. It would also be contrary to the Court's rulings in other areas that the media have no special privileges that are not enjoyed by ordinary citizens. The distinction between media and nonmedia defendants has been rejected by most of the lower courts. A few state courts, however, have restricted the application of *Gertz* to actions by private figures against the media and have applied the ordinary common law to actions by private figures against other private figures.

F. Damages: In *Gertz v. Robert Welch, Inc., supra,* the Court declared that there can be no recovery of either punitive or presumed damages in an action for defamation unless the plaintiff is able to show constitutional malice, that is, knowledge of falsity or reckless indifference to truth or falsity. When the action is brought on the basis of any lesser degree of fault, the plaintiff is only entitled to actual damages, although these damages may include intangible items such as humiliation and embarrassment, etc. As will be seen below, subsequent decisions have raised some uncertainty as to the extent to which this aspect of the *Gertz* case will be applied.

1. In *Dun & Bradstreet, Inc. v. Greenmoss Builders, Inc.,* 472 U.S. 749, 105 S. Ct. 2939, 86 L. Ed. 2d 593 (1985), the Court held that in an action brought by a private figure about matters which are not of public concern or what are sometimes described as matters that are not "newsworthy," the plaintiff may recover punitive or actual damages, if permitted under state law, on a lesser showing of fault than is necessary to meet the actual or constitutional malice

standard. In *Greenmoss Builders,* a majority of the Justices held that the defendant was not a member of the media, but they also indicated that the decision did not turn on this fact. As noted above, a majority of the Justices who decided the *Greenmoss Builders* case has rejected the notion that the First Amendment gives the media some kind of privileged position.

2. A confusing aspect of the *Greenmoss Builders* case is that the Court resurrected the distinction between newsworthy and nonnewsworthy events. This distinction had been made by a plurality of the Court in *Rosenbloom v. Metromedia, Inc.,* 403 U.S. 29, 91 S. Ct. 1811, 29 L. Ed. 2d 296 (1971), an action brought by a private figure against a radio station, but was rejected in *Gertz v. Robert Welch, Inc., supra.* In *Gertz,* a majority of the Court opted to distinguish between defamation actions on the basis of the status of the plaintiff because it was felt that this determination was less subjective than the determination of whether or not the matter in question was one of public interest. The surprising resurrection of the public interest or newsworthiness question is one more indication that, with the changed composition of the United States Supreme Court, the future direction of the Court's intrusion into the law of defamation is, to say the least, uncertain. After *Greenmoss Builders,* it is even possible that the Court might hold that the First Amendment does not apply to some types of defamation.

CHAPTER 16 - QUESTIONS, ANSWERS, AND TIPS

1. **Q:** Any false statement that causes injury to the plaintiff can be the basis for a defamation action by the plaintiff.

   A: False. To be defamatory a statement must not only be false and published to third parties; it must also be such as to tend to harm the plaintiff's reputation so as to lower the plaintiff in the estimation of the community or to cause others to refrain from associating or dealing with the plaintiff. Some courts may simply define defamation as a false statement about the plaintiff that discredits him. It is not necessary for the plaintiff to show that anyone actually believed the defamatory statement, although such evidence will be relevant on the questions of damages.

2. **Q:** Under modern law, a derogatory expression of opinion that carries with it no implication of false facts about the plaintiff can be the basis of a defamation action by the plaintiff.

   A: False. Expression of opinion that do not imply the existence of false defamatory facts are not actionable.

3. **Q:** An oral statement falsely accusing someone of having tuberculosis is actionable as slander per se.

   A: False. The "loathsome disease" category of slander per se only includes venereal and perhaps other sexually transmitted diseases and leprosy.

4. **Q:** Special damages are any pecuniary harm suffered as the direct result of a defamatory statement.

   A: False. To be considered special damages the pecuniary harm must flow from the plaintiff's *lowered reputation* resulting from the defamatory statement. For example, medical expenses incurred by a person who is emotionally upset by a defamatory statement about him are clearly a type of pecuniary harm but, without some further proof, they normally would not be considered as flowing from the damage to his reputation done by the defamatory statement.

5. **Q:** Although neither English common law nor the *Restatement (Second) of Torts* make any such distinction, a significant number of American jurisdictions distinguish between libel per se, which is actionable without allegation and proof of special damages, and libel per quod which is not.

A: True. A majority of American jurisdictions probably follow English common law and the *Restatement (Second) of Torts*, but a significant number do not, but rather require allegation and proof of special damages in some types of libel actions.

6. **Q:** In the United States most jurisdictions treat defamatory statements contained in motion pictures as instances of slander.

A: False

7. **Q:** A charge that all members of a group of 200 have engaged in serious sexual misconduct is unlikely to be held to defame any particular individual member of that group.

A: True. The issue is whether a reasonable person would construe the statement as referring to the activities of any particular member of the group.

8. **Q:** A letter falsely accusing a person who is the addressee of the letter of serious criminal misconduct will provide the basis for an action for defamation, even if the letter is only read by the addressee of the letter.

A: False. To be the basis of an action for defamation, the defendant must have published the defamatory statement to third parties.

9. **Q:** Same facts as Q.8, *supra*, but the addressee of the letter, an able bodied literate person, shows the letter to his attorney. The defamatory letter will now provide the basis for an action for defamation.

A: False. In this situation the publication of the defamatory statement will be attributed to the addressee, not the writer of the letter.

Tip: The law has required that the actual publication of defamatory material by the defendant be either intentional or, at the very least, negligent. Innocent publication is not enough. A person who sends a letter to a blind or incapacitated person can of course reasonably expect that the addressee will ask a third party to read the letter to him, whether such reading of the letter by a third party is intended or not. Under such circumstances, the defendant can certainly be said to have negligently caused the defamatory material to be published to third parties. Likewise, a person who sends a defamatory letter to a child, particularly to an immature child, can reasonably expect the child to show the letter to its parents, whether such reading of the letter by a parent was intended or not.

10. **Q:** In most jurisdictions, it is impossible to defame a dead person.

A: True

Tip: Be aware, however, that sometimes material defamatory of a dead person can be said also to defame living persons who were closely associated with him. For example the statement that a person, now deceased, never married and lived all his life with his mistress is defamatory of a woman who was in fact married to the deceased and who lived with him for many years.

11. **Q:** In the United States, it is now generally the law that any statements made by either a member of Congress or of a state legislator in the course of legislative proceedings are absolutely privileged regardless of whether the statements are germane to the matter under legislative consideration.

   A: True

12. **Q:** A false and defamatory statement made by an inferior federal official in the course of carrying out his official duties is at most qualifiedly privileged.

   A: False. The official is entitled to an absolute privilege for anything he might say so long as it can be said that the subject matter of his statement falls within the "outer perimeter" of his official duties.

   Tip: The significance of identifying the speaker as an "inferior federal official" goes not to whether the speaker is only qualifiedly rather than absolutely privileged but to whether the subject matter of the statement falls within the "outer perimeter" of the federal official's duties. One would expect that, the higher the rank of the official, the broader would be the scope of that official's duties.

13. **Q:** A person who would otherwise be able to claim a reporting privilege to publish some particular statement who knows that the statement is false and defamatory will lose his absolute reporting privilege.

   A: False. Accurate reports of official proceedings and now also of some types of public proceedings, such as the meetings of professional associations, are absolutely privileged regardless of who publishes them.

   Tip: The justification for the reporting privilege is the public's right to know and not any solicitude for the reporter. If the report is not accurate, however, the reporter may even sometimes be subject to an action for defamation even if he believed the report to be true.

14. **Q:** A group as large as a national trade union is too large to permit ordinary members of the union to claim the qualified privilege of common interest should they make false and defamatory statements to other members of their union about people engaged in a dispute with the union.

   A: False

   Tip: The problem in statements made by members of large organizations is that they are likely to be made in union newsletters or church newspapers which often reach non-members. If there is significant foreseeable incidental publication to third parties, the publication may be deemed excessive and the claim of qualified privilege will not be allowed.

15. **Q:** Proof that a person who has made a false and defamatory charge against a public official failed to make any investigation of the truth or falsity of the charge before making it can by itself be sufficient proof that the person making the charge published it in reckless disregard of the statement's truth or falsity.

   A: False

16. **Q:** A person who is otherwise a private figure cannot become a public figure by being involved in a newsworthy event.

   A: False. Although the Court in *Gertz*, has said that such instances would probably be rare, it recognized that fate can sometimes thrust even obscure people into the public limelight.

17. Q: In applying the constitutional requirements now governing actions for defamation, the question of whether someone is or is not a public figure will normally be submitted to the jury.

A: False. The question is always for the court.

18. Q: The reporting privilege, in most jurisdictions, permits a newspapers to report the content of pleadings filed in lawsuit as soon as they are filed with the appropriate court.

A: True

19. Q: According to the English common law and the *Restatement (Second) of Torts* and probably the majority of American jurisdictions, all libel is actionable without allegation and proof of special damages, even if the defamatory nature of the statement is not evident from the statement itself but requires resort to extrinsic facts.

A: True

20. Q: The inducement is the part of the plaintiff's pleadings in a action for defamation in which the plaintiff asserts that the defendant's statement was about him.

A: False. The inducement is that part of the plaintiff's pleadings, usually the complaint, in which the plaintiff alleges any facts that are necessary to show that a statement not defamatory on its face is in point of fact defamatory and/or alleges the facts necessary to permit the conclusion that the defamatory statement refers to the plaintiff. The portion of the plaintiff's complaint in which, after making reference if necessary to facts alleged in the inducement, the plaintiff asserts that the defamatory statement was directed at him is called the colloquium.

Additional Exam Tip: Defamation has always been one of the more technical areas of the law of torts and it remains so despite the general tendency to rationalize and simplify the law. It thus lends itself to true/false questions. As noted on p. 16-18, *supra*, the *Greenmoss Builder's* case has created a considerable amount of uncertainty as to the constitutional principles that apply to defamation actions. Is the Supreme Court on the verge of declaring that defamation actions brought by private figures that do not involve matters of public concern are once more to be governed by the old common law? Unless the court expressly so declares, you should assume that the *Gertz* principles still apply and that in all defamation actions no liability will lie unless the defendant has, at the very least, been negligent or, of course, in the case of public figures and public officials, been guilty of constitutional malice, that is publication with knowledge of falsity or reckless indifference to truth or falsity.

PRIVACY

▶ **CHAPTER SUMMARY**

PRIVACY

Scope of Chapter: The term "privacy" encompasses a whole range of interests from the right to control the use of one's body, as involved in the abortion debate, through the right not to have to use a motorcycle crash helmet. The modern tort of privacy encompasses only a small part of the areas of human activity to which the term privacy has been applied. Following W. Prosser, *Privacy,* 48 Cal. L. Rev. 383 (1960), it has been customary to analyze the modern law of privacy with regard to its attempt to deal with four discrete problems. These are:

1. Publicity which places the plaintiff in a false light;

2. Intrusion upon the plaintiff's seclusion or solitude, or into the plaintiff's private affairs;

3. Public disclosure of embarrassing private facts about the plaintiff; and

4. Appropriation for the defendant's commercial advantage of the plaintiff's name or likeness.

In the discussion that follows, after the presentation of some brief general historical material, we shall discuss in turn each of these aspects of privacy.

I. INTRODUCTION

    A. In General: The tort of privacy is of relatively recent origin. In its early stages of development, it owed much to S. Warren and L. Brandeis, *The Right to Privacy,* 4 Harv. L. Rev. 193 (1890), which argued that a host of common law precedents protecting copyright and confidential relationships could be utilized by the courts to protect the individual's privacy interests. Warren and Brandeis were particularly concerned with the individual's ability to keep his private life from becoming a matter of public knowledge and discussion. As we shall see, despite the development and expansion of the modern tort of privacy, the hopes of Warren and Brandeis with regard to the ability of the individual to keep the public from prying into his private life have largely not been realized.

II. FALSE-LIGHT INVASION OF PRIVACY

    A. Relationship to Defamation: The term false-fight invasion of privacy is used to describe actions for damages brought against those who have made false and personally embarrassing but nondefamatory remarks about the plaintiff. Since the action bears so many analogies to the action for defamation, many of the restrictions that are applied against plaintiffs in defamation actions have been applied to plaintiffs in false-light invasion of privacy actions.

        1. The principal feature of defamation actions which has been carried over to false-light invasion of privacy actions is the requirement that the plaintiff must show fault on the part of the defendant. In *Time, Inc. v. Hill,* 385 U.S. 374, 87 S. Ct. 534, 17 L. Ed. 2d 456 (1967), the Court held that before a plaintiff could recover in the false-light privacy action then before the Court, the plaintiff had to show that the defendant published the material in question either with knowledge of falsity or with reckless disregard of the truth or falsity of the material.

            a. The *Hill* case was decided seven years before *Gertz v. Robert Welch, Inc.,* 418 U.S. 323, 94 S. Ct. 2997, 41 L. Ed. 2d 789 (1974), and moreover, involved someone who would undoubtedly be classified as a public figure, albeit an involuntary one. The question has been raised in a number of the lower courts as to whether, in a false-light invasion of privacy action, a private figure need only show negligence on the part of the person who made the statement that is the subject of the action. Most courts, however, continue to require all plaintiffs in false-light invasion of privacy actions to show constitutional malice. This conclusion seems sensible because a nondefamatory falsehood carries less warning to its maker that care should be used in ascertaining the truth of the statement being made.

2. In recent years, there has been some suggestion not only by the commentators but also by courts that no recovery should be permitted for false-light invasions of privacy. In *Renwick v. News and Observer Pub. Co.*, 310 N.C. 312, 312 S.E.2d 405, *cert. denied*, 469 U.S. 858 (1984), the Court held that North Carolina would not recognize actions for false-light invasions of privacy. Any recovery that might be had for the dissemination of false information about a person could only be obtained in an action for libel or slander. In *Godbehere v. Phoenix Newspapers, Inc.*, 162 Ariz. 335, 783 P.2d 781 (1989), the court would not allow a false-light invasion of privacy action to be brought for statements that concerned the public life or duties of public officials. For the moment, these cases represent a minority view.

17

III. INTRUSIONS UPON THE PLAINTIFF'S SOLITUDE

INTRUSION UPON PLAINTIFF'S SOLITUDE

A. The courts have used this aspect of the invasion-of-privacy tort principally to reach conduct that is quite analogous to conduct that would constitute trespass at common law, but which, for technical reasons, cannot be remedied through the traditional action for trespass. The fact that an action for trespass would lie does not preclude the bringing of an action for invasion of privacy, but insofar as the damages sought in the actions overlap, the plaintiff is not entitled to receive a double recovery. An action for intrusion has two elements: (1) intrusion into a private place, conversation, or matter, (2) in manner highly offensive to a reasonable person. To commit an intrusion, a defendant must penetrate some zone of physical or sensory privacy surrounding the plaintiff or have obtained unwanted access to data about him. Intrusion is proven only if the plaintiff had an objectively reasonable expectation of seclusion or solitude in the place, conversation or data source. *See Restatement (Second) of Torts* § 652B.

Example: In *Hamberger v. Eastman,* 106 N.H. 107, 206 A.2d 239 (1964), the defendant landlord had placed a listening device in the wall of a bedroom before the plaintiffs took possession of the premises. Since the landlord was in possession at the time the listening device was installed, no action for trespass could be brought against him. The court gave relief through an invasion of privacy action.

Other examples would include the unlawful tapping of a telephone and the gaining of entry into a person's home or office through false pretenses.

Example: In order to gain access to a criminal suspect's home, a newspaper reporter/photographer pretends to be a policeman and accompanies police when they go to the suspect's home to interview him. The reporter records the plaintiff's conversations and takes photographs of him. Some of the photographs are subsequently published in the newspaper. The plaintiff may bring an invasion of privacy action. *See Dietemann v. Time, Inc.,* 449 F.2d 245 (9th Cir. 1971), which allows recovery on very analogous facts. In *Wilson v. Layne*, 119 S Ct. 1692 (1999), the Court held that law enforcement officers who allow members of the new media to accompany them when they execute search warrants on private residences, violate the Fourth Amendment.

1. It is not tortious, however, to photograph someone in public. While, as we shall see, there may be some restrictions as to the commercial use that may be made of such a photograph, no one who appears in public may object to the taking of his photograph so long as the photograph is taken in a public place and the physical safety of the person being photographed is not endangered.

   a. It is sometimes difficult to apply the notion of intrusion even to the photographing of someone in a private place. In *Howell v. New York Post, Inc.,* 81 N.Y.2d 115, 612 N.E.2d.

699, 596 N.Y.S.2d 350 (N.Y. 1993), a photographer trespassed at a private psychiatric hospital where the plaintiff was receiving treatment and took pictures of her which were later published in a tabloid-type story. The court ruled against the plaintiff on the apparant bases that she had no proprietary interest in the hospital grounds to object to being photographed there and that the hospital was not a sufficiently private place.

3. People would seem to have a reduced expectation of privacy at work than they enjoy at home. In *O'Connor v. Ortega,* 480 U.S. 709, 107 S. Ct. 1492, 94 L.Ed.2d 714 (1987), the Supreme Court ruled, in a civil-rights context, that a public employee sometimes may enjoy a reasonable expectation of privacy in his or her workplace with regard to searches by a public employer but it recognized that, "operational realities of the workplace," such as actual office practices, procedures, or regulations, frequently may undermine employees' privacy expectation. Applying *O'Conner* in various work enviroments, lower federal courts have inquired into such matters as whether the work area in question was given over to an employee's exclusive use, the extent to which others had access to the work space, the nature of the employment, and whether office regulations placed employees on notice that certain areas were subject to employer intrusions. *See Vega-Rodriguez v. Puerto Rico Telephone Co.,* 110 F.3d 174 (1st Cir. 1997).

4. Invasions into one's "emotional space" have been said to be tortious, even when there is nothing resembling a trespassory invasion of physical space or a public disclosure of embarrassing information. For example, in *Phillips v. Smalley Maintenance Services, Inc.,* 435 So.2d 705 (Ala. 1983), the court allowed an action for invasion of the plaintiff's "emotional sanctum" for damages resulting from being discharged for refusing her supervisor's sexual advances, but the same court found other invasions insuffieciently offensive, such as hearing oneself over the phone being labeled a homosexual when one inquired about a bill. See *Logan v. Sears, Roebuck & Co.,* 466 So.2d 121 (Ala. 1985). Such actions are probably better brought under an intentional infliction of emotional distress theory.

Example: Jacqueline Onassis was unable to enjoin a professional photographer from photographing her in public so long as he refrained from touching her or otherwise endangering her safety. *See Galella v. Onassis,* 487 F.2d 986 (2d Cir. 1973).

2. It is likewise not tortious to continue to follow a person while that person is traveling on the public streets. *Cf. Nader v. General Motors Corp.,* 25 N.Y.2d 560, 307 N.Y.S.2d 647, 255 N.E.2d 765 (1970).

a. Some states have statutes making it a crime to harass a person, as for example by following that person in a public place and inflicting either physical contact or subjecting that person to annoying conduct without legitimate cause. *See* N.Y. Penal Law § 240.25 (McKinney). Such statutes are often called "stalking" statutes. Conduct that would be criminal under such statutes would probably also be the basis for something analogous to a privacy action. It seems doubtful, however, that merely following another person, so long as that person's physical safety is not put in danger, can be made criminal. If the surveillance in question is accompanied by screams and shouts each time the person being followed attempts to speak to someone or if the surveillance materially interferes with a person's ability to engage in normal activities, the applicability of such a statute or indeed the granting of an action for invasion of privacy seems less questionable.

PUBLIC DISCLOSURE OF EMBARRASSING PRIVATE FACTS

IV. **PUBLIC DISCLOSURE OF EMBARRASSING PRIVATE FACTS**

A. **In General:** Although, as noted, this was the aspect of privacy that particularly concerned Warren and Brandeis in their seminal article, this is the area of the tort of privacy which has given the courts the greatest difficulty. If the defendant has secured the embarrassing information about the plaintiff as a result of a relation of confidence, the granting of a remedy does not present insurmountable problems. Indeed, before anyone had heard of the tort of invasion of privacy, patients had been able to bring actions against physicians for disclosure of confidential information, and clients had been able to bring actions against attorneys who violated the attorney-client relationship. The only question in these cases is whether or not the defendant may raise in defense that disclosure was necessitated by the need to protect someone's physical safety or other important interests. When the information has not been obtained in the course of a confidential relationship or by illegal means, to permit a plaintiff to bring an action against someone who has disclosed information that was lawfully gathered is in effect to allow the plaintiff to punish people for making truthful statements about him.

17

1. An action for public disclosure of embarrassing facts was recognized in *Melvin v. Reid,* 112 Cal. App. 285, 297 P. 91 (1931). The case involved a woman who had previously been a prostitute and had been involved as a witness in a sensational murder trial. She subsequently married and was living a very conventional life when the defendants made a movie about the trial, as a result of which her friends and neighbors learned of the plaintiff's lurid past. On the other hand, in *Sidis v. F-R Pub. Corp.,* 113 F.2d 806 (2d Cir. 1940), the court denied an action to a person who had been a child prodigy twenty-five years previously and had subsequently become somewhat of a pathetic recluse. It should be noted that *Melvin v. Reid* was decided at the time when it was thought that movies did not enjoy the same kind of First Amendment protection that was enjoyed by material that appeared in printed form. That distinction, however, is no longer constitutionally sustainable. *See Joseph Burstyn, Inc. v. Wilson,* 343 U.S. 495, 72 S. Ct. 777, 96 L. Ed. 1098 (1952).

2. In *Briscoe v. Reader's Digest Ass'n,* 4 Cal. 3d 529, 93 Cal. Rptr. 866, 483 P.2d 34 (1971), it was held that a man who some eleven years previously had been convicted of truck-hijacking and served time in a federal prison, but who had since lived a respectable life, might be able to bring an action against a magazine which disclosed his past if the jury found that the information disclosed was of very minimal social value, that the intrusion into the plaintiff's personal life would be "grossly offensive to most people," and if the plaintiff had not "voluntarily acceded to a position of public notoriety." On remand, the case was removed to the federal court, which, in an unpublished decision, granted summary judgment for the defendant. The suggestion in *Briscoe* that a cause of action might lie in some circumstances for the disclosure of private facts about a person is somewhat suspect in the light of the U.S. Supreme Court's decisions concerning the publication of the names of people who have been the victims of sexual offenses that we shall examine in the next subsection. Nevertheless, the Supreme Court of California in *Shulman v. Group W Productions, Inc.,* 18 Cal. 4th 200, 955 P.2d 469. 74 Cal. Rptr. 2d 843 (1998), recently reaffirmed, in dicta, its holding in *Briscoe,* that the publication of truthful private facts might be actionable if the facts were not newsworthy.

B. **Disclosure of the Names of Crime Victims:** In a series of cases that includes *Cox Broadcasting Corp. v. Cohn,* 420 U.S. 469, 95 S. Ct. 1029, 43 L. Ed. 2d 328 (1975), and *The Florida Star v. B. J. F.,* 491 U.S. 524, 109 S. Ct. 2603, 105 L. Ed. 2d 443 (1989), the Court struck down statutes making it a crime to publish the names of the victims of sexual offenses that the state courts had construed to permit civil actions against those who violated the statutes. While the Court did not categorically state that one could never be punished for publishing truthful information which one had lawfully obtained, it indicated that if any such punishment in the form of criminal penalties or a civil action were to be upheld, it would have to be because "a state interest of the highest order" was involved.

1. This is not to say that court files involving victims of sexual offenses may not be made confidential or that the custodians of these files may not be forbidden to disclose these reports to other persons. *See* N.Y. Civil Rights Law § 50-b (McKinney), which makes confidential the identity of the victim of a sexual offense who was under eighteen at the time the offense was

committed and forbids the disclosure of any portion of the police report or court files from which the identity of the victim may be ascertained, except when the person seeking the identity of the victim is the person charged with the crime or others involved in the prosecution or has demonstrated to the court that good cause exists for disclosure.

COMMERCIAL APPROPRIATION

17

V. COMMERCIAL APPROPRIATION

A. **In General:** This aspect of the invasion of privacy tort may be usefully summarized in the language of N.Y. Civil Rights Law § 50 (McKinney). That statute makes it illegal for "advertising purposes, or for the purposes of trade" to use "the name, portrait or picture of any living person without having first obtained the written consent of such person, or . . . his or her parent or guardian." A civil remedy, which now also covers the use of a person's voice, is granted by N.Y. Civil Rights Law § 51 (McKinney). It has long been held that the fact that a person's picture or name appears in a newspaper sold for profit does not constitute the use of a person's picture or name for advertising or trade purposes. The states are of necessity required to recognize an exception for newsworthy material. This newsworthiness exception covers not only pictures and reports of great public events but also much more prosaic matters.

Example: It is a spring day. A photographer strolling through a public market takes a photograph of a couple who are embracing. The photograph is published in a newspaper with the caption, "It's spring time." In taking and publishing the photograph, neither the photographer nor the newspaper has invaded the couple's privacy. *Cf. Gill v. Hearst Pub. Co.,* 40 Cal. 2d 224, 253 P.2d 441 (1953).

1. Although the easier cases involve advertisements, it is not the case that any use of a person's name or photograph in an advertisement will necessarily be unlawful. Even advertisements can take advantage of the newsworthiness exception.

   Example: At the conclusion of a successful military campaign, upon the return home of the troops, *X,* a well-known soft drink company, takes out a full-page newspaper advertisement declaring that *X* salutes the conquering heros and also containing material extolling the virtues of the *X* product. Part of the advertisement consists of a news photograph of soldiers marching off to war. *X* has paid *Z,* the owner of the copyright in the photograph, for the right to reproduce the photograph. *A,* one of the soldiers whose faces are recognizable in the photograph, brings an action. If *A* is one of a large group of persons in the photograph, it is doubtful that he can bring an action. The photograph will probably be held to be a photograph of a public event. If *A*'s face were, on the other hand, the only recognizable face in the advertisement, then he most probably could bring an action, even if the image of *A* were taken from a newsreel or a news photograph. As used in the advertisement, the photograph would be held to be of *A,* not of a public event.

2. As we have seen, a person who is photographed in the course of participating in what might be called a public event cannot complain if that photograph is used in a newspaper or television report or even in a television documentary about the event in question. The problem arises when someone is singled out for more extended coverage or, to put it another way and taking the case of a television or motion picture film as an illustration, is, in a manner of speaking, made into an actor.

   Example: In *Taggart v. Wadleigh-Maurice, Ltd.,* 489 F.2d 434 (3d Cir. 1973), *cert. denied,* 417 U.S. 937 (1974), the plaintiff was servicing the portable latrines at the Woodstock Music Festival. The defendants not only photographed him in the performance of his chores, but also engaged him in conversation. In the film "Woodstock," two minutes were devoted to this sequence. The court held that it was a jury question as to whether or not the plaintiff was made into an involuntary performer in the motion picture.

a. A performance may itself be so unusual that it may be considered newsworthy. The question then arises whether it is permissible to photograph and exhibit to others the entire performance.

Example: In *Zacchini v. Scripps-Howard Broadcasting Co.,* 433 U.S. 562, 97 S. Ct. 2849, 53 L. Ed. 2d 965 (1977), the petitioner performed a "human cannonball" act which lasted approximately fifteen seconds. During the act, the petitioner was shot from a cannon into a net about 200 feet away. The petitioner performed this act at a county fair in Ohio. People were charged admission to the fair, but there was no separate fee charged to observe the act. The plaintiff's entire act was shown on a local news broadcast. A divided Court held that there was no constitutional prohibition against a state's making actionable the filming and exhibition, even in a news program, of the plaintiff's *entire act*. Suppose the plaintiff had been paid to perform his act, as in fact was the situation in the *Zacchini* case, but the act was performed in a public park? It is hard to believe that the plaintiff could bring an action against a television station that broadcasts the event on a news program. Even in the circumstances involved in *Zacchini,* if the plaintiff were injured in the course of the act, a television news report of the entire act would be privileged as being "newsworthy."

B. **Descendibility of the Right of Commercial Appropriation:** There have been a number of recent cases concerning the extent to which the right of commercial appropriation of a famous person's name or likeness is descendible to that person's heirs or otherwise survives that person's death. This is a subject more appropriately covered in an intellectual property course. For our purposes, the following brief summary is sufficient. Some courts require that in order for the right of appropriation to survive the person's death, that person must have commercially exploited his name and likeness in his lifetime. In other jurisdictions, either by judicial decision or statute, the right of commercial appropriation is descendible even if the person whose name or likeness is involved had not commercially exploited it before his death. *See* Cal. Civ. Code § 990, *overruling Lugosi v. Universal Pictures,* 25 Cal. 3d 813, 160 Cal. Rptr. 323, 603 P.2d 425 (1979).

CHAPTER 17 - QUESTIONS, ANSWERS, AND SOME TIPS

1. **Q:** An action for false light invasion of privacy permits a person to secure legal redress for false statements about himself that are not defamatory.

   A: True

2. **Q:** Someone who follows another continuously on the public street will probably be liable to an action for invading the physical solitude of the person he is following even if he never approaches within 100 feet of that person.

   A: False. One is free to follow and observe anyone in public places. The possible basis for an action for intentional infliction of emotional distress (or for harassment) would be in a situation that is not only continuous but so close as to put the person whose movements are being monitored in reasonable fear of possible physical violence.

3. **Q:** It is generally not an invasion of privacy for a private person to disclose true but embarrassing facts about another that are contained in public records that are open to public inspection.

   A: True.

4. Q: In violation of an agreement of confidentiality with A, B discloses embarrassing personal facts about A to C. C knows that, in disclosing this information, B is breaching his agreement with A, but C is not a party to this agreement nor was B an agent of C in his dealings with A. C, in turn, reveals this embarrassing information about A to others. A may maintain an invasion of privacy action against C for the revelation of embarrassing personal facts.

A: False. Once B reveals the information to C, the information is, so to speak, in the public domain. If B had revealed the information to C only upon a promise not to pass on the information to anyone else, the matter might be different.

5. Q: A seller of cowboy hats and boots places statements made by a famous cowboy actor into a radio commercial for A's cowboy attire. The cowboy actor never consented to the use of these statements. The cowboy actor probably has an action for commercial appropriation.

A: True. Using someone's voice for advertising or trade purposes is actionable under § 51 of the New York Civil Rights Law and would undoubtedly be sufficient to be the basis of an action in the majority of states in which privacy actions are based upon the common law and not upon statute.

Tip: The key question, which will affect damages, is whether those listening to the commercial can recognize the cowboy actor's voice. If they can, the defendant can be said to be appropriating the cowboy actor's image to sell his products and the damages recoverable will be enhanced considerably.

6. Q: In an action for false-light invasion of privacy, the plaintiff can prevail if he can establish that the defendant should have known that the offending statements were false.

A: False. Most jurisdictions that have considered the matter continue to hold that, to prevail in a false-light invasion of privacy action, a plaintiff must show constitutional malice on the part of the defendant, that is intentional falsehood or reckless indifference to truth or falsity. They have not been prepared to apply the *Gertz* negligence standard in false-light invasion of privacy actions brought by private figures.

Tip: The courts in any particular jurisdiction tend to apply to false-light invasion of privacy actions the same restrictions they apply to defamation actions. A defamatory statement, however, is, by its very nature, more likely to put its maker on notice that care should be taken than would a non-defamatory statement. Undoubtedly, because the need for care is less obvious, the courts that have considered the matter have tended to insist on the plaintiff showing that defendant knew that the statement was false or was recklessly indifferent to the truth or falsity of the statement.

Additional Exam Tip: Be aware that invasion of privacy actions sometimes involve fact patterns that might be the basis for an action for intentional infliction of emotional distress, at least if the defendant's conduct is outrageous enough.

MISUSE OF PROCESS

▶ **CHAPTER SUMMARY**

MISUSE OF PROCESS

Scope of Chapter: In this chapter we shall consider the remedies that are provided by the law of torts for the improper use of the legal process, such as for example, to harass the plaintiff. Perhaps the earliest such remedy was for "malicious prosecution," namely the unjustified initiation of criminal proceedings against another. Over the years, by analogy to the malicious instigation of criminal proceedings, remedies were developed for some abuses of the civil process. We shall consider each of these in turn.

I. MALICIOUS PROSECUTION

18

MALICIOUS PROSECUTION

A. In General: An action for malicious prosecution may be brought by a person who is not guilty of the criminal offense with which he has been charged against a *private* person who without probable cause, initiated or procured the institution of those criminal proceedings. The action will not lie against a public prosecutor or a judge. In order to succeed, the plaintiff must overcome a number of hurdles.

1. ***The plaintiff's innocence:*** The action for malicious prosecution is predicated upon the innocence of the plaintiff. The mere fact that the plaintiff has been acquitted in a criminal prosecution does not prevent the defendant from relitigating the question of the plaintiff's guilt or innocence of the underlying criminal charge. The burden of persuasion on the issue of the plaintiff's innocence will be on the defendant; but it should be noted that malicious prosecution is a civil action and that the defendant merely has to show by a preponderance of the evidence (rather than by the criminal standard of proof beyond a reasonable doubt) that the plaintiff is guilty of the underlying criminal charge.

2. ***Criminal proceedings:*** Criminal proceedings encompass any proceedings in which a governmental body seeks to prosecute a person for an offense and to impose upon that person a penalty of a criminal character. Petty traffic offenses would be included within the term, but not proceedings in which the government incarcerates someone ostensibly for that person's own safety, as, for example, in civil commitment proceedings. A person who has been subjected to wrongful civil commitment may, however, have an action for the misuse of civil process, a subject which we shall discuss in section II of this chapter.

   a. Criminal proceedings are, of course, commenced when a person has been indicted or has had an information filed against her. More generally, a criminal proceeding is considered to have been instituted when any process has been issued for the purpose of bringing the person accused of a criminal offense before an official or tribunal whose function is to determine either the guilt or innocence of the accused or whether the accused shall be held for a later determination of her guilt or innocence. A person who has been lawfully arrested, as, for example, someone arrested under a valid warrant, is a person against whom criminal proceedings have been instituted, and, if the other requirements are met, such a person may be able to bring an action for malicious prosecution.

3. ***Termination of the criminal proceedings in favor of the plaintiff:*** The plaintiff may not bring an action for malicious prosecution unless the criminal proceedings that have been instituted against him have terminated in his favor. The clearest evidence of favorable termination is, of course, an acquittal in a criminal prosecution. Favorable termination, however, may also be shown by the plaintiff's discharge by a magistrate at a preliminary hearing, by a refusal of a grand jury to indict, by the formal abandonment of the proceedings by the prosecutor, or by the quashing of an indictment or information.

4. ***Probable cause:*** Probable cause relates to the reasonable beliefs of the person instigating the prosecution. It has three components: (1) a reasonable belief that the person accused has acted

or failed to act in a particular manner; (2) a reasonable belief that those acts or omissions constitute the offense with which the accused person has been charged; and (3) a reasonable belief on the part of the person making the charge that she is sufficiently informed about the law and the facts to be justified in initiating or continuing the proceedings. In the absence of other evidence, the discharge of the accused by a magistrate during a preliminary hearing is conclusive evidence of the lack of probable cause. So, likewise, in the absence of any contrary evidence, is a refusal of a grand jury to indict the accused. Conversely, the indictment of the accused by a grand jury is certainly evidence that the person who initiated the proceedings had probable cause.

    a.   The conviction of the accused, even if reversed by an appellate tribunal, conclusively establishes the existence of probable cause unless the conviction was obtained by fraud, perjury, or some other illegal means. On the other hand, the acquittal of the accused is not evidence of lack of probable cause. This is because the failure of the tribunal to find that the accused is guilty beyond a reasonable doubt of the offense charged does not mean that there may not have been probable cause to initiate the proceedings against the accused.

    b.   Liability may be avoided if the prosecution was initiated in good faith in reliance upon the advice of an attorney licensed to practice in the jurisdiction in question. If the accuser has made a full disclosure of all the facts of which the accuser is aware and if the accuser has no reason to believe that the attorney has a personal interest in obtaining the conviction of the plaintiff, the accuser will be conclusively presumed to have had probable cause.

    c.   The termination of the proceedings against the accused at the instance of the person who has initiated them or the termination of those proceedings because of the initiator's failure to press the prosecution is evidence of a lack of probable cause. The abandonment of the proceedings by the public prosecutor on her own initiative is not, however, evidence that the accuser acted without probable cause. There are any number of reasons not related to guilt or innocence why the prosecutor might refuse to continue with a particular prosecution.

5.   *Malice:* In order to bring the action, it is generally said that the plaintiff must allege and prove that the prosecution was instituted by the accuser primarily for a purpose other than that of bringing the accused to justice. This requirement is generally referred to as the need to allege and prove malice.

    Example: *A* and *B* are involved in a dispute over a land boundary. *A* seeks to have *B* charged with income tax evasion in order to weaken *B*'s bargaining position in the land dispute. *A* will be chargeable with malice in the sense now being discussed.

    a.   It should be noted that malice is a somewhat artificial concept. If a person has probable cause for making a criminal charge, an action for malicious prosecution may not be brought against that person regardless of the impropriety of the motives which activated him. The lack of probable cause, on the other hand, will be evidence, although not conclusive evidence, that the accuser acted with malice. It should be noted, however, that while an improper purpose is evidence of malice, an improper motive is not evidence of a lack of probable cause. *See Restatement (Second) of Torts* § 669A.

6.   *Function of court and jury:* In an action for malicious prosecution, a number of what are normally thought of as factual issues have traditionally been treated as questions of law to be determined by the court. These questions include whether the proceedings of which the plaintiff complains were criminal in character, whether the proceedings were terminated in favor of the plaintiff, and whether the defendant had probable cause for initiating or continuing the proceedings.

18

II.   MISUSE OF CIVIL PROCESS

A. **In General:** An action may under certain conditions be brought against someone who takes an active part in the wrongful initiation, continuation, or procurement of civil proceedings against another. The action has many analogies to the action for malicious prosecution. In order for the action to lie, the defendant must have instituted, continued, or procured the initiation of civil proceedings against the plaintiff without probable cause and primarily for a purpose other than that of securing the proper adjudication of the claim upon which the proceedings in question were based. As with malicious prosecution, the proceedings must have terminated in favor of the person against whom they were brought. The tort encompasses wrongfully instituted administrative proceedings as well. The issue upon which there is a substantial split in the authorities concerns what kind of damages a plaintiff who has proved all the other elements of the action must show before he can succeed in an action for misuse of civil process.

1. *Probable cause:* A person has probable cause for instituting civil proceedings if that person reasonably believes in the existence of the facts upon which the claim is based and reasonably believes that, under those facts, there may be a valid claim under the applicable law.

    a. One who acts in reliance upon the advice of disinterested counsel, whose advice has been sought in good faith and after a full disclosure of all the known relevant facts, will establish probable cause. It should be noted that, because of the difference in proof required in criminal and civil proceedings, one may in good faith initiate civil proceedings without the same degree of certainty as would be required for the good faith prosecution of a criminal proceeding.

2. In an action for misuse of civil process, the court will, as in an action for malicious prosecution, decide certain essentially factual questions that have now been made "questions of law." These questions that will be decided by the court include the issues of whether a civil proceeding has been initiated, whether any such civil proceeding was terminated in favor of the plaintiff, whether the defendant had probable cause, and whether, in those jurisdictions requiring proof of special damages, the plaintiff has made a sufficient allegation of special damages.

B. **Damages:** The courts in the United States are split on the issue of whether, in order to bring an action for misuse of civil process, the plaintiff must be able to show some kind of special damages.

1. A minority of American jurisdictions hold that no action will lie for misuse of civil process unless the plaintiff can show some sort of interference with the plaintiff's person or property or some other analogous form of special damage. This doctrine is often called the "English" rule. The civil arrest of a person and the attachment of that person's land, chattels, or bank accounts are instances of the requisite special damages. An injunction preventing a person from using and enjoying his lands, chattels, or intangibles would also probably qualify as the requisite special damages.

    a. In some jurisdictions which otherwise follow the English rule, the bringing of repetitious civil proceedings against another person for purposes of harassment will suffice to permit the bringing of an action for misuse of civil process. *See Weisman v. Middleton,* 390 A. 2d 996 (D.C. App. 1978).

2. The majority of jurisdictions in the United States have now abandoned the requirement that the plaintiff must show special damages in order to bring an action for misuse of civil process.

C. There have been a number of attempts in recent years to bring actions for the misuse of civil process against attorneys and others who have instituted actions with little chance of success. Thus far, the courts have refused to allow any liability to lie against an attorney for negligently instituting civil proceedings. *See O'Toole v. Franklin,* 279 Or. 513, 569 P.2d 561 (1977). Any other rule, it is felt, would interfere with an attorney's relations with his client.

1. A number of states now provide for the assessment of litigation costs and attorney fees against parties and attorneys who bring "frivolous actions or assert frivolous defenses." *See* Ga. Code Ann. § 9-15-14 (Supp. 1990). Fed. R. Civ. P. 11 is aimed at the same problem.

2. *Aranson v. Schroeder,* Nos. 93-519, 93-527, 93-564, 1995 N.H. LEXIS 157 (N.H. 1995), ___ N.H. ___, ___ A.2d ___ (1995), appears to be the first case in which a court was prepared to recognize a cause of action for "malicious defense." In that case, the defendant attorney had represented the defendants in a prior action and had apparently raised a defense — ultimately unsuccessful — based on fabricated evidence.

III. ABUSE OF PROCESS

A. **In General:** An action for abuse of process will lie against a person who, in a previous civil or criminal proceeding against the plaintiff, misused that proceeding in order to accomplish some ulterior purpose (*i.e.,* for some purpose other than to obtain a judgment on the merits). The situations giving rise to an action for abuse of process are often analogized to some form of extortion. This tort does not require a showing that the plaintiff would not have been liable in the prior proceeding.

Example: In *Hopper v. Drysdale,* 524 F. Supp. 1039 (D. Mont. 1981), the plaintiff had been involved in a divorce proceeding in which a warrant for his arrest for contempt of court had been issued. At the same time, the plaintiff, who now resided out of state, had brought an action for fraud against his former wife and her attorney. The attorneys in the latter action issued a notice requiring the plaintiff to have his deposition taken. He appeared, gave his deposition, and was arrested under the warrant. It was held that he stated a cause of action for abuse of process. *See also Palmer Ford, Inc. v. Wood,* 298 Md. 484, 471 A.2d 297 (1984) (use of criminal prosecution for purpose of debt collection).

B. **Malicious Abuse of Process:** The Supreme Court of New Mexico recently reviewed the torts of misuse of civil process (called malicious prosecution in New Mexico) and abuse of process and found that they served a common purpose (offering redress to plaintiffs who are improperly made the subject of legal proceedings) and shared similar elements. The court likened the requirement of an ulterior motive in abuse of process actions to the requirement of malice for malicious prosecution. It also compared the institution of proceedings without probable cause, an elenent of malicious prosecution, to the requirement of an act not proper in the regular course of proceedings, an element of abuse of process. The court therefore created a new "malicious abuse of process" tort with the following elements: "(1) the initiation of judicial proceedings against the plaintiff by the defendant; (2) an act by the defendant in the use of process other than such as would be proper in the regular prosecution of the claim; (3) a primary motive by the defendant in misusing the process to accomplish an illegitimate end; and (4) damages." The court added that the plaintiff had to demonstrate that the defendant had a purpose to accomplish an illegitimate end, not merely that he acted with ill will or spite. Termination of proceeding in favor of the plaintiff is not an element of this tort. Demonstrating a lack of probable cause is a means of fulfillilng the second elelment. *See Devaney v. Thriftway Marketing Corp.,* 953 P.2d 277, 124 N.M. 512 (1997).

18

CHAPTER 18 - QUESTIONS, ANSWERS, AND TIPS

18

1. **Q:** In the context of an action for malicious prosecution, the term "malice" includes ill will towards the plaintiff.

   A: True

2. **Q:** In an action for malicious prosecution, it is for the jury to decide, after proper instruction from the trial judge, whether the defendant had probable cause to initiate criminal proceedings against the plaintiff.

   A: False. The question of probable cause is for the court.

   Tip: Although the standard rubric is that questions of fact, even questions of so-called mixed law and fact, such as whether a defendant was negligent or whether a product is defective, are for the jury, there are exceptions. In the field of defamation, for constitutional reasons, whether a plaintiff is a public figure has been made a question of law. In actions for malicious prosecution, the reason the question of probable cause has been made a question of law for the court is in large part historical. The student will just have to memorize these exceptions to normal practice.

3. **Q:** For purposes of fulfilling the requirements for bringing an action for malicious prosecution, criminal proceedings are never considered to have been initiated against a person until he has been arrested.

   A: False. Criminal proceedings against a person are considered to have been initiated when any kind of criminal process, such as an indictment or information, has been issued for the purpose of bringing that person before an official or tribunal whose function it is to determine that person's guilt or innocence or whether that should be held for a later determination of guilt or innocence. It is not necessary that the plaintiff should ever have been arrested.

4. **Q:** A was acquitted of criminal charges in proceedings initiated by B. In a malicious prosecution action brought by A against B, B may not litigate the issue of whether A in fact had committed the criminal offense with which he had been charged

   A: False. Acquittal in a criminal case only establishes that A's guilt has not been proved beyond a reasonable doubt. In a civil action, like malicious prosecution, A's guilt need only be established as more probable than not.

5. **Q:** A judge before whom a criminal defendant is brought enjoys an absolute privilege against a malicious prosecution action, but a public prosecutor who initiates criminal proceedings against an individual only enjoys a qualified privilege that can be defeated by a showing of bad faith.

   A: False. Public prosecutors also enjoy an absolute privilege.

6. **Q:** In most American jurisdictions a plaintiff who brings an action for misuse of civil process must show that, as a result of the defendant's misuse of civil process, he has suffered some form of special damages, such as a physical interference with his person or property.

   A: False. The older, so-called English rule, requiring the plaintiff to allege and prove some sort of special damage in these cases has now been abandoned by most, but by no means all, American jurisdictions.

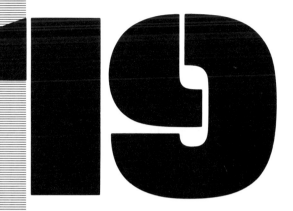

WRONGFUL DEATH
AND LOSS OF CONSORTIUM

▶ **CHAPTER SUMMARY**

WRONGFUL DEATH AND LOSS OF CONSORTIUM

Scope of Chapter: In this chapter, we shall discuss wrongful death and loss of consortium. These actions are often referred to as derivative actions because they are actions brought by plaintiffs who have suffered damage because of an injury to another person. In one sense, these actions are not derivative because the people bringing the actions are seeking recovery for the losses *they* have suffered owing to the injury of the other person; they are not seeking recovery on behalf of the injured person. On the other hand, in most jurisdictions and particularly in wrongful death actions, a wrongful death or loss of consortium action cannot be brought if the injured person would not have had a cause of action himself. To this extent, these actions are indeed "derivative." In the discussion that follows, we shall consider first wrongful death and then loss of consortium. In our discussion of wrongful death, we shall also briefly describe the relationship between wrongful death actions and the various survival statutes that govern what happens when a plaintiff or defendant in an existing action dies before judgment is entered or even before suit is brought.

19

WRONGFUL DEATH

I. **WRONGFUL DEATH**

A. **History:** With the onset of the industrial revolution, the problem of what to do when the family breadwinner was killed started to assume significant social importance. In *Baker v. Bolton,* 170 Eng. Rep. 1033 (K.B. 1808), however, it was held that there was no common law right of recovery for wrongful death. With the increasing industrialization of England, this state of the law became intolerable and was eventually met by Lord Campbell's Act, 9 & 10 Vict. c. 93 (1846). Section 1 of this Act provided that when the death of a person is caused "by wrongful act, neglect, or default and the act, neglect, or default is such as would (if death had not ensued) have entitled the party injured to maintain an action . . . then . . . the person who would have been liable if death had not ensued shall be liable to an action for damages." Section 2 of the Act provided that the action was to be brought "for the benefit of the wife, husband, parent, and child" of the deceased and that "in every such action the jury may give such damages as they may think proportioned to the injury resulting from such death to the parties . . . for whose benefit such action shall be brought."

1. Although Lord Campbell's Act does not by its terms restrict damages to "pecuniary loss," it was soon construed by the courts to impose a pecuniary loss requirement. As we shall see, this pecuniary loss requirement still has some significance in some American jurisdictions.

B. **Survival Statutes:** In the very earliest days of the common law, what we would now call tort actions did not survive the death of either the plaintiff or the defendant. In the fourteenth century, several statutes were enacted that were construed to permit actions for the loss or damage of personal property to survive the death of the plaintiff but not of the defendant. Until the nineteenth century, there was no further change from the ancient rule that all tort actions abated upon the death of one of the parties. Reform began by making all actions for damage to *tangible* property, whether personal or real property, survive the death of either the plaintiff or defendant. Most jurisdictions now also allow actions for damage to intangible property to survive. Although the survival of actions for personal injuries was perhaps somewhat slower in coming, in most jurisdictions such actions now also survive the death of either party. In fact, at the present day, in almost all states, most tort actions now survive the death of either the plaintiff or the defendant and become potential assets or liabilities of the deceased's estate. The most important exceptions are defamation actions and, to a lesser extent, actions for malicious prosecution and possibly for invasion of privacy. In about half of the states, actions for defamation still do not survive the death of either the plaintiff or the defendant.

1. *Relationship to Wrongful Death:* It should be noted that the action for wrongful death established by Lord Campbell's Act is a new cause of action that arises upon the death of the deceased. It does not represent an action of the deceased that survives to the deceased's estate. In the present day, when a person is injured but does not die immediately, the deceased's cause

of action for the damages incurred up to and until the time of death will survive to the deceased's estate. This means that the estate may recover damages for the medical expenses of the deceased prior to death, for the deceased's loss of earning capacity between the period of injury and the time of death, and the deceased's pain and suffering until the time of death. The losses suffered by the deceased's survivors will then, in most states, be recovered in a Lord Campbell's-type action brought by the survivors. To avoid the need for two actions, namely an action under the survival act and one under the wrongful death act, a number of states have merged the two types of action into one action in which the survivors recover for their injuries and the estate recovers for the damages to which it is entitled. See, e.g., Mich. Comp. Laws Ann. § 600.2921.

C. Benefit-of-the-Survivors Statutes: Following the adoption by Parliament of Lord Campbell's Act, similar statutes were enacted in most American jurisdictions. In these statutory schemes, the action is brought primarily for the *benefit of the survivors.* The survivors are limited either to certain named relatives of the deceased, as in Lord Campbell's Act itself, or to the class of persons who would take if the deceased had died intestate.

1. *Benefit-to-the-estate statutes:* A second much smaller general category of wrongful death statutes creates a wrongful death action for the loss occasioned by the deceased's death in favor of the estate of the deceased, although, even under this type of statutory scheme, the damages, once ascertained, are sometimes distributed directly to a designated class of beneficiaries rather than remaining in the estate and becoming subject to the claims of the deceased's creditors. To this extent, although the action is nominally brought on behalf of the estate, the net result resembles that which would be obtained in the more classic benefit-of-the-survivors statutes in which the action is brought directly by the survivors themselves or by an administrator appointed to act on their behalf.

2. *Other methods of handling the problem:* A very few states, including Iowa and New Hampshire, have handled the problem of wrongful death by expanding the scope of their survival statutes to include actions for the death of an individual.

D. Measure of Damages: As noted above in paragraph A, Lord Campbell's Act was construed to limit damages to pecuniary loss. This interpretation was carried over into the United States and indeed, was often actually inserted in the wrongful death statutes modeled upon Lord Campbell's Act that were adopted in most American jurisdictions. It was, thus, for a long time largely impossible to recover anything for the loss of the decedent's companionship. While the law recognized that the death of a wife and mother, even one with no outside employment, represented a substantial pecuniary loss to a surviving husband and minor children, it was often difficult to find a basis for granting any substantial damages to the surviving parents and siblings of minor children. The actual amount of services, assistance, and financial contributions the survivors of a minor child might have been expected to receive, had the deceased child lived, was likely to be relatively small if not altogether nonexistent. To meet this problem, the courts in some states started to interpret pecuniary loss to include the loss of society and companionship, asserting that in the modern day these items had a monetary value and thus were pecuniary losses. In a number of states, the problem was met by legislative enactment which expressly included loss of society, companionship, comfort, guidance, etc., as elements of damages. There are, nevertheless, still a few states which continue to take a very narrow view of what constitutes "pecuniary loss."

1. In the minority of jurisdictions that measure damages by the loss suffered by the estate of the deceased, as well as in those few states that have handled the problem of wrongful death by extension of a state's survival acts, there are three ways of determining the loss suffered by the deceased's estate. These are the present value of the deceased's future accumulations; the present value the deceased's probable future net earnings; and the present value of the deceased's probable gross earnings. The last method is the most generous, and the first is, of course, the least generous. The second method, which focuses on the present value of the probable future net earnings, is the most common and, because it requires deduction of the deceased's own personal expenses, probably comes closest to providing a sum equal to the pecuniary loss recoverable under the more typical loss-to-survivors statutes. It should be noted, however, under a loss-to-the-estate approach, whatever the method of calculating damages, there is no basis for providing anything for the loss of companionship suffered by the survivors. If there is to be any such recovery, it must be on some other basis, such as perhaps individual actions brought by the survivors.

19

E. **Effect of Contributory Negligence:** The contributory negligence of the deceased, which would have affected his recovery if he had lived, has always been held either to be a bar to a wrongful death action or, in a jurisdiction with comparative negligence, to limit the amount of recovery. The effect of the contributory negligence of a beneficiary of the deceased is somewhat more complicated. In those states where the action is viewed as being for the benefit of the estate, the contributory negligence of someone who will eventually share in the distribution of the estate is normally of no relevance. This is also the result achieved in New York, even if the action is brought for the benefit of those persons who would have inherited from the deceased by intestate succession. The rationale is that the nominal plaintiff in these actions is the administrator who prosecutes the claim and then distributes the damages to the persons entitled to them in proportion to their pecuniary injuries as determined after a hearing. In most states in which the wrongful death action is brought for the benefit of the survivors, however, the contributory negligence of one of the survivors will reduce the total damages recoverable and bar or reduce, if comparative negligence is in effect, the contributorily negligent survivor's recovery.

F. **Statutes of Limitations:** In most states, there are special statutes of limitations governing wrongful death actions. Some of the statutes are unclear, however, as to whether the statutory period begins to run at the time of injury or at the time of death. Where the statute is unclear, most courts have held that the statute begins to run from the time of death. A related problem is how to handle a case in which the injured person lingers for a long time and then dies as a result of the original injuries, but after the applicable statute of limitations has run for any tort action that the injured person might have brought. The cases are divided on this issue. In a jurisdiction in which the wrongful death statute closely resembles the provision in Lord Campbell's Act that the action on behalf of the survivors arises "whenever the death of a person shall be caused by wrongful act . . . such as would (if death had not ensued) have entitled the party injured to maintain an action," the tendency is to hold that the action is barred because at the time of death the injured party could not have maintained an action.

G. **Limitations on Recovery:** At one time, more than twenty states had statutory limitations on the amount that could be recovered in a wrongful death action. No state now has any such general limitation. Several states, however, have limitations on the amount of nonpecuniary loss that may be recovered or on the amount that may be recovered by people who are not actually dependents of the deceased.

LOSS OF II. **LOSS OF CONSORTIUM**
CONSORTIUM

A. **Spousal Consortium — History:** At common law, a husband had an action for the loss of the consortium of his injured wife. This action was joined to the wife's action for her own injuries because, prior to the married women's property acts of the nineteenth century, the husband was a necessary party in the wife's action for her own injuries. Although a wife now has the legal capacity to bring an action in her own name, the practice of joining her action with the husband's loss of consortium action has, for obvious reasons of convenience, continued. The husband's action was based upon the loss of his wife's services. Once these losses were shown and, for all intents and purposes, such losses were presumed, the husband could also recover for the loss of his wife's companionship and the opportunity to have sexual relations. Historically, no such action was recognized for a wife's loss of the consortium of her injured husband, undoubtedly, in part, because at common law a wife had no separate legal personality apart from that of her husband.

1. With the passage of the married women's acts, there was no immediate movement toward granting a wife an action for the loss of the consortium of her husband. What happened, rather, was that a number of states abolished the husband's cause of action because the married women's acts gave the wife the sole right to bring an action for her loss of earnings and her inability to perform household services. Beginning, however, with *Hitaffer v. Argonne Co.,* 183 F.2d 811 (D.C. Cir. 1950), the momentum swung the other way. Most states, including many of those that initially abolished the action in response to the married women's acts, now permit either a husband or a wife to bring an action for the loss of consortium of an injured spouse. In England, however, the husband's loss of consortium action, as well as the parents' action for the deprivation of the services of a child and a number of other similar actions, were abolished by the Administration of Justice Act, 1982, c. 53.

   a. In recent years there have been a few cases recognizing a loss of consortium action in situations involving cohabiting, but unmarried, adults. Most of these cases have either been repudiated or not followed. The possibility of the recovery for the loss of consortium by unmarried people, previously recognized by a lower court, was, for example, expressly disapproved in *Elden v. Sheldon,* 46 Cal. 3d 267, 250 Cal. Rptr. 254, 758 P.2d 582 (1988).

B. Parental Consortium: There are a number of jurisdictions which recognize a child's action for the loss of consortium of a parent. *See Berger v. Weber,* 411 Mich. 1, 303 N.W.2d 424 (1981). The majority of states, however, have refused to recognize an action by a child for the loss of the consortium of an injured parent. *See De Angelis v. Lutheran Med. Cir.,* 58 N.Y.2d 1053, 462 N.Y.S.2d 626, 449 N.E.2d 406 (1983).

C. Loss of an Injured Child's Consortium: A very few states recognize such an action. *See Frank v. Superior Court,* 150 Ariz. 228, 722 P.2d 955 (1986). The vast majority of states, even states which recognize a child's action for the loss of consortium of a parent, refuse to recognize a parent's action for the loss of consortium of an injured child. *See Sizemore v. Smock,* 430 Mich. 283, 422 N.W.2d 666 (1988).

D. Effect of Contributory Negligence: Unlike the situation that prevails in wrongful death actions, a few states hold that a loss of consortium action is not barred or, in a comparative negligence jurisdiction, affected by the negligence of the person whose consortium has been lost. *See Fuller v. Buhrow,* 292 N.W.2d 672 (Iowa 1980). This result is justified on the ground that the person bringing the loss of consortium action is trying to recover for his own injuries and that therefore the loss of consortium action should not be affected by the injured person's negligence. Following this theory, in a state which has abolished intrafamily immunities, the injured party should, theoretically, be conceived of as a joint tortfeasor with the person that injured him, at least with regard to an action brought by someone for the loss of the injured person's consortium. *See Lantis v. Condon,* 95 Cal. App. 3d 152, 157 Cal. Rptr. 22 (1979). Most courts, however, continue to reject any suggestion that a claim for loss of consortium is not affected by the negligence of the injured person, that is, of the person the loss of whose consortium is the subject of the action.

CHAPTER 19 - QUESTIONS, ANSWERS, AND TIPS

1. **Q:** Most tort actions now survive the death of either the plaintiff or the defendant.

   A: True. Actions for defamation are one of the principal exceptions. Such actions only survive in about one half of American jurisdictions.

2. **Q:** At one time, the loss of the companionship of the deceased was not considered "pecuniary loss" that could be recovered in a wrongful death action.

   A: True. Although most American jurisdictions now permit, either by statutory amendment or judicial decision, recovery for the loss of the deceased's companionship, a minority of jurisdictions still do not.

3. **Q:** In most states the contributory negligence of the deceased does not serve either to bar recovery or, in a comparative negligence jurisdiction, to reduce recovery in a wrongful death action brought on behalf of the survivors of the deceased.

   A: False.

4. **Q:** In most states the negligence of a beneficiary belonging to a class included in that state's wrongful death statute will not affect the amount that that beneficiary may recover under the state's wrongful death statute.

   A: False. New York is one of the exceptions in this regard.

5. **Q:** Only a very few American jurisdictions will allow the parents of a minor child who has been injured, but not killed, to maintain an action for the loss of the child's consortium against a tortfeasor who has injured the child.

   A: True.

6. **Q:** Most American jurisdictions allow a minor child to bring an action for the loss of the consortium of a parent who against a tortfeasor who has injured but not killed the parent.

   A: False, only a minority of American jurisdictions permit such actions but more jurisdictions permit such actions than permit a parent to recover for the loss of the consortium of an injured child.

   Exam Tips: In answering examination questions, keep in mind that, in most states, wrongful death actions are governed by statute. This means that, although there are many similarities among these statutes, there will also be many differences. A second matter, of which one should be aware, is that the law regarding actions for the loss of the consortium of people who are injured but not killed is in transition. The ability of one spouse to bring an action for the loss of the consortium of an injured spouse is now recognized in almost all American jurisdictions. With regard to other family members the law in any particular jurisdiction could change quite suddenly.

FETAL INJURIES

▶ **CHAPTER SUMMARY**

FETAL INJURIES

Scope of Chapter: Until comparatively recently, a child, even if born alive, was unable to recover for prenatal injuries. *See Dietrich v. Inhabitants of Northampton,* 138 Mass. 14 (1884), in which Judge, later Justice, Oliver Wendell Holmes refused to recognize any such cause of action. The law on this subject has undergone considerable change in the last fifty years. In the discussion that follows, we shall consider first the recovery for physical injuries suffered by a fetus. We shall then discuss actions for what might be called wrongful birth and wrongful life. In a wrongful life action, parents, who claim that but for the negligence of the defendant they would not have conceived the child in question or would have aborted the child, are seeking damages for the care and maintenance of the child. In a wrongful life action, the child is seeking to recover damages for having been brought into existence against someone but for whose negligence the child in question would not have been born. We shall consider each of these in turn.

20

PHYSICAL INJURY TO THE FETUS

I.   PHYSICAL INJURY TO THE FETUS

A.   In General: Since *Bonbrest v. Kotz,* 65 F. Supp. 138 (D.D.C. 1946), the vast majority of jurisdictions have come to recognize that a child who is born alive is able to recover for prenatal injuries. At one time, it was thought that the child had to be viable at the time of injury in order for the child to have an action once it was born. Most of the courts that have recognized a cause of action for prenatal injuries by a child born alive have now abandoned the viability requirement, and there are no recent cases denying a cause of action to a child born alive because, at the time of injury, it was not yet viable.

1.   In recent years, there have been several cases brought by children who were born with birth defects that were the result of tortious conduct that predated the children's conception. Most of the courts that have considered the issue have permitted the child to recover.

   Example: In *Jorgensen v. Meade Johnson Labs. Inc.,* 483 F.2d 237 (10th Cir. 1973), a woman's chromosomal makeup was alleged to have been altered by the defendant's birth control pills. Five years later, she gave birth to twin daughters who, as a consequence, she alleged, were afflicted with Down's Syndrome. It was held that the two children had a cause of action. *But see Abala v. City of New York,* 54 N.Y.2d 269, 445 N.Y.S.2d 108, 429 N.E.2d 786 (1981), which refused to recognize a cause of action for preconception torts.

2.   The few relevant cases are split as to whether a child should be able to bring an action against his mother for injuries caused by her negligence before or during pregnancy. In *Grodin v. Grodin,* 102 Mich. App. 396, 301 NW2d 869 (1980), the court ruled that a child's mother could be held liable for such injury if her conduct was an unreasonable exercise of parental discretion. In a similar action, however, another court refused to recognize such a right, fearing that it would force the courts to scrutinize a pregnant woman's every act or omission before and during her pregnancy. *See Stallman v. Youngquist,* 125 Ill.2d 267, 126 Ill. Dec. 60, 531 N.E.2d 355 (Ill. 1988).

   a.   An important issue is the significance of whether the mother knew or should have known, at the time of her alleged misconduct, that she was pregnant. Such knowledge may well be necessary before many courts will recognize a duty on the mother's part to refrain from behavior potentially harmful to her unborn child. Actual knowledge of pregnancy would of course be less important if liability is recognized for prenatal injury due to the mother's negligence prior to conception. To adopt such a view would be to recognize a duty in a woman to properly care for her own body throughout her fertile years, regardless of pregnancy or her knowledge thereof. For further discussioon, *see 78 A.L.R. 4th* 1082 (1991).

B. Wrongful Death of a Fetus: The majority of jurisdictions now permit a wrongful death action to be brought on behalf of a fetus that is delivered still-born. *See Amadio v. Levin,* 509 Pa. 199, 501 A.2d 1085 (1985). Unlike the situation with regard to a child who is born alive, in order for there to be an action for the wrongful death of a fetus, the fetus must have been viable at the time of injury. Such a requirement would seem essential, given the fact that the states are not permitted to prohibit abortion in the early stages of pregnancy.

1. In a number of jurisdictions, it has been held, however that a fetus is not a "person" within the meaning of that state's wrongful death statute. *See Giardina v. Bennett,* 111 N.J. 412, 545 A.2d 139 (1988). This means that in those jurisdictions no action can be brought for the death of a fetus. An important issue is the significance of whether the mother knew or should have known, at the time of her alleged misconduct, that she was pregnant. Such knowledge may well be necessary before many courts will recognize a duty on the mother's part to refrain from behavior potentially harmful to her unborn child. Actual knowledge of pregnancy would of course be less important if liability is recognized for prenatal injury due to the mother's negligence prior to conception. To adopt such a view would be to recognize a duty in a woman to properly care for her own body throughout her fertile years, regardless of pregnancy or her knowledge thereof. For futher discussion, *see* 78 A.L.R. *4th* 1082 (1991).

   a. The Third Circuit recently held that a state does not offend the Equal Protection Clause when it allows wrongful death actions in cases where a child already born dies due to prenatal injuries but bars actions regarding stillborn children. The state may treat stillborn children differently from children who survived birth because stillborn children are not "persons" within the meaning of the Fourteenth Amendment, but, dependng on state law, the parents of a stillborn child may recover in a separate action for emotional distress caused by the stillbirth. *See Alexander v. Whitman,* 114 F.3d 1392 (3rd. Cir. 1997), *cert. denied,* 118 S.Ct. 367, 139 L.Ed.2d 286 (1997).

II. WRONGFUL BIRTH

WRONGFUL BIRTH

A. In General: In these cases the parents are typically seeking recovery for medical and other expenses incurred because a child was either conceived or carried to term owing to the negligence of the defendant. The cases are of two general types. The first concerns a child, usually a healthy child, who was born as a result of a negligently performed sterilization procedure or because of an ineffective birth-control device. The second type of case typically concerns the birth of a child whose conception was intentional. The gist of the action, in this latter group of cases, is either that the parents would not have conceived a child if they had known of the possibility of genetic defects or that, having conceived the child, the child would have been aborted and not have been carried to term if appropriate tests had been administered or the risks of producing a defective child had been adequately explained.

1. *Defective Children:* Almost all courts will permit the parents of a defective child to recover the costs of caring for that child if, but for the negligence of the defendant, the parents would have not conceived the child or brought the child to term, . Some courts expressly limit those damages to the *increased* costs of raising the defective child over those costs that would have been incurred for raising a healthy child. Most of the courts that allow recovery for some or all of the costs of raising a defective child require a showing by the parents that they would have obtained an abortion but for the lack of knowledge caused by the defendant doctor's negligence in not informing them of the child's condition prior to birth. *See Keel v. Banach,* 624 So.2d 1022 (Ala. 1993). At least one state has not recognized a parental claim for wrongful birth due to the difficulty of proving this proposition. *See Wilson v. Kuenzi,* 751 S.W.2d 741 (Mo. 1988). Some states have rejected the condition that parents should ever have to mitigate damages by aborting the fetus or putting the child up for adoption, citing these

20

actions as "highly personal matters" that should not affect recovery. *See Marciniak v. Lundberg,* 153 Eid. 2d 59, 450 N.W.2d 22243 (1990), a case involving a healthy but unwanted child.

    a.   In actions seeking damages for wrongful birth, parents have often also sought to recover for their emotional injuries. A few states have recognized such a cause of action, but the majority position would appear to be against permitting such recovery.

2.   ***Unwanted-but-Healthy Children:*** The courts are divided on the question of whether the parents of an unwanted-but-healthy child can recover the costs of rearing that child against someone whose tortious conduct resulted in the child's conception. The trend in the United States is to deny recovery for the costs of rearing a healthy child and only to permit recovery for the costs incurred by the mother in carrying the unwanted pregnancy to term and the attendant pain and suffering that accompanied the pregnancy and birth.

    a.   There are, however, a minority of courts which allow recovery for the costs of raising an unwanted but healthy child. Typically, these courts have required such recovery to be offset by the benefits that the parents derive from the child's aid, society, and comfort. *In Marciniak v. Lundberg,* 153 Wis.2d 59, 450 N.W.2d 243 (1990), the court did not require any such offset. It reasoned that, by deciding to have the improperly performed sterilization, the plaintiffs had chosen to forego the benefits of parenthood. Consequently, they should not have those benefits forced upon them by offsetting the benefits of parenthood against the costs of raising a child.

        (1)   When determining whether to offset damages, courts may take into account the reasons that parents did not want children. At least one court has suggested that, when parents wanted to avoid having children due to fears of producing a handicapped child or of the dangers to the mother's health from pregnancy and childbirth, the courts should not impose the costs of raising the child on a negligent doctor when those risks do not materialize, but, when the parents wanted to avoid having children to conserve family resources or for career or lifestyle reasons, the courts should recognize no offset for benefits derived from raising the child. *See Hartke v. McKelway,* 707 F.2d 1544 (D.C. Cir. 1983).

    b.   As noted, the majority of jurisdictions do not allow the parents to recover for the costs of rearing an unwanted-but-healthy child. One reason for doing so may be the implicit recognition that parents who do not wish to be saddled with the cost of raising a healthy-but-unwanted child could take steps to mitigate those expenses either by aborting the fetus or putting the child up for adoption after it is born.

        (1)   The few actions brought by the siblings of unwanted children claiming that owing to the addition of another child, they have been deprived of some of their parents' care and attention have been uniformly unsuccessful.

3.   ***Pregnancy as the result of misrepresentations between sexual partners:*** Courts have been loathe to recognize an action by one sexual partner against another for misrepresentations about the possibility of pregnancy in cases where the sexual encounter that resulted in pregnancy would allegedly not have occurred but for the first partner's reliance on the second's misrepresentation. Where a man brought an action against a woman for misrepresenting to him that she was practicing contraception, the court held that the state's interests in securing support for the child and the woman's interest in the privacy of her sexual relations prevailed over the plaintiff's interests. *See Welzenbach v. Powers,* 139 N.H. 688, 660 A.2d 1133 (1995). Where a man falsely assured a woman that he had had a vasectomy, the courts held that the birth of a normal, healthy child precluded inquiry into representations made between the parties regarding birth control. *See C.A.M. v. R.A.W.,* 237 N.J. Super, 532, 568 A.2d 556 (1990). An action did lie against a man who falsely represented he was sterile, however, where pregnancy complications forced a woman to undergo a procedure that rendered her sterile. The court allowed the action due to the harm that resulted to the mother. *See Barbara A. v. John G.,* 145 Cal. App. 3d 369, 193 Cal. Rptr. 422 (1983).

III.   WRONGFUL LIFE

A.   **In General:** These are actions brought by a child who was born in a defective state, such as a child born a paraplegic or with serious genetic defects, or perhaps even by a healthy child born out of wedlock. The gist of the action is that the child would rather not have been born. In the case of a defective child, the claim is that, if the parents had been properly advised, they either would not have conceived the child or would have aborted it. Such claims have thus far been uniformly rejected. Various reasons are given for this result. One of the most frequent is that general damages in such a situation are impossible to assess. Another reason given is that life in our society is always presumed to be better than the alternatives. Thus, while the parents of a defective child who can show that, but for the negligence of the defendant, they would have aborted the child can recover some or all of their costs of rearing that child, the defective child will recover nothing for having been born.

CHAPTER 20 - QUESTIONS, ANSWERS, AND TIPS

1.   **Q:** In most of the jurisdictions that recognize a cause of action on behalf of a child born alive for prenatal injuries, it is not necessary that the fetus should have been viable at the time of the injury.

     A: True.

2.   **Q:** In most of the jurisdictions that have considered the issue, a wrongful death action will not lie for the death of a still-born fetus.

     A: False. Most jurisdictions recognize the action.

     Tip: Since wrongful death actions are, in most states, of statutory creation whether or not an action will lie for the wrongful death of a still born fetus will depend on the wording and construction of the jurisdiction's wrongful death statute. In a number of jurisdictions, the courts have held that a "fetus" is not a person within the meaning of the state's wrongful death statute.

3.   **Q:** In most American jurisdictions, tortious acts that have occurred prior to a child's conception may not serve as the basis for an action for pre-natal injuries.

     A: False

4.   **Q:** Prior born children have a cause of action for the wrongful death of an unwanted sibling because the presence of the unwanted child, even it if is healthy, will inevitably diminish the care and attention that the parents can devote to their prior-born children.

     A: False

5. **Q:** A child born with genetic birth defects that his mother's physicians negligently failed to discover during the period during which abortion was safe and legal has a cause of action for wrongful life against the negligent physician.

 A: False

DAMAGES

▶ **CHAPTER SUMMARY**

DAMAGES

Scope of Chapter: Damage issues pervade the law of torts. Special aspects of damages are discussed in other chapters of this book. Damage to personal property by trespass or conversion is discussed in Chapter 2. The liability of multiple defendants, including claims for contribution and indemnity, is discussed in Chapter 6. Claims for purely economic loss for products liability are discussed in Chapter 11, and for misrepresentation in Chapter 12. Chapter 15 discusses special damage problems associated with constitutional torts, Chapters 16 and 18 deal with special damage rules for defamation and for malicious prosecution. Chapter 19 deals with damages for derivative tort claims, and Chapter 22 discusses statutory changes in rules of damage recovery. Damage issues arise in other chapters as well, as, for example, with regard to recovery for emotional distress.

21

This chapter is primarily concerned with general tort damage principles, particularly as they arise in the context of personal injury claims. The usual rule does not allow recovery for pure economic loss in tort, but there are developing exceptions to this rule, for instance, in negligent misrepresentation and in products liability. Some cases, moreover, allow recovery by plaintiffs having no business relationship with the defendant for pure business losses resulting from defendant's conduct. *See People Express Airlines v. Consol. Rail Corp.,* 100 N.J. 246, 495 A.2d 107 (1985) (tank car accident produced toxic fumes causing evacuation of plaintiff's business office, resulting business losses recoverable). The problem in these areas is in deciding where to draw the line as to the plaintiffs who can recover.

TYPES OF DAMAGES

I. TYPES OF DAMAGES

A. General and Special Damages: The basic procedural distinction between general and special damages is that the latter must be specially pleaded while the former need not be. As a general proposition, damages that are mechanically calculable, such as medical expenses, must be specially pleaded. Damages for pain and suffering are typically considered to be general damages, and they are recoverable without detailed specification either in pleading or in proof. *See Restatement (Second) of Torts § 904.*

1. Recoverable damages in tort are typically for past lost earnings and lost future earning capacity, for past and future medical expenses, and for pain and suffering caused by the defendant's tortious conduct. The pain and suffering item often includes recovery for other intangibles such as disfigurement, loss of the enjoyment of life, and the like.

B. Limiting Rules on Compensatory Damages: There are a number of restrictions on matters that can be presented to the jury. Other rules affect the plaintiff's recovery on principles akin to contributory fault. Finally, there are limitations on recoverable damages imposed by statute or by court rule.

1. Typically, interest on tort claims prior to judgment is not recoverable, although in some jurisdictions this rule has been changed by statute or court decision. The traditional reason for this rule is that interest is not allowed on damages that are unliquidated or that are uncertain in amount. On the other hand, the no-interest rule provides a disincentive to settlement, since the defendant loses nothing by delaying payment of a valid claim.

2. Damages for personal injury are not taxable as income, even though such damages include recovery for lost income or lost earning capacity, as well as for out-of-pocket losses such as medical expenses and intangible or noneconomic losses such as pain and suffering. I.R.C. § 104(a)(2). The general rule is that the jury is not to be instructed or told about the nontaxability of tort recoveries. The U.S. Supreme Court, however, held that the jury should be told to take into account the nontaxability of damages in awarding recovery under the Federal Employers Liability Act, *Norfolk & Western R.R. v. Liepelt,* 444 U.S. 490, 100 S. Ct. 755, 62 L.Ed.2d 689 (1980), and a few state courts have followed this rule in state law cases as well, *see, e.g., Blanchfield v. Dennis,* 292 Md. 319, 438 A.2d 1330 (1982). Tort actions based

on other federal statutes are also likely to be influenced by *Liepelt*. In 1996, Congress passed an amendment to 26 U.S.C. § 104 to make tort recoveries for emotional distress and punitive damages subject to income tax.

3. A more general principle regarding the irrelevance of income or benefits coming from sources other than the tortfeasor, as the result of a tort, is the collateral source rule. This rule provides that the tortfeasor is not entitled to any credit for sums received by the victim from insurance, gratuitous aid, remarriage, and the like, as a result of the tort, nor is the jury to be told that the victim has received such outside income or benefits. The rationale for this rule is that the tortfeasor should not benefit from advantages resulting from the victim's own thrift or good relations. A number of jurisdictions by statute, however, require the jury to reduce *recovery* for collateral benefits received by the victim in order to prevent double recovery. In all events, sums paid to the claimant by the tortfeasor, or by actual or assumed cotortfeasors, as a result of the tort are not considered collateral sources and are credited against the tort recovery.

4. Most courts instruct the jury to reduce damages for future medical expenses and lost earning capacity to their present value. Present value is determined by calculating how much money would be required at the present time in order to produce a designated sum of money in the future, if the present sum were invested at a rate which the claimant could reasonably be expected to earn. *See Restatement (Second) of Torts* § 913A. Typically juries are not asked to reduce awards for future pain and suffering to present value, probably because the method of calculating such awards is so discretionary in the first place that it makes little sense to reduce the award by a mechanical rule. An award of punitive damages is not reduced by a present-value calculation, since such damages are designed to punish the tortfeasor presently, and they do not represent future damages.

   a. Most courts say that inflation should not be considered in calculating an award of future pecuniary damages, except to the extent that the inflationary factor may affect the rate used to discount future damages to present value. A few courts, however, have concluded that the prospect of future inflation offsets any financial advantage of receiving future damages before they accrue, so that a reduction of future pecuniary damages to present value need not be made. *See, e.g., Beaulieu v. Elliott*, 434 P.2d 665 (Alaska 1967).

5. There is a division of authority regarding whether the plaintiff can ask the jury to place a monetary value on the plaintiff's pain and suffering, broken down into small units of time, *e.g.,* so much money per minute, per hour, or per day and the like for the entire period during which the plaintiff is expected to suffer. *See* annot., 3 A.L.R. 4th 940 (1983). Those courts that do not allow the argument consider it to be misleading. In all events, the jury cannot be asked to calculate damages for pain and suffering based on what *they themselves* would charge to undergo such pain, since this argument is unduly prejudicial. D. Dobbs, *Remedies,* at 545 (1973). Some level of awareness is a prerequisite for recovering for pain and suffering. *McDougald v. Garber,* 73 N.Y.2d 246, 538 N.Y.S.2d 937, 536 N.E.2d 372 (1989).

6. It is widely stated that the tortfeasor takes his tort victim as he finds him. Thus, if the victim is predisposed to nervous disorder and this disorder is precipitated by the defendant's conduct, the defendant can be held liable for triggering the disorder. *Bartolone v. Jeckovich,* 103 A.D.2d 632, 481 N.Y.S.2d 545 (1984). The jury, however, is entitled to consider the likelihood of such injury resulting anyway in determining whether the defendant has "caused" the plaintiff's injury.

   Example: Defendant negligently ran into an alcoholic, causing him to suffer *delirium tremens* resulting in death. In assessing damages, the jury was entitled to consider the likelihood of the deceased's death in any event from alcoholism. *McCahill v. N.Y. Transp. Co.,* 201 N.Y. 221, 94 N.E. 616 (1911).

If the plaintiff is unusually sensitive, she may not be able to recover for damages resulting from such extrasensitivity unless the defendant is aware of that sensitivity. If a person suffers a nervous breakdown on being casually touched by another, this would likely be considered an unusual reaction for which no recovery would be allowed. Persons may also be expected to suffer a certain amount of harsh language and criticism for which no damages for emotional distress will be allowed.

DUTIES OF
PLAINTIFF AND
OF THE COURT **II.** **DUTIES OF THE PLAINTIFF AND OF THE COURT**

A. **Avoidable Consequences:** The plaintiff is obligated to take reasonable steps to mitigate or reduce damages caused by the tortfeasor, as, for example, by seeking medical or other treatment. In determining what is reasonable in this regard, the jury is entitled to consider the cost, risk, and pain involved in seeking medical treatment, and the likelihood of success. *Zimmerman v. Ausland,* 266 Or. 427, 513 P.2d 1167 (1973). The jury is also entitled to take into account plaintiff 's circumstances, as, for example, her religious beliefs that cause her to be opposed to certain medical treatment. *Christiansen v. Hollings,* 44 Cal. App. 2d 332, 112 P.2d 723 (1941). It has been held, however, that applying the doctrine of avoidable consequences to one who refused a blood transfusion is not a violation of the constitutional guarantee of the free exercise of religion. *Munn v. Southern Health Plan, Inc.,* 719 F. Supp 525 (N.D. Miss. 1989).

1. As we have seen in Chapter 5, *supra,* courts are divided regarding the duty of the plaintiff to wear a seat belt in an automobile. Some courts treat this as part of the avoidable consequences doctrine, so that plaintiff 's damages will be reduced by the amount of damages *caused* by her unreasonable failure to wear a seat belt. *Spier v. Barker,* 35 N.Y.2d 444, 363 N.Y.S.2d 1026, 323 N.E.2d 164 (1974). Other courts view such failure as a form of contributory negligence, which in a comparative fault jurisdiction would reduce the plaintiff 's damages by the percentage of fault attributable to the unreasonable failure to wear a belt. *See Curry v. Moser,* 89 A.D.2d 1, 454 N.Y.S.2d 311 (1982). Some jurisdictions by statute place a percentage limit on the maximum amount by which plaintiff's recovery can be reduced for such failure, *e.g.,* Iowa Code § 321.445(4)(b)(2) (Supp. 1990) (5% maximum), and still other jurisdictions either by court decision or by statute generally prohibit consideration of plaintiff 's failure to wear a seat belt.

B. **Judicial Control of Damages:** A court has the power to order a new trial if damages are so excessively high or low as to shock the conscience of the court or to suggest passion, prejudice, or caprice on the part of the jury. In addition, many courts will grant a new trial unless the plaintiff will agree to a specified reduction (*remittitur*) in damages where they are too high, or unless the defendant will agree to a specified increase (*additur*) where the damages are too low. The U.S. Supreme Court held that an additur denies the plaintiff 's federal constitutional right to trial by jury *in a federal court. Dimick v. Schiedt,* 293 U.S. 474, 55 S. Ct. 296, 79 L.Ed. 603 (1935). State courts are divided on the question of whether additur violates a state constitutional right to trial by jury *in a state court. See* annot., 11 A.L.R. 2d 1217 (1950). The right to trial by jury is controlled by state, rather than federal, law in a civil case in state court unless the plaintiff 's suit is based on a federal cause of action.

PUNITIVE
DAMAGES **III.** **PUNITIVE DAMAGES**

A. **Basis of Liability:** Exemplary or punitive damages can be awarded in the jury's discretion against a defendant guilty of willful, wanton, or reckless misconduct or conduct in callous disregard of the rights of others. Some courts require proof by clear and convincing evidence in order to justify an award of such damages, but the majority allow recovery based on a preponderance of the evidence. In the case of a corporate defendant, some courts require the conduct giving rise to such damages to be committed by a person in a managerial position, but most courts only require that the conduct be committed by any employee acting within the scope of her employment. Some states require that the trial of punitive damages be bifurcated (tried separately) from the rest of the case, to avoid jury prejudice.

1. Typically, punitive damages cannot be awarded against a municipality, and the United States retains sovereign immunity from the award of such damages. There have been questions raised as to whether very large punitive awards constitute a denial of due process, and a number of courts and commentators have expressed concern about the fairness of repeated punitive awards in multiple cases arising out of the same conduct of the defendant. Statutory restrictions on punitive awards are considered in Chapter 22.

2. Courts generally allow the plaintiff to introduce evidence of the defendant's wealth, to assist the jury in assessing punitive damages. *Pluid v. B.K.,* 948 P.2d 981 (Alaska 1997). Some courts permit the jury to consider attorney's fees incurred by the plaintiff in assessing punitive damages. *St. Luke Evangelical Lutheran Church v. Smith,* 568 A.2d 35 (Md. 1990). A majority of courts that have considered the matter do not allow punitive damages to be awarded against the estate of a tortfeasor who dies after committing the tort. *G.J.D. v. Johnson,* 669 A.2d 378 (Pa. Super. 1995) Punitive damages are taxable by the federal government as income, 26 U.S.C. § 104 (1997).

3. In *BMW v. Gore,* 116 S. Ct. 1589 (1996), in assessing the constitutionality of an award of punitive damages, the Court said the punitive award must bear a "reasonable relationship" to the compensatory award. The jury should consider the "civil or criminal penalties that could be imposed for comparable misconduct," and the degree of reprehensibility of the defendant's misconduct. In the *Gore* case, the Court said, the jury in assessing punitive damages erroneously considered similar conduct of the defendant in other jurisdictions where such conduct would not have provided a basis for awarding punitive damages.

IV. NEGLIGENT INFLICTION OF EMOTIONAL DISTRESS

A. Intentional infliction of emotional distress was considered in Chapter 2. Courts generally allow recovery for emotional distress when accompanied by personal injury. In addition, courts allow recovery of emotional distress unaccompanied by physical injury if the plaintiff is the direct victim of defendants's negligence. *Corgan v. Muehling,* 574 N.E. 2d 602 (Ill. 1991) (sexual relation of defendant psychologist with plaintiff patient).

1. Courts widely allow bystanders to recover for negligent infliction of emotional distress if they receive a physical impact from, or are in the zone of danger of, the tort. In addition, the bystatnder can recover if she is closely related to a physically injured victim, and witnesses the victim's injury. *Dunphy v. Gregor,* 64
    2 A. 2d 372 (N.J. 1994). The court is *Migliori v. Airborne Freight Corp.,* 690 N.E. 2d 413 (Mass. 1998), held that a rescuer of a tort victim could not recover for negligent infliction of emotional distress because the rescuer was unrelated to the victim.

2. The cases divide on when a person can recover in neglignence for emotional distress arising out of fear of contracting HIV or AIDS. Some courts require actual exposure to the virus of disease, *Bain v. Wells,* 936 S.W.2d 618 (Tenn. 1997), while others permit recovery for reasonable fear of exposure. *Madrid v. Lincoln Cnty. Med. Cntr.,* 923 P.2d 1154 (N.M. 1996).

CHAPTER 21 – QUESTIONS, ANSWERS, AND TIPS

1. **Q:** What are the reasons pro and con for allowing interest on unliquidated tort claims?

   A: Pro: without such damages the defendant lacks sufficient incentive to settle; Con: the damages are uncertain in amount.

   Tip: Neither of these arguments is definitive. Tort damages become fixed on judgment, and the appropriate interest rate can then be fixed retroactively. Imposing an incentive to settle assumes the defendant should be encouraged to settle, although such encouragement may be inappropriate if the defendant reasonably thinks the claim is invalid.

2. **Q:** What is the difference between a collateral source, and a sum paid to the tort victim by a tortfeasor or assumed cotortfeasor?

   A: The collateral source is not normally credited against any tort claim, while the payment by a tortfeasor or supposed cotortfeasor is so credited.

   Tip: A collateral source payment does not come directly from a tortfeasor, although the tortfeasor is the indirect cause of such payment. The distinction can be nebulous, however, as for example where A tortiously floods B's land, and the water from the flood freezes so B is able to sell the resulting ice at a profit. This situation looks as if the defendant directly conferred the benefit, but the benefit would not have materialized without the ingenuity either of the plaintiff or a third person.

3. **Q:** Are the reasons the same for not reducing to present value damages for pain and for punitives?

   A: No. Damages for pain and suffering are typically not reduced because of their intrinsically non-financial character, while punitives do not represent future damages but are presently imposed.

   Tip: The reduction of future damages to present value is based on the somewhat doubtful assumption that the average tort victim will in fact invest her tort recovery in the financial market. Perhaps the present value rule is merely intended to encourage such investment.

4. **Q:** What is the difference between the eggshell-skull doctrine (take your victim as you find her) and the extrasensitivity rule?

   A: There is no duty, absent notice, to assume someone is extrasensitive, but there is a duty to compensate for unforeseen damages of the general sort that are foreseeably caused by a tortious act.

   Tip: If a tort victim were known by the tortfeasor to be extrasensitive, then the tortfeasor would be liable for any unforeseen damages of the general sort foreseeably caused to the victim under the eggshell-skull doctrine.

5. **Q:** Is unreasonable failure to avoid consequences treated the same as contributory or comparative fault?

   A: It depends on whether the failure is treated as fault or as cause.

   Tip: If the plaintiff's contributory fault is treated as conduct which helps cause a tort to happen, then such failure would not be treated as causal fault since the tort has already happened when the failure to mitigate occurs.

6. **Q:** Why should additur be treated differently from remittitur for purposes of a constitutional right to a jury trial?

   A: Theoretically a jury has agreed to a lower figure that is contained within the jury verdict, but not to a higher one.

   Tip: This answer does not explain why the court makes the acceptance of remittitur or additur conditional on approval by the plaintiff or defendant, respectively, in lieu of a new trial. Probably the new trial option is not of constitutional dimension, but is merely a procedural rule. But see *Johansen v. Combust. Engr.*, 170 F. 3d 1320 (11th Cir. 1990).

7. **Q:** Punitive damages are intended to punish the defendant and not to compensate (i.e., make whole) the plaintiff.

   A: This statement is not entirely accurate in jurisdictions that allow an award of attorneys fees as part of punitive damages.

   Tip: Arguably an award of attorneys fees to a plaintiff as part of punitive damages would not be taxable as income to the plaintiff since such fees are not punitive in nature but are compensatory to the plaintiff.

8. **Q:** What is the difference between a direct and an indirect victim of negligently inflicted emotional distress?

   A: An indirect victim as a bystander must prove close relation and witnessing of the injury to the direct victim, unless the victim can recover as one in the zone of danger or because she suffered a physical impact.

   Tip: The distinction between direct and indirect victim is not clear. Perhaps the indirect victim doctrine should be limited to the bystander who is not in direct peril or who is not highly foreseeable.

21

NOTES

STATUTORY CHANGES

▶ **CHAPTER SUMMARY**

STATUTORY CHANGES

Scope of Chapter: Statutory changes continually occur in tort law, and much of tort law is now codified at the federal or state level. Sometimes these statutes provide only administrative remedies, but in many cases they provide the basis for common law remedies as well. In the mid-1970s and again in the mid-1980s, however, different approaches to statutory changes in tort law were taken. These approaches were characterized by statutory retrenchments on tort law recovery, primarily in response to perceived "explosions" in the number and amount of tort recoveries as well as "crises" in the availability or affordability of liability insurance. There is little doubt about the insurance crises, although the causes or reasons for such crises are hotly debated. There is also considerable debate about the nature, causes, and extent of the perceived litigation "explosions."

In response to these concerns, a number of statutory retrenchments in the tort field were enacted, primarily at the state level. This chapter will examine some of the major changes in this area. The concerns illustrated by these changes should be compared with the tort alternatives considered in Chapter 23.

I.   **TYPES OF CHANGES**

A.   **Statutes of Limitation:** Numerous statutes of limitations exist in the various jurisdictions. They govern the time within which a suit can be brought. They often differ according to the type of injury incurred (*e.g.,* personal injury, or property damage), the activity regulated (*e.g.,* medical malpractice or products liability), or the legal theory of recovery (*e.g.,* negligence, warranty, or contribution). The lengths of time (*e.g.,* one year, three years, ten years) they provide within which suit must be brought vary widely, as do the types of circumstances (*e.g.,* minority, fraudulent concealment, continuing duty to warn) that will stop, or "toll," the running of the statutory period.

1.   Probably the most common rule for determining when the statutory period begins is the discovery rule. This rule begins the statutory period at the time when the plaintiff discovers, or should discover, that she has a right to sue.

a.   In response to the perceived tort crises, many jurisdictions enacted *statutes of repose.* Under such statutes, the limitation period begins to run from a fixed date, regardless of whether the plaintiff has discovered or could discover that he has a cause of action, and regardless of whether he has even been injured. Typical examples are products liability statutes of repose, which run from the date the product is first sold for use or consumption, *e.g.,* Tenn. Code Annot. § 29-28-103. Others involve real estate construction, with the period running from the date of completion of the construction, and medical malpractice statutes running from the date of treatment. Congress enacted the General Aviation Revitalization Statute, 49 U.S.C. § 40101 Note (1994), providing an 18-year statute of repose from the date of sale for private aircraft. Congress enacted the General Aviation Revitalization Statute, 49 U.S.C. § 40101 Note (1994), providing an 18-year statute of repose from the deed of sale for private aircraft. These statutes provide certainty, but at the expense of fairness to the litigant.

B.   **Damage Caps:** Other jurisdictions have enacted caps on the amount of recoverable damages. These damage limits vary widely in context and in amount. Some statutes limit the total amount recoverable. Others limit the amount recoverable for pain and suffering or for punitive damages. Such statutes also provide a degree of certainty, but at the expense of flexibility and individual determinations.

C.   **Several Liability:** As noted in Chapter 6, a number of jurisdictions have by statute abolished or limited joint liability and adopted several liability for cotortfeasors responsible for the same injury. These statutes take a variety of forms, for example, from abolishing joint liability entirely, to abolishing it for pain and suffering recovery, or abolishing it where the defendant's fault is less than that of the plaintiff. *See* Wright, *Joint and Several Liability,* 21 U.C. Davis L. Rev. 1141 (1988). Another approach is to apportion the nonrecoverable portion attributable to an insolvent defendant between or among the other at-fault parties. Thus, if plaintiff were 10% at fault, defendant A 40% at fault, and insolvent defendant B 50% at fault, the damages would be apportioned 20% to the plaintiff and 80% to defendant A. See *Restatement of the Law (Third): Apportionment of Liability* § 30C (1998). Some statutes place the risk of nonrecovery from a cotortfeasor on the plaintiff, rather than the defendant. It is debatable whether this approach is appropriate, especially when the defendants are master and servant or are acting in concert, or where the plaintiff is free of fault.

D. Implied Statutory Preemption: A notable recent trend is to find implied statutory or regulatory preemption of common law causes of action.

Examples: The federal cigarette warning law impliedly preempts a common law cause of action for failure to warn. *Cipollone v. Liggett Group Inc.,* 112 S.Ct.2608 (1992). The Nat'l Traffic and Motor Vehicle Safety Act impliedly preempts a claim for failure to provide airbags. *Wood v. GM Corp.,* 865 F.2d 395 (1st Cir. 1988).

It is clear that the legislature may expressly preempt a common law tort cause of action. It is less common to find implied preemption, however, because it is widely recognized that statutory standards are the result of political compromise and are not intended to fix the common law standard of responsibility. See *Medtronic, Inc. v. Lohr,* 116 S.Ct.2240 (1996).

CONSTITUTIONAL AND POLICY CONSIDERATIONS

II. CONSTITUTIONAL AND POLICY CONSIDERATIONS

A. Unconstitutionality: Many of the above statutes have been challenged on various grounds of unconstitutionality — including due process, equal protection, "open court" provisions of state constitutions, and many other grounds. A number of the challenges have been successful, with no clear pattern emerging. The propriety and success of such challenges depend on the level of constitutional scrutiny used and on the point at which the court is willing to draw the line between considerations of constitutionality and considerations of policy.

B. Policy: Without regard to the constitutionality of such statutes, it may be questioned whether such enactments are sound as a matter of policy. An interesting historical comparison is the guest passenger statutes, which prevent a guest (nonpaying) passenger from recovering from his host driver for injuries caused by the driver's negligence. Such statutes once existed in about half the states. Now they are largely repealed or overturned as unconstitutional. *See Henry v. Bauder,* 213 Kan. 751, 518 P.2d 362 (1974). The statutory classifications proved unfair and too rigid, and they were ultimately riddled with exceptions that made the statutes seem arbitrary and capricious in application. It is difficult to remove flexibility from the tort law without destroying its utility.

CHAPTER 22 – QUESTIONS, ANSWERS, AND TIPS

1. **Q:** What were the nature and causes of the liability insurance crises in America in the mid-1970s and mid-1980s?

    A: The crises consisted of sharp increases in insurance premiums and unavailability of insurance coverage. The causes of the crises are not clear.

    Tip: The insurance industry has claimed the crises were caused by runaway tort liability and runaway tort recoveries. The plaintiffs bar and consumer groups claim the crises were caused by competitive underpricing of insurance premiums during periods of high interest rates (i.e., times of favorable investment of premiums), and sharp increases of those premiums and withdrawal of high-risk coverage during periods of low interest rates.

2. Q: What is the difference between a statute of limitation and a statute of repose, and why might the latter be unconstitutional?

A: A statute of limitation typically runs from the date of reasonable discovery by the plaintiff of her cause of action, while a repose statute runs from a time such as the date of sale, date of construction, or date of treatment, and may expire before any injury ever occurs. Some courts have thought it unconstitutional to cut off a claim before it can ever be brought.

3. Q: What are the advantages and disadvantages of damage caps?

A: They give a degree of certainty of outcome, as least in the individual case, but at the price of individualized justice.

Tip: Some damage awards may be excessive, but this problem can be handled by judicial remittitur. A one-measure-for-all damage cap rule works like a procrustean bed.

4. Q: In a comparative fault-several liability jurisdiction there may be no greater reason for placing on the plaintiff the risk of non-recovery from a third-party tortfeasor than on the defendant.

A: True.

Tip: Assuming the equities are in balance, perhaps the risk of non-recovery for the fault of a third party should be reallocated proportionately between the plaintiff defendant. E.g.: plaintiff 10% at fault, defendant 30%, and judgment-proof third party 60%; reallocate third party fault 15% to plaintiff and 45% to defendant, with a final allocation of 25% and 75% between plaintiff and defendant, respectively.

5. Q: Tort law is characterized by bright-line rules.

A: False.

Tip: The goal of tort law is to provide individualized justice. The result is that most issues tend to be left to the jury as questions of fact rather than of law.

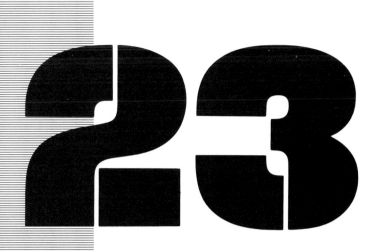

TORT LAW ALTERNATIVES

▶ CHAPTER SUMMARY

TORT LAW ALTERNATIVES

Scope of Chapter: Many people, particularly academics, decry the slowness, costliness, and unpredictability of the tort system of recovery. *See* J. O'Connell, *Ending Insult to Injury* (1975). As a method of compensation, it is considered inefficient. Moreover, it is debatable whether the system works as an effective deterrent to tortious activity, particularly the activity of individuals.

One approach has been to retrench on tort law recovery. This approach has been considered in Chapter 22. The present chapter examines alternatives to the tort system.

23

PARTIAL ALTERNATIVE SYSTEMS

I. PARTIAL ALTERNATIVE SYSTEMS

A. **Workers' Compensation:** Death and injury in the workplace took an appalling toll in this country during the nineteenth and early twentieth centuries. Workers were often unable to recover in tort because of the defenses of contributory negligence, assumption of the risk, and the fellow-servant rule, which relieved an employer of liability for injuries caused by a co-employee.

1. Beginning in the 'teens of the twentieth century, various jurisdictions in this country began to enact workers' compensation statutes providing for compensation for workplace injuries that arise out of and in the course of employment, without regard to fault. The statutes typically provide for partial replacement of wages (usually not more than two-thirds of average wages), medical expenses, some recovery for disfigurement, and death benefits. Almost all of the statutes provide a maximum recoverable amount, with no recovery for pain and suffering. The remedies are typically provided in lieu of any tort remedy the worker might otherwise have against his employer.

    a. These statutes have been subject to a number of criticisms. Typical are complaints that the compensation is inadequate and the payment scales too rigid. There has been a considerable amount of litigation concerning such matters as what sorts of injuries arise out of and in the course of employment and the extent of medical or physical disability. Also, there has been considerable uncertainty about the nature and extent of workplace diseases covered by workers' compensation.

        (i) As a result of these dissatisfactions, several exceptions have developed to the workers' compensation exclusivity rule (which precludes any employee tort claim against his employer). One exception is where the employer intentionally injures an employee. California, by statute, makes the employer liable in tort for causing injury to an employee by the removal of or failure to install point-of-operation guards on punch presses. West's Annot. Cal. Labor Code § 4558 (1982). Almost all jurisdictions allow the employee to sue a third party, such as a machine manufacturer, in tort for workplace injuries caused by the third party. Some jurisdictions then allow the third party to seek contribution against the employer, thus circumventing the workers' compensation exclusivity-of-remedy rule. *Dole v. Dow Chem. Co.*, 30 N.Y.2d 143, 331 N.Y.S.2d 382, 282 N.E.2d 288 (1972).

B. **No-Fault Automobile Insurance:** Less than half the states provide for no-fault auto insurance, whereby the owner or her passengers or pedestrians may recover medical expenses and lost wages — usually up to a designated maximum — caused by an automobile accident involving the owner's vehicle, without regard to fault. If two or more cars are involved in an accident, each owner and his passengers recover against that owner's own insurer. See 29 U. Memph, L. Rev. 69 (1998).

1. The no-fault plans are of two basic types. One, the "add-on" plan, allows the insured to recover in tort against any available tortfeasor, with the no-fault benefits credited against any such

recovery. The other plan provides for no-fault benefits exclusively up to a designated threshold — either of expenses incurred or seriousness of injury — after which point the insured can bring a claim in tort against any available tortfeasor. None of the no-fault plans provides no-fault compensation as the completely exclusive remedy.

C. **Public and Private Insurance:** Social Security, Medicare, and Medicaid provide wage and medical benefits to many retired, disabled, and indigent persons in this country, without regard to fault. In addition, many people have medical benefits and some have wage benefits provided through private individual, or employment group, insurance policies.

II. TOTAL ALTERNATIVE SYSTEMS

A. **Alternative Dispute Systems:** Arbitration, negotiation, and like systems have become widely used in this country as an alternative to tort and other adversarial litigation. These alternative systems are typically, at least in part, fault-based, but they seek compromise instead of confrontation and they attempt to minimize the costs and delay of litigation.

TOTAL ALTERNATIVE SYSTEMS

B. **The New Zealand System:** Effective in 1974, New Zealand essentially abolished its tort system in favor of a comprehensive no-fault scheme. The scheme is financed by taxes on employers, automobile owners, and taxpayers in general. It covers only accidental injuries, except that disability from workplace disease is also covered. It provides medical and wage benefits and some benefits for loss of enjoyment of life.

1. The New Zealand system has been criticized for not providing an adequate safety incentive, either by rate structure or otherwise. Also, recent indications are that the system is proving much more expensive to operate than anticipated. *See* Miller, *The Future of New Zealand's Accident Compensation Scheme,* 11 U. Haw. L. Rev. 1 (1989).

III. POLICY CONSIDERATIONS

POLICY CONSIDERATIONS

A. One possibility is to provide a no-fault system with a parallel tort system. This is the approach of some of the auto no-fault plans and of workers' compensation in England and Australia. The approach enables persons to pursue goals of both compensation and deterrence. Such a dual system may, however, prove too costly to operate unless it is carefully regulated.

CHAPTER 23 – QUESTIONS, ANSWERS, AND TIPS

1. **Q:** Worker's compensation provides an exclusive rule of recovery by an employee against her employer for injuries arising out of and in the course of employment.

A: False. Many jurisdictions allow an employee to sue her employer in tort for injuries intentionally caused by the employer.

Tip: Note also that workers comp. only covers personal injuries and diseases arising in the workplace. A dignitary tort claim (e.g., defamation) or an intangible property claim (e.g., wrongful discharge) may lie outside the exclusivity rule and may be brought in tort.

2. **Q:** No-fault auto insurance, where adopted in the United States, is the exclusive remedy for personal injuries arising out of automobile accidents.

A: False. All American plans provide for an alternative tort remedy, either for damages in excess of the no-fault benefits or for damages above a certain threshold measured either in terms of expenses incurred or seriousness of injury.

Tip: No-fault typically does not cover property damage, and it may be inapplicable in accidents between citizens of different states depending on governing choice-of-law rules.

3. **Q:** The New Zealand no-fault system, administered by the government from tax revenues, provides insurance coverage for all injuries and deaths caused by accident or disease.

A: False. Non-workplace-contracted diseases are not covered by the New Zealand plan.

Tip: The rising costliness of the New Zealand no-fault system may be due to inadequate funding, abuse of the system, or a combination of both. It is unclear what effect, if any, the general abolition of the tort system in New Zealand has had on safety incentives in that country.

IMMUNITIES

▶ **CHAPTER SUMMARY**

IMMUNITIES

Scope of Chapter: There have traditionally been a number of situations in which, because of the defendant's status, the plaintiff has been unable to recover damages for injuries inflicted by the defendant. At one time, these immunities from suit were much more extensive than they are at present. The whole trend of modern legal development has been to abolish or limit immunities from suit. Immunities from suit nevertheless still exist and in some areas are likely to continue to exist for the foreseeable future. Traditionally, in the United States, three general types of immunities have been recognized: those of governmental entities; those of charitable institutions; and the immunity of family members from suits by other members of their family. We shall discuss each of these in turn.

24

GOVERNMENTAL IMMUNITIES

I.   GOVERNMENTAL IMMUNITIES

A.   Suits against the United States: Until the enactment of the Federal Tort Claims Act in 1946, the sovereign immunity of the United States, with some minor statutory exceptions for maritime torts and certain types of property damage, barred all tort actions against the federal government. Those injured by the activities of federal officials could only obtain relief by either bringing an action against the official involved, if such an official could be identified, or by petitioning Congress, which gave some recompense for some tort claims against the government by means of private acts.

1.   The Federal Tort Claims Act, the principal provisions of which are codified as 28 U.S.C. §§ 1346, 2671–80, provides that the United States shall be liable in tort "in the same manner and to the same extent as a private individual under like circumstances, but shall not be liable for interest prior to judgment or for punitive damages." 28 U.S.C. § 2674. Even when a govenment employee's failure to perform procedures required by a federal agency's regulations causes injuries to others, the government avoids liability if state law would not hold a private party performiing a similar service liable for omitting such procedures. *See Zabala Clemente v. United States,* 567 F.2d 1140 (1st Cir. 1992). There are a number of specific exceptions to the liability of the United States which are outlined in 28 U.S.C. § 2680. The principal exceptions to liability follow immediately below.

2.   *The discretionary function exception:* Under 28 U.S.C. § 2680(a), the government is not liable for any act or omission of one of its employees who has exercised due care in the execution of a statute or regulation regardless of whether such statute or regulation is valid. More importantly, the government is not liable for any action or omission of a federal employee in the "exercise or performance or the failure to exercise or perform a discretionary function or duty," regardless of whether the discretion involved has been abused.

a.   What is a discretionary function has proved to be very difficult to determine. Some courts have attempted to give some meaning to the discretionary function exception by distinguishing between the planning functions of government to which the discretionary function applies and the operational functions of government to which it does not. There is no simple test. The Supreme Court's first, and perhaps most famous, engagement with the problem, *Dalehite v. United States,* 346 U.S. 15, 73 S. Ct. 956, 97 L. Ed. 1427 (1953), is, to say the least, not very helpful.

Example: Consider two cases involving the operation of Yellowstone Park. In *Smith v. United States,* 546 F.2d 872 (10th Cir. 1976), the court held that, even if the decision to leave a section of Yellowstone Park as an "undeveloped natural area" was the exercise of a discretionary function, the decision not to post warning signs near a superheated thermal pool was not the exercise of a discretionary function. The court, however, upheld the decision of the district court that the action was barred by the plaintiff's contributory negligence. In the second case, *Martin v. United States,* 546 F.2d 1355 (9th Cir. 1976), *cert. denied,* 432 U.S. 906 (1977), the government's decision to close the garbage dumps in Yellowstone Park was held to be the exercise of a discretionary function.

Example: In *United States v. S.A. Empresa de Viacao Aerea Rio Grandense (Varig Airlines),* 467 U.S. 797, 104 S. Ct. 2755, 81 L. Ed. 2d 660 (1984), the Court unanimously held that the discretionary function exception barred a tort action premised upon the FAA's conduct in certifying the aircraft in question for use in commercial aviation. At the same time, the Court has also held that the failure of agency personnel to follow applicable requirements established by statute or regulation can be the basis of an action under the Tort Claims Act. *See Berkovitz v. United States,* 486 U.S. 531, 108 S. Ct. 1954, 100 L. Ed. 2d 531 (1988).

b. In a more recent case, the Court held that, even if the plaintiff is injured as a result of the day-to-day activities of a government agency, if the supposedly tortious government activity is the result of choices that are guided by statutory policies, the action will be barred by the discretionary function exception. *United States v. Graubart,* 499 U.S. 315, 111 S. Ct. 1267, 113 L. Ed. 2d 335 (1991).

3. As originally enacted, 28 U.S.C. § 2680(h) carved an exception from the coverage of the Tort Claims Act for claims "arising out of assault, battery, false imprisonment, false arrest, malicious prosecution, abuse of process, libel, slander, misrepresentation, deceit, or interference with contract rights." Exception "(h)" is sometimes described as the intentional tort exception. In 1974, exception "(h)" was amended to provide that the Tort Claims Act would apply to claims arising from the conduct of "investigative or law enforcement officers" with regard to claims for "assault, battery, false imprisonment, false arrest, abuse of process, or malicious prosecution."

a. In *Sheehan v. United States,* 896 F.2d 1168 (9th Cir. 1990), the appeals court held that an action by a federal employee who sought recovery for intentional infliction of emotional distress resulting from sexual harassment by the plaintiff's supervisor was not barred by the enumerated intentional tort exceptions and thus could be brought under the Tort Claims Act. It is unclear if this case will be followed. The Supreme Court has yet to rule on the issue.

4. There are a number of other exceptions which include claims arising "out of the loss, miscarriage, or negligent transmission of letters or postal matter," claims arising out of the assessment or collection of taxes or customs duties, claims arising out of the "combatant activities of the military or naval forces or the coast guard during time of war," and "[a]ny claim arising in a foreign country."

a. The Court has construed the Tort Claims Act as not to permit an action against the government by a serviceman whose injuries "arise out of or are [incurred] in the course of activity incident to service." *See Feres v. United States,* 340 U.S. 135, 71 S. Ct. 153, 95 L. Ed. 152 (1950).

5. The Court has also construed the Tort Claims Act to exclude the liability of the United States on a strict liability theory. *See Laird v. Nelms,* 406 U.S. 797, 92 S. Ct. 1899, 32L. Ed. 2d 499 (1972).

6. ***Relationship to an action against a government employee:*** As originally enacted, the Tort Claims Act did not prohibit an injured person from pursuing a remedy against both the United

24

States and the employee whose conduct caused the plaintiff's injury, although a judgment in an action against the United States was a complete bar to a similar tort action against the employee. In 1961, however, the Tort Claims Act was made the exclusive remedy for persons whose injuries arose out of the operation of a motor vehicle. In 1988, the remedy against the United States was made exclusive with regard to any action based on tort against the employee. 28 U.S.C. § 2679(b)(1).

a. Although the Tort Claims Act now provides the exclusive remedy for ordinary tort actions arising out of acts or omissions of government employees, the Tort Claims Act, as now amended, expressly does not bar any so-called civil right actions against government employees, that is, the Tort Claims Act does not bar actions against government employees arising out of violations of the Constitution or of federal statutes. 28 U.S.C. § 2679(b)(2).

b. The question has arisen whether the Tort Claims Act's barring of actions against federal employees for torts committed during the course of their employment operates when an action against the United States is also barred because the tort occurred in a foreign country. The Court has held that it does. *United States v. Smith*, 499 U.S. 160, 111 S. Ct. 1180, 113 L. Ed. 2d 134 (1991).

7. ***Procedure:*** All actions under the Federal Tort Claims Act must first be filed with the appropriate federal agency within two years after the claim arises. 28 U.S.C. § 2401(b). If the claim is filed within the appropriate period, the statute of limitations is then tolled for a period of six months after the claim is denied by the agency. Actions under the Tort Claims Act are tried to a judge sitting without a jury. If a plaintiff obtains an award of damages under the Act, attorneys fees are limited to 25% of the judgment or settlement obtained in an action filed in the courts and to 20% of any award obtained through administrative settlement. It is a crime for an attorney to demand or receive any greater fee.

(2) While the courts are prepared to recognize that a state has substantial discretion in deciding what type of highway plan to adopt, once it has adopted a plan and has decided on specific ways to implement that plan, the failure to implement the plan within a reasonable period of time can subject the state to liability. *See Friedman v. State of New York,* 67 N.Y.2d 271, 493 N.E.2d. 893, 502 N.Y.S.2d 669 (1986).

B. **Suits against the States:** It has long been held that the states have, like the United States, a residual "sovereign immunity." This sovereign immunity was invoked by the various states to avoid suits brought against them by those who had been injured by the actions of state employees in the course of their duties. As the role of government became more pronounced, the pressures to abolish the states' immunity from suits increased. The first abolitions of sovereign immunity were by statute. New York, in 1920, became one of the first states to do so. In what is now N.Y. Jud. Ct. of Claims Act § 8 (McKinney), the state waived immunity and assumed liability "in accordance with the same rules of law as applied to actions . . . against individuals or corporations." In many other states, abolition was more gradual, with the states' acceptance of liability often being confined to a limited number of situations such as claims arising out of the dangerous condition of public property or the negligent operation of motor vehicles. Many states also developed a distinction between so-called proprietary functions and governmental functions. This is a distinction that was developed primarily in connection with the immunity of units of local government. We shall discuss the distinction in paragraph C.3., below, when we discuss the liability of such governmental units.

1. Beginning with *Muskopf v. Corning Hosp. Dist.,* 55 Cal. 2d 211, 11 Cal. Rptr. 89, 359 P.2d 457 (1961), which abolished the immunity of state as well as local government, sovereign immunity was abolished by judicial decision in a number of states. Judicial abolitions of

sovereign immunity have sometimes been followed by the reimposition of sovereign immunity by the legislature or, more commonly, by the passage by the legislature of a tort claims act setting forth the types of cases for which suit may be brought against the state.

2. At the present time, over three-quarters of the states have either totally abolished the doctrine of sovereign immunity or substantially modified it.

    a. Those states which have enacted statutes only modifying, but not totally abolishing, sovereign immunity typically recognize liability for motor vehicle accidents, medical malpractice, and accidents caused by the dangerous condition of state roads and property.

    b. Even in a state which has totally abolished the state's sovereign immunity, the courts have recognized on the state level something like the discretionary function exception recognized under the Federal Tort Claims Act. To make sure that liability is not imposed for functions that would fall within this category, California, for example, by statute (Cal. Gov. Code Ann. § 818.2 (West)) declares that a public entity shall not be liable for "adopting or failing to adopt an enactment or . . . failing to enforce any law"; for issuing or failing to issue, suspend, or revoke a permit or license (*id.* at § 818.4); or for failing to inspect or for negligently inspecting the property of private parties (*id.* at § 818.6).

       (1) There are a number of states which permit claims against the state government but limit the amount of damages that are recoverable, *e.g.,* III.–S.H.A. ch. 37, § 439.8 (705 ILCS § 505/8)($100,000 per claimant except for claims arising out of the operation of motor vehicles); N.C. Gen. Stat. § 143-291(a) ($150,000 per injured person).

       (2) While the courts are prepared to recognize that a state has substantial discretion in deciding what type of highway plan to adopt, once it has adopted a plan and has decided on specific ways to implement that plan, the failure to implement the plan within a reasonable period of time can subject the state to liability. *See Friedman v. State of New York*, 67 N.Y. 2d 271, 493 N.E. 2d 893, 502 N.Y.S.2d 669 (1986).

3. There are a few states that still purport completely to retain the doctrine of sovereign immunity. One such state is Arkansas, whose constitution declares that "[t]he State of Arkansas shall never be made a defendant in any of her courts." (Ark. Const. Art. 5, § 20.) Nevertheless, Arkansas has provided an administrative procedure for resolving claims against the state and also requiring the state to pay the actual damages judicially assessed against state employees for acts or omissions committed in the good faith performance of their official duties. Following a judicial abolition of sovereign immunity, the Missouri legislature (Vernon's Ann. Mo. Stat. § 537.600) reimposed immunity except with regard to claims arising from automobile accidents or out of the dangerous condition of government property. There is so much variation among the states that an outline such as this cannot hope to give a complete picture of the current state of the law.

C. **Suits against Local Governments:** Under English common law, units of local government were not considered to share in the sovereign immunity of the Crown. They were treated as one type of corporate body such as the Oxford and Cambridge Colleges and later the great trading corporations like the East India Company. The analogy between municipal corporations and private corporations was carried over to colonial America and was still strong at the time of the American Revolution. The nineteenth century, however, brought general corporation laws. When private corporations became common and not merely rare entities, the analogy between municipal corporations and private corporations was no longer readily accepted. As a result, by judicial decision or by amendment of the state constitutions, municipal corporations came to be seen as exercising general governmental powers and thus, to some extent, sharing in the immunities of state governments.

Example: The earliest American case illustrating this movement is *Mower v. Leicester,* 9 Mass. 247 (1812), misconstruing the earlier English case, *Russell v. The Men of Devon,* 100 Eng. Rep. 359 (K.B. 1788), which merely held that an action against an unincorporated entity, namely "the men dwelling in the county of Devon," for damage done because of a bridge being out of repair, failed for want of a proper party defendant.

1. Since units of local government do not share in the sovereign immunity of a state, the Eleventh Amendment of the United States Constitution, which has been interpreted to forbid a suit in federal court against the state without its consent, has never been held to prevent suit in federal court against municipalities.

2. The immunity of municipalities and other units of local government from suit has now either been abolished or substantially limited in scope in most states.

3. Many of the states which still take a restrictive view of the extent to which governmental immunity has been abolished will permit an action against a unit of local government if the activity involved is considered to be a proprietary function rather than a governmental function. The distinction first arose, when governmental immunity was much more widespread, in order to ameliorate the harsh consequences of that doctrine.

    a. The government-proprietary distinction has proved difficult to apply to the myriad activities of governmental entities. In some states, the maintenance and operation of a public swimming pool has been held to be a governmental function; in others, it has been held to be a proprietary function. Even within the same jurisdiction, the application of the distinction is not always clear. *Compare Aylward v. Baer,* 745 S.W.2d 692 (Mo. App. 1987), which held that the installation and maintenance of street lights was a governmental function, with *Lamar v. City of St. Louis,* 746 S.W.2d 160 (Mo. App. 1988), which held that an action could be brought against a city for alleged negligence in barricading a street excavation because the excavation was made for the purposes of installing water mains, the court having previously held that the construction and operation of a municipal water system was a proprietary function.

4. Arkansas is one of the few states that purports to grant complete immunity to units of local government. Ark. Stat. Ann. § 21-9-301. At the same time, however, undoubtedly in recognition of the harshness of such a doctrine, units of local government are required to maintain liability insurance, and a direct action is permitted against the insurer. If the local government entity is uninsured, the entity loses its immunity up to the minimum amount of insurance required under the Arkansas Finacial Responsibility Act. There is, again, so much local variation that it is impossible for an outline such as this to pretend to any degree of completeness.

CHARITABLE
IMMUNITY

II. **CHARITABLE IMMUNITY**

A. **In General:** The doctrine of charitable immunity is an American invention, although the American cases adopting it did rely on *dicta* in some mid-nineteenth- century English cases that were overruled by the House of Lords in *Mersey Docks & Harbour Bd. Trustees v. Gibbs,* 11 Eng. Rep. 1500 (1866). One of the first American cases adopting the doctrine of charitable immunity was *McDonald v. Massachusetts Gen. Hosp.,* 120 Mass. 432 (1876), which held that a charitable corporation was not liable in tort, at least when the plaintiff was a charitable patient. This result, if limited to the beneficiaries of charitable organizations, could be justified on the ground that these beneficiaries should be prevented from "biting the hand that feeds them." The doctrine of charitable immunity, however, was extended beyond beneficiaries. One of the principal justifications for the doctrine was that it was contrary to the intention of those who had donated funds to the charitable organization to expend those funds for the payment of tort judgments. *Parks v. Northwestern University,* 218 Ill. 381, 75 N.E. 991 (1905), is perhaps the most famous case associated with this so-called "trust-fund" theory.

1. The first complete judicial abrogation of the doctrine of charitable immunity was *President and Directors of Georgetown College v. Hughes,* 130 F.2d 810 (D.C. Cir. 1942). Previously, some states had restricted the doctrine by allowing recovery when the charity had been negligent in its choice of personnel or by construing the purchase of liability insurance as a waiver of immunity or by limiting the doctrine to actions brought by beneficiaries of the charity.

2. The doctrine of charitable immunity has now been totally abolished in at least 80% of the states.

   a. In those states where the charitable immunity doctrine continues to have some application, it is usually confined to actions brought by beneficiaries of a charity, and in some states there are statutory limits on damages. New Jersey combines both these approaches. Under N.J. Stat. Ann. 2A:53A-7 and 53A-8 (West), the New Jersey legislature in 1959 reinstated traditional charitable immunity with regard to actions based on negligence brought by beneficiaries of all charities including religious organizations except hospitals. As to hospitals, the liability to anyone who has been a beneficiary to whatever degree of a charitable hospital is limited to $10,000 per occurrence.

III. FAMILY IMMUNITIES

A. **Interspousal Immunity:** At common law, a wife had no legal personality separate from that of her husband. The possibility of one spouse bringing an action against another thus could not arise. With the enactment of the married women's property acts of the nineteenth century, it became possible for a married woman to sue her husband (or to be sued by him) with regard to disputes over property, and that included tort actions involving property interests. Most courts, however, refused to construe these acts as affecting tort actions by one spouse against another for personal injuries. The need to preserve family harmony, to keep the state from intruding into the marital relationship, and to prevent collusive suits were frequently-given justifications.

   1. With the passage of time, more and more states either by statute or judicial decision began to abolish the doctrine of interspousal immunity. Some states which did not immediately abolish the doctrine started to permit an action where one of the spouses was dead at the time of suit or the marriage had ended in divorce or the injury arose out of an automobile accident in which insurance coverage was present. Some states also permitted one spouse to bring suit against another for intentional torts.

   2. At the present time, the majority of states have completely abolished interspousal immunity. In a number of other states, it has been limited in the ways noted in the preceding paragraph. In a few states the doctrine of interspousal immunity still exists in something approaching its former vigor.

B. **Parent-Child Immunity:** Like charitable immunity, this is a tort doctrine that has no English counterpart. It is totally American in origin. The modern trend to abolish tort immunities has limited the range of application of the parent-child immunity, but not to the same extent as has been the case with regard to the interspousal immunity. The need to preserve parental authority as well as a general desire to preserve family harmony have been given as reasons for not abolishing the immunity.

1.   The parent-child immunity applies to personal injury actions between parents and *unemancipated* minor children. A child becomes emancipated by operation of law when the child marries or when the child achieves majority, unless the child is so infirm that it cannot support itself and continues to live, unmarried, in its parent's home. A child will also be considered emancipated if the parents abandon it or fail to discharge their legal duty to support the child. Parents can, in addition, emancipate a child by surrendering their right to the custody and control of the child.

2.   At present, in close to half of the states, the doctrine of parent-child immunity has been completely abolished or abolished with some slight qualification. In about two-thirds of the states that have abolished the doctrine, when an action is brought by a child against its parent, the conduct of the parent, following *Gibson v. Gibson,* 3 Cal. 3d 914, 92 Cal. Rptr. 288, 479 P.2d 648 (1971), is to be judged according to what "an ordinarily reasonable and prudent parent [would] have done in similar circumstances." In the other states that have substantially abolished the doctrine of parent-child immunity, the doctrine is abolished except when, following *Goller v. White,* 20 Wis. 2d 402,122 N.W.2d 193 (1963), the alleged negligent act involves an exercise of reasonable parental authority over the child or when the alleged negligent act involves an exercise of ordinary parental discretion with regard to such matters as the provision of food, clothing, housing, and medical care. States following the *Goller* case, with its reservation of a residual parental immunity from suits by minor children where parental authority and parental discretion are involved, have tended to restrict the types of cases to which these exceptions will apply.

      Example: In *Thoreson v. Milwaukee & Suburban Transp., Inc.,* 56 Wis. 2d 231, 201 N.W.2d 745 (1972), a mother who left her three-year-old son watching television in her home while she went to a neighbor's house was found liable in a third-party suit for contribution by a bus company in the path of whose bus the little boy ran. The court held that the *Goller* exceptions were not intended to cover this sort of routine care. On the other hand, in *Holodook v. Spencer,* 36 N.Y.2d 35, 364 N.Y.S.2d 859, 324 N.E.2d 338 (1974), the New York Court of Appeals refused to recognize a child's cause of action for negligent supervision because it felt that the major effect of recognizing such an action would be to make possible claims for contribution against the parents by those who had tortiously injured a minor child.

      Example: A New York court also rejected the notion that parents who negligently *create a risk* that results in injury to a child could be held liable for the injury. The court so ruled even though the decision that led to the risk, drawing hot water for the child's bath and then leaving the child in the room, did not involve a *choice* to expose the child to risk. The dissent argued that the court should disallow parental immunity because the dangerous condition was created by an instrumentality in control of the parent and did not involve a choice about how much freedom or responsibility to give the child. The majority rejected this as a standard for evaluating liabilty. *See Zikely v. Zikely,* 98 App. Div. 2d 815, 470 N.Y.S.2d 33 (N.Y. App. Div. 1983).

3.   In addition to the jurisdictions that have substantially abolished parent-child immunity, perhaps another third of the states have abolished the doctrine in automobile negligence cases or, in a few instances, in automobile negligence cases in which the parent has liability insurance. A number of states, however, retain the parent-child immunity in something like its former vigor.

4. Questions concerning contribution can arise if a family member succeeds in an action against a third party who in turn is able to establish that a spouse, child, or parent of the plaintiff was also at fault and partly the cause of the plaintiff's injuries. In some, probably most, jurisdictions contribution will only be allowed if the plaintiff could have brought an action against the family member in question. In some jurisdictions contribution is available even if the person against whom contribution is sought could have claimed immunity in an action by the plaintiff. *See Bishop v, Nielsen,* 632 P.2d 864 (Utah 1981).

CHAPTER 24 - QUESTIONS, ANSWERS, AND TIPS

24

1. **Q:** No tort action may be brought against the United States unless it falls within a category of suits against the United States that has been explicitly authorized by Congress.

    A: True

2. **Q:** No common-law tort action may be brought against a federal official for the negligent operation of a government automobile in the course of the federal official's performance of his governmental functions.

    A: True. The remedy against the United States under the Federal Tort Claims Act is exclusive.

3. **Q:** Actions brought under the Federal Tort Claims Act are normally tried by a judge and jury.

    A: False. Juries are not available in actions brought under the Federal Tort Claims Act.

4. **Q:** No action may be brought against the United States for defamation.

    A: True

5. **Q:** The Supreme Court has held that the United States may be held strictly liable in tort for the unavoidable miscarriage of an ultra-hazardous or abnormally dangerous activity being carried on by an instrumentality of the United States.

    A: False

6. **Q:** Municipalities are considered to be arms of the state government and thus to share in the sovereign immunity of the state to the same extent as an instrumentality of the state, such as, for example the state prison system.

    A: False

7. **Q:** The Eleventh Amendment of the United States Constitution, which forbids certain suits against the states to be brought in federal courts, does not prevent suits against municipalities from being brought in the federal courts.

    A: True. Although municipalities, in most states, were for a time immune from tort liability, it was on the ground of governmental immunity. For purposes of constitutional law, municipalities were never considered to share the sovereign immunity of state governments.

24

8. **Q:** In a jurisdiction in which suit can be brought against a municipality, a tort action for damages cannot be brought against a municipality for failure to appropriate sufficient money to purchase an adequate fleet of fire trucks.

A: True. Despite the large-scale abrogation of governmental immunity, certain activities and functions of government are considered governmental and decisions concerning these functions are not subject to judicial examination with regard to their wisdom or adequacy.

9. **Q:** The defense of charitable immunity still exists in about one half of the states.

A: False. Most American jurisdictions have abolished the doctrine of charitable immunities.

10. **Q:** Interspousal immunity has been completely abolished in all states.

A: False. It has been completely abolished in the majority of states but only partially in some and in a few exists almost in its complete common-law form.

11. **Q:** The doctrine of parent-child immunity did not exist at English Common law.

A: True. It is a late nineteenth century American development.

12. **Q:** Some states that have abolished parent-child immunity still do not allow a child to bring an action against its parents based on the claim that the parents were negligent in exercising parental discretion with regard to matters such as the provision of clothing, housing, and education.

A: True

Exam Tip: Because questions regarding immunities are so jurisdiction specific and, in the case of governmental immunities, often governed by statute, they are unlikely to be the subject of a detailed examination question. It usually will be enough for the student to note that an immunity problem is present, either because a governmental entity is involved, or because the action involves family members. A question turning on a possible charitable immunity, although vestiges of the doctrine remain in some states, is unlikely.

EXAM PREPARATION

Exam Preparation   EP-2

EXAM PREPARATION

This section includes four sample essay questions and answers and thirty-eight sample True-False questions and answers. Before attempting to answer the essay questions, the student may wish to re-read the material in Chapter 1, II. Because law school professors differ with regard to the way they structure their examination questions, the essay questions are constructed to cover not only different subject matters but also the different styles that law professors may use in constructing their examinations.

SAMPLE ESSAY QUESTIONS

QUESTION 1

D is a physician and professor at a medical school who is engaged in research on toxic materials. D is also an avid gardener. D's garden has been under attack from moles which are attracted to the garden to eat grubs that feed on the root systems of the plants. In the course of his research, D has come across an experimental pesticide that seems very effective — that is, it is highly toxic, at least, to insects and small rodents — but seems entirely to lose its toxic quality after a few months' exposure to air, water, and sunlight. The pesticide is supplied in white tablets that bear a resemblance to generic aspirin, although they are somewhat larger than the standard 500 mg. aspirin tablet. The pesticide is applied by dissolving a number of the tablets in water and then spraying the solution around the plants. D decides to bring home a quantity of tablets and to see if they will eliminate the grubs and thus end his confrontation with the moles. As supplied to the laboratory, the pesticide comes in a large plastic jar. D takes an old and battered empty 250-tablet aspirin bottle, fills it with about 100 tablets of the pesticide, and puts the bottle in the pocket of his raincoat. While D is walking to his car, the sky clears up, and it becomes hotter. D takes off his raincoat and puts it on the passenger seat. As he is driving home, D remembers that he should buy some milk. He stops at a supermarket and rushes in to get the milk and pays for it in the "express" check-out lane. He does not lock the car. The store is not in what might be called a "high-crime neighborhood." D is in the store less than five minutes. While D is in the store, Z steals the coat. Z is an unemployed musician living with some friends until he can find some work.

A few days later X, a graduate student at the university, visits Z's friends. She complains of a headache. Z's friends remember seeing an aspirin bottle in Z's room and, after going in and getting it, offer it to X. X takes two tablets with water. Upon returning to the home she has shared for a year with Y, a male fellow student, she starts to feel ill and eventually goes into convulsions. Y watches what is happening in horror as X thrashes about. With much difficulty, he manages to get X into his car and drive her to the medical center. For many hours X's life is in danger, but she survives. Y stays with X during most of this period and even helps administer the emetics that are given to her to help her regurgitate everything in her stomach. It is a traumatic experience for him. X is left with some residual damage to her stomach and esophagus. She is, however, eventually able to resume most of her previous activities.

X eventually learns from various sources that the aspirin bottle with the pesticide belonged to D from whom it was stolen as described above.

X brings an action for damages against D.

Y brings an action for (a) loss of consortium and (b) negligent infliction of emotional suffering against D.

The two actions are combined. Before they come to trial, X and Y are married.

If you were a trial judge trying this case with a jury, how would you rule on D's motions for a directed verdict after the presentation of the evidence described above?

QUESTION 2

X was the wife of Z and lived with Z in a medium-size city in one of the southwestern states. Z was employed as a bookkeeper in the accounting department of the City Board of Education. X was a housewife. In 1975, she and Z had been married fifteen years and had three children. In the years 1973–75, thirteen women in their late twenties and early thirties were found partially clothed and strangled with bits of their own clothing in wooded areas around the city in which X and Z lived. The murders had a pattern in that the victims were all recently divorced women who frequented singles bars. In 1975, Z was arrested for these murders. X was in total shock. She never suspected that her husband led a double life. Z was tried and convicted for three of the murders and sentenced to death. Although it was never judicially determined that Z was responsible for the other ten murders, there is a substantial factual basis for believing that he was responsible for these killings also.

The arrest and trial of Z in 1975 was a cause celebre. The fact that X was Z's wife was reported in the national press and on nationwide television. X was constantly being sought for interviews. Generally she refused to say anything but on a few occasions spoke to reporters about the fine home life that she, Z, and her children had had, and she several times said that Z had been a good provider, a good husband, and good father. Owing to the strictures on the application of the death penalty that have been imposed by the numerous decisions of the United States Supreme Court on the subject, the final appeals from Z's conviction were not disposed of until 1978. There then followed a long series of habeas corpus petitions on his behalf in both the state and federal courts. The entire process was not completed until 1985. Z was eventually executed in 1986. In 1987, D, a monthly magazine, decided to run an article about serial killers. The murders committed by Z were a prominent part of this article. In the course of preparing the article, one of D's reporters tried to interview X, but she refused to talk to him. By this time, X had moved to a distant city and was living a somewhat retiring life. Her children having all grown up, X lived by herself. She supported herself by working as a part-time bookkeeper for a local dentist. In the article about serial killers, in which Z's exploits were prominently featured, it was stated that an attempt was made to interview X, but that X "who was now unemployed and has become a total recluse just barely subsisting" refused to speak to D's reporter. The article then went on to say: "This is curious because when Z was being tried X often spoke to reporters who paid her as much as $5,000 for the privilege of interviewing her. Perhaps the reason that she would not speak to us is that we subscribe to a higher standard of journalism and never pay to interview people who are involved in public events."

It turns out that, although X was on several occasions offered a substantial amount of money for "the story of her life with Z," she in point of fact had never accepted any such offers nor had she ever accepted any money from anyone on the occasions when she had spoken to reporters in 1975. In 1986, shortly after Z was executed, X talked to a law school seminar (twenty students and one professor) studying the death penalty for which X was paid a $200 honorarium. The reporter who wrote the article testified that he had heard that X had been offered money by several tabloids, and he had assumed that she had accepted money for the interviews which she had given. The reporter also testified as to why he stated in the article that X was "unemployed" and had become a "total recluse just barely subsisting." He replied that, after X refused to see him, he asked her neighbors about X. The neighbors whom he spoke to said that they hardly knew X and that she kept pretty much to herself and did not go out much. He concluded from this that the plaintiff was an unemployed recluse and wrote the article on this assumption. He did not investigate the matter further because he did not consider it important.

X brings an action against D. You are a trial judge trying the case with a jury. D moves for a directed verdict. How would you rule on this motion? If you deny the motion, in whole or in part, include in your answer some indication of the key issues that you would send to the jury? Explain your answers.

QUESTION 3

Plaintiff's (P's) sister (S), who is an employee of the Farmers Home Administration (Fm HA) and also P's guardian, inspected P's house to determine if it were eligible for a loan. She failed to discover in her inspection that the house was built over an abandoned underground mine shaft. She certified the house as eligible for a loan, which the U.S. government then made to P. After the improvements were made, the mine shaft collapsed, and P's house was badly damaged as a result.

Discuss P 's possible tort claims against the U.S. government and S.

QUESTION 4

D, a bus driver, was driving a bus containing twenty elderly persons down a steep narrow mountain road en route to a senior citizens function when the bus brakes suddenly gave way. The bus very quickly reached a high rate of speed. There was no safe place to pull off the road, since on one side was a steep rock wall and on the other a deep precipice.

Ahead of the bus was a runaway-truck pulloff, which provided the only chance the driver had of saving the lives of her passengers and of herself. Five school children were awaiting a school van pickup at the entrance to the pulloff, and the driver could not use the pulloff without hitting the children. The driver's horn failed to function when she attempted to use it.

Assume the driver had no reason to know that the brakes or horn of her bus would fail.

If the driver tries to miss but in fact hits the children, will she be liable in tort to them? If she does not attempt to use the pulloff, will she be liable in tort to her passengers?

ANSWERS TO ESSAY QUESTIONS

QUESTION 1

D's motion for a directed verdict against X, denied.

D's motion for a directed verdict against Y, granted.

This question presents two principal issues: was D negligent toward X, and was D's conduct the proximate cause of X's injuries? There is also a subsidiary issue as to whether X was contributorily negligent. In Y's action against D, two additional issues are presented. First, can someone who is not married to another person at the time of injury recover for loss of the injured person's consortium? Second, can someone who is not physically threatened with injury recover for negligent infliction of emotional distress under the circumstances presented in the question?

I.   X 's ACTION AGAINST D

A. **The Negligence Issue**

By putting the toxic pesticide tablets in an empty aspirin bottle, D could be said to be negligent to anyone whom D reasonably could expect might find the bottle; that is, D could foresee an appreciable risk of injury to anyone who might find the bottle and in ignorance take some of the tablets thinking that they were aspirin tablets. To use an alternative terminology that some professors might prefer, because such a risk of injury was foreseeable, D owed the persons who might be exposed to such a risk a duty of care. Militating against any such obligation is the fact that the aspirin bottle was old and battered and the fact that the tablets were slightly larger than ordinary aspirin tablets. It might be argued that these factors would be sufficient to alert anyone who came upon the bottle to treat the contents with some care, particularly someone who came upon the bottle in circumstances where there was no independent suggestion other than the bottle itself and the color and shape of the tablets that these were in fact aspirin tablets, such as, would be the case for a person who might come upon the bottle lying on the ground seemingly abandoned.

At the time that D put the tablets in the bottle and placed the bottle in a pocket of his raincoat, it is hard to argue that someone like X was put in any kind of danger by D's conduct. If X were a member of D's household who could conceivably be expected to come across the bottle once D had taken it home, it would be a different matter. But D did more than merely place the bottle in a pocket of his raincoat, D left the bottle in his raincoat pocket when he went into the supermarket. If D had spent a great deal of time in the supermarket and if the raincoat were particularly valuable, a strong case could be made that D should have foreseen and, given the fact that a poisonous substance was in its pocket, guarded against the theft of his coat. This conclusion would be reinforced if the store were located in a high-crime neighborhood. The store, however, was not located in a high-crime neighborhood, and there is no indication that the raincoat was particularly valuable. Nevertheless, D was clearly aware that, if the coat were lost or stolen, the bottle could come into the hands of an unsuspecting person. Under the circumstances, it is undoubtedly a jury question as to whether, in putting the pesticide tablets in an old aspirin bottle and placing that bottle in his raincoat and then leaving the coat in a place where it might be stolen, D was negligent toward someone like X who eventually came across the bottle and ingested some of the tablets thinking that they were aspirin.

B. The Causation Issue

Even if D were found negligent, however, the question arises as to whether D's conduct was the legal cause of X's injuries. There is no question but that D's conduct was the actual cause, or cause in fact, of X's injuries. The difficult issue is whether D's conduct was the proximate cause of X's injuries. The analysis on this issue will follow pretty much the same general line as the analysis used in deciding the negligence issue. There is no question but that D could foresee that, if he were to misplace the battered old aspirin bottle containing the pesticide, some unwary person might take some of the tablets thinking they were aspirin, particularly if, as is the case here, some seemingly knowledgeable third person vouched for the genuineness of the product. There is furthermore no question that, if D left the bottle in the pocket of a coat placed on a seat in an unlocked car that might attract the interest of a thief, the bottle might get into the hands of third persons who did not know what its contents were. Whether D could foresee that the coat would be stolen when it was left for only five minutes in an unlocked car is undoubtedly a jury question, but a jury finding that he could have foreseen this event would not be unreasonable.

The difficult question on the causation issue is whether the act of Z in stealing the coat cuts off the chain of causation either because the consequent ingestion of the stolen pills was unforeseeable or, even if foreseeable, should not be held to have been legally caused by D owing to the greater moral responsibility of Z. The argument that D's responsibility should be cut off is strengthened by the fact that X would not have taken the tablets thinking they were aspirin if it were not for the further intervening and most probably negligent conduct of Z's friends who suggested to X that the bottle contained aspirin.

Many courts might grant a directed verdict for D on the causation issue on the ground that the intentional intervening acts of Z and the highly negligent acts of Z's friends cut off any chain of proximate causation between D's conduct and X's injuries. The modern trend in tort law, however, is to impose liability upon negligent parties, even if the injury would not have occurred without the intentional criminal acts of a third person, if those intentional criminal acts are highly foreseeable. Many courts would therefore let the case go to the jury on the issue of causation and allow the jury to determine whether D's conduct was the proximate cause of X's injury on the ground that the intervening acts of Z were highly foreseeable and that the subsequent negligent conduct of Z 's friends was also foreseeable.

C. Subsidiary Issues

The final issue confronting X is her own possible contributory negligence. Factors pointing toward her negligence include the fact that the tablets were contained in a battered old bottle and, although not as strongly supporting a conclusion of contributory negligence, the fact that the tablets were slightly larger than ordinary aspirin tablets. While a judge might rule that X was not contributorily negligent as a matter of law, most courts would probably let this issue go to the jury as well.

II. Y 's ACTION

A. Loss of Consortium

The modern trend is to deny actions for loss of consortium brought by persons who do not, at the time of injury, have a legally recognized family relationship with the injured person, the loss of whose consortium is being sought in the action. The fact that X and Y married subsequent to the accident and before trial might be said to have strengthened Y 's case but, given cases like *Elden v. Sheldon,* 46 Cal. 3d 267, 250 Cal. Rptr. 254, 758 P.2d 582 (1988), it seems unlikely that a court would let Y get to the jury on this count.

B. Negligent Infliction of Emotional Distress

The action for negligent infliction of emotional distress presents a more difficult question. In a jurisdiction that still follows the impact rule, Y would not have a cause of action unless it is claimed that Y 's holding of X while she was in the throes of convulsions generated the requisite impact. This argument is hard to make because Y voluntarily held X in his arms while he tried to get her to the hospital. Of course, if X had injured Y in the course of her convulsions, there is no question but that Y might have had a cause of action against D, subject to the problems of establishing D's negligence and the requisite causation discussed above in connection with X 's case, but that did not happen here. At any rate, almost no jurisdiction follows the impact rule any more.

In a jurisdiction which requires that a plaintiff must himself have been threatened with physical injury in order to recover for the negligent infliction of emotional suffering, Y would again probably not have a claim. Nothing D did threatened Y with physical injury unless it could be maintained that Y feared that X would strike him while she was in the throes of her convulsions, a claim that seems somewhat belied by the facts.

In the growing number of jurisdictions that follow *Dillon v. Legg,* 68 Cal.2d 728, 69 Cal. Rptr. 72, 441 P.2d 912 (1968), the question becomes more difficult. Certainly Y witnessed serious injury to X under visually traumatic circumstances. He does not, however, seem to have suffered any physical injury or illness as a result of his emotional trauma. If Y were a close relative of X at the time of injury, there seems little doubt but that, subject to the need to establish D's negligence and the causal considerations discussed above, Y would have a cause of action, at least in a jurisdiction that has dispensed with the physical injury or illness requirement. Y 's problem is that at the time of X 's injury he did not have any legally recognized close family relationship to X. The court in *Dillon* confined its decision to close relatives and this restriction was reaffirmed in *Thing v. La Chusa,* 48 Cal. 3d 644, 257 Cal. Rptr. 865, 771 P.2d 814 (1989). *See also Elden v. Sheldon, supra.*

The final theory under which Y might try to recover for negligent infliction of emotional suffering is as a "direct victim" of *D*'s conduct as recognized in *Molien v. Kaiser Found. Hosp.,* 27 Cal. 3d 916, 167 Cal. Rptr. 831, 616 P.2d 813 (1980). Under this theory, *Y* need not show physical injury or illness as a result of his emotional trauma. Subsequent California cases, however, have made it clear that merely witnessing injury to another person does not make one a direct victim. *See Ochoa v. Superior Court,* 39 Cal. 3d 159, 216 Cal. Rptr. 661, 703 P.2d 1 (1985).

QUESTION 2

D's motion for a directed verdict on a claim for false-light invasion of privacy, granted.

D's motion for a directed verdict on a claim for defamation, denied.

As just noted, *X* could possibly bring an action for false-light invasion of privacy and for defamation. Each of these possible actions will be discussed in turn.

I.   FALSE-LIGHT INVASION OF PRIVACY

A.   Premise for a False-Light Invasion of Privacy Action

A false-light invasion of privacy action would be premised on the statement that *X* "was now unemployed and has become a total recluse just barely subsisting." Even though *X* has the burden of persuasion on the issue of falsity, there is no basis upon which a judge could conclude that *X* has not come forward with enough evidence to present that issue to a jury. Indeed, all the evidence that has been presented would appear conclusively to establish that the statement was indeed false. While a few jurisdictions, such as North Carolina, have refused to recognize a false-light invasion of privacy action, most jurisdictions will recognize the action.

The question that is then presented is whether *X* has shown sufficient fault on the part of *D*. The prevailing view is that, even if the plaintiff is not a public figure or public official, to succeed in a false-light invasion of privacy action the plaintiff must show constitutional malice, that is, the plaintiff must show clear and convincing evidence that the defendant knew that the statement in question was false or that the defendant made the statement in reckless disregard of its truth or falsity. Although it is a close question, it is hard to say that the reporter was guilty of the requisite degree of fault in concluding that *X* was an unemployed recluse who was just barely subsisting. Certainly there is no basis for concluding that the reporter stated something that was known by him to be false. It is a much closer question as to whether or not the reporter might be said to be reckless. The Court has held that the mere failure to investigate is not by itself enough to show a reckless disregard of truth or falsity. There must be some showing that the reporter exhibited a conscious indifference to the truth. It is relevant in this regard that *X* refused to speak to the reporter. On these facts, although they are indicative of a high degree of negligence on the part of the reporter, a court would probably grant a directed verdict for *D*. A contrary decision, however, that is, a decision to send the question of the reporter's reckless indifference to the truth to the jury, would not be insupportable.

II.   DEFAMATION

A.   *X*'s other cause of action is for defamation.

The statement that *X* often spoke to reporters who paid money in order to interview her about her life with *Z* is capable of being considered defamatory in that many people would think poorly of a person who tried to obtain financial advantage from the fact that her husband was being tried in a sensational murder case. They would think of her as mercenary and unfeeling and this would lead to the lowering of her reputation among a substantial segment of the community. At least a jury could so find. A modern judge would probably rule that the other statement declaring that

EP

X was an unemployed total recluse just barely subsisting was not defamatory on the ground that reasonable people would not think poorly of someone in X's situation who was unemployed and/ or a recluse (indeed X was socially withdrawn) and/or just barely subsisting.

In a minority of states which distinguish between libel *per se* and libel *per quod,* the situation is more difficult. In a jurisdiction which limited the libel *per se* category to those defamatory statements which fall within the slander *per se* categories, X would probably not have a cause of action, at least without allegation and proof of special damages. In the instant case, X has neither alleged nor proven any special damages. If it is a jurisdiction which distinguishes between libel *per se* and libel *per quod* on the basis of whether or not the defamation is clear on the face of the statement made, X would probably have a cause of action. The defamatory nature of the statement does not depend on the allegation and proof of any extrinsic facts, that is on facts not contained in the article itself.

As a preliminary matter, the question arises as to whether the statement in question that X had been offered money by reporters for the privilege of interviewing her is true. The only evidence, even remotely bearing on that question, to suggest that it might be true is the fact that in 1986 X received an honorarium for attending a law school seminar. The statement in question, however, was that X took money from reporters in 1975. Accordingly, although the plaintiff has the burden of persuasion on the issue of truth or falsity, there is not a scintilla of evidence to support a conclusion that the statement that X received money when she was interviewed by reporters in 1975 is true.

The difficult question is what standard of fault, if any, must X show in order to recover. On this issue the first question is whether X is a public figure. There is no question that at the time of Z's murder trial X was a public figure, albeit an involuntary one. After the passage of twelve years, however, it is not clear that she continues to enjoy the status of a public figure. The question of whether someone is a public figure is a question of law to be decided by the court. Given the way the Supreme Court has ruled in cases like *Hutchinson v. Proxmire,* 443 U.S. 111, 99 S. Ct. 2675, 61 L. Ed.2d 411 (1979), and *Wolston v. Reader's Digest Ass'n,* 443 U.S. 157, 99 S. Ct. 2701, 61 L.Ed.2d 450 (1979), the Court would probably conclude that X had lost her status as a public figure. If X were still a public figure, she would have to show constitutional malice and, as indicated above, there is a strong argument that she has not met that burden. Taking X to be a private figure at the time the article in question was published, it seems clear that X has shown that D was at least negligent. Certainly there is ample evidence to permit the jury so to find.

The question arises then as to what damages a jury would be entitled to award X. She is certainly entitled to actual damages which can include humiliation, embarrassment, and any injuries that she might show to have directly flowed from her loss of reputation in the community. As to whether or not she can secure presumed or punitive damages under *Dunn & Bradstreet, Inc. v. Greenmoss Builders, Inc.,* 472 U.S. 749, 105 S. Ct. 2939, 86 L. Ed.2d 593 (1985), the question is more difficult. There is one obvious difference between this case and *Greenmoss Builders,* namely that the defendant is a member of the media. Nevertheless, most of the judges who decided the *Greenmoss* case did not think that the distinction between media and nonmedia defendants was a permissible one. Thus, the mere fact that a media defendant is involved here will not conclusively determine whether or not X can get presumed or punitive damages. On the other hand, *Greenmoss Builders* was restricted to cases in which the material in question was not a matter of public interest, that is the published material was not "newsworthy." In this case, it would be hard to rule that the material in question was not newsworthy. Under these circumstances, the strictures on the recovery of damages contained in *Gertz v. Robert Welch, Inc.,* 418 U.S. 323, 94 S. Ct. 2997, 41 L.Ed.2d 789 (1974), would govern. X's recovery would therefore be limited, as already noted, to her actual damages.

QUESTION 3

The United States can be liable under the Federal Tort Claims Act (FTCA) for the unprivileged negligent torts of its employees committed during the course of employment. For the most part, the U.S. government is not liable for intentional torts, and there is no evidence of intent to harm here. The U.S. government is not strictly liable under the FTCA. In any event, the mine shaft is not an abnormally dangerous condition created by S, nor did S cause the subsidence of the house by the removal of subjacent land support (two possible bases for strict liability).

Whether or not S was negligent in failing to discover the abandoned mine shaft may depend on the scope of her duties of inspection as an Fm HA employee. Her duty may extend only to an examination of the soundness or fitness of the house. Alternatively, even if she were expected to examine the land, the mine shaft may have been concealed and not reasonably discoverable.

If S were negligent, the U.S. government may be immune under one of the exceptions to the FTCA. The exceptions most likely to be raised are those of discretionary immunity and misrepresentation.

EP

The discretionary immunity exception normally applies only when policy-level decisions are made. The inspection and certification of a house for a loan seem to be fairly routine activities to which the immunity would not apply.

It is unclear if S can be considered to have made a representation to P because her certification (the possible misrepresentation) was made to her employer. Normally an action for misrepresentation arises only when a misstatement is made to and relied upon by a third party. Assuming this is a misrepresentation, to which the immunity applies, an action might still he for negligent inspection. The cases are divided as to whether negligent conduct that precedes the misrepresentation can be treated as a separate basis for suit. The distinction may lie in how closely the conduct and the statement are related.

If the U.S. government is liable for the employment-related negligence of S, then S is not liable since, under the FTCA, the exclusive remedy is against the U.S. government. If, however, the U.S. government is immune, for example because of the misrepresentation exception, then S could possibly be independently liable for a nondiscretionary tortious act. Alternatively, S could be liable for conduct outside the scope of her employment S as P's guardian may owe an independent or antecedent duty to P to discover or be aware of the underground mine shaft.

A number of jurisdictions retain family immunity. But this immunity does not normally apply to actions against guardians nor to actions not involving personal injury.

One situation in which both S and the U.S. government could be liable to P is if S were negligent in her nonemployment as well as in her employment capacity. Thus, if S as a sister and guardian should have known of the mine shaft, and as a government inspector she should also have discovered the shaft, then both she and the U.S. government could be liable to S.

QUESTION 4

The question states that the driver had "no reason to know" that the brakes or horn of "her" bus would fail. Stating that the bus belongs to the driver seems to eliminate the possibility of looking to some other owner for faulty maintenance, and there is no suggestion of negligent repair.

The *Restatement* distinguishes between "reason to know" and "should know," with the latter term imposing a higher standard of investigation or inquiry. It may be that the driver should have known of the defective brakes or horn, even though she had no reason (no special indication) for knowing.

Likely there is a statutory duty of brake and horn maintenance. Depending on the jurisdiction, violation of such a statute may constitute negligence *per se* to which there is no defense of due care. If this is the case, then the driver will be strictly liable to whomever she injures as a result of the statutory violations.

It can clearly be inferred that the lack of adequate brakes was the cause of the accident. It is less clear that the lack of horn was causal. Sounding the horn may have caused the children to avoid injury, if the driver chose the pulloff; if she did not, the horn would have been of little help to the bus passengers.

It does not appear that the driver could rely on a defense of self-defense if she chose to hit the children, since the children presented no active (as opposed to passive) threat of death or serious bodily injury to her or her passengers.

Perhaps the children were at fault in blocking the entrance to the pulloff. It does not appear whether they were properly standing at a designated school van pickup point. Even if they were standing at an improper place, their fault would only be contributory negligence which might reduce their recovery under comparative fault, taking into account their age, intelligence, and experience as compared with children of like abilities.

The defense of public necessity applies only when the public at large is threatened. It is doubtful if twenty-one people (the bus passengers and driver) would be sufficient for this purpose. The defense of private necessity is not a complete defense: the actor is permitted to act, but must pay for any damage done. In any event, these defenses are typically applied to the taking of property, and it would be very surprising if a court would hold that they would apply to the taking of life or limb.

The driver may have a defense of sudden emergency for whichever course of conduct she follows. At most, however, this defense will present a jury question.

Much of tort law — negligence, intentional nuisance, and strict liability — takes a balancing approach to determining liability. The risk is weighed against the utility of the defendant's action and the burden of taking precautions. It is unclear how a risk-utility analysis would apply in this situation. Balancing numbers of lives would weigh in favor of nonliability for hitting the children, but an opposite result might be reached if ages were weighed. The driver (and, constructively, the passengers) set the risk in motion and should perhaps be liable for doing so — particularly if there is statutory liability for nonmaintenance of the bus. On the other hand, the children may be causally responsible for blocking the pulloff entrance. There is no legal authority, in any event, for allowing a person to take innocent lives in order to save other innocent lives.

There is no evidence that D was negligent in hitting the children while attempting to use the pulloff, since the facts state that D "could not use the pulloff without hitting the children." Her conduct may, however, have been intentional or at least reckless.

If D does not attempt to use the pulloff, there should be no liability to the bus passengers absent proof of common law or statutory fault in maintaining the bus. Assuming D had no right or privilege to hit the children in order to save the passengers' lives, there was then no reasonable alternative available to D to save the lives of the passengers.

TRUE/FALSE QUESTIONS

1. In an action for slander that does not fall into one of the slander *per se* categories, the plaintiff can discharge his obligation to allege and prove special damages by showing that he has suffered a nervous breakdown that has required an extensive and expensive hospital stay.

2. In deciding whether a physician has made an adequate disclosure to a patient about to undergo an inherently risky course of treatment, the trend in the United States is to judge the adequacy of the physician's disclosure by the standard of what other physicians would have done in like circumstances.

3.   A person bringing an action for battery can recover substantial damages even in the absence of any serious physical injury.

4.   A member of the United States Armed Forces who was injured through the negligence of an army bus driver while being transported from one military base to another may bring an action against the United States under the Federal Tort Claims Act.

5.   X mails a letter which is lost owing to the negligence of postal employees. X may not bring an action against the United States under the Federal Tort Claims Act.

6.   X, a salesman, is on his way to close a large purchase agreement with a customer. Owing to the negligence of Y there is a multicar pileup on the freeway. Although X is not hurt, he is unable to get off the freeway for the several hours it takes for the freeway to be cleared. As a consequence, X is unable to close the sale and loses a very large commission. X may bring an action against Y to recover damages for his lost commission.

7.   In most jurisdictions, the defendant has the obligation of alleging and proving the plaintiff's contributory negligence.

8.   In an action for defamation, it is for the jury to decide whether the plaintiff is a public figure.

9.   If a private figure brings an action for defamation and the subject matter of the defamation concerns a matter of public interest, the plaintiff must show that the defendant either knew that the material in question was false, or that the defendant published the statement in question in reckless disregard of its truth or falsity.

10.   In an action for negligence in which the plaintiff secures from the trial judge a res ipsa loquitur instruction, that is, the jury is instructed that it may infer the defendant's negligence from the fact of the plaintiff's injury, the ultimate burden of persuasion in most jurisdictions remains with the plaintiff.

11.   The doctrine of res ipsa loquitur can be invoked even if the defendant knows no more about what caused the plaintiff's injury than does the plaintiff.

12.   If X is negligent toward Y but Y would not have been injured except for the intervening conduct of a third party, Y cannot bring an action based on negligence against X.

13.   In the course of cutting his grass, X injures Y. The injury is solely due to his negligence in running into his lawnmower. X has a duty to come to Y's assistance.

14.   At common law, a person who had been invited to someone's house for a social occasion and who was injured while there was classified as an invitee for purposes of determining the tort liability of the host.

15.   The parole board meets to discuss whether to grant a parole to X, a person convicted of child abuse who has served ten years and is now eligible for parole. A petition signed by a great many people urging that X not be paroled is presented to the parole board. The board grants X a parole. Shortly thereafter, X molests another child. Even in a jurisdiction which no longer retains governmental immunity, the molested child and his parents may not bring an action against the parole board.

16.   A babysitter watches in horror as the child under her care is killed owing to the negligent conduct of D, whose negligence is the sole cause of the accident. The babysitter herself was not close enough

to have been put in any physical danger herself. She nevertheless suffers severe emotional trauma which requires medical treatment. The babysitter may not bring an action for damages against D.

17. At common law, anyone who trespassed on another's land could be shot.

18. Under *Restatement (Second) of Torts* § 402A, the manufacturer of a drug is liable for the unforeseen consequences that occur from the use of the drug even if the manufacturer did not know and could not have reasonably known at the time of injury that the drug posed that danger.

19. In actions governed by federal law, the jury must be instructed that damage awards for personal injury are not subject to federal income taxation.

20. Under the Supremacy Clause, actions brought in the state courts are subject to the same requirements as noted in Question 19.

21. The majority rule in the United States is that damages for pain and suffering may be recovered on behalf of a person who has been comatose from the moment of injury.

22. In most American jurisdictions, there is no necessary correlation between the punitive damages that may be recovered and the compensatory damages that have been recovered.

23. In a wrongful death action, the services that the deceased performed for other members of the family are not an item that falls within the category of "pecuniary loss."

24. In most jurisdictions in the United States, parents of an injured child may not recover for the loss of that child's consortium.

25. In most jurisdictions in the United States, the parents of a healthy child may not recover the costs of raising that child against a negligent physician but for whose negligence the child would not have been conceived.

26. A public person who suffers emotional trauma as a result of a vicious parody that exaggerates in a ludicrous manner the fact that the public person has a tendency to stutter, particularly when he becomes excited, will be unable to bring an action against those responsible for the parody either on a theory of intentional infliction of emotional distress or of invasion of privacy.

27. Under the *Restatement (Second) of Torts,* if the defamatory nature of an alleged libel is not clear on the face of the statement, the plaintiff may not bring an action without alleging and proving special damages.

28. If matter is covered by the reporting privilege, it may be published even though the publisher knows as a fact that the matter is false.

29. Someone who is entitled to a qualified privilege, as, for example, someone who shares a common business interest with the person to whom a statement is made, may avoid liability for any statements that come with the scope of that privilege even if the person making the statement has exhibited reckless indifference to whether or not the statement is true.

30. Federal officials acting within the scope of their duties have no greater privileges with regard to the publication of defamatory material than officials of business corporations exercising a similar degree of authority.

31. A person whose picture has been taken in a public place may not bring an action for invasion of privacy against the person who took the photograph.

32. X attends a football game. Y seated on the other side of the stadium watches X with binoculars during the entire course of the game, which lasts over three hours. X becomes aware that he is being watched. X may bring an action against Y for invasion of privacy.

33. An action for malicious prosecution cannot be brought against a public prosecutor.

34. At common law, a private person could not arrest someone who had committed a misdemeanor that did not involve a breach of the peace.

35. A state official who is acting in direct violation of state law will, nevertheless, be considered to be acting "under color of state law" for purposes of an action under 42 U.S.C. § 1983.

36. The president of the United States has a complete immunity from civil rights actions for any conduct in which the president has engaged in the course of the president's duties.

37. The general rule in the United States is that an exceptionally gifted child may not bring an action for damages against its parents who, though they could easily afford to do so, refuse to take their gifted child out of a crime-ridden school and send the child to a private school that caters to the needs of the exceptionally gifted child.

38. In an action for malicious prosecution, the question of whether the defendant had probable cause to initiate a criminal prosecution is a question of fact to be decided by the jury.

EP

ANSWERS TO TRUE-FALSE QUESTIONS

1. False, *see* Ch. 16, I.C.1.

2. False, *see* Ch. 3, II.F.3.b.(2).

3. True, *see* Ch. 2, II.B. and D.

4. False, *see* Ch. 24, I.A.4.a.

5. True, *see* Ch. 24, I.A.4.

6. False, *see* Ch. 13, III.

7. True, *see* Ch. 5, I.A.1.

8. False, *see* Ch. 16, III.D.2.

9. False, *see* Ch. 16, III.E. *See also* Ch. 16, III.F.2.

10. True, *see* Ch. 3, III.A.2.

11. True, *see* Ch. 3, III.A.

12. False, *see* Ch. 8, III.A.

13. True, *see* Ch. 4, III.A.1.a.

14. False, *see* Ch. 4, II.A. and B.

15. True, *see* Ch. 24, I.B.2.b.

16.   True, *see* Ch. 4, I.A.2.a.(1).

17.   False, *see* Ch. 4, II.B.1.

18.   False, *see* Ch. 11, II.A.1.

19.   True, *see* Ch. 21, I.B.2.

20.   False, *see* Ch. 21, I.B.2.

21.   False, *see* Ch. 21, I.B.5.

22.   True, *see* Ch. 21, III.A.

23.   False, *see* Ch. 19, I.D.

24.   True, *see* Ch. 19, II.C.

25.   True, *see* Ch. 20, II.A.2.

26.   True, *see* Ch. 17, IV.A.

27.   False, *see* Ch. 16, I.D.

28.   True, *see* Ch. 16, II.B.2.

29.   False, *see* Ch. 16, II.C.4.

30.   False, *see* Ch. 16, II.B.3.c.

31.   True, *see* Ch. 17, III.A.1.

32.   False, *see* Ch. 17, III.A.2.

33.   True, *see* Ch. 18, I.A.

34.   True, *see* Ch. 2, III.F.1.

35.   True, *see* Ch. 15, I.A.

36.   True, *see* Ch. 15, III.A.1.

37.   True, *see* Ch. 24, III.B.

38.   False, *see* Ch. 18, I.A.6.

GLOSSARY

GLOSSARY

A

Abnormally dangerous activity. An activity, as set forth in *Restatement (Second) of Torts* § 520, giving rise to strict liability on the part of the actor for damages caused thereby. It includes blasting, crop spraying, keeping wild animals, storing large quantities of water *(Rylands v. Fletcher)*, and the like. The activity typically involves a high degree of risk, cannot reasonably be made safe, is not a matter of common usage, and may be inappropriate to the place where it is carried on. The activity is often associated with the use of land and with the invasion of the activity from the land of the defendant onto that of the plaintiff.

Action on the case. Under common law writ pleading, such an action was used to describe what in modern pleading is usually described as an action in negligence.

Assumption of the risk. The defense of voluntary exposure by the plaintiff to a known risk. Where comparative fault applies, the exposure if unreasonable may reduce the plaintiff's recovery by the percentage of such unreasonableness compared to the total fault, rather than bar recovery entirely. If the exposure amounts to express or implied consent, however, it can bar recovery entirely, regardless of whether comparative fault is used in the jurisdiction.

Assault. An intentional physical act or gesture that puts another in fear of an imminent battery.

Attractive nuisance. An attractive but dangerous condition on land, imposing on the landowner a duty of due care to protect foreseeable trespassing minors against harm from the condition.

Avoidable consequences. Damages that the plaintiff, as a reasonable person, is expected to prevent or avoid. *See* Mitigation of Damages.

B

Battery. The intentional harmful or offensive physical contact with another without privilege to do so.

Burden of persuasion. The burden placed on the plaintiff of persuading the jury or fact finder, usually by a preponderance of the evidence, as to the facts or inferences of fact necessary to recovery, or, in the case of the defendant, of the facts or inferences necessary to sustain a defense.

Burden of proof. Sometimes used as a synonym for "burden of persuasion." It is also sometimes used to describe the burden placed on the plaintiff, or the defendant in the case of a defense, to persuade the judge that there is a reasonable dispute of fact, or of the inferences to be drawn from the facts, so that the claim or defense should be submitted to the jury or fact finder for determination instead of being determined by the judge. If the judge makes the determination, it is often said to be a determination "as a matter of law," *i.e.,* a matter of fact or inference about which reasonable persons cannot differ.

Bystander. A tort victim whose injury is not directly related to the commission of a tort. There may be no proximate cause, no duty owed, or no foreseeability of the injury so that the victim will be unable to recover. Usually such a victim can recover if he suffers foreseeable personal injury, but recovery is less likely if the damage suffered is pure economic loss or merely mental distress.

C

Cause in fact. Actual (as opposed to proximate or legal) cause. Some courts define actual cause in terms of a "but for" analysis — but for the defendant's act or omission, the injury would not have occurred. Other courts use a substantial-factor analysis — if the defendant's conduct is a substantial factor in causing the injury she may be liable, even though the injury may have occurred only as a result of the defendant's conduct combining with another cause or causes or even if another cause might alone have caused the injury.

Collateral source rule. The rule prohibiting a credit against plaintiff's tort recovery of any benefits (such as unemployment benefits, health insurance, and the like) received by the plaintiff from any source other than the defendant or a cotortfeasor of the defendant.

Common law. Any judge-made law, as distinguished from statutory law. The term "common law" is also used to distinguish the English and English-based judicial systems from the European or civil law systems that are based on a codified body of law (the Civil Code). The civil law is applied in the State of Louisiana.

Comparative fault. The rule by which a plaintiff's damages are reduced by a percentage equal to the percentage of the plaintiff's own causal fault. Under pure comparative fault, the plaintiff can recover as long as her fault is not the sole proximate cause of her injury. Under modified comparative fault, the plaintiff will be barred from all recovery if her fault is as great as (or, in some jurisdictions, greater than) that of the defendant. Some jurisdictions apply comparative fault (or comparative causation) rules when the defendant is sued either in strict liability or in negligence, while other jurisdictions limit its application to negligence actions. Where there is more than one defendant, the jurisdictions differ regarding whether the plaintiff's fault is compared to each defendant or to all of the defendants as a group.

Compensatory damages. Damages (typically for lost earnings, medical expenses, and pain and suffering) intended to make the plaintiff whole, or to restore him — insofar as is possible by a monetary award — to the condition he was in prior to his injury. Compensatory damages are distinguished from nominal damages and from punitive damages.

Concert of action. Action by defendants taken pursuant to a common plan, design, or agreement — either express or implied. Most courts impose joint liability on the defendants for tortious injury resulting from such action.

Concurrent tortfeasors. Tortfeasors whose tortious actions combine to cause an injury. If the damages resulting from the injury are theoretically or practically indivisible, many jurisdictions impose joint liability on the tortfeasors for the damages. Other jurisdictions require the court or jury to apportion the damages between or among the defendants on the basis of cause and/or fault, with each defendant only severally liable to the plaintiff for her portion of the damages caused.

Consent. Conduct of the plaintiff indicating his willingness to permit the defendant to act tortiously toward him. A valid consent is a complete bar to recovery.

Consortium, Loss of. Loss of marital companionship resulting from the tortious acts of another. A spouse may typically state a claim against the tortfeasor for such loss.

Constitutional tort. A tort committed by one acting as an agent, or apparent agent, of the federal or of a state government and involving a violation of the U.S. Constitution (usually, a violation of one of the first ten amendments).

Constructive knowledge. Imputed knowledge, or knowledge implied by law, as opposed to actual knowledge.

Contributory negligence. The failure of a person to exercise due care for her own safety.

Contribution. An action, often statutory, whereby a tortfeasor who has paid more than her equitable share of damages to a claimant seeks recovery over and against a cotortfeasor for the amount of such excess payment. Shares of contribution are variously computed on the basis of fault or causation or on equal shares.

Conversion. The intentional exercise of control over another's personal property which is of such seriousness that the person exercising the control is required to pay full value for the property.

Covenant not to sue. An agreement by a tort victim not to sue an apparent tortfeasor of the victim. Such an agreement is usually made in return for a sum of money paid by the tortfeasor to the victim. The effect of the agreement is to relieve the tortfeasor from any further liability to the victim for the tort, although it does not relieve joint tortfeasors from liability even if the right to sue is not reserved as to them.

D

Defamation. An untrue statement, either written or spoken by the defamer and read or heard by a third person, that injures the defamed person's reputation by holding him up to ridicule, contempt, hatred, distrust, and the like.

Duty. The underlying basis for imposing liability, either in tort or in any other field of law. The determination of whether a duty is owed involves mixed questions of law, fact, and policy.

F

False light invasion of privacy. The making of a false public statement by one about another that portrays the other in a contemptible or embarrassing light. There is considerable overlap between this tort and that of defamation, with the result that some courts do not recognize false light invasion of privacy as a separate tort.

Fault. Action or failure to act arising out of negligence, recklessness, or intentional misconduct. If the conduct is also willful, wanton, or malicious, it may provide the basis for an award of punitive damages.

Foreseeability. The possibility or likelihood that a

given act or omission will give rise to a particular consequence. If the consequence is unforeseeable, then generally there is no liability in tort for that consequence. Many courts treat foreseeability and proximate cause as interchangeable concepts.

I

Immunity. A statutory or common law rule protecting a defendant from liability for his tortious acts.

Impact rule. The rule requiring physical impact to the claimant, however slight, as a result of the tortfeasor's act or omission before the claimant can recover from the tortfeasor for negligent infliction of emotional distress.

Imputed negligence. A situation where the negligence, and sometimes the contributory negligence, of one person is imputed to another, *e.g.*, where the negligence of an employee acting within the scope of her employment is imputed to her employer, thereby making the employer vicariously liable for the employee's negligence.

Indemnity. A claim by one tortfeasor against a cotortfeasor to share liability to the tort victim. Traditionally, the indemnity claim is for recovery over in full, on the ground that the indemnitee is only secondarily or vicariously liable. However, some courts allow recovery over for partial indemnity based on relative degrees of fault, cause, or responsibility, and where this is done, a claim for indemnity closely resembles one for contribution.

Intent. The state of mind of a tortfeasor necessary in order to impose a liability for intentional torts. For many intentional torts, the necessary intent is the desire to cause the consequences of one's act, or the knowledge or belief that such consequences are substantially certain to occur. For other intentional torts, such as trespass to land, intentional nuisance, and some forms of conversion, the only necessary intent is to do an act that may result in unintended consequences.

Intervening cause. The cause of an injury not attributable to the tortfeasor, for which, however, the tortfeasor may be responsible unless it is a superseding cause.

Intrusion upon seclusion. One of the invasion-of-privacy torts, consisting of the intrusion upon the privacy of another, or of her affairs, in a manner that would be considered highly offensive to a reasonable person.

Invitee. A business visitor or a visitor on public premises who is owed a duty of reasonable care by the owner or occupier of the premises.

J

Joint liability. The liability of two or more tortfeasors for the same tort, arising out of their joint or concurrent activity. Each tortfeasor is liable for the full amount of the claimant's damages, and the claimant can collect all or part of her damages from any one of the tortfeasors up to the full amount of her damages. *Compare* Several Liability.

L

Last clear chance. A doctrine that relieves the plaintiff of his contributory negligence when the defendant has the last clear chance to avoid the accident. The doctrine is applied in one or more of the following situations: (1) the plaintiff is helpless and the defendant is aware of the plaintiff's helplessness; (2) the plaintiff is inattentive and the defendant is aware of the plaintiff's inattentiveness; and (3) the plaintiff is helpless and the defendant should be aware of the plaintiff's helplessness. Most courts apply the doctrine in situation (1), fewer in (2), and fewer still in (3). Where comparative fault applies, usually the doctrine of last clear chance is not applied.

Legal cause. A term sometimes used for Proximate Cause.

Libel. Written defamation.

Licensee. A social guest to whom a landowner or land occupier owes a duty of care to protect from unreasonable dangers on the land of which the occupier is aware and the guest is unaware.

M

Malice. At common law, willful, wanton, or spiteful misconduct. For purposes of defamation, constitutional or actual malice is knowing or reckless disregard by the defamer of whether her defamatory statement is true or false.

Malpractice. Professional negligence, as by a doctor, lawyer, accountant, and the like.

***Mary Carter* agreement.** An agreement (named after a case involving the Mary Carter Paint Company) whereby a tortfeasor settles with the plaintiff, conditioned on recovery of all or part of the settlement by the settlor depending on whether or how much the plaintiff is able to collect from any nonsettling cotortfeasor(s). Some courts hold such agreements invalid as against public policy, while other courts hold that the jury or fact finder must be told of the existence and terms of the agreement where the settling tortfeasor remains in the case as a nominal defendant.

Misfeasance. Tortious misconduct. *Compare* Nonfeasance.

Misrepresentation. A tortious misstatement.

Mistake. An error of judgment or of fact. In some situations (*e.g.*, self-defense) reasonable mistake is a defense, while in others (*e.g.*, trespass to land), it is not.

Misuse. The use of a product in an unintended way. Misuse of a product will normally not excuse the product supplier from liability unless the misuse is unforeseeable.

Mitigation of damages. Damages that the plaintiff as a reasonable person is expected to prevent or avoid. *See* Avoidable Consequences.

N

Necessity. The need to act to protect a public or a private interest. Public necessity is a complete defense, but at least where the plaintiff's interest is of the same order as that of the defendant, a defendant typically must pay for damages he causes out of private necessity (*i.e.*, out of protection of himself or a limited number of other persons, as opposed to protection of the public at large).

Negligence. The failure of a person to exercise reasonable care under the circumstances, proximately causing damage to another person.

Nominal damages. Damages awarded to a plaintiff not as compensation, but as the vindication of a right violated by the defendant. A plaintiff may recover nominal damages (*e.g.*, $1) for trespass to land not resulting in any discernible damage.

Nonfeasance. Tortious failure to act. *See* Misfeasance.

Nuisance. A private nuisance is a substantial and unreasonable interference with one's use and enjoyment of her land. A public nuisance is a similar interference with a right common to the public, often involving the violation of a criminal statute.

O

Offensive contact. A contact that offends the sensibilities of the ordinary person.

Ordinary care. The degree of care required of a reasonable person under the particular circumstances involved.

P

Premises liability. The liability of an owner or occupier of real property toward those who come onto or near the property. In many jurisdictions, the liability varies according to the status of the entrant (whether trespasser, licensee, or invitee), but the modern trend is to impose a duty of care on the owner or occupier toward all entrants.

Prima Facie case. The amount of evidence necessary to enable a proponent (usually the plaintiff) to get her case before a jury or fact finder.

Privacy, Invasion of. A general term that includes four separate torts: (1) intrusion into seclusion; (2) publication of private facts; (3) a publication presenting the plaintiff in a false or undesirable appearance (false light); and (4) appropriation of name or likeness.

Privilege. A right accorded to one by law for policy reasons to commit without liability acts that, without the privilege, would be tortious.

Products liability. The liability of a product supplier for a defective condition in the product when it leaves the supplier's hands, causing foreseeable injury to another. This liability can be based on breach of warranty, negligence, or strict liability in tort.

Proximate cause. The legal cause of an accident. Some courts speak of proximate cause in terms of foreseeability, while others speak in terms of the direct, natural result of an act. The determination of proximate cause usually involves considerations of social policy.

Public interest. A matter whose publication will not justify a claim for invasion of privacy through the publication of private facts and also a matter that invokes constitutional free speech protections in the law of defamation.

Public person. A public official or public figure who is constitutionally required to prove by clear and convincing evidence, in order to recover for defamation

G

about himself, that the defamer spoke or wrote with constitutional or actual malice (*i.e.,* with knowing or reckless disregard of the truth).

Publication. For purposes of defamation, the making of a defamatory statement by one person to another about the plaintiff. If the statement is read or heard only by the plaintiff or by no one, there is no actionable defamation.

Punitived damages. Damages awarded against a defendant for willful, wanton, malicious, or reckless tortious misconduct, intended to punish the wrongdoer and to provide a deterrent to others. Also called exemplary damages because of the deterrent or exemplary nature of the damages for others.

Pure economic loss. Pecuniary loss unaccompanied by any *physical* damage to person or property.

R

Reasonable care. The same as Ordinary Care.

Reasonable person. A person who acts with that degree of care expected of an ordinary person under the circumstances. One so acting will not be found negligent, although the action may give rise to strict liability and to liability for some intentional torts.

Reason to know. An indication known to a person that should put him as a reasonable person on notice of a fact, event, or condition.

Reckless conduct. Conduct that is flagrantly disregardful of the rights of others — usually a sufficient basis for awarding punitive damages.

Release. An agreement whereby a claimant, in return for some consideration (usually money), agrees to release a tortfeasor from liability. It has much the same effect as a covenant not to sue.

Res ipsa loquitur. A negligence doctrine whereby the plaintiff is relieved from the burden of introducing evidence to prove a specific act of negligence when she suffers injury from an occurrence that ordinarily does not happen in the absence of negligence, and the thing or event that caused the injury is fairly attributable to or under the control of the defendant.

S

Scienter. Actual knowledge.

Self-defense. The privilege to use force to protect oneself from harm.

Several liability. The division of liability between two or more cotortfeasors based on the degree of fault, cause, or responsibility of each tortfeasor. Under this rule of liability, no tortfeasor is liable for the fault, etc. of another tortfeasor. *Compare* Joint Liability.

Should have known. The state of mind that would cause a reasonable person to apprehend a fact, event, or condition.

Slander. Spoken or unwritten defamation for which proof of special damages is required, unless it is slander per se.

Slander per se. A slander of one in one's trade or profession, accusing a woman of unchastity, accusing one of having a loathsome disease, or of having committed a crime involving moral turpitude. Special damages need not be proven in order to recover for slander per se.

Special damages. Damages that must be specially pleaded. In the case of defamation, damages resulting in the loss of something of monetary value, emotional distress being insufficient for this purpose.

Statute of limitations. The time within which a lawsuit must be filed, usually running from the date of reasonable discovery of the cause of action.

Statute of repose. The time within which a lawsuit must be filed, usually running from some fixed date (such as the date of a sale of a product or the date of completion of a building), regardless of whether the claimant knows, has reason to know, or should know that she has a cause of action or whether she has even suffered any injury or harm.

Strict liability. Liability imposed without regard to the fault of the person held legally responsible.

Superseding cause. An unforeseeable intervening cause or a cause that breaks the chain of proximate cause.

Survival statute. A statute allowing the estate of a tort victim to sue for any tort committed against the victim before her death, where the victim was unable to vindicate the tort claim before her death.

T

Thin-skull doctrine. The doctrine providing that if a tortfeasor injures one with an unusual susceptibility (*e.g.,* hemophilia), he will be liable for the injury resulting from that susceptibility.

Transferred intent. The doctrine whereby if one attempts to commit an intentional tort (said to include, however, only the torts of assault, battery, false imprisonment, trespass to land, and trespass to chattel) on *A*, and unintentionally injures *B* instead, the tortfeasor will be liable to *B*.

Trespasser. One on land without permission, to whom the landowner owes a duty not to injure intentionally.

Trespass to chattel. The substantial and wrongful deprivation of one's right to possession of a chattel (tangible personal property).

Trespass to land. The entry onto (or over or under) the land of another without privilege to do so.

V

Vicarious liability. The liability of a principal for the tortious acts of an agent.

W

Willful and wanton misconduct. Intentional, malicious, or reckless misconduct, which is usually sufficient to justify a claim for punitive damages.

Workers' compensation. The statutory right of an employee to claim fixed benefits (primarily loss of earnings and medical expenses) from her employer for injury or disease arising out of and in the course of employment.

Wrongful birth. A claim by parents for damages because of the birth of a child resulting from the failure of a healthcare provider to prevent the birth by diagnosis or by sterilization.

Wrongful death. An action by designated survivors of a deceased person against another who tortiously caused the death of that person.

Wrongful life. An action brought by a person born with a handicap or disease, owing to the failure of a healthcare provider to prevent that person's birth by proper diagnosis or by sterilization.

Z

Zone of danger rule. A rule followed by some courts that a person cannot recover for negligent infliction of emotional distress caused from seeing another tortiously injured, unless that person was himself in danger of being injured by the defendant's tortious conduct.

G

NOTES

TABLE OF AUTHORITIES

TABLE OF CASES

TA

TA

TA

TA

TA

TA

TA

TA

TA

TA

TA

TA

TA

TABLE OF AUTHORITIES

TA

United States Code

TA

TA

CROSS-REFERENCE CHART

CR

TORTS Casenote Law Outlines Cross-Reference Chart	Shulman 3rd. Ed. 1976	Keeton 2nd. Ed. 1989	Franklin 6th Ed. 1996	Epstein 6th Ed. 1995	Prosser 9th Ed. 1994	Dobbs 3rd. Ed. 1997	Henderson 5th Ed. 1999	Robertson 2nd Ed. 1998	Shapo 1990	Christie 3rd. Ed. 1997	Phillips 2nd 1997
CHAPTER 2: Intentional Torts and Defenses											
I. Assault	1010-1022	81-85	811-813	9, 40-42, 66-70, 963-964, 1025-1026	33-36	41-48	749-753	8-18	16-19	41-52	51-54
II. Battery	1010-1039	25-80	811-813	4-31, 70-72, 243, 963-964	29-33	20-40	11-13, 20-80	19-20	27-49	41-52	39-50
III. False Imprisonment	956-962, 1039-1048	95-99	814-820	72-82	36-47	49-51	759-761	21-25	49-63	1258-1267	55-66
IV. Intentional Infliction of Emotional Distress	959, 1011-1018	85-94	820-835	82-91	47-62	486-490	768-770	26-34	64-79	49-51, 1031-1064	67-79
V. Trespass to Land	1049-1055	100-106	588-594	9-11, 56-64	62-74	52-53	437-440	35-43		55-58	101-110
VI. Trespass to Chattel	1049-1055	100-102	1077	10-11	74-76	56-57		44-46		58-60	93-101
VII. Conversion		100-102	1077	642-651	76-88	53-56		44-46		60	93-101
VIII. Defenses	1022-1032		835-852	12-66, 80-81	90-129	63-88	439	47-80	103-161	61-100	113-152
CHAPTER 3: Negligence											
I. Introduction		123-143	22-112	165-167, 168-189	130-132	90-93	175-178	81-83	163-174	102-104	199
II. Standard of Care	140-249	144-221	31-40	168-170, 189-250	143-200	94-125	179, 221-266	84-106	175-238	105-144	199-203
III. Proof of Negligence	249-284	223-235	75-97	291-317	227-254	143-152, 161-177	201-212, 236-239	107-124	541-609	153-231	203-280
CHAPTER 4: Special Situations											
I. Negligent Infliction of Emotional Distress		415-422	226-257	552-558	566-572	493-510		241-280	709-761	501-535	79-80
II. The Liability of Possessors of Land	157-159, 570-644	255-264	165-188	559-620	461-506	304-320, 451-456	252-256	281-307	177-206	537-561	281-318
III. The Failure to Aid - Affirmative Duties	350, 369	236-240	116-140	620-640		418	267-293	226-240	799-804	459-500	700-709
CHAPTER 5: Plaintiff Misconduct											
I. Contributory Negligence	374-403	280-291	382-387	319-349	566-572	242-262	241	414-436	296-303	337-342	628-630
II. Assumption of Risk	412-428	305-330	405-430	354-373	581-594	245-251	412-415	437-452	239-295	374-395	646-665
III. Comparative Fault	428-440	291-305	387-402	373-398	572-581	262-278	417	414-436	303-319	343-373	632-645

TORTS Casenote Law Outlines Cross-Reference Chart	Shulman 3rd. Ed. 1976	Keeton 2nd. Ed. 1989	Franklin 6th Ed. 1996	Epstein 6th Ed. 1995	Prosser 9th Ed. 1994	Dobbs 3rd. Ed. 1997	Henderson 5th Ed. 1999	Robertson 2nd Ed. 1998	Shapo 1990	Christie 3rd. Ed. 1997	Phillips 2nd 1997
IV. The So-called Seat Belt Defense	393-402	288-290	403-405	397				437-442		396-398	667-673
CHAPTER 6: Multiple Defendants, Contributions and Indemnity											
I. Joint Liability	115-119, 291-296	353-357	322-325	399-450	344-353	742-749	119-124, 131-133	634-645	611-629	411-420	1288-1297
II. Several Liability	299-306	355-377	325-341	399-450	344-353	742-749	119-124, 131-133	634-645	611-629	411-420	1288-1297
III. Contribution		356-369	399-402	441-450	369-389	719-737	132	632-633	643-652	422-424	1298-1308
IV. Indemnity		356-369	680-688	428-431	369-389	719-722		532-633	630-643	405-406	1298-1308
CHAPTER 7: Actual Cause											
I. In General	285-287		293	467-491	255-283	180-202	110	125-182		234-264	809-866
CHAPTER 8: Proximate Cause											
I. The Direct Cause Test	287-289	331-336		509-512, 532-539	284-315	202-204	297	189-191		282-283	867-885, 898-911
II. The Reasonable Foreseeability Test	355-373	371-390		509-542	284-315	215, 225-226	297-309	189-219	662-670, 1141-1165	270-273	898-911
III. The Intervening Cause	290-291	336-339, 397-407		505-506	315-342	223-238	328-329	210	671-698	232-236	912-930
IV. Liability to Rescuers	351-354	393-395	375-377	508-509		216		198	762-767	335-336	700-709
CHAPTER 9: Vicarious Liability											
I. The Rationale for the Rule	103-112	504-506	22	464-466	638	551-576	149-161	335-346	198-199	400-411	451
II. Typical Situations of Vicarious Liability	101-138	506-527		450-466	638-660	551-576	149-151, 160-161	334-346	199-206	400-404	451-484
III. Imputed Contributory Negligence				349-354	660-663	576				406-411	451-484
CHAPTER 10: Strict Liability for Animals and for Abnormally Dangerous Activities											
I. Animals	97-99	134, 135, 528-534, 570, 571	431-472	102-103, 607-610, 651-654	664-669	586-587	481-485	540-541		562-568	423-430
II. Abnormally Dangerous Activities	64-78	537-561	431-472	659-662	669-686	602	148-150	541-545	176-177, 428-434	568-612	431-450

CR

CROSS-REFERENCE CHART

TORTS Casenote Law Outlines Cross-Reference Chart	Shulman 3rd Ed. 1976	Keeton 2nd Ed. 1989	Franklin 6th Ed. 1996	Epstein 6th Ed. 1995	Prosser 9th Ed. 1994	Dobbs 3rd Ed. 1997	Henderson 5th Ed. 1999	Robertson 2nd Ed. 1998	Shapo 1990	Christie 3rd Ed. 1997	Phillips 2nd 1997
CHAPTER 11: Products Liability											
I. Theories of Recovery	675-682	635-676	473-492	761-771, 747-752	695-719	612-624	508-526	551-602	368-374	624-630	
II. Bases of Recovery	675-746	699-719		781-862	695-719	625-658	507-508, 553-554, 587-598	560-582	374-400	643-711	491-511
III. Definitions of Defectiveness	726-731	626-699	492-550	781-862	720-764	625-650	507-508	560-579	374-390	640-643	511-521
IV. The Parties	675-682, 702-725	635-659		771-777, 851-862	769-775, 792-806	687-699	508-512	603-611		635-639	522-580
V. Transactions Covered by Products Liability	736-743			761-768, 779-781		690-699	535-536	603-611	419-434	635-639	522-580, 584-585
VI. Defenses	720-736				775-781	660-664	537-539, 543-545	551-554	401-418	712-727	580-587
CHAPTER 12: Nondisclosure and Misrepresentation Causing Only Pecuniary Loss											
I. Nondisclosure	790-794, 798-804		1118-1139	1305-1311	1015-1022	985-988	929-932, 943-948			995-997	1020-1033
II. Deceit or Fraudulent Misrepresentation	747-790	986-1015	1118-1139	1286-1315	1013-1015	971-980	916-917		80-92	982-996	1020-1033
III. Negligent Misrepresentation	804-823	1015-1039	1118-1139	1315-1328	1013-1015	973	932-943		87	997-1015	1020-1033
IV. Innocent Misrepresentation	770-777	997-999	1118-1139			980-982	942-946		87	980	1020-1033
V. Defenses	784-789	991-998				971-989				61-101, 337-398	1020-1033
VI. Damages	770-784	1048-1052		1311-1315	1068-1072	971, 976-977	916-917			991-992	
CHAPTER 13: Business Torts											
I. Product Disparagement or Injurious Falsehood		1145-1158, 1201-1222	588-612	1101-1102, 1339-1340	1073-1085	944-947			98		
II. Interference with Contract or with Prospective Economic Advantage		1304, 1305	1140-1165	1341-1355	1073-1123	960-969	966-975		965-991	1016-1030	1035-1067
III. Negligent Interference				1343-1355		960-969					
CHAPTER 14: Nuisance											
I. The Rationale for Nuisance	71-86	572-634	588-612	682-725	810-842	590-593	444-447	615-630	813-865	951-979	589-626
II. Damages	84-86	608-622	588-612	712	810-842	960-969	446	619-630	827-839, 850-851	961-962	589-626

TORTS Casenote Law Outlines Cross-Reference Chart	Shulman 3rd. Ed. 1976	Keeton 2nd. Ed. 1989	Franklin 6th Ed. 1996	Epstein 6th Ed. 1995	Prosser 9th Ed. 1994	Dobbs 3rd. Ed. 1997	Henderson 5th Ed. 1999	Robertson 2nd Ed. 1998	Shapo 1990	Christie 3rd. Ed. 1997	Phillips 2nd 1997
CHAPTER 15: Civil Rights (or Constitutional) Torts											
I. Actions Against State Officials	128-138	267				398-409		490-495, 499-502	1142-1155	1329-1336	1079-1134
II. Actions Against Federal Officials	120-128	267		955-966		388-398		474-499	1165-1189	1316-1329	1079-1134
III. Immunities from Civil Rights Action				954-978		413-416			1190-1204	1318-1329	1079-1134
CHAPTER 16: Defamation											
I. The Common Law Action for Defamation	840-865	1159-1186	876-902	1083-1144	842-946	912-916	829-839		867-881	1106-1132	931-932
II. Common Law Defense for an Action for Defamation	841-879	1201-1246	902-928	1144-1169	842-946	912-916	832-839		896-928	1132-1191	931-932
III. Constitutional Developments	880-952	1054-1064, 1121-1158, 1187-1200	928-1017	1169-1214		916-928	842-847		881-896	1032-1087	931-932
CHAPTER 17: Privacy											
I. Introduction				1215-1223		937-947	867-871			8-16, 1192	986-1019
II. False-light Invasions of Privacy	988-989	1065-1069, 1134-1145	1059-1069	1260-1268		944-947	900-906		928-946	1194-1201	986-1019
III. Intrusions Upon the Plaintiff's Solitude	953-962	1089-1095, 1276	1069-1092	1268-1284		990-993	871-889		958-964	1194, 1201-1218	101, 986-1019
IV. Public Disclosure of Embarrassing Private Facts	968-988	1276-1286	1028-1059	1241-1260		937-941	886-890		947-957	1218-1241	986-1019, 1056
V. Commercial Appropriation		1280-1282	1092-1117	1223-1241		953-959	906-913		938-946	8-16, 1192-1194, 1216, 1241-1257	
CHAPTER 18: Misuse of Process											
I. Malicious Prosecution	1049-1056	1247-1275		902	886-1013	929-932				1268-1286	80-92
II. Misuse of Civil Process		1224-1229			886-1013	933-935				1268-1286	80-92
CHAPTER 19: Wrongful Death and Loss of Consortium											
I. Wrongful Death	1024-1032	438-440, 443-451	16	914-920	546-565	531	378-380	373-385	513-539	831-847	1249-1263, 751

CR

TORTS Casenote Law Outlines Cross-Reference Chart	Shulman 3rd. Ed. 1976	Keeton 2nd. Ed. 1989	Franklin 6th Ed. 1996	Epstein 6th Ed. 1995	Prosser 9th Ed. 1994	Dobbs 3rd. Ed. 1997	Henderson 5th Ed. 1999	Robertson 2nd Ed. 1998	Shapo 1990	Christie 3rd. Ed. 1997	Phillips 2nd 1997
III. Loss of Consortium		453-458	247	920-922		539		384-385		835-836	1263, 1255
CHAPTER 20: Fetal Injuries											
I. Physical Injury to the Fetus	553-557					520			516-523	848-854	745-750
II. Wrongful Birth		440-443	257-268			521	383-384	373-385		855-870	751-768
III. Wrongful Life			257-268			521	390-392	373-385		855-870	751-768
CHAPTER 21: Damages											
I. Types of Damages	460-569	423-457		863-897	507-545	758-788	615-700	347-411	447-494	734-762	1087-1286
II. Duties of the Plaintiff and the Court	474-476, 535-545	429, 430		338-341, 396-397		772-782		308-323	494-512	758-762	1135-1186
III. Punitive Damages	530-534	36-43, 479-481, 742-753	650-672	922-938	530-545	782-785	694-700	385-404	494-512	792-804	1263-1286
CHAPTER 22: Statutory Changes											
I. Types of Changes				438-440, 892-894		278-297		465-470		913-915	1092
II. Constitutional and Policy Considerations						797-814	30-34			904-950	
CHAPTER 23: Tort Law Alternatives											
I. Partial Alternative Systems	781-909		718-800	1014-1079	1190-1213	829-877, 893-903	722-732, 234-235		993-1085	917-950	1440-1445, 1325-1398
II. Total Alternative Systems			718-800	1071-1079	1190-1213		744, 8		1085-1112	915-917	1419-1436
III. Policy Considerations		829-833, 846-858, 906-909	718-800		1213-1214	797-814			997-998, 1005-1031, 1083-1085	905-913	1405-1408
CHAPTER 24: Immunities											
I. Governmental Immunities	120-137	265-275	197-225	954-978		387-416	428-430	474-509	1115-1204	1316-1340	770-795
II. Charitable Immunity	137, 138	275-277	198	945-946		385-386	430			1341-1343	796-797
III. Family Immunities		277-280	188-197	939-945		381-384	431-435	510-513		1344-1358	798-808

CR

INDEX

INDEX

ID

ID

ID

ID

ID

ID

ID

ID

ID

Announcing the First *Totally Integrated* Law Study System

CASENOTE LEGAL BRIEFS

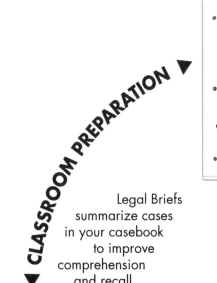

CLASSROOM PREPARATION

EXAM PREPARATION

Legal Briefs
summarize cases
in your casebook
to improve
comprehension
and recall.

Case briefs
cross-referenced
to *Outline* for
further discussion
of cases & law.

CASES AND MATERIALS ON TORTS

CASEBOOK

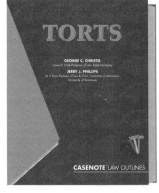

CASENOTE LAW OUTLINES

Outline cross-referenced to most
casebooks to help prepare for class & exams.

PERIODIC REVIEWS

CASENOTES PUBLISHING COMPANY INC.

"Preparation is nine-tenths of the law. . ."

DISCOVERY AND DISCLOSURE

the Ultimate Outline

➤ **RENOWNED AUTHORS:** Every **Casenote Law Outline** is written by highly respected, nationally recognized professors.

➤ **KEYED TO CASENOTE LEGAL BRIEF BOOKS:** In most cases, **Casenote Law Outlines** work in conjunction with the **Casenote Legal Briefs** so that you can see how each case in your textbook relates to the entire subject area. In addition, **Casenote Law Outlines** are cross-referenced to most major casebooks.

➤ **FREE SUPPLEMENT SERVICE:** As part of being the most up-to-date legal outline on the market, whenever a new supplement is published, the corresponding outline can be updated for free using the supplement request form found in this book.

CASENOTE LEGAL BRIEFS™

PRICE LIST EFFECTIVE JULY 1, 1999 ● PRICES SUBJECT TO CHANGE WITHOUT NOTICE

Ref. No.	Course	Adaptable to Courses Utilizing	Retail Price
1265	ADMINISTRATIVE LAW	ASIMOW, BONFIELD & LAVIN	20.00
1263	ADMINISTRATIVE LAW	BREYER, STEWART & SUNSTEIN	21.00
1266	ADMINISTRATIVE LAW	CASS, DIVER & BEERMAN	19.00
1260	ADMINISTRATIVE LAW	GELLHORN, B., S., R. & F.	19.00
1264	ADMINISTRATIVE LAW	MASHAW, MERRILL & SHANE	20.50
1267	ADMINISTRATIVE LAW	REESE	19.00
1262	ADMINISTRATIVE LAW	SCHWARTZ	20.00
1350	AGENCY & PARTNERSHIP (ENT.ORG)	CONARD, KNAUSS & SIEGEL	23.00
1351	AGENCY & PARTNERSHIP	HYNES	23.00
1281	ANTITRUST (TRADE REGULATION)	HANDLER, P., G. & W.	19.50
1283	ANTITRUST	SULLIVAN & HOVENKAMP	20.00
1611	BANKING LAW	MACEY & MILLER	19.00
1305	BANKRUPTCY	JORDAN, WARREN & BUSSELL	19.00
1058	BUSINESS ASSOCIATIONS (CORPORATIONS)	KLEIN & RAMSEYER	21.00
1059	BUSINESS ORGANIZATIONS (CORPORATIONS)	SODERQUIST, S., C., & S.	23.00
1040	CIVIL PROCEDURE	COUND, F., M & S	21.00
1043	CIVIL PROCEDURE	FIELD, KAPLAN & CLERMONT	22.00
1049	CIVIL PROCEDURE	FREER & PERDUE	18.00
1041	CIVIL PROCEDURE	HAZARD, TAIT & FLETCHER	21.00
1047	CIVIL PROCEDURE	MARCUS, REDISH & SHERMAN	21.00
1044	CIVIL PROCEDURE	ROSENBERG, S. & D.	22.00
1046	CIVIL PROCEDURE	YEAZELL	19.00
1311	COMM'L LAW	FARNSWORTH, H., R., H. & M.	21.00
1312	COMM'L LAW	JORDAN & WARREN	21.00
1310	COMM'L LAW (SALES/SEC.TR./PAY.LAW [Sys.])	SPEIDEL, SUMMERS & WHITE	24.00
1313	COMM'L LAW (SALES/SEC.TR./PAY.LAW)	WHALEY	22.00
1314	COMMERCIAL TRANSACTIONS	LOPUKI, W., K. & M.	21.00
1320	COMMUNITY PROPERTY	BIRD	19.50
1630	COMPARATIVE LAW	SCHLESINGER, B., D., H.& W.	18.00
1048	COMPLEX LITIGATION	MARCUS & SHERMAN	19.00
1072	CONFLICTS	BRILMAYER	19.00
1071	CONFLICTS	CRAMTON, C. K., & K.	19.00
1070	CONFLICTS	ROSENBERG, HAY & W.	22.00
1073	CONFLICTS	SYMEONIDES, P., & M.	22.00
1086	CONSTITUTIONAL LAW	BREST & LEVINSON	20.00
1082	CONSTITUTIONAL LAW	COHEN & VARAT	23.00
1088	CONSTITUTIONAL LAW	FARBER, ESKRIDGE & FRICKEY	20.00
1080	CONSTITUTIONAL LAW	GUNTHER & SULLIVAN	21.00
1081	CONSTITUTIONAL LAW	LOCKHART, K., C., S. & F.	20.00
1085	CONSTITUTIONAL LAW	ROTUNDA	22.00
1089	CONSTITUTIONAL LAW (FIRST AMENDMENT)	SHIFFRIN & CHOPER	17.00
1087	CONSTITUTIONAL LAW	STONE, S., S. & T.	21.00
1103	CONTRACTS	BARNETT	23.00
1102	CONTRACTS	BURTON	22.00
1017	CONTRACTS	CALAMARI, PERILLO & BENDER	25.00
1101	CONTRACTS	CRANDALL & WHALEY	22.00
1014	CONTRACTS	DAWSON, HARVEY & H.	21.00
1010	CONTRACTS	FARNSWORTH & YOUNG	20.00
1011	CONTRACTS	FULLER & EISENBERG	23.00
1013	CONTRACTS	KESSLER, GILMORE & KRONMAN	25.00
1016	CONTRACTS	KNAPP & CRYSTAL	22.50
1012	CONTRACTS	MURPHY & SPEIDEL	24.00
1015	CONTRACTS	ROSETT	23.00
1019	CONTRACTS	VERNON	22.00
1502	COPYRIGHT	GOLDSTEIN	20.00
1501	COPYRIGHT	NIMMER, M., M. & N.	21.50
1218	CORPORATE TAXATION	LIND, S. L. & R	16.00
1050	CORPORATIONS	CARY & EISENBERG	21.00
1054	CORPORATIONS	CHOPER, COFFEE, & GILSON	23.50
1350	CORPORATIONS (ENTERPRISE ORG.)	CONARD, KNAUSS & SIEGEL	23.00
1053	CORPORATIONS	HAMILTON	21.00
1058	CORPORATIONS (BUSINESS ASSOCIATIONS	KLEIN & RAMSEYER	21.00
1057	CORPORATIONS	O'KELLEY & THOMPSON	20.00
1059	CORPORATIONS (BUSINESS ORG.)	SODERQUIST, S., C. & S.	23.00
1056	CORPORATIONS	SOLOMON, S., B. & W.	21.00
1052	CORPORATIONS	VAGTS	20.00
1300	CREDITOR'S RIGHTS (DEBTOR-CREDITOR)	RIESENFELD	23.00
1550	CRIMINAL JUSTICE	WEINREB	20.00
1029	CRIMINAL LAW	BONNIE, C., J. & L.	19.00
1020	CRIMINAL LAW	BOYCE & PERKINS	24.00
1028	CRIMINAL LAW	DRESSLER	23.00
1027	CRIMINAL LAW	JOHNSON	22.00
1021	CRIMINAL LAW	KADISH & SCHULHOFER	21.00
1026	CRIMINAL LAW	KAPLAN, WEISBERG & BINDER	20.00
1205	CRIMINAL PROCEDURE	ALLEN, KUHNS & STUNTZ	19.00
1206	CRIMINAL PROCEDURE	DRESSLER & THOMAS	24.00
1202	CRIMINAL PROCEDURE	HADDAD, Z., S. & B.	22.00
1200	CRIMINAL PROCEDURE	KAMISAR, LAFAVE & ISRAEL	21.00
1204	CRIMINAL PROCEDURE	SALTZBURG & CAPRA	19.00
1300	DEBTOR-CREDITOR (CREDITORS RIGHTS)	RIESENFELD	23.00
1304	DEBTOR-CREDITOR	WARREN & WESTBROOK	23.00
1224	DECEDENTS ESTATES (TRUSTS)	RITCHIE, A. & E.(DOBRIS & STERK).	23.00
1222	DECEDENTS ESTATES	SCOLES & HALBACH	23.50
	DOMESTIC RELATIONS (see FAMILY LAW)		
3000	EDUCATION LAW (COURSE OUTLINE)	AQUILA & PETZKE	27.50
1670	EMPLOYMENT DISCRIMINATION	FRIEDMAN & STRICKLER	19.00
1671	EMPLOYMENT DISCRIMINATION	ZIMMER, SULLIVAN, R. & C.	20.00
1660	EMPLOYMENT LAW	ROTHSTEIN, KNAPP & LIEBMAN	21.50
1350	ENTERPRISE ORGANIZATION	CONARD, KNAUSS & SIEGEL	23.00
1342	ENVIRONMENTAL LAW	ANDERSON, MANDELKER & T.	18.00
1341	ENVIRONMENTAL LAW	FINDLEY & FARBER	20.00
1345	ENVIRONMENTAL LAW	MENELL & STEWART	19.00
1344	ENVIRONMENTAL LAW	PERCIVAL, MILLER, S. & L.	20.00
1343	ENVIRONMENTAL LAW	PLATER, A., G. & G.	19.00
1217	ESTATE & GIFT TAXATION	BITTKER, CLARK & McCOUCH	17.00

Ref. No.	Course	Adaptable to Courses Utilizing	Retail Price
	ETHICS (see PROFESSIONAL RESPONSIBILITY)		
1065	EVIDENCE	GREEN & NESSON	22.00
1066	EVIDENCE	MUELLER & KIRKPATRICK	19.00
1064	EVIDENCE	STRONG, BROUN & M.	24.50
1062	EVIDENCE	SUTTON & WELLBORN	24.00
1061	EVIDENCE	WALTZ & PARK	21.00
1060	EVIDENCE	WEINSTEIN, M., A. & B.	24.50
1244	FAMILY LAW (DOMESTIC RELATIONS)	AREEN	24.00
1242	FAMILY LAW (DOMESTIC RELATIONS)	CLARK & GLOWINSKY	21.00
1245	FAMILY LAW (DOMESTIC RELATIONS)	ELLMAN, KURTZ & BARTLETT	22.00
1243	FAMILY LAW (DOMESTIC RELATIONS)	HARRIS, T. & W.	21.00
1243	FAMILY LAW (DOMESTIC RELATIONS)	KRAUSE, O., E. & G.	26.00
1240	FAMILY LAW (DOMESTIC RELATIONS)	WADLINGTON	22.00
1231	FAMILY PROPERTY LAW (WILLS/TRUSTS)	WAGGONER, A. & F.	22.00
1360	FEDERAL COURTS	FALLON, M. & S. (HART & W.)	21.00
1360	FEDERAL COURTS	HART & WECHSLER (FALLON)	21.00
1363	FEDERAL COURTS	LOW & JEFFRIES	18.00
1361	FEDERAL COURTS	McCORMICK, C. & W.	22.00
1364	FEDERAL COURTS	REDISH & SHERRY	19.00
1690	FEDERAL INDIAN LAW	GETCHES, W. & W.	22.00
1089	FIRST AMENDMENT (CONSTITUTIONAL LAW)	SHIFFRIN & CHOPER	17.00
1700	GENDER AND LAW (SEX DISCRIMINATION)	BARTLETT & HARRIS	21.00
1510	GRATUITOUS TRANSFERS	CLARK, L., M., A., & M.	20.00
1651	HEALTH CARE LAW	CURRAN, H., B. & O.	23.00
1650	HEALTH LAW	FURROW, J., J. & S.	19.50
1640	IMMIGRATION LAW	ALEINIKOFF, MARTIN & M.	18.00
1641	IMMIGRATION LAW	LEGOMSKY	21.00
1690	INDIAN LAW	GETCHES, W. & W.	22.00
1371	INSURANCE LAW	KEETON	23.00
1370	INSURANCE LAW	YOUNG & HOLMES	19.00
1503	INTELLECTUAL PROPERTY	MERGES, M., L. & J.	21.00
1394	INTERNATIONAL BUSINESS TRANSACTIONS	FOLSOM, GORDON & SPANOGLE	17.00
1393	INTERNATIONAL LAW	CARTER & TRIMBLE	18.00
1392	INTERNATIONAL LAW	HENKIN, P., S. & S.	19.00
1390	INTERNATIONAL LAW	OLIVER, F., B., S. & W.	24.00
1331	LABOR LAW	COX, BOK, GORMAN & FINKIN	21.00
1471	LAND FINANCE (REAL ESTATE TRANS.)	BERGER & JOHNSTONE	20.00
1620	LAND FINANCE (REAL ESTATE TRANS.)	NELSON & WHITMAN	21.00
1452	LAND USE	CALLIES, FREILICH & ROBERTS	19.00
1421	LEGISLATION	ESKRIDGE & FRICKEY	17.00
1480	MASS MEDIA	FRANKLIN & ANDERSON	17.00
1312	NEGOTIABLE INSTRUMENTS (COMM. LAW)	JORDAN & WARREN	21.00
1541	OIL & GAS	KUNTZ, L., A., S. & P.	20.00
1540	OIL & GAS	MAXWELL, WILLIAMS, M. & K.	20.00
1561	PATENT LAW	ADELMAN, R., T. & W.	24.00
1560	PATENT LAW	FRANCIS & COLLINS	25.00
1310	PAYMENT LAW [SYST.][COMM. LAW]	SPEIDEL, SUMMERS & WHITE	24.00
1313	PAYMENT LAW (COMM.LAW / NEG. INST.)	WHALEY	22.00
1431	PRODUCTS LIABILITY	OWEN, MONTGOMERY & K.	24.00
1091	PROF. RESPONSIBILITY (ETHICS)	GILLERS	15.00
1093	PROF. RESPONSIBILITY (ETHICS)	HAZARD, KONIAK, & CRAMTON	20.00
1092	PROF. RESPONSIBILITY (ETHICS)	MORGAN & ROTUNDA	15.00
1030	PROPERTY	CASNER & LEACH	23.00
1031	PROPERTY	CRIBBET, J., F. & S.	23.50
1037	PROPERTY	DONAHUE, KAUPER & MARTIN	20.00
1035	PROPERTY	DUKEMINIER & KRIER	20.00
1034	PROPERTY	HAAR & LIEBMAN	22.50
1036	PROPERTY	KURTZ & HOVENKAMP	21.00
1033	PROPERTY	NELSON, STOEBUCK, & W.	22.50
1032	PROPERTY	RABIN & KWALL	22.00
1038	PROPERTY	SINGER	20.50
1621	REAL ESTATE TRANSACTIONS	GOLDSTEIN & KORNGOLD	20.00
1471	REAL ESTATE TRANS. & FIN. (LAND FINANCE)	BERGER & JOHNSTONE	20.00
1620	REAL ESTATE TRANSFER & FINANCE	NELSON & WHITMAN	20.00
1254	REMEDIES (EQUITY)	LAYCOCK	22.00
1253	REMEDIES (EQUITY)	LEAVELL, L., N. & K-F.	23.00
1252	REMEDIES (EQUITY)	RE & RE	25.00
1255	REMEDIES (EQUITY)	SHOBEN & TABB	24.50
1250	REMEDIES (EQUITY)	RENDLEMAN	27.00
1310	SALES (COMM. LAW)	SPEIDEL, SUMMERS & WHITE	24.00
1313	SALES (COMM. LAW)	WHALEY	22.00
1312	SECURED TRANS. (COMMERICIAL LAW)	JORDAN & WARREN	21.00
1310	SECURED TRANS.	SPEIDEL, SUMMERS & WHITE	24.00
1313	SECURED TRANS. (COMMERCIAL LAW)	WHALEY	22.00
1272	SECURITIES REGULATION	COX, HILLMAN, LANGEVOORT	20.00
1270	SECURITIES REGULATION	JENNINGS, M., C. & S.	20.00
1680	SPORTS LAW	WEILER & ROBERTS	19.50
1217	TAXATION (ESTATE & GIFT)	BITTKER, CLARK & McCOUCH	17.00
1219	TAXATION (INDIV. INCOME)	BURKE & FRIEL	21.00
1212	TAXATION (FEDERAL INCOME)	FREELAND, LIND & STEPHENS	20.00
1211	TAXATION (FEDERAL INCOME)	GRAETZ & SCHENK	19.00
1210	TAXATION (FEDERAL INCOME)	KLEIN & BANKMAN	20.00
1218	TAXATION (CORPORATE)	LIND, S., L. & R.	16.00
1006	TORTS	DOBBS	21.00
1003	TORTS	EPSTEIN	22.50
1004	TORTS	FRANKLIN & RABIN	19.50
1001	TORTS	HENDERSON, P. & S.	22.50
1000	TORTS	PROSSER, W., S., K., & P.	25.00
1005	TORTS	SHULMAN, JAMES & GRAY	24.00
1281	TRADE REGULATION (ANTITRUST)	HANDLER, P., G. & W.	19.50
1410	U.C.C.	EPSTEIN, MARTIN, H. & N.	17.00
1510	WILLS/TRUSTS (GRATUITOUS TRANSFER)	CLARK, L., M., A. & M.	20.00
1223	WILLS, TRUSTS & ESTATES	DUKEMINIER & JOHANSON	21.00
1220	WILLS	MECHEM & ATKINSON	22.00
1231	WILLS/TRUSTS (FAMILY PROPERTY LAW)	WAGGONER, A. & F.	22.00

CASENOTES PUBLISHING CO., INC. ● 1640 FIFTH STREET, SUITE 208 ● SANTA MONICA, CA 90401 ● (310) 395-6500

E-Mail Address- casenote@westworld.com ● Website- www: http://www.casenotes.com